Toddlers & Twos

BIBLE
Quest

A Bible Story Curriculum for all ages

A Bible Story Curriculum For Birth To Two

TODDLERS & TWOS is a part of the BIBLEQUEST curriculum. It emphasizes teaching the overall story of the Bible, helping very young children encounter the Bible story and begin their faith journey as disciples of Jesus Christ. The overall story of the Bible—a story of God's incarnation, love, justice, and salvation, a story of God's good news—and our interpretation and expression of that story are essential gifts to the new century.

The activities in each session of TODDLERS & TWOS are carefully tailored to the abilities and interests of the children. Because people learn in a variety of ways, the sessions provide opportunities for visual, musical, artistic, linguistic, kinesthetic (movement), individual, and group experiences with the Bible story.

This Leader's Guide is to be used with the audio CD packaged in the back of this book.

Writers

Linda Ray Miller

Joyce Riffe

Judy Knopf

Diana McDonald

Illustrator

Robert S. Jones

Editor

Linda Ray Miller

Cover Art

DigitalVision

BIBLE QUEST is an ecumenical project. Nine partners participated in the development, writing, editing, and production of these resources. BIBLE QUEST is published jointly by the Christian Church (Disciples of Christ), The Church of the Brethren, Cumberland Presbyterian Church, Moravian Church in America (Southern Province), The Presbyterian Church in Canada, Presbyterian Church (U.S.A.), The United Church of Canada, The United Church of Christ, and The United Methodist Church.

All scripture quotations, unless otherwise indicated, are from the *New Revised Standard Version Bible,* copyright 1989 by the Division of Christian Education of the National Council of Churches of Christ in the U.S.A. In some instances, the text has been adapted for inclusivity. Used by permission.

Every effort has been made to trace copyrights on the materials included in this publication. If any copyrighted material has nevertheless been included without permission and due acknowledgment, proper credit will be inserted in future printings after notice has been received.

www.biblequestlink.com

© 2000 Bible Quest Publishers

Printed in the U.S.A.

Table of Contents

Leader's Guide   Toddlers & Twos

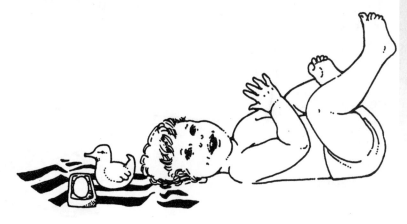

How To Use This Guide

Do I have to Do All This?

You will notice that the sessions are not dated and that there are more than 52 of them. (56 to be exact!) This means that you will not use every session. Look ahead to make sure that you do the Thanksgiving session at Thanksgiving, and the Easter session at Easter. Arrange the other sessions around these dates. Look through all of the lessons to see which ones you want to leave out and steal ideas from the "left out" sessions.

✎ Each week we have tried to provide you with more activities than you can possibly use. There are also usually two or three ways to tell the Bible story. While you should plan for more activities than you think you need, feel free to leave out an activity if you do not have time to prepare for it, or if your children do not respond well to it. Substitute favorite activities from previous sessions. Tailor this resource to meet YOUR needs!

✎ We have provided you with a CD to teach you the music. Don't worry if you can't sing, the toddler's can't either! And, they do not care whether you are in tune or not. They just love music. So use it!

✎ Two products that are indespensible to this resource are the Activity Pak and the Bible Story Picture Cards. These are published quarterly and are sold separately.

Wherever two or three are gathered.....
One of the first things you need to know about this age is that it is frustrating for children and teachers to try to gather a whole class together for anything. Most activities are preceded by the sentence, "Gather two or three children." This means that you should repeat the same activity several times during the session, each time with a different group of children. And if a child comes up again while you are playing with a game and they have already done it once, let them do it again. Repetition is important. The only thing you will want to be aware of is that each child in your class should hear the Bible story at least once during the morning. But you can tell the story in any center or activity! Don't wait to share the story until you have all the necessary props. Tell it again, and again, and again.

Especially the first few weeks, you will need to capture the attention of the two year old with some activity in order to lessen anxiety when parents leave. Each week there is one activity under "Prepare For The Story" that is designed to do just that. It will usually be play dough, a sand box, or a water table activity. DO NOT NEGLECT THIS ACTIVITY!

Supplies To Get You Started

Teacher scissors, non-toxic white glue, large crayons, stapler, staples, construction paper, drawing paper, various colors of tempera paint, play dough (see recipe on page 232), CD player, building blocks, toy kitchen set, baby dolls, toddler toys

Welcome to the wonderful world of Toddlers & Twos!

Forget everything you have ever heard about the "terrible twos". This is a delightful age to work with. The children will change almost before your eyes from baby-like creatures that whimper and cry to convey their needs into young children that can use complete sentences. The stories you tell the children this year will be brand new to them. That may be a bit hard to believe, but few of your children have even heard the story of Baby Jesus! You get to introduce the Bible to a whole group of children. How Awesome!

So, are you nervous? Good! You should be. You have answered a very important call from God to teach these precious children. It is normal to be a little bit nervous. But here is the best part - because God has called you to this work, God will support you in it. So, say a little prayer before your children arrive, pray daily for each of your children by name, and ask God to strengthen you and guide you. And don't forget to call on those whom God has provided to help you - your pastor, Christian Education worker, or denominational professionals.

May God bless your work!

Linda Ray Miller
Development Editor

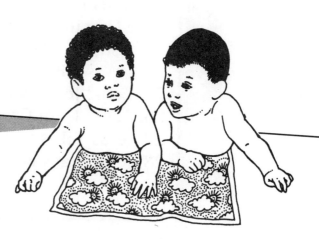

Session Outlines

Fall

1. Let's Go to Church Psalm 122:1
2. We Are Happy at Church Psalm 100:2
3. God Loves Me Psalm 100:5
4. Noah Builds an Ark Genesis 6:9-22; 7:6-10
5. Noah Finds Dry Ground Genesis 7:17-18; 8:5
6. Noah Sees a Rainbow Genesis 8:3-20a; 9: 12-16
7. Moses is Born Exodus 2:1-10
8. Ruth Chooses Ruth 1:1-22
9. Boaz is Kind to Ruth Ruth 2:1-4:13
10. Obed is Born Ruth 4:13-22
11. David Is Chosen 1 Samuel 16:1-13
12. David Plays His Harp 1 Samuel 16:14-23
13. David and Jonathan 1 Samuel 18: 1-5
14. Thanksgiving Psalm 9:2

Winter

15. Mary is Told About Jesus Luke 1:26-38
16. Mary and Joseph Get Ready Luke 2:4-5
17. Mary and Joseph Look For a Place to Stay Luke 2:6-7
18. Jesus is Born Luke 2:6-7
19. The Shepherds See Baby Jesus Luke 2:8-20
20. Wise Men See Baby Jesus Matthew 2:11
21. Jesus Lived in a Family Mark 6:3 and Luke 4:22
22. I Live in a Family Mark 6:3 and Luke 4:22
23. Jesus is a Baby Luke 2:7, 12
24. I Was a Baby Luke 2:7, 12
25. Look! Jesus is Growing Luke 2:40, 52
26. Look! I Am Growing Luke 2:40, 52
27. Jesus Takes a Trip Luke 2:41-42
28. Jesus Stays Behind Luke 2: 43-51

Bible people were glad to worship God. We are glad to go to church to worship God.

Bible Verse:

I was glad when they said to me, "Let us go to the house of the Lord!" (Psalm 122:1)

Resources:

Bible
CD
Activity Pak (Fall)
   page 8 (figures 1, 3, 5)
   page 3 ("Many Kinds
   of Churches" picture)
   Songbook
Bible Story Picture Cards

Supplies:

nametags
play dough (see recipe
   on p. 232)
CD player
worship items: (cross,
   Bible, pastor's stole,
   fancy candlesticks
dress-up clothes
hand mirror
lightweight fabric scraps
   or scarfs
newsprint or shelf paper
masking tape
crayons
teacher scissors
black felt-tip marker
building blocks
round blocks
toy rolling pins
chairs

Let's Go to Church ....

Enter the Bible Story

Read Psalm 122:1: This Bible verse is part of a song that expresses the joy that pilgrims felt at being in the city and the temple as they came to Jerusalem. Psalm 122 is known as the pilgrim song and was perhaps sung by those leaving Jerusalem after an exciting visit. It expresses their happiness at having been invited to join the band of travelers going to Jerusalem and at having seen the wonderful city that was home to God's earthly house, the temple.

Think About It: The religious pilgrims who sang this song were happy to have an opportunity to visit the great city of Jerusalem and God's earthly house there. What ways in addition to singing do you think the religious pilgrims might have expressed their joy at visiting the "house of the Lᴏʀᴅ?" Were they chatting, laughing and friendly with others as they walked along the road?

Are you joyful on Sunday morning because you have the opportunity to go to church, or are you hurried and under stress as you prepare yourself and your family to leave home? Do you greet friends and others at church with a happy, accepting attitude?

How dangerous do you think it was for pilgrims to travel in those times? Is it dangerous for you to go to church today? Is it dangerous for people in some parts of the world to go to church today?

Through the Week: Imagine a large group of travelers singing with joy as they walk out of the city. How will you help children sing happily at church? We want children to come to know that their church is a very special place where they are welcomed, valued, and loved, and where they experience happy times with friends and teachers.

Pray: I am glad, God, for the opportunity to attend my church and to serve it. I am especially happy to be able to live my faith with the children in my class. Help me to keep before me the joy of being together with children in my class.

The Story and Young Children

Children can know that people long ago sang happy songs while visiting a special place to worship God. They can be helped to have happy experiences as they come to their own church and can have opportunities to express joy at church. The Sunday school experience may be for some children their first regular time away from parents, although many children may be away from home in a caregiving arrangement as parents work. Toddlers may still have some measure of stranger anxiety. As a teacher it is up to you to help young children feel happy and at home in the church setting. Basic foundations are being laid at church that will give toddlers and two-year-olds either positive or negative lifelong feelings about the church.

Room Setup: Set up the room with many choices, including the choices mentioned in the Learning Centers. Have a few toddler manipulative toys available as well, such as simple puzzles (no more than four big pieces) and Duplo blocks. The important thing to remember is that we want each child to immediately see something that looks interesting and worth playing with.

Learning Centers

Work with two or three children at a time in each learning center.

Conversation Center

You will need: play dough, round blocks, toy rolling pins, CD, CD player, Songbook, large piece of newsprint or shelf paper, masking tape, crayons, teacher scissors, black felt-tip marker.

Get ready: Gather the children around a table and sit down with them; engage them in conversation. For the scribble banner, cover the table with paper and tape it so the paper doesn't slide.

- Play With Play Dough, Activity 1b
- Talk About Coming to Church, Activity 1c
- Make a Scribble Banner, Activity 4b

Building Center

You will need: building blocks.

Get ready: Provide enough blocks for toddlers to share.

- Retell the Bible Story, Activity 2b
- Build Block Churches, Activity 3c

Storytelling Center

This should be an open area where you may gather children for storytelling or to listen and respond to music. It would be helpful to have this center on a carpeted area.

You will need: Bible, Activity Pak—p. 8 (figures 1, 3, 5), CD, CD player, Songbook, fabric scraps or scarfs, hand mirror.

Get ready: Prepare storytelling figures (see Activity Pak—p. 2).

- Tell the Bible Story, Activity 2a
- Retell the Bible Story, Activity 2b
- Tell Another Story, Activity 3b
- Enjoy Music, Activity 4a

Family Living Center

You will need: CD, CD player, Songbook, dress-up clothes, chairs.

Get ready: Make a car or a bus by arranging chairs.

- Pretend Going to Church, Activity 3d

Discovery Center

You will need: Activity Pak—p. 3 ("Many Kinds of Churches" picture), CD, CD player, Activity Pak Songbook, items for worship.

Get ready: Display some things that one would see in your worship service: a cross, a Bible, candlesticks, a pastor's stole. Place only things that the children can touch. Untouchable items will create stress.

- Look at Worship Items, Activity 1d
- Look at a Poster, Activity 3a

A Happy Walk

Joshua walked with his mother and father on the dusty road. Everyone was leaving the big city.

"I am happy that we went to the house of the Lord," said Joshua's mother.

"Yes, it was beautiful there," said Joshua's father.

Joshua and his family sang: "I was glad when they said to me, 'Let us go to the house of the Lord!' "

1 Prepare

for the Story

 Welcome Each Child

Do this as each child enters.

Stoop to the child's eye level and welcome each child by name. Be prepared to learn new names, since this may be the child's first session of a new church school year, and some or all of the children may be new. You can place a piece of masking tape with each child's name on his or her back as a reminder to you during the session, if you teach toddlers or younger two-year-olds. Nametags hung about the neck with yarn will work with older two-year-olds. Wear a nametag yourself to help parents get to know you.

Say: "I am so happy you have come to church today." Involve children in an interesting or comforting activity. The play dough activity can catch the interest of hesitant children and will involve them quickly in an experience in which they feel they have some measure of control.

 Play With Play Dough

Do this in the Conversation Center.

Sit with children at a low table as they enjoy manipulating play dough. (Rule: "The play dough stays *on* the table.") Provide round blocks or toy rolling pins for smoothing dough, or provide items with which children can make interesting prints in the dough. As children work, listen to the song "I Was Glad" (CD, Songbook). Sing along with the recording and encourage children to sing with you. Manipulate the play dough in rhythm with the song. The words are included in the Songbook.

 Talk About Coming to Church

Do this in the Conversation Center.

Let the children continue working with play dough. After singing "I Was Glad" **say:** "Do you know what 'the house of the Lord' is? It is our church. I am glad that all of us have come to church today." Sing "I Came to Church Today" (CD, Songbook).

 Look at Worship Items

Do this in the Discovery Center.

With one or two children, look at the items you have gathered. (Suggested items include a cross, a Bible, candlesticks, and a pastor's stole.) Help the children identify each item. Remember that this may be the first time some of them have seen these items. Place only things that the children can touch.

2 Tell

the Story

 **Tell the Bible Story**

Do this in the Storytelling Center.

Gather one or two children. **Say:** "I am happy to be at church today. Are you? What do we do when we are happy? I smile when I am happy. Do you?" Let the children see their smiling faces in a hand mirror.

Show the Bible figure of the little boy (figure 5). **Say:** "This little boy's name is Joshua. He is very happy. I'll tell you why he is happy." Tell the Bible story using the figures of the Bible man, woman, and boy (figures 1, 3, 5). Hold up the appropriate figure(s) as each one or all three is named in the story. Sing "I Was Glad" (CD, Songbook) with the children.

 Retell the Bible Story

Do this in the Storytelling Center or the Building Center.

Let the children play with the Bible story figures (figures 1, 3, 5). Help them remember the words that each figure said. **Ask:** "What did the mommy say? What did the daddy say? What did the family sing?"

Build a square of blocks for the temple and another square of blocks for the home. Move the figures from temple to home as you sing "I Was Glad" (CD, Songbook).

3 Connect
with the Story

a **Look at a Poster**
Do this in the Discovery Center.

Look at the Many Churches Poster (Activity Pak—p. 3). **Ask:** "What are these buildings?" Tell the children the buildings are churches, even though each looks different. Remind the children that people are happy to go to each of the special churches. **Say:** "We are happy to come to our special church too." Sing "All the Way to Church" (CD, Songbook) with the children.

b **Tell Another Story**
Do this in the Storytelling Center.

Robin peeked into her new classroom. She was not sure she wanted to go in.

"Hello, Robin," said Mrs. Evans. "I'm glad you have come to church. We have some new play dough today. Come in and see how soft it is." Robin and Mrs. Evans played with the soft play dough. It was fun. Then Robin played with the blocks, heard a story, and sang songs. Robin had a good time in her new class.

"Bye, bye," Robin said when it was time to go home. All the way home Robin sang, "I was glad when they said to me, 'Let us go to the house of the Lord.'"

c **Build Block Churches**
Do this in the Building Center.

Help the children learn to stack blocks on top of one another. As you stack the blocks, talk about building churches. **Say:** "Oh, look, this is a TALL church. Now let's build a little church. This church is very LONG."

d **Pretend Going to Church**
Do this in the Family Living Center.

Invite the children to dress up and go to church in a car or bus. Sing "All the Way to Church" (CD, Songbook) as the children play.

4 Celebrate
the Story

a **Enjoy Music**
Do this in the Storytelling Center.

Say: "I am so happy we have all come to church today. Let's sing a song about how happy we are to come to church." Sing "I Was Glad" (CD, Songbook) with the children. Give each child a piece of lightweight fabric or a scarf. Encourage each to dance and move the fabric as the song is played on the CD. Repeat the song several times.

Sing "All the Way to Church" (CD, Songbook) with the children, joining hands to walk in a circle for the first two verses. Then add the motion "jumping." Let the children suggest other motions.

b **Make a Scribble Banner**
Do this in the Conversation Center.

Let the children stand around the table to scribble with crayons on the paper.

Sing or play today's songs on the CD as the children work, modeling how they can move the crayons to the rhythm of the music. Carefully remove the paper from the table when the children have finished. The teacher can cut it into small "banners" for each one to take home. Leave one large piece to make a banner for the classroom.

Print today's Bible verse in large letters on your class banner or on the children's banners if you have time.

c **Say Goodbye**
Recall today's Bible story. Encourage the children to say or sing the Bible verse with you. **Say:** "I am glad (*name one of the children*) came to church today." Repeat this for each child. **Pray:** "Thank you, God, for our church. We are happy to come to church."

Have a helper at the door to ensure that anxious children do not leave until someone comes for them. Tell parents about today's Bible story and make sure that each child has today's Bible Story Picture Card. Point out to parents the room banner the class made today. Be sure the children take home their banners.

Tip
Make the stories more personal. Substitute your name and that of the children in contemporary stories.

Look Back
Today we wanted children to hear that people long ago were happy to go to church.

Did each child have a chance to hear the story?

We also wanted children to feel happy to come to church today.

Did the children have joyful experiences in the class today? Were some children's experiences not so joyful?

How can these children be helped to be happy at church in the next session?

How has the Bible story spoken to you as you prepared for and carried out the session?

What have the children taught you?

Look Ahead
The next session is entitled, "We Are Happy at Church." Many ideas explored in this session can be carried over into the next. Plan to use all three songs again.

Use play dough again to help hesitant or new children feel comfortable.

Bible people were glad to worship God. We are glad to go to church to worship God.

Bible Verse:
Worship the LORD with gladness. (Psalm 100:2)

Resources:
Bible
CD
Activity Pak (Fall)
   pages 5, 8 (figures
    1–12)
   page 3 ("Many Kinds
    of Churches" picture)
   Songbook
Bible Story Picture Cards

Supplies:
play dough (see
   recipe on p. 232)
craft sticks
construction paper
felt-tip markers
teacher scissors
masking tape
posterboard
glue
3- to 5-ounce paper cups
magazines
building blocks
round crackers
soft cream cheese
small paper plates
plastic knives
raisins
sliced pimentos
two or three
   cardboard boxes large
   enough to hold two
   children
CD player
pocketbooks
dress-up clothes
chairs
worship items from last
   week

We Are Happy at Church ....

Enter the Bible Story

Read Psalm 100:2: This Bible verse is part of a hymn sometimes sung by a procession of people as they approached the temple. These hymns were used in a variety of settings, both for public, corporate worship and by individuals in their own private worship.

Think About It: We are reminded by this hymn that the oldest roots of our own faith were set firmly in joyous feelings of coming to be in the presence of God in God's own special place. Reflect on the following questions as you prepare to help children experience this ancient joy.

    People going to the temple anticipated a happy time. What did they experience at the temple that made them happy? What do you experience at church that makes you happy? What can you help children experience at church that will help them feel happy?

Through the Week: Today's Bible verse, like the one for the previous session, reminds us that the Jewish people were a singing people and that their faith was often a singing and musical faith. Think of ways that we express our own faith in music today.

Pray: I am happy, God, to be able to live the joy of my own faith with the children in my class. Help me to provide happy classroom experiences for the children.

The Story and Young Children

    Children can hear that people long ago had happy times at God's special place, the temple. They can be helped to experience happy times at their own church.

    In the last session you may have welcomed reluctant children and those who were feeling stranger anxiety. You may continue to be especially challenged to help some of the children feel happy and at home in the church setting. The play dough activity may be repeated today, as it is soothing and often quickly engages hesitant children.

    One aspect of feeling happy at church is to experience friendships there. Children this age are just beginning these experiences. Activities that help children notice and respond positively to others are an important part of feeling happy about coming to church. Several of today's suggested learning experiences encourage noticing and responding to others.

Room Setup: Set up the room with many choices, including the choices mentioned in the Learning Centers. Have a few toddler manipulative toys available as well, such as simple puzzles (no more than four big pieces) and Duplo blocks. The important thing to remember is that we want each child to immediately see something that looks interesting and worth playing with.

Learning Centers

Conversation Center

You will need: play dough, CD, CD player, Songbook, yellow construction paper, felt-tip marker, Activity Pak—p. 3 ("Many Kinds of Churches" picture), posterboard, teacher scissors, smiling people cut from magazines, glue, round crackers, soft cream cheese, raisins, pimentos, small paper plates, plastic knives, small paper cups, craft sticks.

Get ready: Cut circles from yellow construction paper. Draw a smiling face on each circle. Cut a variety of smiling people from magazines or catalogues. Cut a large door in one sheet of posterboard. Tape the second sheet of posterboard behind the first, leaving the door free to open and shut. Pour a small amount of glue into a 3- or 5-ounce paper cup.

- Play With Play Dough, Activity 1b
- Take a Smiley Face Walk, Activity 1c
- Make a Happy Faces Church, Activity 3a
- Make Happy Face Snacks, Activity 4b

Discovery Center

You will need: worship items (see Session 1).

Get ready: Repeat the display of things that one would see in your worship service. Remember to place only things that the children can touch. Untouchable items create stress.

Building Center

You will need: building blocks, Activity Pak—p. 5 (figures 4, 6, 10), CD, CD player, Songbook.

Get ready: Provide enough blocks for toddlers to share. You may use wooden unit blocks or large cardboard or plastic blocks.

- Build Block Churches, Activity 3c

Storytelling Center

Create an open area where the children can gather for storytelling or to listen to music.

You will need: two or three large cardboard boxes, Bible, Activity Pak—pp. 5, 8 (figures 1–12), CD, CD player, Songbook.

Get ready: Prepare storytelling figures (see Activity Pak—p. 2).

- Tell the Bible Story, Activity 2a
- Play in a Friendly Box, Activity 2b
- Tell Another Story, Activity 3b
- Enjoy Music, Activity 4a

Family Living Center

You will need: pocketbooks, dress-up clothes, chairs, CD, CD player, Songbook.

- Pretend Going to Church, Activity 1d

We Are Happy at Church

Sarah liked going with her mother to worship God. They went to a special place to worship. All the people were smiling. Sometimes there was singing. Sometimes there was dancing.

Sarah's mother said, "Everyone is happy to come to the house of the Lord." Sarah and her mother were glad to be with the people worshiping God.

1 Prepare

for the Story

a   Welcome Each Child
Do this as each child enters.

Stoop to the child's eye level and welcome each child by name. You may need to use masking tape or construction paper nametags as you did in the previous session. Again, wear a nametag yourself to help parents get to know you.

Say to each child: "I am happy to see you at church today. We are going to have a happy time at church." Be prepared to involve children in an interesting or comforting activity.

b   Play With Play Dough
Do this in the Conversation Center.

Use play dough prepared for the previous session. Sit with the children as they play with the play dough. Provide items for children to manipulate the dough as they did in the last session.

Draw children's attention to a smiley face that you have drawn with a craft stick in flattened dough. **Say** to the children: "When I'm happy, I smile just like this smiley face." As children work, listen to the CD song "I Was Glad" (CD, Songbook).

Sing along, inviting children to sing with you. Manipulate the play dough in rhythm with the song.

c   Take a Smiley Face Walk
Do this in the Conversation Center.

Before class begins, tape all but one of the smiley faces around the room at the children's eye level. Show the reserved smiley face to the children. Hold hands and walk around the room. Have the children point to a smiley face whenever they see one.

d   Pretend Going to Church
Do this in the Family Living Center.

Invite children to act out going to church as they did in the previous session. Provide dress-up clothes, pocketbooks, and chairs to make cars or buses. Encourage the children to "ride in cars or buses" with their friends as they go to church. Sing "All the Way to Church" (CD, Songbook) as the children play.

2 Tell

the Story

a   Tell the Bible Story
Do this in the Storytelling Center.

Gather one or two children. Show children the little girl Bible figure (figure 6).

Say: "This little girl's name is Sarah. I know a story about her." Tell the Bible story, using the mother (figure 3) and the other figures (figures 1, 2, 5-12) to represent people in the happy crowd. Hold up the appropriate figure as each one is named in the story. Show the crowd figures talking and dancing as these actions are mentioned in the story.

Open a Bible and **say:** "Sarah and her mother and all of the people were glad to go to church. The Bible says: 'Worship the LORD with gladness.'" Invite the children to repeat the verse with you.

b   Play in a Friendly Box
Do this in the Storytelling Center.

Invite the children to climb in and out of boxes together.

As two children sit in the same box, **say:** "Terry and Doug are sharing a box. It's fun to play with our friends at church."

As the children share a box, sing the following song to the tune of "London Bridge":

(*Name the two children*) are in the box,
In the box, in the box.
(*Name the two children*) are in the box,
Both together.

3 Connect

with the Story

a **Make a Happy Faces Church**
Do this in the Conversation Center.

Write the name of your own church over the door on the posterboard. Invite the children to fill the church with happy people. Let them choose and glue the pre-cut figures behind the doors. Show the children how to "touch" the glue in the paper cup and then "touch" the posterboard before placing the cut picture. **Talk** about all of the different people who come to church: "Matt has found a baby to come to our church. Joan found a grandmother. Remember that we have many friends at church. Everyone is happy to come to church."

b **Tell Another Story**
Do this in the Storytelling Center.

One, two, three. Scott stacked the blocks to make a tower. "What a good tower you have made," said Mrs. Ito.

Amy came over to look at Scott's tower. "I like your tower," said Amy.

Scott had happy times at church. There were blocks to play with. There were stories to hear and songs to sing. There were good friends and nice teachers. Scott was glad to be in God's special place, the church.

c **Build Block Churches**
Do this in the Building Center.

Encourage children to build block churches. Let the children use the figures (figures 1-12) to walk along block roads to church.

Sing "All the Way to Church" (CD, Songbook) as children build or "walk" the figures.

4 Celebrate

the Story

a **Enjoy Music**
Do this in the Storytelling Center.

Say: We have had some happy times at church today. I'm glad we came to church." Sing "I Was Glad" (CD, Songbook) with the children. Engage the children in acting out today's action verse, "When I'm Happy" (CD, Songbook). Invite children to find a friend and to hold the friend's hand. (Make sure each child has a friend. The teacher can be a friend to make an even number. Groups of three are also acceptable.) Lead children in walking around the room with their friends as you sing "All the Way to Church" (CD, Songbook). Let the children dance to the music of the CD.

b **Make Happy Face Snacks**
Do this in the Conversation Center.

Give each child a cracker on a paper plate and a plastic knife. Let the child spread a small amount of cream cheese on the cracker. Help the child add raisin eyes and a smiling pimento mouth. As children enjoy eating their smiley faces, remember today's Bible verse. **Pray:** "Thank you, God, for good crackers to eat. Thank you for our church."

c **Say Goodbye**

Recall today's Bible story. Encourage the children to say the Bible verse with you. **Say:** "I am glad (*name a child*) came to church today." Repeat this for each child. **Pray:** "Thank you, God, for our church. We are glad to come to church."

Be sure to have a teacher or helper at the door to ensure that anxious children do not leave until someone comes for them. Tell parents about today's Bible story and make sure that each child has today's Bible Story Picture Card. Show the parents the "Nurturing Your Child's Faith" section of the card. Point out to parents the happy faces church the class made.

Tip
Make the stories more personal. Substitute your name and that of the children in the contemporary stories.

Look Back
Did each child have an opportunity to hear the story and the Bible verse today?

Today we wanted children to experience happy times at church. Did the children have good experiences? Did anyone who was not happy in the previous session have a better time today?

How did you help them? How can you continue to help children who are feeling uncomfortable about coming to Sunday school?

Look Ahead
The next session is entitled "God Loves Me." Children will be exploring "God's big love." Several activities will involve the use of heart shapes. The heart pattern can be found on page 235 in this book.

Session

3

Psalm 100:5

We know that God made us, and that God loves and cares for us and all of nature.

Bible Verse:
God loves me forever.
(Psalm 100:5, paraphrased)

Resources:
Bible
CD
heart pattern (p. 235)
Activity Pak (Fall)
    page 8 (figures 1, 7)
    page 21 (matching hearts game)
    Songbook
Bible Story Picture Cards

Supplies:
CD player
construction paper
tape
teacher scissors
play dough
heart-shaped cookie cutters and other items to make heart prints
dolls and doll items
magazines
crayons or felt-tip markers
nature items
building blocks
colorful fall leaves
child-sized rocking chair
clothesline or bulletin board
clothespins

Optional Supplies:
doll furniture and equipment
cardboard box
cotton swabs
tempera paint
heart-shaped stickers

16

God Loves Me!.......

Enter the Bible Story

Read Psalm 100:5: This Bible verse is part of the same hymn used in the previous session. It is a psalm of thanksgiving. The Hebrews were not talking about the flow of seconds, minutes, hours, days, and years that we live when they stated that God's love is forever. Rather, they meant the flow of *history*. God's love surrounds God's people throughout the events that happen to them and the experiences they have from generation to generation.

Think About It: We are told by this hymn that God loves us forever. Reflect on the following questions as you prepare to help children know that God loves them with a very big love. What does it mean to say that God loves us *forever*? Does it mean that God loves us every minute of our lives? Does it mean that God loves us through all of our experiences, during good times and bad? Does it mean that God loves us when we are faithful and even when we are not? How do we show children what God's love is like?

Through the Week: As we noted in the last session, Psalm 100 expresses joyous thanksgiving to God for God's greatness and for the goodness to us that grows from that greatness. Continue to think of ways in which we can help children express joy.

Pray: Thank you, God, for your love, which surrounds me all the days of my life. Help me to be aware of your love, especially as I try to model love for the children in my classroom.

The Story and Young Children

Children can hear that people long ago expressed happiness and thanksgiving for God's love. We can give them opportunities to experience love and to express their own happy feelings of thankfulness for God's love. Young children learn what God's love is like as their parents, teachers, and caregivers show love to them. Adults model God's love for children. This is both our greatest privilege and our greatest responsibility. The first thing that should happen to any child in our class is that he or she should experience *love* from *us*.

Young children learn with their senses in concrete ways. They are naturally curious about the world around them and often notice small things in nature that adults overlook. The beauties and wonders of the natural world help children understand the concept of God's love. God provides these wonders to supply our needs or to give us pleasure, because God loves us very much.

Room Setup: Collect pictures of things that God provides for us (nature items, food, water, families, pets) and arrange a display of these on a low bulletin board or a clothesline strung *above* the children's heads but low enough so that pictures hung from it with clothespins are at the children's eye level.

Learning Centers

Work with two or three children at a time in each learning center.

Conversation Center

You will need: heart pattern (page 235) play dough, heart-shaped cookie cutters, items to make heart prints, construction paper, teacher scissors, crayons or felt-tip markers (optional: cotton swabs, tempera paint).

Get ready: Set out the play dough, or prepare new dough using the recipe on p. 232. Use the heart pattern (page 235) to cut paper hearts from different colors of construction paper.

- Continue Using Play Dough, Activity 1b
- Decorate With Bible Verse Hearts, Activity 4b

Building Center

You will need: building blocks.

Get ready: Provide enough blocks for toddlers to share. You may use wooden unit blocks or large cardboard or plastic blocks.

Family Living Center

You will need: baby dolls, child-sized rocking chair, doll items.

Get ready: Set out the dolls and the doll items for the children to use.

- Show Love to Babies, Activity 1d

Storytelling Center

You will need: Activity Pak—p. 8 (figures 1, 5), Bible, colorful fall leaves, CD, CD player, Songbook (optional: cardboard box).

Get ready: Prepare Bible story figures (see Activity Pak—p. 2).

- Tell the Bible Story, Activity 2a
- Retell the Bible Story, Activity 2b
- Tell Another Story, Activity 3b
- Enjoy Music, Activity 4a

Discovery Center

You will need: nature objects (a rock, a shell, potted plant), Activity Pak—p. 21 (matching hearts game), pictures of things God provides, tape, clothesline or bulletin board, clothespins.

Get ready: Cut pictures of animals, people, plants, and food from magazines. Tape these at the children's eye level around the room. Set out nature items in the Discovery Center. Remember to set out only things that children can touch and that are too large to fit into children's mouths.

- Play a Matching Hearts Game, Activity 1c
- Look at Pictures, Activity 3a
- Find Signs of God's Love, Activity 3c

God's Big Love

Micah and his father sat on the roof of their home.
"Look at all the stars, Micah," Father said.
"Where do the stars come from?" Micah asked.
"God made the stars and many things for us," Father said. "God made the stars, the moon, and the sun. God loves us very much."
"God loves me forever," Micah said.
"God loves me forever too," Father said.

 # Prepare

for the Story

 a **Welcome Each Child**

Do this as each child enters the room.

Using the heart pattern (p. 235), cut a heart shape for each child from red construction paper. (Or buy heart-shaped stickers.) Fasten a paper heart to your clothes with masking tape.

Stoop to the child's eye level and **say:** "I'm glad to see you today, (*child's name*). I have something special for you today that says, 'I love you.'" Fasten a heart on each child with tape.

Be prepared to involve children in activities and to comfort children who still need special help.

 b **Continue Using Play Dough**

Do this in the Conversation Center.

Use play dough again if it is still in good condition. It remains a comforting activity and one that new and uneasy children may have come to expect.

Add heart-shaped cookie cutters or items that make heart-shaped prints in the dough today. Tell the children that hearts mean, "I love you."

 c **Play a Matching Hearts Game**

Do this in the Discovery Center.

Separate the cards in the matching hearts game (Activity Pak—page 21). For younger children use only the red and blue hearts.

Ask the children to sort the cards into two piles—a red pile and a blue pile. With older children use more colors. With the oldest children you may also wish to play a matching game where the cards are turned face down and the children search for matches. As children play, tell them that hearts mean, "I love you" and that they remind us that God loves us.

 d **Show Love to Babies**

Do this in the Family Living Center.

Have the children show loving care to the baby dolls.

As they play with the dolls, encourage conversation about ways in which we show love: "Ruth is loving the baby. She is rocking her to sleep. Seth is being so gentle with the baby."

 # Tell

the Story

a **Tell the Bible Story**

Do this in the Storytelling Center.

Show children the little boy (figure 5). **Say:** "This little boy's name is Micah. One night he and his father went to a special place. They climbed way up to the roof of their house." (Option: Make a simple Bible-times house from a cardboard box. Use this house as a prop with the figures as you tell the story.) Tell the Bible story while acting it out with the Bible figures (figures 1, 5). Open a Bible and **say:** "The song that Micah and his father sang is in the Bible: 'God loves me forever.'" Invite the children to repeat the verse with you.

 b **Retell the Bible Story**

Do this in the Storytelling Center.

Invite the children to practice acting as twinkling stars before you retell the story.

Have them hold up their hands, move their fingers, and say, "Twinkle, twinkle, twinkle."

Invite the children to join you in the action version of today's Bible verse after you have finished the story:

God's love is very, very big.
(*Make a big circle with arms raised overhead.*)
God loves me forever.
(*Place both hands on chest.*)
God's love is very, very big.
(*Make a big circle with arms raised overhead.*)
God loves you forever.
(*Point to someone else.*)
God's love is very, very big.
(*Make a big circle with arms raised overhead.*)
God loves us all forever.
(*Spread arms wide.*)

3 Connect
with the Story

a **Look at Pictures**
Do this in the Discovery Center.

Invite the children to explore pictures in the display. Talk with the children about the pictures. As you look at each picture, tell the children that God provides for us whatever is pictured.

Say: "God loves us so much that God gives us good bananas to eat." **Pray**: "Thank you, God, for (*name item*)."

b **Tell Another Story**
Do this in the Storytelling Center.

"Come and see," said Erin's teacher, Mr. Frost. Erin ran to the window and looked out. What a surprise! The big green tree that had been outside all summer had turned to red!

"God plans for many trees to change color," Mr. Frost said. "When we see the pretty colors, we can remember that God loves us and makes the world beautiful for us." Erin was happy for God's love and for pretty trees.

c **Find Signs of God's Love**
Do this in the Discovery Center.

If you have a window in your classroom low enough for children to see out, and if your view is an appropriate one for today's session, let the children look out the window to find signs of God's love, such as a tree, flowers, grass, a squirrel, and birds.

Or let the children investigate the nature items in the Discovery Center, with adult supervision.

4 Celebrate
the Story

a **Enjoy Music**
Do this in the Storytelling Center.

Say: "We heard (are hearing) a story today about how much God loves us. I am happy that God loves us forever."

Sing "Show How Much God Loves Us" (CD, Songbook). Add suggested verses and engage children in the other songs that you have learned in in the past three sessions (CD, Songbook).

Repeat the action verse "When I'm Happy" from the last session. Say the action verse "God's Big Love."

b **Decorate With Bible Verse Hearts**
Do this in the Conversation Center.

Let each child choose a colored heart. Write today's Bible verse on the heart with a black marker.

Let the children decorate the hearts with crayons or markers. (Option: Let children decorate their hearts by applying paint with cotton swabs if you have an older group. Use good quality swabs so that the cotton does not come loose when dipped in paint.)

Recall today's Bible verse as the children work.

Help the children hang their hearts on the clothesline gallery or tape them about the room.

c **Say Goodbye**

Recall today's Bible story, inviting children to say the Bible verse with you.

Say: "I am happy that God loves you, (*name one of the children*)." Repeat this for each child in the class. **Pray**: "Thank you, God, for your love."

Be sure to have a teacher or helper at the door to ensure that anxious children do not leave until someone comes for them. Tell parents about today's Bible story and make sure that each child has today's Bible Story Picture Card.

Show the parents the "Nurturing Your Child's Faith" section of the card. Give children their Bible verse hearts to take home.

Tip
Make the stories more personal. Substitute your name and that of the children in the contemporary stories.

Look Back
Did each child have an opportunity to hear that God loves her or him today? How did the children hear this? a story? a song? a Bible verse?

We wanted children to have happy feelings and to express them today. Did you observe children acting in happy ways? How?

Can you name something new that you learned today?

Look Ahead
Next week you will begin studying Bible stories with Noah and the ark. Look ahead and prepare a sandbox for the children to play with (see p. 234). Try to find a toy Noah's ark and lots of toy animals for the children to play with. Make a brown construction paper ark, using the pattern on p. 245 and the instructions on p. 21.

Session

4

Genesis 6:9-22;
7:6-10

Noah followed
God's will. We too
must follow God's
will for us.

Bible Verse:
Noah did all that
God told him to
do.
(Genesis 6:22,
adapted)

Resources:
Bible
CD
ark pattern (page 245)
Activity Pak (Fall)
   pages 5, 8 (figures
   2, 11, 12)
   page 16 (animal
   couples)
   Songbook
Bible Story Picture Cards

Supplies:
sand table or large
   plastic container
   with sand (see p.
   234)
sand toys
toy animals
toy Noah's ark
stuffed pet animals
pet items, such as
   feeding dishes, pet
   beds, and
   grooming brushes
pictures of animals
   from magazines
glue
posterboard
small paper cups
CD player
building blocks
large blocks or boxes
brown construction
   paper
small cardboard box
   such as one that
   granola bars or
   instant oatmeal
   might come in
teacher scissors

Noah Builds an Ark..............................

Enter the Bible Story

Read Genesis 6:9-22; 7:6-10: Today's story tells the beginning of the story of Noah. We will take three weeks to tell the story fully.

Think About It: We often greet the tasks that God calls us to do with more than a bit of skepticism: What? Me teach two-year olds? What could I teach them? God, surely you mean for me to spend my vacation at the Grand Canyon and *not* in Honduras on some mission trip! Reflect on the following questions as you prepare to tell the story and to help children retell the story: What has God called you to do recently? Have you been listening for God's call in your life? What is hard or improbable about what God calls you to do?

Through the Week: We have spent three weeks telling the children that we come to church for happy times, and that we are glad to be at church. We now begin studying Bible stories. Remember that it is not important for children of this age to absorb every detail of the Bible story. Keep focused on how much God loves us and how much God loved the animals. God used Noah to save the animals and the people from the flood. Consider how you will make the story come alive for your children.

Pray: Thank you, God, that you loved all of creation so much that you did not allow it to be destroyed. Help me to pass on that love to the children I teach.

The Story and Young Children

   This is not really a story for children, even though it has lots of animals and Noah's ark is used as a decorating theme in many nurseries. The Noah story is really a story of how God became so disappointed in human beings' wickedness that all of creation was threatened with extinction. It is a story of one man who was a bit more righteous than everyone else in his generation (and remember just how righteous his generation was), and how God used Noah to save creation.

   Young children cannot conceive of a God they cannot see. God, to them, is only visible through the actions of significant adults in their lives. Judgment is another concept that children have difficulty with. How could a toddler do something so bad that God would want to destroy the world? When you tell this story, focus on things that children *do* understand, such as the fact that God loved the world and did not let it be destroyed.

Room Setup: Cut pictures of animals from magazines. Place these pictures all around the room at the children's eye level. A low bulletin board will work well, as will hanging pictures from a clothesline with clothespins, if you have one.

Learning Centers

Conversation Center

You will need: magazines, teacher scissors, large piece of posterboard, shallow cups, glue.

Get ready: Cut animal pictures from magazines.

• Make an Animal Banner, Activity 1d

Building Center

You will need: building blocks, toy animals, large blocks or boxes.

Get ready: Provide enough blocks for toddlers to share. (Option: Decorate a cardboard box to represent the ark.)

• Play With Toy Animals, Activity 1c
• Build a Boat, Activity 3c

Discovery Center

You will need: Activity Pak—pp. 5, 8 (figures 2, 11, 12), sand table or plastic box, play sand, sand toys, toy Noah's ark set.

Get ready: Put plastic animals and a plastic boat in the sandbox.

• Play With Sand, Activity 1b
• Retell the Bible Story, Activity 2b

Family Living Center

You will need: toy pets, pet supplies.

Get ready: Set out pet dishes and supplies so that they are available to the children.

• Take Care of Pets, Activity 3a

Storytelling Center

You will need: Bible; CD, CD player, Songbook; Activity Pak—pp. 5, 8 (figures 2, 11, 12) and 16 (animal couples); ark pattern (p. 245); small box with open top; brown construction paper, teacher scissors.

Get ready: Prepare Bible story figures (see Activity Pak—p. 2). Use the pattern on page 245 to trace an ark onto brown construction paper. Cut it out. Tape the ark shape onto a small box so that it can stand alone. Leave the top of the box open so that you may put animals into the box.

• Tell the Bible Story, Activity 2a
• Learn a Song, Activity 2c
• Tell Another Story, Activity 3b
• Enjoy Music, Activity 4a
• Sing an Action Song, Activity 4b

Noah Builds a Boat

"There is going to be a big flood," God told Noah. "You must build a big boat to save the animals."

"No, no, Noah!" said Noah's neighbors. "It is silly to build a boat!"

Noah did all that God told him to do.

"You must find two of every kind of animal to put on the boat," God told Noah.

"No, no, Noah!" said Noah's neighbors. "It is silly to get all those animals!"

Noah did all that God told him to do.

"You must put your family on the boat," God told Noah.

"No, no, Noah!" said Noah's neighbors. "Don't get on the boat with all those animals!"

Noah did all that God told him to do.

21

1 Prepare
for the Story

 Welcome Each Child
Do this as each child enters the room.

Stoop to the child's eye level and welcome each child by name. Use nametags if you have trouble remembering children's names.

Say to each child: "I am so happy you have come to church today."

Be prepared to involve children in an interesting or comforting activity. The sandbox should draw a lot of attention.

Children whose interest has been caught have an easier time saying goodbye to their parents or caregivers.

 Play With Sand
Do this in the Discovery Center.

Encourage the children to run the sand through their fingers. Point out that the sand feels smooth.

Say: "I wonder why there is a boat in the sand? Boats don't go in the sand! They go in water! Today we will hear a story about a boat in the sand."

 Play With Toy Animals
Do this in the Building Center.

Place a variety of animals along with the blocks in the Building Center. Encourage the children to use the animals in their play.

 Make an Animal Banner
Do this in the Conversation Center.

Gather one or two children. Pour glue into a small cup shallow enough for children to get their fingers into. Set out the animal pictures you have cut from magazines. Let each child choose a picture.

Show the children how to "touch" the glue and then "touch" the picture to get a small amount of glue on the back of an animal picture. Then allow the child to put a picture of the animal on the posterboard. Repeat until the posterboard is covered with the animals that God created. Talk with the children about their animals as you work.

Say: "What an interesting animal you chose, Eliza. Can you tell me its name? I am glad that God made so many different kinds of animals."

2 Tell
the Story

 Tell the Bible Story
Do this in the Storytelling Center.

Tell the children that today's story comes from the Bible. Show the figure of Noah (figure 2). **Say:** "This man's name is Noah. God had a special job for him to do." Tell the story, using the figures and the animal couples (figures 2, 11, 12 and Activity Pak—p. 16) at appropriate times. Open a Bible. **Say:** "The Bible says Noah did all that God told him to do." Ask the children to repeat the Bible verse with you.

 Retell the Bible Story
Do this in the Discovery Center.

Place the storytelling figures (figures 2, 11, 12) or the toys in the sandbox. **Say:** "God told Noah to build a big boat." Set up the boat in the sand while repeating the Bible verse. Then **say:** "God told Noah to get the animals into the boat." Have the children put all the animals in the boat while repeating the Bible verse. **Say:** "God told Noah to put his family in the boat." Have the children put the people in the boat while repeating the Bible verse. Keep repeating until all children have had a chance to place the animals and people in the boat. The more the children repeat the story, the more they will remember it.

 Learn a Song
Do this in the Storytelling Center.

Say: "Noah's boat is called by a special name. It's called an ark." Sing "The Animals on the Ark" (CD, Songbook) with the children.

After singing all of the printed verses, ask the children what other animals were on the ark and what sound those animals make. (Note: Younger toddlers do not have the language skills to name animals, but older twos will enjoy adding animals.)

3 Connect

with the Story

a Take Care of Pets

Do this in the Family Living Center.

Set out the pet items. Let the children enjoy playing with the toy pets. **Ask:** "Do you have a pet? What do you do to help take care of your pet?" Remind the children that Noah had to care for many "pets."

b Tell Another Story

Do this in the Storytelling Center.

Zachary came running into the Sunday school classroom. He ran straight to Mr. Peters. He said "Cat! Cat!"

Zachary's grandmother said, "Zachary is trying to tell you that we got a new cat at our house."

"How wonderful, Zachary," said Mr. Peters. "What is your cat's name?"

"Patches," said Zachary.

"Patches is a wonderful name for a cat," said Mr. Peters. "Do you help to take care of Patches?"

"He sure does," said Zachary's grandmother. "He helps to put out food and water, and he is learning how to be gentle with the kitty."

"I am so glad that God made cats," said Mr. Peters. "And I am glad that God wants us to take care of them."

"Me too," said Zachary.

c Build a Boat

Do this in the Building Center.

Gather two or three children. **Say:** "God told Noah to build a big boat. Let's pretend to be Noah and build a big boat." Use large blocks and make a big boat—big enough for the children to climb into. Collect all of the animals from around the room and gather them into the boat after it is built.

Say: "I am glad God told Noah to save all of the animals."

4 Celebrate

the Story

a Enjoy Music

Do this in the Storytelling Center.

Sing "The Animals on The Ark" (CD, Songbook), adding as many animals as you and the children can think of. You may wish to add movements as you sing.

Enjoy other songs and action verses that you have learned in Sunday school.

b Sing an Action Song

Do this in the Storytelling Center.

Sing "When Noah Built The Ark," using the motions (CD, Songbook).

As the children add other animals, let them suggest the motions they should use.

c Say Goodbye

Recall today's Bible story, encouraging children to say the Bible verse with you. **Say:** "I am glad (*name one of the children*) came to church today." Repeat this for each child in the class.

Pray: "Thank you, God, for Noah. We are glad he did what you told him to do."

Be sure to have a teacher or helper at the door to ensure that anxious children do not leave until someone comes for them. Tell parents about today's Bible story and make sure that each child has today's Bible Story Picture Card.

Show the parents the "Nurturing Your Child's Faith" section of the card. Point out the animal banner to the parents.

Tip

Make the stories more personal. Substitute your name and that of the children in the contemporary stories.

Look Back

Today we wanted each child to hear that God told Noah to do something, and Noah did it.

Did each child have a chance to hear the story?

We also want children to continue to experience happy times when they come to church. Was each returning child glad to come to your room? If not, what did you do? Did each new child feel welcomed?

What did the children teach you today?

Look Ahead

Next week we will let the children play with water. This is a favorite activity for toddlers, but it must be thought out ahead of time. Read the instructions carefully. You are also invited to use fingerpaint. If you feel this is too messy, there is another craft activity (leaf rubbings) in the lesson plan. You may choose to do either one or both.

**Genesis
7:17-18; 8:5**

God brought Noah, his family, and all the animals safely to dry land. But they had to wait a long time for God to do this.

Bible Verse:
God remembered Noah and the animals.
(Genesis 8:1, adapted)

Resources:
Bible
CD
Activity Pak (Fall)
   page 8 (figure 2)
   page 16 (animal couples)
   Songbook
Bible Story Picture Cards

Supplies:
large plastic tub or dishpan
water
water play items
blue fingerpaint
fingerpaint paper or freezer paper
cover-ups
pet items
leaves or leaf shapes
thin paper
large green crayons
masking tape
CD player
green paper leaf or piece of green cloth
cleanup supplies
clothesline and clothespins
building blocks
brown construction paper ark made last week

Noah Finds Dry Ground............

Enter the Bible Story

Read Genesis 7:17-18; 8:5: This week we continue the story of Noah with the account of the long period of time that Noah and his family were on the ark with all of the animals. The flood caused the earth to return to its pre-Creation state: "The earth was a formless void and darkness covered the face of the deep" (Genesis 1:1). But this time the earth was not empty—there was a little rudderless boat floating on the water. And God remembered the creatures on the boat and caused the rain to stop. Eventually, the wind blew the waters away enough to cause dry land to appear. But still Noah and the animals could not leave the ark. They had to stay until they knew that the land could support them. So Noah sent out birds to look for food. The evidence of the leaf was enough to tell Noah that life would once again flourish on the earth and that God had not forgotten the remnant of creatures floating in the boat.

Think About It: "Lord, give me patience, and I want it right now!" Sound familiar? We all want what we want when we want it. We do not like to wait. Reflect on the following questions as you prepare to teach the children this week: What does it mean to you when the psalmist says, "Wait for the LORD" (Psalm 27:14)? What do you have trouble waiting for? What is it that you do not mind waiting for?

Through the Week: What do you think it was like to be confined to a large boat for a long time? The Bible says that it rained for forty days and forty nights, which is another way of saying a long, long time. Then there was a longer time waiting for some dry land to appear. The animals were dependent on Noah and his family for food and for cleaning up.

Pray: God, thank you for being with me during the hard times—when I get so tired of waiting for an end to the situation that is bothering me. Remind me that your presence is with me always.

The Story and Young Children

We are living in a culture that believes in "instant gratification." We get irritated when our food does not cook in the microwave in less than five minutes. How quickly we forget what our lives were like even ten years ago. Have you had the experience of being interrupted by a child while you are talking to someone else? The child will simply repeat the request even louder if you do not respond. We tend to think that we are forgotten when we have to wait a long time for anything. Does Mommy remember where she left me? Does the teacher remember that I want to talk to her? We emphasize during this lesson that just because we have to wait does not mean we are forgotten. Mommies, daddies, teachers, and God remember children.

Room Setup: Set up a place for water play today. Be sure to have lots of towels and waterproof coverups to protect clothing, since toddlers love to splash in water.

Learning Centers

Conversation Center

You will need: short-sleeved adult-size shirts, paper towels, soapy water, clothesline and clothespins, blue fingerpaint (see p. 233), fingerpaint paper or freezer paper, several large leaves (or leaf shapes cut from cardboard), large green crayons with the paper removed, thin paper (newsprint or typing paper), masking tape.

Get ready: Put a circle of masking tape on each leaf and place the leaf on the table, tape side down. This will keep the leaf in place while the children are rubbing. Tape a piece of paper to the table on top of the leaf.

- Use Blue Fingerpaint, Activity 1c
- Make Leaf Rubbings, Activity 3a

Building Center

You will need: building blocks.

Get ready: Provide enough blocks for toddlers to share. You may use wooden unit blocks or large cardboard or plastic blocks.

Family Living Center

You will need: pet items from last week.

Get ready: Set out items from last week.

- Take Care of Pets, Activity 1d

Storytelling Center

This should be an open area where you may gather children for storytelling, or to listen and respond to music.

You will need: Bible; leaf, piece of green paper, or scrap of green cloth; CD, CD player, Songbook; Activity Pak—p. 8 (figure 2) and 16 (animal couples); ark shape (p. 234); brown construction paper ark (see Session 4).

- Tell the Bible Story, Activity 2a
- Retell the Bible Story, Activity 2b
- Tell Another Story, Activity 3b
- Enjoy Music, Activity 4a
- Play a Waiting Game, Activity 4b

Discovery Center

You will need: a large plastic tub or several dishpans, water, items for water play (funnels, scoops, small containers, floating items such as corks and toy boats).

Get ready: See p. 234 for information on setting up for water play. Use an adult monitor to keep splashing to a minimum. Prepare waterproof coverups (see p. 233).

- Enjoy Water Play, Activity 1b

The Dove Finds a Leaf

Noah and the animals were in the big boat a long, long time. God remembered Noah and the animals.

One day Noah sent out a dove to see if there was a place to stop the boat.

The dove brought back a green leaf. Noah knew there was a place to stop the boat.

Noah was glad that God had planned for dry land.

 **Prepare**

for the Story

a **Welcome Each Child**
Do this as each child enters the room.

Stoop to the child's eye level and welcome each child by name.

Say to each child: "I remember you, (*name of child*), and I am so happy to see you again."

b **Enjoy Water Play**
Do this in the Discovery Center.

Gather one or two children. If the children were present last week, **say**: "Last week there was sand in here. I wonder where the sand went? Now there is all water." Tell the children that they will hear a story about a time when there was no sand, only water.

c **Use Blue Fingerpaint**
Do this in the Conversation Center.

Gather one or two children. Put a paint smock or a short-sleeved adult shirt on each

child to protect his or her clothing. Give each child a large piece of fingerpaint or freezer paper. (Freezer paper is thicker than copy paper or newsprint and will hold up well under small fingers.)

Pour a small amount of blue fingerpaint onto the center of the paper. Tell the children that they are going to make a picture of water. Let the children enjoy the sensation of paint on their hands.

Be sure to have paper towels as well as soapy water handy for cleanup. Put each child's name on her or his picture and hang it on the wall or on your clothesline.

d **Take Care of Pets**
Do this in the Family Living Center.

Let the children enjoy playing with the toy pets again this week.

Recall last week's story and remind the children that Noah had to take care of a lot of "pets."

 **Tell**

the Story

a **Tell the Bible Story**
Do this in the Storytelling Center.

Gather one or two children. Show the children the brown construction paper ark from last week. Remind children who were present last week of the story of Noah building the ark. Tell the children that all of the animals are now inside the ark, and Noah is looking for a place to stop the boat so they can all get off.

Tell the Bible story, using Noah (figure 2) and the animals (Activity Pak—p. 16) at the appropriate times. Open a Bible and **say**: "Even though Noah and the animals had to wait a long, long time, God did not forget them. The Bible says, 'God remembered Noah and the animals.'"

Ask the children to repeat the Bible verse with you.

b **Retell the Bible Story**
Do this in the Storytelling Center.

Gather one or two children. Ask the children to echo your words and motions

as you retell the story.
Noah and the animals were in the big boat a long, long, time.
(*Sigh and put your head on one hand.*)
And God remembered Noah and the animals.
(*Smile and hold up one finger.*)

Noah looked everywhere for dry land, but did not see any.
(*Hold hand up to your forehead; look around.*)
And God remembered Noah and the animals.
(*Smile and hold up one finger.*)

Noah sent out a dove to look for land.
(*Flap your arms like a bird.*)
And God remembered Noah and the animals.
(*Smile and hold up one finger.*)

The dove brought back a green leaf.
(*Flap your arms like a bird.*)
Because God remembered Noah and the animals.
(*Smile and hold up one finger.*)

3 Connect
with the Story

a Make Leaf Rubbings
Do this in the Conversation Center.

Gather one or two children. Give each child a green crayon from which you have removed the paper. Show the child how to rub the crayon across the paper to make a rubbing of the leaf that you taped to the table. Put the child's name on the paper and remove it from the table, replacing the paper on top of the leaf for the next child.

b Tell Another Story
Do this in the Storytelling Center.

Gather one or two children and tell the story:

Akia was angry. She wanted to fingerpaint, but Mrs. Johnson told her that she had to wait her turn until Shelby was finished.

Akia tried to grab Shelby's arm to make her stop fingerpainting. Mrs. Johnson said, "No, no, Akia. It is time to wait. I will remember that you want to fingerpaint. Why don't you play with the blocks until it is your turn?"

Akia went to where Montez was playing with the blocks. She and Montez built a big tower with the colored blocks.

"Akia," said Mrs. Johnson, "Shelby is finished. I remember that you want to fingerpaint. It is your turn now."

Akia was happy as she played with the squishy paint. She was glad Mrs. Johnson remembered.

4 Celebrate
the Story

a Enjoy Music
Do this in the Storytelling Center.

Gather one or two children. Sing "The Animals on the Ark" (CD, Songbook), using motions, if you wish.

Remind the children that God loved Noah and his family and all the animals so much that God caused the water to go away so that they could stop the boat.

Sing "Show How Much God Loves Us" (CD, Songbook). Sing other songs that the children have learned and enjoyed in previous weeks.

b Play a Waiting Game
Do this in the Storytelling Center.

Put a leaf, paper, or cloth on a table in plain sight. Gather several children in a circle.

Say: "Let's pretend we're waiting for the water to go away." Ask the children to sit very still for about ten seconds and wait. Then point to one of the children and say, "You be the dove and find us a leaf."

Tell the child to go to the table, get the "leaf," and bring it back to the circle. When the child returns, have the children cheer.

Replace the "leaf" on the table and play again, this time picking a different "dove." Repeat until all the children have a chance to be the "dove."

c Say Goodbye
Recall today's Bible story. Encourage the children to say or sing the Bible verse with you. **Say:** "I am glad that God remembers (*name one of the children*)." Repeat this for each child in the class.

Pray: "Thank you, God, for remembering us. We will remember how much you love us."

Have a teacher or helper at the door to ensure that anxious children do not leave until someone comes for them. Tell parents about today's Bible story and make sure that each child has today's Bible Story Picture Card. Show the parents the "Nurturing Your Child's Faith" section of the card. Send the fingerpaint pictures home with the children if they are dry enough. If not, find a safe place for them to dry until next week. Be sure the children take home their leaf rubbings.

Tip
Make the stories more personal. Substitute your name and that of the children in the contemporary stories.

Look Back
Did you remember all of the children? Did each child have a chance to hear the Bible story today?

What activities went well today? What activities could use some improvements?

Are the children adjusting well to being left at Sunday school by their parents?

What are some ways you can help make arrival time more pleasant for everyone?

Look Ahead
Next week we will return to sand play (see p. 234). We will be making rainbows by pasting squares of tissue paper. Prepare the colored tissue paper ahead of time.

God always keeps promises, just as in the time of Noah.

Bible Verse:
God said, "I have put a rainbow in the clouds." (Genesis 9:13, adapted)

Resources:
Bible
CD
Activity Pak (Fall)
   pages 5, 8
   (figures 2, 4, 8, 9)
   page 16 (animal couples)
   page 4 ("Noah and the Rainbow" picture)
   Songbook
Bible Story Picture Cards

Supplies:
large piece of paper or posterboard
two-inch squares of colored tissue paper in rainbow colors
brown construction paper ark made in Session 4
glue
3- to 5-ounce paper cups
toy animals
sandbox (see p. 234)
CD player
pet supplies
large plastic margarine container with lid
straws
liquid dishwashing soap
prism, cut glass, or small mirror and glass of water
animal crackers
napkins
building blocks
plastic animals
(optional: Noah's ark toy)

28

Noah Sees a Rainbow······

Enter the Bible Story

Read Genesis 8:3-20; 9:12-16: We end the story of Noah with the story of the promise about the rainbow that God gave to Noah and to us all.

Think About It: One of the two-year-olds in my class breaks into a big smile and comes running to me with arms stretched out whenever she sees me. Of course she is rewarded with a big kiss and a hug. This always makes me feel special. We have other ways of showing love to one another. A phone call to see if someone is okay, a note received in the mail, a small gift for no reason at all—these all help us know that we are special to someone else. Reflect on the following questions as you prepare to tell the story and to help children retell the story this week: What reminds you that you are loved? What do you do to tell others that they are special to you? How do you know that God loves you? What signs do you see in your daily life that remind you of God's great love? How can you show the children in your class how special they are and how much God loves them?

Through the Week: Find some way this week to show the children and their parents that you are thinking of them and praying for them. Try to bring a rainbow into someone else's life.

Pray: Thank you, God, for the many ways we experience your love. Help us to notice these signs of love as we go through our busy lives. Remind us of how special we are to you. Amen.

The Story and Young Children

Toddlers may or may not have seen a rainbow. Nevertheless, we can tell them about the rainbow so that the first time they see one, they will remember that God loves them. Because we have not focused on the fact that the flood was sent because God was so disappointed in humanity's behavior, we will not focus on the fact that the rainbow is the sign that the flood will not happen again. Instead, with children of this age, it is most appropriate to say that God sends a rainbow to tell us that we are loved.

Room Setup: Place a prism where light will shine through it (and where it will be out of the children's reach). Or hang a piece of cut glass in a window. You can also place a small mirror in a glass of water and set it in a window sill. If you do not have a window, you may use the light from a film projector or a slide projector. (Always keep cords and projectors away from the children.)

Learning Centers

Conversation Center

You will need: a large piece of paper or posterboard on which you have drawn a rainbow; two-inch squares of tissue paper in red, orange, yellow, green, blue and purple; glue; napkins and animal crackers.

Get ready: Cover the top of a low table with a large piece of paper or posterboard. Before the children arrive, draw seven arcs on the paper to make a rainbow with six "bands" of color. You may choose to use fewer colors if you have a small class. Pour glue into small paper cups.

• Make a Rainbow, Activity 1b
• Make a Snack to Share, Activity 4b

Discovery Center

You will need: sandbox and toys (see p. 234); a prism, cut glass, or small mirror and glass of water; margarine container with lid, paper punch, water, liquid dishwashing soap, drinking straws (optional: Noah's ark toy).

Get ready: Punch two holes in the lid of the container. Pour about ½-cup water in the container and add 1 tablespoon dishwashing soap. Place the lid on the container.

• Play With Sand, Activity 1d
• Make a Bubble Machine, Activity 3a
• Enjoy Rainbows, Activity 4a

Building Center

You will need: building blocks, plastic animals.

• Play With Toy Animals, Activity 1c

Storytelling Center

This should be an open area where you may gather children for storytelling, or to listen and respond to music. It would be helpful to have this center on a carpeted area.

You will need: Bible; Activity Pak pp. 5, 8 (figures 2, 4, 8, 9), p. 16 (animal couples), and p. 4 ("Noah and the Rainbow" picture); CD and CD player, Songbook; brown construction paper ark (see Session 4).

•Tell the Bible Story, Activity 2a
•Retell the Bible Story, Activity 2b
•Sing a Song, Activity 2c
•Tell Another Story, Activity 3b

Family Living Center

You will need: stuffed toy animals; pet supplies.

• Take Care of Pets, Activity 2d

Noah Sees a Rainbow

Noah, his wife, his family, and all the animals were glad to be on dry land. They had been on the boat for a long, long time. They were glad that God had saved them from the big flood. They were glad that God had remembered them and had planned for dry land.

"I have put a rainbow in the clouds," God said. "When you see the rainbow, remember that I love you forever."

1 Prepare

for the Story

a **Welcome Each Child**
Do this as each child enters the room.

Stoop to the child's eye level and welcome each child by name. **Say:** "I am so happy to see you, (*name of child*). We are going to make a rainbow today."

Encourage each child to find an activity that interests her or him.

 **Make a Rainbow**
Do this in the Conversation Center.

Show the children how to "touch" the glue and then "touch" a square of tissue paper to place a small amount of glue on the paper or posterboard. Then help the children glue their squares onto the larger piece of paper, filling each band with a different color.

Remember that rainbows do not have to be perfect, and some paper may wind up in the wrong section. Tell the children and parents that mistakes lend character to your rainbow.

Hang the rainbow close to your Storytelling Center when you have filled all the bands. (Option: You may wish to color your rainbow with markers or crayons.)

c **Play With Toy Animals**
Do this in the Building Center.

Place a variety of animals in the Building Center, along with the blocks. Encourage the children to use the animals in their play. Let the children use blocks to build a boat for the animals.

Remind the children that the animals needed new houses and barns after they got off the ark.

d **Play With Sand**
Do this in the Discovery Center.

Encourage the children to feel the sand with their fingers.

Say: "I wonder how Noah and his family felt when they finally got off the boat and got to feel dry ground again."

Pretend to get all the animals off the boat if you have a Noah's ark toy for this session.

2 Tell

the Story

a **Tell the Bible Story**
Do this in the Storytelling Center.

Gather two or three children. Show the children the brown construction paper ark made in Session 4. Tell the Bible story, using the figures (figures 2, 4, 8, 9 and Activity Pak—p. 16) in the appropriate places. Open a Bible and **say:** "The Bible says, 'God said, "I have put a rainbow in the clouds."'" Invite the children to say the Bible verse with you.

b **Retell the Bible Story**
Do this in the Storytelling Center.

Gather two or three children. Show the children the "Noah and the Rainbow" poster (Activity Pak—p. 4). Talk about the things they see in the poster. If your children are verbal enough, ask them to tell you the story using the poster.

c **Sing a Song**
Do this in the Storytelling Center.

Listen to "The Rainbow Song" (CD, Songbook). Repeat the song, and this time sing along with it. Play the song again and encourage the children to dance to the music.

d **Take Care of Pets**
Do this in the Family Living Center.

Let the children enjoy playing with the toy pets again this week. Tell the children they are showing the animals that they love them.

Connect

with the Story

a **Make a Bubble Machine**

Do this in the Discovery Center.

Make a bubble machine out of a large plastic margarine container. Punch two holes in the lid of the container.

Pour about 1/2-cup water in the container and add about 1 tablespoon liquid dishwashing soap. Place the lid on the container.

Give each child a drinking straw. Have the children practice blowing through the straw. Let the children blow air on their hands. Be sure each child understands that he or she is to blow, not suck, through the straw.

Insert the straw into one of the holes of the bubble machine. Have the child blow through the straw to make bubbles come out of the other hole.

Place the bubbles in a spot where light can shine on them after each child has had a turn. The light should cause the bubbles to appear to have rainbow colors on them. Help the children see the colors in the bubbles.

Say: "Rainbows help us remember that God promises to love and care for us."

b **Tell Another Story**

Do this in the Storytelling Center.

Tracy dipped her straw into the bubble machine. She took a deep breath and blew. She laughed and laughed as bubbles came floating out of the bubble machine.

"Look!" said Tracy. "Look at all my pretty bubbles."

"I see your bubbles," said Mr. Thomas. "And do you see the colors? There are rainbows in your bubbles."

"I have rainbows in my bubbles!" Tracy said with delight.

"The light shining through your bubbles make the rainbows appear," said Mr. Thomas.

"Rainbows make me happy," said Tracy.

"And rainbows help us remember that God loves us," said Mr. Thomas. "And that makes me happy too."

Celebrate

the Story

a **Enjoy Rainbows**

Do this in the Discovery Center.

Use a prism or cut glass to catch sunlight and reflect it off the walls of the room. Or place a small mirror in a glass of water. Have the mirror leaning against the side of the glass. Place the glass where it will get direct sunlight and be out of the children's reach.

Remind the children that rainbows remind us of God's love.

 Make a Snack to Share

Do this in the Conversation Center.

Enjoy eating animal crackers. Hand out napkins. Place two animal crackers on each child's napkin. Help the children identify the animals.

Remind the children that God told Noah to bring two of every kind of animal on the big boat. Noah did what God told him to do. Noah knew that God would

take care of his family and the animals on the boat.

c **Say Goodbye**

Recall today's Bible story, encouraging the children to say the Bible verse with you.

Say: "I am glad (*name one of the children*) came to church today." Repeat this for each child in the class.

Pray: "Thank you, God, for our church. We are happy to come to church."

Be sure to have a teacher or helper at the door to ensure that anxious children do not leave until someone comes for them. Tell parents about today's Bible story and make sure that each child has today's Bible Story Picture Card.

Show the parents the "Nurturing Your Child's Faith" section of the card. Point out to parents the rainbow made by the class.

Tip
Make the stories more personal. Substitute your name and that of the children in the contemporary stories.

Look Back
Did each child have an opportunity to hear the story of the rainbow?

What activities worked well with your children? Which activities did not go so well? What could you do to improve them?

Did all of the children feel loved today?

Look Ahead
For next week's story on Moses you will need to gather baskets. You will also bring back the water play activities and will need something to represent water in your Building Center.

31

Children need to feel safe and loved. Teachers and parents can help children feel this way by rocking them.

Bible Verse:
Moses was put in a basket and placed on the river.
(Exodus 2:3, paraphrased)

Resources:
Bible
CD
Activity Pak (Fall)
    pages 5, 9 (figures 6, 13, 14, 16)
    page 12 (Baby Moses)
Songbook
Bible Story Picture Cards

Supplies:
CD player
pictures of water
items for water play
    (see p. 234)
towels
baskets
blocks
toy boats
small blue rug, carpet square, or large piece of blue paper
baby dolls, doll items, blankets
thin paper plates
construction paper
stapler and staples
crayons or felt-tip markers
teacher scissors
child-sized rocking chair, rocking boat, or other rocking toy
blue scarfs, fabric scraps, ribbon, or paper streamers
bulletin board or clothesline and clothespins
dishpan

Moses Is Born.........

Enter the Bible Story

Read Exodus 2:1-10: These verses tell the story of Moses as a baby. Moses' sister Miriam is part of this story, although his older brother Aaron, who is present in later stories about Moses, is not mentioned. The name of the book of the Bible in which we find the story of the baby Moses is "Exodus." This is from the Greek language and means "going out." It is the story of the nation of Israel "going out" from slavery in Egypt to wander in the wilderness for many years under the leadership of Moses. It is during this period of wandering that Moses received the Ten Commandments from God.

Think About It: Moses became a hero of the Hebrew people, a leader whom they followed in times of trouble and risk. Reflect on the following questions as you prepare to help children know a story about this important person in the history of Israel: What would have happened to Israel if Moses' mother and sister had not taken such good and clever care of him? Would the history of Israel have been different without this leader? How would our own personal histories have been different if those who cared for us in babyhood and childhood had been different? How do our actions affect the childhood of the children we care for and teach? How can we make a difference in their lives?

Through the Week: The Bible often tells something about the birth and babyhood of the important people described in its stories. What can you remember about other babies in the Bible? What do you recall about the births of Isaac, Obed, and, of course, Jesus? Rocking a baby is one of life's most common experiences.

Pray: We are grateful, God, that we can know the wonderful stories of people from Hebrew history. Help us make this story of Moses come alive in the lives of the children we teach.

The Story and Young Children

Children can know that Moses was an important person in the Bible. They can hear the story of baby Moses and how his mother and sister cared for him. Children in this age group may have observed their parents or others caring for a baby. They can be reminded that when they were babies, their parents and caregivers cared for them. Imitating and acting out caring play with dolls is a good activity for toddlers and two-year-olds.

Room Setup: Display the pictures of water that you used in Session 5. Set out a variety of baskets near the "Baby Moses" poster (Activity Pak—p. 12). Provide children with something that rocks back and forth. If you have younger children, provide an adult rocker so that teachers may rock children. Because in today's story Moses was placed at the edge of the river, water play and experiences are good for use in this session. Children will enjoy repeating some of the water play activities from the lesson on Noah two weeks ago.

Learning Centers

Work with two or three children at a time in each learning center.

Conversation Center

You will need: thin paper plates, construction paper, stapler, staples, crayons or markers, teacher scissors, CD, CD player, Songbook.

Get ready: Cut construction paper in thirds to make 9-by-4-inch sheets.

• Make Paper Plate Baskets, Activity 3a

Discovery Center

You will need: dishpans, items for water play, towels, water pictures, teacher scissors, a variety of baskets, baby doll, baby blanket.

Get ready: Place dishpans on a low table and fill with an inch or two of water. Cut pictures of water from magazines. Place the pictures of water on a clothesline or bulletin board.

• Enjoy Water Play, Activity 1b
• Explore Water Pictures, Activity 1c
• Explore Baskets, Activity 1d

Family Living Center

You will need: child-sized rocking chairs or rocking boat, CD, CD player, Songbook.

• Enjoy Rocking, Activity 4b

Storytelling Center

This should be an open area where you can gather children for storytelling, or to listen and respond to music.

You will need: Bible; Activity Pak—pp. 5, 9 (figures 6, 13, 14, 16) and p. 12 ("Baby Moses" picture), CD, CD player, Songbook; blue scarfs, fabric scraps, ribbon or paper streamers; blue rug or paper cutout (optional: doll, blanket, basket).

• Tell the Bible Story, Activity 2a
• Retell the Bible Story, Activity 2b
• Sing a Song, Activity 2c
• Tell Another Story, Activity 3c
• Enjoy Music, Activity 4a

Building Center

Provide enough blocks for toddlers to share. Use wooden blocks or large cardboard or plastic blocks.

You will need: boats; blue rug or carpet square or winding river cut from blue posterboard.

• Play With Toy Boats, Activity 3b

Back and Forth

Back and forth. Back and forth. Mother rocked baby Moses.

Back and forth. Back and forth. Big sister Miriam rocked baby Moses.

Mother fixed a special basket. She put baby Moses in the basket.

Mother and Miriam took the basket and put it on the water at the edge of the river.

Back and forth. Back and forth. The water rocked baby Moses in the basket. The baby was safe because Miriam watched him. Miriam loved baby Moses.

Prepare
for the Story

a Welcome Each Child
Do this as each child enters the room.

Have the water sounds (CD) playing as the children enter the room. (Use the "repeat" button on your CD player to repeat the selection for longer play.)

Stoop to the child's eye level and welcome each child by name. **Say** to each child: "Listen. Do you hear something special?"

b Enjoy Water Play
Do this in the Discovery Center.

Give the children turns to play in the water, one child at a time to a dishpan. Let the children enjoy manipulating the water with their hands and with the toys.

Help the children tell what the water looks like and how it feels. Tell the children that today they will hear a story about a river full of water.

c Explore Water Pictures
Do this in the Discovery Center.

Talk with the children as they enjoy looking at pictures. Help the children describe what they see in the pictures. For younger children this may mean helping them say words such as *water*, *lake*, or *river*. Tell the children that today they will hear a story about a baby who floated on water in a little basket.

d Explore Baskets
Do this in the Discovery Center.

Invite the children to explore the baskets. How do they look? How do they feel? Help them see how the baskets are alike and how they are different. Tell the children that today they will hear a story about a baby who slept in a basket. Give the children turns to place the baby doll into each basket. Make it a game to see into which basket the baby will fit: "No, Michael, that basket is too little for a baby! Let's try another basket."

Tell
the Story

a Tell the Bible Story
Do this in the Storytelling Center.

Gather one or two children. Show the children the "Baby Moses" picture (Activity Pak—p. 12).

Let the children tell you what they see. Help younger children with words such as *water*, *basket*, and *reeds*. Open the Bible and **say**: "The Bible tells a story about this little baby. His name is Moses."

Tell the Bible story, acting it out with the Bible figures (figures 6, 13, 14, 16). (Option: Use a baby doll, baby blanket, and a real basket as you tell the story.)

Look at the Bible and **say**: "The Bible says, 'Moses was put in a basket and placed on the river.'" Invite the children to repeat the Bible verse with you.

b Retell the Bible Story
Do this in the Storytelling Center.

Have "Water Sounds" (CD) playing as you retell the story. At each place where the story says "back and forth," have the children rock their imaginary babies.

Pantomime with the children preparing the basket with a blanket at the corresponding place in the story, or let the children each have a real basket and blanket to prepare.

After preparing the basket **say**: "Listen! Do you hear the water? I hear the river. Let's go down to the river. We have something special to do there." Move to the "river" (a blue rug or paper cutout) and place the real or imaginary babies in the baskets in the river.

c Sing a Song
Do this in the Storytelling Center.

Play "Little Baby Moses" (CD, Songbook) while you pretend to rock a baby. Then sing the song and pretend to put your baby to sleep.

Finally, sing the song as you pretend to float your baby on the river.

34

3 Connect
with the Story

a **Make Paper Plate Baskets**
Do this in the Conversation Center.

Give each child a paper plate. Let the children decorate their paper plates with crayons or markers. Let each child choose a color of construction paper for a handle.

Fold the construction paper lengthwise over on itself several times to make a handle for the basket. Slightly turn up two opposite sides of the plate and staple the folded paper handle firmly to the bowed-up undersides of the plate. The handle should be short enough to hold the sides in a slightly turned-up position to make a basket.

Remind the children as they work that baby Moses rocked in a basket on the water. Sing the song "Little Baby Moses" (CD, Songbook).

b **Play With Toy Boats**
Do this in the Building Center.

Provide toy boats and pretend water for the children to play with.

c **Tell Another Story**
Do this in the Storytelling Center.

Hannah liked to watch her baby brother Jason. He was lying on a blanket on the floor kicking his legs and smiling. Suddenly Jason stopped smiling and began to cry.

"Jason is tired," said Mother as she picked him up and cradled him in her arms. Mother placed Jason in the baby swing and turned the swing on.

Back and forth went the swing. Soon Jason stopped crying. His eyes closed. He was fast asleep.

"I have to go into the kitchen to wash the dishes," Mother said to Hannah. "Would you stay here and watch Jason? You can call me if he wakes up."

Hannah played with her toys near Jason's swing. She was glad to help Mother keep Jason safe.

4 Celebrate
the Story

a **Enjoy Music**
Do this in the Storytelling Center.

Sing "Little Baby Moses" (CD, Songbook). Invite the children to rock imaginary babies in their arms to the rhythm of the song as you sing it again.

Play "Water Sounds" (CD) and encourage the children to pretend to be water and to move their bodies to the water sounds. Give them blue scarfs, fabric scraps, ribbon, or paper streamers to move like water.

b **Enjoy Rocking**
Do this in the Family Living Center.

Invite the children to rock in a chair or a boat. Recall today's Bible story as the children rock.

Sing "Little Baby Moses" (CD, Songbook) as the children rock. Let the children pretend to fall asleep while rocking.

c **Say Goodbye**

Recall today's Bible story, encouraging the children to say the Bible verse with you. **Say**: "Moses was a little baby. (*Name one of the children*) was once a baby like Moses and now is growing bigger." Repeat the last sentence for each child in the class. **Pray**: "Thank you, God, for stories in the Bible about special people like baby Moses."

Have a teacher or helper at the door to match children with family members. Give the children their paper plate baskets to take home. Tell parents about today's Bible story and make sure that each child has today's Bible Story Picture Card. Show the parents the "Nurturing Your Child's Faith" section of the card.

Tip
Make the stories more personal. Substitute your name and that of the children in the contemporary stories.

Look Back
Did each child have an opportunity to experience the story of baby Moses today?

Did the children hear the story? sing it? act it out?

We wanted children to know that Moses' mother and sister cared for him. Did the children feel cared for in our class today? In what ways did they experience love and care during the session?

Look Ahead
Next week we will learn about Ruth and how she helped Naomi when she was sad. Prepare play dough for next week's lesson. Gather pictures of people showing emotion. Note: There are three sessions on Ruth. You may wish to combine two of them in order to finish this quarter's sessions with the Thanksgiving session.

Friends show their love by caring for and being with sad or sick people.

Bible Verse:
Ruth said, "Where you go, I will go." (Ruth 1:16, adapted)

Resources:
Bible
CD
Activity Pak (Fall)
    page 21 (matching hearts game
    page 23 ("Ruth and Naomi" picture
    Songbook
Bible Story Picture Cards

Supplies:
play dough
construction paper
paper plates
glue
small paper cups
craft sticks
small suitcases
dress-up clothes
building blocks
CD player
magazines
teacher scissors

Ruth Chooses........

Enter the Bible Story

Read Ruth 1:1-22: This familiar story has much to teach us about how we respond to others. In this story Ruth made a deliberate choice—a choice that many of us, given the same circumstances, would not have made. Moab and Israel did not have a happy co-existence. In fact, it was unusual for an Israelite family to live in Moab, much less to allow their sons to take Moabite wives. When Naomi became a widow, life took an unexpected turn. A woman on her own could barely raise enough food to survive. So when Orpah and Ruth became widows in a family without men, their society expected them to return to their mother's tent and find new husbands. Orpah did what was expected. Ruth, out of love and compassion for her mother-in-law, rebelled against society and went with Naomi to a place where she would be treated as a foreigner.

Think About It: Ruth is a beautiful story of love and commitment between women. Reflect on the following questions as you prepare to help the children learn how we care for others: How do you feel when something or someone is taken from you? Are you willing to admit your anger towards God? Does true faith ever include doubting or questioning God? How do you comfort someone whose grief or pain you do not understand? What would cause you to go against tradition or societal expectations in order to help someone else?

Through the Week: Take time to notice others around you. How are they feeling? What can you deduce from their body language, facial expressions, reactions to stress? Think about feelings from a toddler's point of view. Feelings can be frightening if you do not know what they are and how to control them. How will you help your children experience feelings this week? How will you teach them to control their feelings?

Pray: God, thank you for the ability and the call to help others in times of trouble, and to accept help for ourselves.

The Story and Young Children

When we are born, the entire universe revolves around us. If we are lucky, we have people surrounding us who respond to our every wish. They feed us when we are hungry, change our diapers when we are wet, and comfort us when we are in distress. Infants do not cry just to irritate adults. They cannot conceive the fact that adults have feelings. Infants cry to communicate that something is wrong. This is the only language they have. The children you teach still are not adept at using language to communicate their needs. They are increasingly surrounded by others who do not cater to their every whim. They are likely to communicate their frustration by biting, hitting, or screaming. They do this because they are children—not because they are bad. This story teaches children that God wants us to help people who are hurt. We can use this story to help children understand that others have feelings, and that each of us should be a friend to everyone— especially those in pain.

Room Setup: Add suitcases and dress-up clothes to the Family Living Center. Set out play dough and tools, including craft sticks, in the Conversation Center.

Learning Centers

Work with two or three children at a time in each learning center.

Conversation Center

This should be a table around which you can gather the children. Sit down with the children and engage them in conversation.

You will need: play dough, craft sticks, construction paper shapes, paper plates, glue, small paper cups.

Get ready: Prepare play dough. Make dough according to the recipe on page 232 or use commercial dough. Cut small circles and big arcs out of construction paper scraps.

- Play With Play Dough, Activity 1b
- Make Happy and Sad Faces, Activity 3a

Discovery Center

You will need: Activity Pak—p. 21 (matching hearts game), emotion pictures (see below).

Get ready: Separate the cards in the matching hearts game if you did not do so in Session 3. Gather pictures from magazines or old curriculum of people displaying various emotions.

- Play a Matching Hearts Game, Activity 1c
- Explore Pictures, Activity 4b

Family Living Center

Include a toy kitchen set and props appropriate to the lesson.

You will need: a few small suitcases and dress-up clothes.

- Play "Going on a Trip," Activity 1d

Building Center

- Play With Blocks, Activity 2d

Storytelling Center

This should be an open area where you can gather children for storytelling, or to listen and respond to music. It would be helpful to have this center on a carpeted area.

You will need: Activity Pak—p. 23 ("Ruth and Naomi" picture"), CD, CD player; Songbook; Bible.

- Tell the Bible Story, Activity 2a
- Retell the Bible Story, Activity 2b
- Sing a Song, Activity 2c
- Tell Another Story, Activity 3b
- Sing a Song, Activity 3c
- Enjoy Music, Activity 4a

Ruth Takes Care of Naomi

Naomi was sad. Her husband had died. Her sons had died. She decided to move a long way away. She wanted to go home to Bethlehem.

She said goodbye to Ruth.

But Ruth said, "I will go with you. I will take care of you. You will not be alone."

37

1 Prepare

for the Story

a **Welcome Each Child**
Do this as each child enters the room.

Stoop to the child's eye level and welcome each child by name. **Say** to each child: "I am so happy you have come to church today."

b **Play With Play Dough**
Do this in the Conversation Center.

Draw the children's attention to a smiley face that you have drawn in the play dough with a craft stick. Some of the children will remember this activity from Session 2.

Say: "When I am happy, I have a *big* smile on my face."

Help the children draw happy faces in the clay. Then draw the children's attention to a sad face that you have drawn in the play dough.

Say: "Sometimes I am sad, and then I have a sad face." Help the children draw sad faces in the play dough.

c **Play a Matching Hearts Game**
Do this in the Discovery Center.

Gather one or two children. Ask the children to match the hearts (Activity Pak—p. 21) by colors.

You may wish to sort the cards into piles. Or give the children some cards, show them one of the remaining cards, and **ask:** "Who has a card to match this one?" The oldest children may enjoy playing "Concentration" with the cards.

Remind the children as you play that hearts mean, "I love you" and that just as God loves us, we should love one another.

d **Play "Going on a Trip"**
Do this in the Family Living Center.

Allow the children to play as if they are preparing to go on a trip. Talk about the things they would need to put in their suitcases if they were going a long way away.

2 Tell

the Story

a **Tell the Bible Story**
Do this in the Storytelling Center.

Gather one or two children. Show the children the "Ruth and Naomi" picture (Activity Pak—p. 23). **Say:** "Look at this woman. Her name is Naomi. Doesn't she look sad? I think the other woman is helping her. Her name is Ruth. Let me tell you a story about them."

Tell the children the story. Open a Bible and say the Bible verse. **Say:** "God loves us so much that God gave us friends to be with us when we are sad." **Pray:** "Thank you, God, for friends when we are sad."

b **Retell the Bible Story**
Do this in the Storytelling Center.

Gather one or two children. Say the following action verse:

Naomi was sad. "Boo, hoo, hoo!"
(*Rub eyes as if crying.*)
"I want to go home! Boo, hoo, hoo!"

(*Rub eyes as if crying.*)
Ruth said, "Don't cry, Naomi."
(*Wag head back and forth.*)
"I will go with you."
(*Put both hands on chest.*)
"I love you, Naomi."
(*Wrap both arms around yourself in a big hug.*)

c **Sing a Song**
Do this in the Storytelling Center.

Gather two or three children. Play "Ruth and Naomi" (Songbook). Play it again and encourage the children to act out the story as they listen.

d **Play With Blocks**
Do this in the Building Center.

As the children play with blocks, encourage them to make a new house for Naomi, back home in Bethlehem.

3 Connect
with the Story

a Make Happy and Sad Faces
Do this in the Conversation Center.

Gather one or two children. Give each child a paper plate. Put some glue in a paper cup. Show each child how to "touch" the glue with one of their fingers and then touch a scrap of construction paper.

Give each child three circles and one arc cut from construction paper. Help the children glue on their paper plates two construction paper circles as eyes, one construction paper circle as a nose and a construction paper arc to make a mouth. Notice that if you glue the arc pointing up, it looks like a happy face. If the arc is pointing down, it looks like a sad face.

Let the children make one of each face. While you work, talk about Ruth and Naomi and how Ruth knew Naomi was sad and wanted to help Naomi feel better.

b Tell Another Story
Do this in the Storytelling Center.

Brandon was crying. He was sad because his daddy had gone away and left him at Sunday school.

Mrs. Park picked up Brandon and held him. "It's okay, Brandon," said Mrs. Park. "Daddy will come back soon. You are safe here. We love you."

Deysha came over to Mrs. Park and Brandon. She patted him on the back, very gently. "We love you," said Deysha.

Brandon stopped crying. He and Deysha went to play with the blocks. Mrs. Park was happy. Brandon was happy. Deysha was happy. They were glad they had a special place to play and to learn about being loved.

c Sing a Song
Do this in the Storytelling Center.

Sing the song "If You're Happy and You Know It" (CD, Songbook). Use these verses:

1. If you're happy and you know it, clap your hands. (*Clap hands.*)
2. If you're sad and you know it, cry a tear. (*Rub eyes and say, "Boo, hoo."*)
3. If you're angry and you know it, stomp your feet. (*Stomp feet.*)
4. If you're scared and you know it, stand and shake. (*Hold arms close to chest and shake while looking scared.*)

Add other verses at the suggestions of the children.

4 Celebrate
the Story

a Enjoy Music
Do this in the Storytelling Center.

Play "Happy Music" (CD) and ask the children to dance around and act happy. Then play "Sad Music" (CD) and ask the children to dance around sadly.

If there is time, enjoy other songs that you have learned today or in past weeks.

b Explore Pictures
Do this in the Discovery Center.

Have the children look at the various pictures of people showing emotions.

As you look at each picture, **talk** about the emotion: "That man looks angry, doesn't he, Sean? What should he do now?" (*Use words, not hitting.*)

c Say Goodbye

Recall today's Bible story. Have the children say the Bible verse with you. **Say:** "I am glad (*name one of the children*) came to church today. Were you happy or sad to come today?" Repeat this for each child in the class. **Pray:** "Thank you, God, for friends who love us. When we are sad, we know they will help us."

Have a teacher or helper at the door to match children with their caregivers. Tell parents about today's Bible story and make sure that each child has today's Bible Story Picture Card.

Show the parents the "Nurturing Your Child's Faith" section of the card. Be sure the children take home their happy and sad faces.

Tip
Make the stories more personal. Substitute your name and that of the children in the contemporary stories.

Look Back
Did each child have an opportunity to experience the story of Ruth and Naomi today? Did the children hear the story? sing it? act it out?

We wanted children to know that people can feel sad, or happy, or angry.

Did the children experience activities that helped them know that feelings are good? Are the children prepared to help someone else when that person is sad?

Look Ahead
Next week we will be using wheat stalks for painting. These can be found at most craft stores or at places that sell dried or artificial flowers. Be on the lookout for them or a suitable alternative.

Ruth chose to love and care for Naomi, just as God loves and cares for us.

Bible Verse:
Be kind to one another.
Ephesians 4:32

Resources:
Bible
CD
Activity Pak (Fall)
   page 5, 8, 9 (figures 1, 3, 4, 15, 23)
   page 20 ("Boaz Shares" activity)
   Songbook
Bible Story Picture Cards

Supplies:
CD player
empty boxes and cans of grocery items
toy food
toy grocery cart or basket
play dough (see p. 232)
cookie cutters
tempera paint (only one color)
paper
wheat stalks
short-sleeved adult shirts
large resealable plastic bag
ingredients for trail mix
napkins
building blocks
two small boxes such as those that checks come in

Boaz Is Kind to Ruth.........................

Enter the Bible Story

Read Ruth 2:1–4:13: Ruth saw that Naomi got home to Bethlehem and then set out to provide for her. It was going to be difficult at best for two women living alone to provide for themselves. In addition, the field was not a safe place for an unaccompanied female—especially a foreigner. There was a great risk of harassment and perhaps even violence from the young men. But Boaz made it clear that she was under his protection. She was to stay close to his young women, and he warned his young men not to bother her. Moreover, he told them to pull grain from the sheaves that they had already gleaned from the field and to drop the grain deliberately in her path. Ruth went home with much more grain than she could have reasonably expected. Small wonder, then, that Naomi began to plan how to get Boaz to act as their protector and benefactor.

Think About It: Many of the stories of the Bible, particularly in the Hebrew Scriptures, portray the mighty acts of God in human history. However, in this story God acts through the ordinary—the everyday lives of common people. In fact, God is hardly mentioned at all in the text! Reflect on the following questions as you prepare to tell the story and to help children retell the story: Have you ever experienced God working in your life in some ordinary event? If so, which event? Why do we concentrate so much of our attention on the dramatic interventions of God? Is God always at work in our lives? Or does God act only at special moments?

Through the Week: Notice the acts of God in your day-to-day life.

Pray: Thank you, God, for using the ordinary events of our lives to show us your love. Thank you for using ordinary people like me. Amen.

The Story and Young Children

Toddlers do not understand the concept of sharing. In their eyes the entire world is theirs by right. Seeing another child with an attractive toy is reason enough, to them, for biting, scratching, or simply taking the toy away. We must understand the situation from the children's point of view and then help them reinterpret it. The important lesson in this story for children is that of sharing. Ruth and Naomi needed food once they got settled into their new home. Boaz had heard of Ruth's kindness in caring for Naomi, and he in turn was kind to Ruth in allowing her to gather all the grain she could carry. Naomi and Ruth had an abundance of food because of Boaz's kindness.

Room Setup: Gather empty boxes and cans of common grocery items to play grocery store. Tape closed empty boxes such as cereal, cake mixes, or rice. Open cans from the bottom, if possible, and check carefully for sharp edges that could cut little fingers. Ask parents to provide these items occasionally; we will use a pretend grocery store several times during the year, and the boxes may not last long.

Learning Centers

Conversation Center

This should be a table around which you may gather the children. Sit down with the children and engage them in conversation.

You will need: play dough, cookie cutters, tempera paint, paper, wheat stalks (available at most craft stores), short-sleeved adult shirts that button down the front, large resealable plastic bag, napkins, ingredients for trail mix (cereal, goldfish crackers, raisins, banana chips, and so forth).

- Play With Play Dough, Activity 1b
- Paint With Wheat Stalks, Activity 3a
- Make a Snack to Share, Activity 4b

Family Living Center

This would include a toy kitchen set and props appropriate to the lesson.

You will need: empty boxes and cans of grocery items, toy food, toy grocery cart or basket. (See note in Room Setup on preparing empty cans or boxes.)

Get ready: Set out common grocery items on a shelf or countertop.

- Play Grocery Store, Activity 1c

Discovery Center

You will need: Activity Pak—p. 20 ("Boaz Shares" activity), small boxes such as those that checks come in.

Get ready: Glue the pictures of Ruth and Boaz onto separate small boxes such as checks come in. Separate the sheaves of grain. Place them all in the Boaz box.

- Retell the Bible Story, Activity 2b

Building Center

- Play With Blocks, Activity 3c

Storytelling Center

You will need: Activity Pak—pp. 5, 8, 9, 17 (figures 1, 3, 4, 15, 23); CD, CD player, Songbook, Bible.

- Tell the Bible Story, Activity 2a
- Sing a Song, Activity 2c
- Tell Another Story, Activity 3b
- Enjoy Music, Activity 4a

Boaz Is Kind to Ruth

Ruth helped Naomi move to her new home. Then she went out to get some grain to eat.

"You may get your grain from my field," Boaz said. "I have heard that you have been kind to Naomi. May God bless you for being kind."

Ruth got a lot of grain from Boaz's field. She took it to Naomi. Naomi was happy to have so much food. Ruth was glad that Boaz was kind.

1 Prepare

for the Story

a Welcome Each Child
Do this as each child enters the room.

Stoop to the child's eye level and welcome each child by name. **Say** to each child: "I am so happy you have come to church today."

Be prepared to involve children in an interesting or comforting activity.

b Play With Play Dough
Do this in the Conversation Center.

Set out the play dough and cookie cutters. Pretend to make cookies for our friends as you play with the dough.

c Play Grocery Store
Do this in the Family Living Center.

Set out common grocery items on a shelf or countertop. If you have a toy grocery shopping cart or a basket, let the children put all the boxes and cans in their cart or basket, then take them out and put them back on the shelf.

While the children are playing, talk to them about how their caretakers go grocery shopping to provide food for them to eat.

2 Tell

the Story

a Tell the Bible Story
Do this in the Storytelling Center.

Gather one or two children. Show the children the storytelling figure of the young woman (figure 3).

Say: "This is Ruth. She is helping Naomi. I know a story about how this man, Boaz, helped her." Tell the Bible story, using the storytelling figures (figures 1, 3, 4, 15, 23) at the appropriate time.

Open a Bible and say the Bible verse. Ask the children to repeat the verse with you. Sing the Bible verse in the song "Be Kind to One Another" (CD, Songbook). Ask the children to sing with you.

b Retell the Bible Story
Do this in the Discovery Center.

Set out the "Boaz Shares" game (Activity Pak—p. 20). **Say**: "Look at Ruth. I think she is hungry. She needs some food." Then **say**: "Look at Boaz. He is not hungry. He has *lots* of food. Let's help him share his food." Take sheaves of grain and place them in the Ruth box one at a time while repeating the following verse.

One, two, three, what do you see?
Boaz giving Ruth some grain,
How kind is he?

When all of the grain is on the Ruth card, place it back on the Boaz card and repeat the verse.

c Sing a Song
Do this in the Storytelling Center.

Gather two or three children. Sing the following song to the tune of "Are You Sleeping?" (The tune is the same as the one for the song "Ruth and Naomi" on the CD). You may wish to use the storytelling figures (1, 3, 4, 15, 23) as you sing.

Where are you going?
Where are you going?
Naomi asked Ruth,
Naomi asked Ruth.
Going to get some grain,
Going to get some grain.
For our food,
For our food.

I will help you,
I will help you.
Boaz told Ruth,
Boaz told Ruth.
Help you get some grain,
Help you get some grain.
For your food,
For your food.

3 Connect
with the Story

a **Paint With Wheat Stalks**
Do this in the Conversation Center.

Gather two or three children. Protect their clothing from the paint by having each one wear an adult, short-sleeved shirt buttoned in the back.

Hold up a bundle of wheat stalks and **say**: "This is a sheaf of wheat." Move the sheaf through the air. **Ask**: "What sound do you hear?"

Separate the stalks and give one to each child. Let the children examine the stalks. Notice how dry they are and how they tickle your skin when you gently draw it across your cheek or arm. Notice the seed head and the long fingers of chaff that grow off the seed head.

Say: "This is the part that Ruth and Naomi could make into bread." Hold the stalk by the straw end and carefully dip the chaff into paint and move it across the sheet of paper. Help the children paint with their wheat stalk. When the child is finished, put his or her name on the paper and hang it on the wall or on your clothesline to dry.

b **Tell Another Story**
Do this in the Storytelling Center.

Aaron was playing with the blocks. He could build a big tall tower with his blocks and then knock them down. Aaron was having fun.

Shamika came over to the blocks. She wanted to have fun with the blocks. But Aaron had all of the blocks. She tried to take them away from Aaron, but Aaron bit her.

"No, no," said Mrs. Jennings. "We do not bite in Sunday school. We share. Shamika, would you like to play with the blocks?"

Shamika nodded her head.

"Aaron, could you share some blocks with Shamika?" Aaron gave Shamika some blocks.

c **Play With Blocks**
Do this in the Building Center.

Encourage the children to share as they play with blocks.

4 Celebrate
the Story

 Enjoy Music
Do this in the Storytelling Center.

Sing this week's Bible verse, "Be Kind to One Another" (CD, Songbook). Play the song on the CD. Invite the children to dance. Sing other favorites from the CD.

 Make a Snack to Share
Do this in the Conversation Center.

Recall the story of Ruth and Naomi needing food to eat and how Boaz shared with them. Ask the children to wash their hands in preparation for a snack.

Put a cup or two of each ingredient in a plastic bag. Allow each child to shake the bag to mix the ingredients. When each child has had a chance to shake the bag, scoop a small amount for each child out and place it on a napkin. **Say**: "We all helped make this snack. We are sharing our snack together."

 Say Goodbye

Recall today's Bible story. Have the children say or sing the Bible verse with you, "Be Kind to One Another" (Songbook, CD).

Say: "I am glad (*name one of the children*) shared with us today." Repeat this for each child in the class. **Pray**: "Thank you, God, for Ruth and Boaz. Help us learn to share like they did."

Be sure to have a teacher or helper at the door to match children with their caregivers.

Tell parents about today's Bible story and make sure that each child has today's Bible Story Picture Card. Show the parents the "Nurturing Your Child's Faith" section of the card. Point out to parents the wheat paintings, and show them the wheat stalks that the children used. Be sure the children take home their paintings.

Tip
Make the stories more personal. Substitute your name and that of the children in the contemporary stories.

Look Back
Did each child have an opportunity to hear the story of Ruth and Boaz today? Did they hear it? act it out? sing it?

What activities worked well with your children? Which activities did not go so well? What could you do to improve them before using them again?

Look Ahead
Which children were absent today? Which children have you not seen in a while? Make a point this week to call the parents of those who were absent and tell them that you have missed them.

Next week we get to play with baby things as we celebrate the birth of Ruth and Boaz's baby, Obed. You may wish to have a baby from your church nursery come for a visit with its mother. Make arrangements for this ahead of time.

God gives us families to love and care for us.

Bible Verse:
They named him Obed.
(Ruth 4:17)

Resources:
Bible
CD
Activity Pak (Fall)
    pages 5–8, 9 (figures 1, 3, 4, 16)
    Songbook
Bible Story Picture Cards

Supplies:
CD player
baby dolls
doll blankets
doll care items
play dough (see p. 232)
cookie cutters
    (gingerbread people shape)
rocking chair
cotton swabs
white construction paper
tempera paint (two or three colors)
3- to 5-ounce paper cups
short-sleeved adult shirts
magazine pictures of families
building blocks
bulletin board or clothesline and clothespins
(optional: picture box, rocking chair)

Obed Is Born..........

Enter the Bible Story

Read Ruth 4:13-22: Naomi finally found happiness again in the birth of her grandson, Obed. Don't you love a story with a happy ending? Two women bereft of the male support so necessary in their culture find a husband for the younger woman, and a baby boy is born. Naomi, who complained in the first chapter that God had afflicted her and brought her misfortune, was proven wrong in the fourth chapter. The neighborhood women celebrated with Naomi the birth of this son, who would be her sustainer in her old age. But then there is a twist to the story. They also praised Ruth as being better to her than seven sons. What? The entire story has been focused on the importance of sons, and then this foreigner is more important than seven of them? And then, a final dramatic twist: This Moabite woman became the great-grandmother of the great King David! The irony of a cursed foreigner being in any way involved with the genealogy of the greatest of Hebrew rulers is astonishing.

Think About It: The fullness in life that was lost in the beginning of the story was completely restored. The harvest was over, and the famine was dispelled. Naomi's family was restored in the marriage of Ruth and Boaz and the birth of their son, Obed. Through apparent human emptiness, God worked to bring fullness. Reflect on the following questions as you prepare to help children hear this story of God's providence: When has your life lost its fullness and meaning? At these times, how did God work to restore that fullness of life? What made you aware of God's restoration?

Through the Week: Notice the many blessings that are present in your life today. Give thanks to God for your blessings.

Pray: Thank you, God, for being with me when I feel empty and alone. Help me to give you the glory when my emptiness is filled.

The Story and Young Children

This story, much like that of baby Isaac, tells of a birth that happened after all hope had given up. Naomi had decided that she would never have grandchildren. Ruth had given up hope of having a husband and family when she moved away from her own people. After all, why would any Hebrew want to marry a Moabite? Hopefully, your children's experience with babies has been that the babies are wanted, and the birth of a child has been an occasion for great joy. But sadly, that is not always the case. Be alert to those children who may have heard comments intimating that babies only mean more trouble. Help them experience the hope and joy in this birth.

Room Setup: Set out baby dolls and baby care items in the Family Living Center. Display pictures of families on a bulletin board or clothesline.

Learning Centers

Work with two or three children at a time in each learning center.

Conversation Center

This should be a table around which you may gather the children. Sit down with the children and engage them in conversation.

You will need: play dough, gingerbread person cookie cutters, cotton swabs, white construction paper, two or three colors of tempera paint, small paper cups, short-sleeved adult shirts that button down the front.

- Play With Play Dough, Activity 1d
- Make a Card for Grandparents, Activity 3a

Discovery Center

You will need: bulletin board or picture box, magazine pictures of families. (Be sure to include different family configurations, including single parents, three generations, one child, and many children.)

- Enjoy a Visitor, Activity 1c
- Look at Pictures, Activity 3c

Building Center

Provide enough blocks for toddlers to share.

You will need: blocks, a small baby doll.

- Build a House for Obed, Activity 4b

Storytelling Center

This should be an open area where you may gather children for storytelling or to listen and respond to music. It would be helpful to have this center on a carpeted area.

You will need: Bible; Activity Pak—pp. 5, 8, 9 (figures 1, 3, 4, 16), CD, CD player, Songbook, a baby doll, a rocking chair.

- Tell the Bible Story, Activity 2a
- Retell the Bible Story, Activity 2b
- Do a Fingerplay, Activity 2c
- Sing a Song, Activity 2d
- Tell Another Story, Activity 3b
- Enjoy Music, Activity 4a

Family Living Center

This would include a toy kitchen set and props appropriate to the lesson.

You will need: baby dolls, doll blankets, doll care items.

- Care for Dolls, Activity 1b

Obed Is Born

Ruth and Boaz had a baby boy. They were very happy. Ruth and Boaz named him Obed.

They brought Obed to see his grandmother, Naomi. Naomi loved her baby grandson.

All of the neighbors were happy to see the new baby in Naomi's family.

Prepare
for the Story

a **Welcome Each Child**

Do this as each child enters the room.

Stoop to the child's eye level and welcome each child by name. **Say** to each child: "I am so happy you have come to church today."

Be prepared to involve children in an interesting or comforting activity.

b **Care for Dolls**

Do this in the Family Living Center.

Involve children in conversation about babies as they pretend to care for dolls: Do they have babies in their homes? Can they identify things as "baby things" and "big girl" or "big boy" things?

c **Enjoy a Visitor**

Do this in the Discovery Center.

Invite a family in your church that has a young baby to visit your class. Ask the parents or guardians to describe how happy they were to bring a baby into their family.

Talk about the things that one needs for babies to grow and to be safe and healthy. Show the children how to gently stroke the skin of an infant, if parents or guardians give permission.

d **Play With Play Dough**

Do this in the Conversation Center.

Gather two or three children. Let them mold and shape the play dough as they want. Use a cookie cutter to make a small person.

Say: "Look, I have a little girl (or boy). Let's make Sarah's family." Make a "cookie" to represent Sarah and others to represent each member of her family.

Say: "Look, here's Sarah, and Mommy, and Daddy, and brother Justin."

Tell
the Story

a **Tell the Bible Story**

Do this in the Storytelling Center.

Gather one or two children. Show the children the adult figures and identify them as Ruth, Naomi, and Boaz (figures 1, 3, 4). If needed, review the stories from the last two weeks.

Tell the Bible story, bringing out the picture of Ruth and Obed (figure 16) at the appropriate time. Open a Bible; say the Bible verse. Have the children repeat it with you.

b **Retell the Bible Story**

Do this in the Storytelling Center.

Gather one or two children. Let them take turns holding the baby doll and rocking it while you play "Naomi's Lullaby" (CD, Songbook). Or have all of the children hold pretend babies and rock at the same time.

c **Do a Fingerplay**

Do this in the Storytelling Center.

Say the following fingerplay with the children:

This is Obed's family. (*Fold fingers down.*) Here's Mama Ruth. (*Hold up one finger.*) Here's Papa Boaz, (*Hold up a second finger.*) Grandma Naomi, (*Hold up a third finger.*) And baby Obed. (*Hold up a fourth finger.*) Thank you, God, for families. (*Fold hands as in prayer.*)

d **Sing a Song**

Do this in the Storytelling Center.

Gather two or three children. Sing the following song to the tune of "Are You Sleeping?"

You may wish to use the storytelling figures as you sing.

Who is with you?
Who is with you?
Naomi asked Ruth,
Naomi asked Ruth.
Here's your baby, Obed,
Here's your baby, Obed.
Hold him near.
Hold him near.

3 Connect

with the Story

a | Make a Card for Grandparents
Do this in the Conversation Center.

Gather two or three children. Protect clothing by putting a shirt on each child, buttoned down the back. Give each child a piece of paper.

Pour a small amount of paint in the bottom of each cup. Show each child how to gently dip his or her cotton swab into the paint and then use it to draw on the paper. Tell the children that they are making a picture for their grandparents. If any child does not have living grandparents, he or she may make the painting for someone else.

Say: "I wonder if Obed ever made things for his grandmother, Naomi."

b | Tell Another Story
Do this in the Storytelling Center.

"We're going on a trip, Shelby!" said Mama. She was putting clothing in a suitcase. "We're going to see Grandma!"

Shelby remembered Grandma. Grandma was big and soft. Shelby liked to sit in her lap. Grandma always had time to play with Shelby. She did not have to go to work or cook dinner.

"Go see Grandma!" said Shelby. She was glad that she had a grandma.

c | Look at Pictures
Do this in the Discovery Center.

Display the pictures of families on a bulletin board or in a picture box. Invite the children to talk about the pictures: Is there a family that looks like theirs? Is there a family that looks like Obed's?

Say: "God provides families to take care of children like you."

4 Celebrate

the Story

a | Enjoy Music
Do this in the Storytelling Center.

Sing "I Am in a Family" to the tune of "Mary Had a Little Lamb." Use the music to "Jesus Had a Family" (CD).

I am in a family, family, family.
I am in a family,
God gave them to me.

Then sing the song using each child's name.

Joseph's in a family, family, family.
Joseph's in a family,
Count them, one, two, three.

After singing, list everyone in Joseph's family, holding up fingers as you name them: "Mommy, Granny, Emma, and Joseph. One, two, three, four—four people in Joseph's family!" Sing other songs that the children have enjoyed this year.

b | Build a House for Obed
Do this in the Building Center.

Gather one or two children. Tell the children that the baby's name is Obed.

Invite the children to build a house for Obed. Help the children make the house for the doll, with beds or chairs or other things that the children name. Ask questions to see what else the house will need. **Ask**: "Where will Obed eat? Where will Obed sleep?"

c | Say Goodbye

Recall today's Bible story, encouraging children to say the Bible verse with you. **Say**: "I am glad (*name one of the children*) has a family." Repeat this for each child in the class. **Pray**: "Thank you, God, for our family. We are glad that our family loves us."

Be sure to have a teacher or helper at the door to match children with their caregivers.

Tell parents about today's Bible story and make sure that each child has today's Bible Story Picture Card. Show the parents the card for grandparents that the children have made. Ask them to help the child deliver it.

Tip
Make the stories more personal. Substitute your name and that of the children in the contemporary stories.

Look Back
Did every child have the opportunity to hear the story of Obed? Did they hear of Obed in the Building Center? the Family Living Center?

What activities interested the children? Which activities caused little response?

Are the children using words to communicate with you? Avoid the temptation to give them items that they merely point to. Encourage the use of words.

Look Ahead
Next week you will be introducing the children to David. See p. 237 and prepare the crowns ahead of time. Also locate your sandbox materials and toy sheep or farm animals.

Session

11

1 Samuel 16:1-13

God chooses people to do special things.

Bible Verse:
The Spirit of God came upon David. (1 Samuel 16:13, adapted)

Resources:
Bible
CD
sheep pattern (p. 236)
crown pattern (p. 237)
Activity Pak (Fall)
  pages 8, 9, 17 (figures 2, 17, 18, 20)
  page 24 ("Samuel Chooses David" picture)
  Songbook
Bible Story Picture Cards

Supplies:
sandbox (see p. 234)
small toy sheep or other farm animals
glue
3- to 5-ounce paper cups
cotton balls
yellow construction paper
small pieces of colored paper
toy pets and pet items
masking tape
CD player
snacks (orange, apple, and banana slices)
napkins
stapler and staples
building blocks
teacher scissors
(optional: star- or circle-shaped stickers)

48

David Is Chosen.........................

Enter the Bible Story

Read 1 Samuel 16:1-13: The Bible story for today tells the story of David being chosen by God to replace Saul as king of Israel. Saul was chosen because the people wanted a king. Samuel was the messenger from God who anointed Saul to be king. But Saul began to disobey the instructions that God sent through Samuel. So God told Samuel to find another king. As Samuel went to Bethlehem, he was fearful that Saul would find out. When Samuel reached Bethlehem, the elders were fearful, indicating that Samuel held significant power as a judge and priest. It is believed that David was about fifteen years old at the time of this anointing. It would be seven years before he actually became king. The anointing by Samuel is one way that God prepared David for the task ahead of him. How is God preparing you for the task ahead of you?

Think About It: After Saul became disobedient to God, God looked for a man who would be obedient. David seemed to fit the job. In comparison to David's brothers, Samuel thought David was inferior. But God looks on the heart, and what God saw in David's heart was much more important than his outward appearance. Reflect on these questions as you prepare to tell the story and to help the children retell the story: How do you think David felt when he was chosen? What questions does this story raise for you? What issues connect your life with the story? God chose David to be the king of God's chosen people. How has God chosen you?

Through the Week: Think of the story from Samuel's point of view. Think of the story from the brothers' point of view. Think of the story from Jesse's point of view. Think of the story from David's point of view.

Pray: God, thank you for looking not only on outward appearances. Help me to have the love and devotion to you that David had.

The Story and Young Children

Although children cannot grasp fully the concept of being used by God, they can understand that David was chosen because he loved God. The story of David being chosen holds a very special message for children and adults. David was very young when he was chosen by God. God doesn't wait until we are adults before using us. God watched over David as he grew and knew that even at a young age David wanted to serve and praise God. The children can know that they are loved by God and that God can choose us, even when others think we are not big enough for the job.

Room Setup: Place the "Samuel Chooses a King" poster (Activity Pak—p. 24) in the Storytelling Center. Have the CD playing music as the children enter. Place pictures of people God has chosen—your pastor, parents, teachers, Bible characters—around the room.

Learning Centers

Conversation Center

You will need: crown pattern (page 237), sheep pattern (page 236); 3- to 5-ounce paper cups; cotton balls; yellow construction paper; small pieces of colored paper for jewels; glue; stapler and staples; orange slices, apple slices, and banana slices; napkins (optional: star- or circle-shaped circles).

Get ready: Make a copy of the sheep pattern for each child. Using the crown pattern, cut the yellow construction paper into crown shapes. Prepare the snack so that the children will get to make choices.

- Make Sheep, Activity 1c
- Make Crowns, Activity 3a
- Choose a Snack, Activity 4b

Discovery Center

You will need: sandbox (see p. 234), small toy sheep or other farm animals.

- Play With Sand, Activity 1b

Family Living Center

You will need: toy pets and items used to take care of pets.

- Take Care of Pets, Activity 1d

Building Center

- Make Animal Pens, Activity 2d

Storytelling Center

You will need: Activity Pak—pp. 8, 9, 17 (figures 2, 17, 18, 20), p. 24 ("Samuel Chooses David" picture); CD, CD player, Activity Pak Songbook, Bible.

- Tell the Bible Story, Activity 2a
- Retell the Bible Story, Activity 2b
- Say an Action Verse, Activity 2c
- Tell Another Story, Activity 3b
- Enjoy Music, Activity 4a

David Is Chosen

God told Samuel that soon there would be a new king. God said, "Go to Jesse's house, and I will show you the new king."

Samuel went to Jesse's house. Who would be the new king? Was it big, handsome, Eliab? Was it big, strong Abinadab? Maybe it was Shammah? There were lots of handsome young men at Jesse's house. But it was not any of them.

Samuel said, "Do you have any more sons?"

Jesse said, "Well, there's David, but he's too little. He's out taking care of the sheep"

When Samuel saw David, God said to Samuel, "He is the one!"

Samuel told David, "Be happy! God has chosen you for a special job. You will be king and will help the people love and serve God."

1 Prepare

....

for the Story

a **Welcome Each Child**

Do this as each child enters the room.

Stoop to the child's eye level and welcome each child by name. **Say** to each child: "I am so happy you have come to church today."

b **Play With Sand**

Do this in the Discovery Center.

Let the children play with the animals in the sandbox.

Say: I wonder how you take care of sheep? What do they eat? Let's pretend that the grass is over here. What do they drink? Let's pretend the water is over here. Come over here, sheep. Whew! It's a lot of work to take care of sheep."

c **Make Sheep**

Do this in the Conversation Center.

Gather two or three children. Give each child a copy of the sheep (page 236) and several cotton balls. Pour a small amount of glue into a small paper cup. Show each child how to dip the cotton ball into the glue and then stick it on the paper. Allow each child to fill the outline of the sheep with cotton.

Say: "Today we will hear a story about a boy who took care of sheep for his father."

d **Take Care of Pets**

Do this in the Family Living Center.

As children play in this center today, encourage them to take care of pets. Tell the children that David took care of sheep.

2 Tell

....

the Story

a **Tell the Bible Story**

Do this in the Storytelling Center.

Gather two or three children. **Say**: "Look at this man. His name is Samuel. He is a special messenger from God."

Tell the Bible story, using the storytelling figures at the appropriate times. (figures 2, 17, 18, 20). Open a Bible and **say** the Bible verse. "The Spirit of God came upon David." Ask the children to say the verse with you.

b **Retell the Bible Story**

Do this in the Storytelling Center.

Gather two or three children. Show them the picture "Samuel Chooses a King" (Activity Pak—p. 24).

Say: "Samuel is trying to pick a new king from all of these men. Which one do you think he will choose? Will he choose this one? (*Point to the first man in the line.*) Nooooo! (*Shake your head.*) Will he choose this one? (*Point to the next man in the line.*) Nooooo!" (*Shake your head.*)

Continue in the same way with all of the young men in the line. When you get to the last boy, **say**: "Yes! He will choose this one! Hooray!"

Let the children cheer. Then ask the children to repeat the Bible verse with you.

c **Say an Action Verse**

Do this in the Storytelling Center.

Perform the following action verse with the children:

Clap your hands
(*Clap three times.*)
And slap your knee.
(*Pat your knees three times.*)
Jump up high,
(*Jump in place.*)
'Cause God chose me!
(*Point to self.*)

Repeat several times as long as the children show interest.

d **Make Animal Pens**

Do this in the Building Center.

Tell the children that one way we take care of animals is by giving them pens or fences to keep them safe. Help the children build pens for the toy animals.

3 Connect
with the Story

a **Make Crowns**
Do this in the Conversation Center.

Gather two or three children. Give each child a crown shape (page 237) that you have cut out ahead of time, a paper cup with a small amount of glue in the bottom, and several pieces of brightly colored paper.

Show the children how to "touch" the glue and then "touch" the pieces of paper to glue them onto the crown. (Option: You may use circle- or star-shaped stickers.) Help the children decorate their crowns.

As the children work, remember the Bible story. **Say:** "God chose David to be a king. I wonder what God is choosing (*name of child*) to be?" When the crown is decorated, staple the ends together and place it on each child's head. **Say:** "God chooses (*name*)!"

b **Tell Another Story**
Do this in the Storytelling Center.

Ms. Rankin looked around the room. All of the toys were scattered all over. The room was a mess!

"Oh, no," said Ms. Rankin, "What shall I do? I need some helpers to pick up all of these toys."

Ms. Rankin looked around the room. She said, "I choose Jeffrey to help put the blocks back on the shelf." Jeffrey went running to the Building Center and began to put the blocks away.

Then she said, "I choose Anne-Marie to put the baby dolls back in their beds." Anne-Marie began putting the babies in the beds and put the blankets on top of them.

Then Ms. Rankin said, "I choose Justin and Teesha to put the crayons and paper away."

Ms. Rankin kept on choosing children to do special jobs. Soon the room was clean, and the children were ready for a story.

c **Choose Helpers**

After telling the story above, choose the children to do special jobs in the room. Wrap masking tape, sticky side out, on the children's hands and ask them to pick up the scraps of paper left from making crowns. They will find they only have to touch the scraps with the tape, and the scraps will be picked up.

Make sure that all toys are put away before it is time to go.

4 Celebrate
the Story

a **Enjoy Music**
Do this in the Storytelling Center.

Celebrate the fact that you are all chosen by dancing to "Having Fun Today" (CD, Songbook). Follow the simple instructions in the song. Sing other songs that the children have enjoyed this year.

b **Choose a Snack**
Do this in the Conversation Center.

Provide fresh orange, apple, and banana slices. **Ask** each child: "Which do you choose?" (It is okay to choose all three, providing the child is willing to eat them.)

Talk to the children about the choices they made. Affirm that all choices—even the choice not to eat at all—are good choices. Help the children clean up after their snack.

c **Say Goodbye**

Recall today's Bible story, encouraging children to say the Bible verse with you. **Say:** "I am glad that God chose (*name one of the children*)." Repeat this for each child in the class.

Pray: "Thank you, God, for choosing us. Help us to do what you ask us to."

Be sure to have a teacher or helper at the door to make sure anxious children do not leave until someone comes for them. Tell parents about today's Bible story and make sure that each child has today's Bible Story Picture Card.

Show the parents the "Nurturing Your Child's Faith" section of the card. Be sure the children take home their crowns and sheep.

Tip
Make the stories more personal. Substitute your name and that of the children in the contemporary stories.

Look Back
Did all of the children have a chance to hear the story today? Did they talk about David in the Building Center? the Conversation Center?

Do different activities seem to draw different children?

What choices were you able to affirm for the children?

Look Ahead
Next week we will use music extensively in the session. You might wish to have a visitor come with a musical instrument to play for the children.

51

Session

12

1 Samuel 16:14-23

God gives us music, which makes us feel happy.

Bible Verse:

David took the harp and played it, and Saul would feel better.
(1 Samuel 16:23, *Good News Bible*, paraphrased)

Resources:

Bible
CD
Activity Pak (Fall)
    pages 9, 17 (figures 17, 19, 20)
    Songbook
Bible Story Picture Cards

Supplies:

CD player
crayons or markers
cardboard tubes
bingo markers or
    colored dot stickers
shoebox
rubber bands
autoharp instrument
toy guitar or other toy
    musical instruments
rhythm instruments
    such as sand blocks
building blocks
basket

David Plays His Harp......................

Enter the Bible Story

Read 1 Samuel 16:14-23: The Bible story for today tells the story of David being asked to come and play his harp for King Saul. By this time in the story of King Saul, Saul was aware that he has fallen out of favor with God. This naturally made him very depressed. His friends suggested bringing in a young musician, David, to make him feel better. Saul was unaware at this time that Samuel had already anointed David to be the next king. It demonstrates the character of David that he was immediately loved by Saul.

Think About It: This story is a wonderful example of how music can be used in ministering to those who are depressed or distressed. Reflect on the following questions as you prepare to tell the story: How has music been a comfort or help to you? Do you notice a difference in your mood when you listen to different kinds of music? classical? jazz? popular? hymns and spiritual songs?

Through the Week: Think about Saul's experience and try to see the story from Saul's point of view. Think of the story from David's point of view.

Pray: God, thank you for music and for those who make music that brings us closer to you.

The Story and Young Children

Young children at this age enjoy music. Music is often used to calm or comfort infants and young children. Music with a strong beat can get children excited and marching or dancing around the room. One way to get an entire group of toddlers focused at once is to bring out a musical instrument and to begin to play. (Granted, the focus doesn't last long, but it's there!) While young children cannot understand the concept of mental illness and music's effect, they do know that music makes them feel good.

Room Setup: Today is a musical day. Make sure that there are musical instruments that can be used for playing and for celebrating.

Learning Centers

Work with two or three children at a time in each learning center.

Conversation Center

This should be a table around which you may gather the children. Sit down with the children and engage them in conversation.

You will need: cardboard tubes (paper towel rolls); bingo markers, colored dot stickers, or crayons and markers.

• Make Musical Instruments, Activity 3a

Discovery Center

You will need: CD, CD player; Songbook; an autoharp instrument, a toy guitar, or a shoebox and rubber bands.

Get ready: If you don't have access to a stringed musical instrument, make one by stringing rubber bands across the open side of a shoebox.

• Play With a Harp, Activity 1b

Family Living Center

This would include a toy kitchen set and props appropriate to the lesson.

• Use Songs in Play, Activity 1d

Building Center

Provide enough blocks for toddlers to share. You may use wooden unit blocks or large cardboard or plastic blocks.

• Make Drums, Activity 1e

Storytelling Center

You will need: Bible; CD and CD player, Songbook; Activity Pak—pp. 9, 17 (figures 17, 19, 20); basket; musical instruments that the children have made, or toy instruments that you have purchased. Or use any toy that makes a noise—like beating on a large hollow block or shaking a toy that has pieces inside it.

Get ready: Prepare storytelling figures (see Activity Pak—p. 2)

• Talk About Happy and Sad Music, Activity 1c
• Tell the Bible Story, Activity 2a
• Retell the Bible Story, Activity 2b
• Sing Another Song, Activity 2c
• Tell Another Story, Activity 3b
• Play a Game, Activity 3c
• Enjoy Music, Activity 4a
• Enjoy a Visitor, Activity 4b

David Plays His Harp

King Saul was sad. His friends did not know what to do to make him happy.

Then one of his friends said, "I know, let's get David to come and play his harp for the king."

David loved to play his harp. David came and played music for King Saul.

David's music made King Saul feel better.

1 Prepare

for the Story

a Welcome Each Child

Do this as each child enters the room.

Stoop to the children's eye level and welcome each child by name. **Say** to each child: "I am so happy to see you today. How are you feeling?"

Be prepared to involve children in an interesting or comforting activity.

b Play With a Harp

Do this in the Discovery Center.

Gather one or two children. **Say:** "Do you see my harp? I can use my harp to sing songs of praise to God. When we play, we must strum gently on the strings."

Let each child pluck the strings of the instrument you brought. Hold the instrument and guide the children's hands to ensure that they play gently.

While strumming your instrument sing "Play the Harp" or songs that the children have learned in previous sessions (CD, Songbook). **Say:** "Today we will hear a story about a boy who played a harp."

c Talk About Happy and Sad Music

Do this in the Storytelling Center.

Gather two or three children. Play "Sad Music" (CD). **Say:** "This music makes me feel very sad." Invite the children to dance around sadly.

Say: "Today we will hear a story about a king who was very sad. But when he heard music, he was happy." Play "Happy Music" (CD). **Say:** "This music makes me feel happy." Invite the children to dance around happily.

d Use Songs in Play

Do this in the Family Living Center.

As the children play in this center, encourage them to sing cleanup songs as they work or lullabies as they hold babies.

e Make Drums

Do this in the Building Center.

As the children play with blocks, encourage them to explore the sounds they can make by hitting blocks together or by pounding on large blocks with their hands.

2 Tell

the Story

a Tell the Bible Story

Do this in the Storytelling Center.

Gather two or three children. Tell the Bible story, using the storytelling figures (figures 17, 19, 20) at the appropriate times. Open a Bible and say the Bible verse. Invite the children to say the verse with you.

b Retell the Bible Story

Do this in the Storytelling Center.

Gather two or three children. Do the following action verse:

King Saul was sad.
(*Make a sad face and sigh heavily.*)
His friends did not know what to do.
(*Hold up both hands at shoulder height; shake your head and look perplexed.*)
Then one friend had an idea!
(*Raise your eyebrows and your index finger with excitement.*)
"Let's get David! David can help the king!"

(*Run in place.*)
David played his harp for King Saul.
(*Pantomime playing a guitar or harp.*)
King Saul was happy to hear the music.
(*Clap your hands and make a happy face.*)

c Sing Another Song

Do this in the Storytelling Center.

Sing "David Played the Harp". This song is sung to the tune of "The Farmer in the Dell." Pretend to strum a harp as you sing.

O David played the harp,
O David played the harp.
He sang songs of praise to God,
O David played the harp.

King Saul heard the harp,
King Saul heard the harp,
He clapped his hands in praise to God,
King Saul heard the harp.

3 Connect
with the Story

a **Make Musical Instruments**
Do this in the Conversation Center.

Gather two or three children. Give each child a cardboard tube and a bingo marker. (These markers are found in many drug or variety stores and make a nice round dot when placed on the paper.)

If you choose not to use the bingo markers, use colored dot stickers instead. Or let the children use markers or crayons to decorate their paper towel rolls. When the cardboard is decorated, show the children how to hold it up to their mouths and "toot" a song.

b **Tell Another Story**
Do this in the Storytelling Center.

"Bedtime for Hannah," Daddy said. Daddy helped Hannah put on her pajamas and brush her teeth. Then he tucked her into bed.

"Good night, Hannah," said Daddy. Daddy left Hannah alone so she could go to sleep. But Hannah did not go to sleep. She was afraid.

"Daddy! Daddy! Come here!" cried Hannah.

"What's the matter?" Daddy asked.

"I can't sleep," said Hannah. "Sing me a song."

Daddy sang Hannah a song. Soon Hannah was no longer afraid. She went sound asleep.

c **Play a Game**
Do this in the Storytelling Center.

Ask one child to sit in the center of a circle and pretend to be sad. **Say** with the children: "Poor Saul, he's so sad."

Have the children play their instruments. Then have everyone say, "Are you happy now, Saul?" If Saul says no, play your instruments again. If Saul says yes, have everyone cheer. Then choose another child to be Saul.

4 Celebrate
the Story

a **Enjoy Music**
Do this in the Storytelling Center.

Gather two or three children. Invite the children to bring their instruments to the Storytelling Center with them. Or provide a basket of rhythm instruments. Let each child choose an instrument to play.

Sing happy songs from the CD and Songbook, such as "I Was Glad." Sing quieter songs, such as "Little Baby Moses." Sing songs of praise to God. Celebrate by dancing to "Having Fun Today."

b **Enjoy a Visitor**
Do this in the Storytelling Center.

Invite a visitor who plays a musical instrument to visit your class today. Ask the visitor to show the children how the instrument makes music. Have the visitor play some tunes that the children know.

Teach the children to sit quietly while the music is playing and to applaud when the music is over.

c **Say Goodbye**
Recall today's Bible story, encouraging children to say the Bible verse with you.

Say: "I am glad (*name one of the children*) was in Sunday school today." Repeat this for each member of the class.

Pray: "Thank you, God, for music. We are glad that music makes us feel better."

Be sure to have a teacher or helper at the door to ensure that anxious children do not leave until someone comes for them. Tell parents about today's Bible story and make sure that each child has today's Bible Story Picture Card.

Show the parents the "Nurturing Your Child's Faith" section of the card. Tell parents about some of the songs the class sang today.

Be sure the children take home their instruments.

Tip
Make the stories more personal. Substitute your name and that of the children in the contemporary stories.

Look Back
What feelings did the children express today?

Did each child experience being called by name?

What is it that you now know about the story and about the students that you did not know before this session?

What could you change about the lesson to make it better?

Look Ahead
Next week we will be talking about friends. What can you do to foster friendships among your students?

Session

13

1 Samuel 18:1-5

David and Jonathan were friends.

Bible Verse:
A friend loves at all times.
(Proverbs 17:17)

Resources:
Bible
CD
Activity Pak (Fall)
  pages 8, 17 (figures 5, 20)
  Songbook
Bible Story Picture Cards

Supplies:
CD player
large piece of newsprint or shelf paper
masking tape
crayons
felt-tip markers, including a black one
instant-developing camera and film
construction paper
tape
paper plates
table
play dishes
simple snack such as graham crackers and juice
clear self-adhesive paper or laminating machine
lightweight scarfs, pieces of cloth, or paper streamers
paper punch
yarn
building blocks

David and Jonathan........................

Enter the Bible Story

Read 1 Samuel 18:1-5: The Bible story for today tells the story of David and the close friendship he had with Saul's son, Jonathan. As the king's eldest son, Jonathan was next in line for the throne. It says much about David and Jonathan's relationship that Jonathan never seemed to be disturbed once he realized that David was to be the next king. It also says much that after David became king, when most of Saul's family was put to death (a common practice at the time), David spared Jonathan's son, Mephibosheth.

Think About It: This passage is the introduction to one of the best examples in the Bible of love, loyalty, and friendship between two individuals. Reflect on the following questions as you prepare to tell the story and to help children retell the story: How do you think Jonathan felt when he heard about the exploits of David? How important is it for us to have a "best friend"?

Through the Week: Think of your friends this week. We often use different friends at different times. For instance, you might have one friend you go see when you want to have a good time, but another that you want to be with you if you go to the hospital.

Pray: Thank you, God, for my friends. Help me to be as much a blessing to them as they are to me. Amen.

The Story and Young Children

Happily, most toddlers and two-year-olds still think of everyone as their friends. Because they are often still at the center of their universe, they cannot yet imagine that everyone is not madly in love with them. If they are lucky, they will be several years older before they learn anything to the contrary. However, children of this age are not good at being friends. This is the concept that we must teach them. The children can know that God wants them to do kind things and to love God and their friends.

Room Setup: Tape paper to the Conversation Center table so that the children can begin their scribbling as they arrive. Make place mats for the Family Living Center. Locate an instant-developing camera for the Discovery Center.

Learning Centers

Work with two or three children at a time in each learning center.

Conversation Center

This should be a table around which you may gather the children. Sit down with the children and engage them in conversation.

You will need: CD, CD player, a large piece of newsprint or shelf paper (heavier paper works better), masking tape, crayons, a black felt-tip marker, paper plates, a simple snack such as graham crackers and juice.

- Make a Scribble Banner, Activity 1b
- Make Paper Plate Handprints, Activity 3a
- Share a Snack, Activity 4b

Discovery Center

You will need: an instant-developing camera and film, construction paper, tape, felt-tip markers, paper punch, yarn.

- Make a Friends Picture Book, Activity 1c

Building Center

Provide enough blocks for the toddlers to share. You may use wooden unit blocks or large cardboard or plastic blocks.

- Play "Going to Visit a Friend," Activity 1d

Family Living Center

This would include a toy kitchen set and props appropriate to the lesson.

You will need: a table, play dishes, construction paper, clear self-adhesive paper, felt-tip marker (optional: laminating machine).

Get ready: Draw the outline of a plate, cup, and spoon onto a piece of construction paper with a felt-tip marker. Cover the place mat with clear self-adhesive paper for durability (or laminate with a machine).

- Play "A Friend Is Coming to Dinner," Activity 3c

Storytelling Center

You will need: Activity Pak—pp. 8 and 17 (figures 5, 20), Songbook, Bible, CD, CD player; lightweight scarfs, pieces of cloth, or paper streamers.

- Tell the Bible Story, Activity 2a
- Retell the Bible Story, Activity 2b
- Sing a Song, Activity 2c
- Tell Another Story, Activity 3b
- Enjoy Music, Activity 4a

David and Jonathan Are Friends

David and Jonathan were friends.

David played his harp for Jonathan. Jonathan shared his things with David.

David and Jonathan liked to be with each other.

Jonathan was sad when David was away. When David came back, Jonathan was glad.

David was happy to have a good friend like Jonathan.

 **Prepare**

for the Story

a Welcome Each Child

Do this as each child enters the room.

Stoop to the children's eye level and welcome each child by name. **Say** to each child: "I am so happy to see my friend, *(child's name)*."

Be prepared to involve children in an interesting or comforting activity.

b Make a Scribble Banner

Do this in the Conversation Center.

Cover the table with newsprint or shelf paper. Tape the paper in place. Let the children stand around the table to scribble with the crayons on the paper.

Sing or play music (CD) as the children work, modeling for them how they can move the crayons to the rhythm of the music. Allow time for all the children to contribute to the banner.

While the children work, **say**: "We are all friends in this class. This is a big banner that all of our friends helped with." When the children have finished, carefully remove the paper from the table.

Print today's Bible verse, "A friend loves at all times," in large letters on your class banner. Hang the banner on the wall for all to enjoy.

c Make a Friends Picture Book

Do this in the Discovery Center.

Take pictures of the children playing with their friends in all of the centers. Make sure you have at least two or three pictures of each child.

When the film is developed, tape the pictures to construction paper. Write the names of the friends pictured in big block letters. Display the pictures in the Discovery Center.

Talk to the children about the pictures. **Say**: "Who is that working with the blocks? I think they are sharing. They are friends." When you have a nice collection of pictures, assemble them into a book by using a paper punch and yarn. On the cover of the book, write "A Friend Loves at All Times."

Play "Going to Visit a Friend"

Do this in the Building Center.

Gather two or three friends. Use the blocks to build a small house. Then build another house some distance away. Use the blocks to build a road between the two houses. With your fingers pretend to "walk" from one house to another. **Say**: "I think I will go see my friend, Brandi." Carry on a conversation with your friend (your other hand) and then go back home.

 Tell

the Story

a Tell the Bible Story

Do this in the Storytelling Center.

Gather two or three children. Tell the Bible story, using the figures of David and Jonathan (figures 5, 20).

Open a Bible and **say** the Bible verse: "A friend loves at all times." Invite the children to repeat the verse with you.

b Retell the Bible Story

Do this in the Storytelling Center.

Locate the fingerplay "David and Jonathan Go Visiting" (Songbook). The fingerplay is long but repetitious. Encourage the children to imitate your motions, particularly as you go "up and down and up and down."

Sing a Song

Do this in the Storytelling Center.

Locate the song "Jonathan Was David's Friend" (Songbook, CD). Sing the song to the tune of "London Bridge." Repeat the song and encourage the children to sing along with you.

Jonathan was David's friend,
David's friend, David's friend.
Jonathan was David's friend,
Friends forever!

3 Connect
with the Story

a **Make Paper Plate Handprints**
Do this in the Conversation Center.

Gather two or three children. Give each child a paper plate. Have the child place a hand in the middle of the plate.

Trace around the child's hand with a crayon. Write the child's name inside the handprint. Let the children decorate the plates with crayons.

Say: "We have many friends in our class. Each one is special. Let's place our hands on our banner to show all of our friends."

Tape each handprint to the scribble banner made earlier.

b **Tell Another Story**
Do this in the Storytelling Center.

Jacob looked into his new Sunday school class. "Hello, Jacob," said Mr. Jason. "I am glad you are in our class."

Jacob was not glad. He did not know any of the children in his new class. He wanted his mommy.

Mr. Jason said, "Amy, would you be Jacob's new friend?" Amy came over and patted Jacob on the back. She took him to the blocks and showed him how to build a bridge. Then they went to sing a song with Mrs. Shimaki. Then Mr. Barnes told them a story.

Jacob was happy. He had a new friend.

c **Play "A Friend Is Coming to Dinner"**
Do this in the Family Living Center.

Make place mats ahead of time for the Family Living Center. Draw the outline of a plate, cup, and spoon onto a piece of construction paper with a felt-tip pen.

Cover the place mat with clear self-adhesive paper for durability. (You can laminate these, if you choose.) Make just enough place mats for the number of dishes that you have.

Gather two or three children. **Say:** "Let's pretend that our friend is coming to dinner. We have to set the table. Let's see, where does the plate go? What goes on the little circle? Are we ready? Now let's find a friend to eat with us."

4 Celebrate
the Story

a **Enjoy Music**
Do this in the Storytelling Center.

Play "A Friend Loves at All Times" (CD, Songbook). Let the children dance to the music with the cloth or paper streamers.

Sing along with the music as you dance. Choose other favorite songs and sing and dance together.

b **Share a Snack**
Do this in the Conversation Center.

Ask the children to sit down for a snack. Ask them to pass the snack to each other.

Say: "Justine, would you pass your friend Thompson a cracker? Akia, please give a napkin to all of your friends."

c **Say Goodbye**

Recall today's Bible story. Have the children say or sing the Bible verse with you.

Say: "I am glad (*name one of the children*) is my friend." Repeat this for each child in the class.

Pray: "Thank you, God, for our friends."

Be sure to have a teacher or helper at the door to match children with parents or caregivers. Tell parents about today's Bible story and make sure that each child has today's Bible Story Picture Card.

Show the parents the "Nurturing Your Child's Faith" section of the card. Point out to parents the scribble banner and the friends picture book that the class made. Have the children take home their handprints, if you choose to remove them from the scribble banner.

Tip
Make the stories more personal. Substitute your name and that of the children in the contemporary stories.

Look Back
What feelings did the children express today?

Did each child experience being called by name?

What is it that you now know about the story and about the students that you did not know before this session?

What could you change about the lesson to make it better?

Look Ahead
The next lesson in this book is the Thanksgiving lesson. You should be teaching this on the Sunday before or after Thanksgiving. Look ahead to plan for teaching the Christmas story close to Christmas Day.

Session

14

Psalm 9:2

We are thankful to God for all God's blessings.

Bible Verse:
I will sing praise to God. (Psalm 9:2, *Good News Bible*, adapted)

Resources:
Bible
CD
Activity Pak (Fall)
   page 17 (figures 21, 22)
   page 20, top (fruit color cutouts)
   Songbook
Bible Story Picture Cards

Supplies:
CD player
index cards
clear self-adhesive paper or laminating machine
basket
books and simple puzzles about food
paper plates
pictures of food pre-cut from magazines or seed catalogs
glue
small paper cups
empty boxes and cans of grocery items
toy food
toy grocery cart or basket
rhythm instruments
large bowl
spoons
table knife (teacher use only)
plain or vanilla yogurt
sliced banana
building blocks
(optional: sweetening such as sugar, honey, jam, or jelly; fruit)

Thanksgiving...........

Enter the Bible Story

Read Psalm 9: The psalms testify to the truth that God is the center of creation, life, and history. Each psalm falls into one of a variety of categories. Some psalms, such as Psalm 9, combine more than one category in a single psalm. This psalm is made up of two different parts. The first part, verses 1–12, is a hymn of thanksgiving. The first twelve verses, which praise God, serve as a long introduction to the rest of the psalm, which is known as a lament. The lament expresses sorrow and despair over some form of alienation from God.

Think About It: The Hebrew people were a people who were grateful to God and who often expressed that gratitude. The Book of Psalms contains many songs of thanksgiving. Reflect on the following questions as you prepare to help children express thanks to God in this session: Can you think of other psalms that express thanksgiving to God? Look through the Book of Psalms for passages of gratitude and praise. What are some of the phrases used to convey thanks? How can we help the children we teach express thanks to God?

Through the Week: There have been recent reminders all around us of the Thanksgiving holiday. In our present culture, however, this national emphasis on giving thanks is often swallowed up by our rush toward the Christmas celebration. Take time to give thanks in your own life and family and to plan ways to help the children you teach focus on giving special thanks to God.

Pray: Thank you, God for all that we are and have and know. Help us remember that all of our gifts from you come with corresponding responsibilities to use the gifts well.

The Story and Young Children

Children can hear that God cares for us and plans for food. They can have opportunities to give thanks for God's care and for God's bountiful provisions for us. At this time of year the results of the harvest are all around us in grocery stores and at roadside markets. Fruit and vegetable displays are beautiful to see, and young children can enjoy exploring them with adult supervision. Children can experience the colors, the textures, the smells, and the tastes of all that God provides.

Room Setup: Provide books about food on a low shelf or in a basket near floor pillows or a folded quilt in a quiet corner. Place on a low table puzzles that picture food. Collect empty food boxes, paper bags, and other items for the children to create a grocery store in the Family Living Center. (See Session 9 for more instruction.)

Learning Centers

Work with two or three children at a time in each learning center.

Conversation Center

You will need: paper plates, pictures of food cut from magazines or seed catalogs, glue, plain or vanilla yogurt, table knife (for teacher use), large bowl, small paper cups, spoons, sliced banana (optional: sugar, honey, jelly, or jam for sweetening).

Get ready: Pour a small amount of glue into paper cups.

- Make Food Plates, Activity 1d
- Make Yogurt Pudding, Activity 4b

Family Living Center

You will need: empty boxes and cans of grocery items, toy food, toy grocery cart or basket.

Get ready: See Session 9 on preparing empty cans or boxes. Set out common grocery items on a shelf or countertop.

- Play Grocery Store, Activity 3c

Building Center

Provide enough blocks for toddlers to share. You may use wooden unit blocks or large cardboard or plastic blocks.

Discovery Center

You will need: picture books and puzzles about food; index cards, precut magazine pictures of foods; Activity Pak—p. 20, top (fruit color cutouts); basket; glue; clear self-adhesive paper or laminating machine. (Option: You may wish to use real fruit.)

Get ready: Glue a different food picture to each of several index cards. Cover the cards with clear self-adhesive paper for durability, or laminate with a machine.

- Explore Food Cards, Activity 1b
- Enjoy Books and Puzzles, Activity 1c
- Enjoy Fruit Color Cutouts, Activity 3a

Storytelling Center

You will need: Activity Pak—p. 17 (figures 21, 22), CD, CD player, Activity Pak Songbook, Bible, rhythm instruments.

Get ready: Prepare storytelling figures (see Activity Pak, p. 2)

- Tell the Bible Story, Activity 2a
- Retell the Bible Story, Activity 2b
- Sing a Song, Activity 2c
- Tell Another Story, Activity 3b
- Enjoy Music, Activity 4a

Father and Daniel Are Grateful

Father and Daniel worked together in the hot sun. They were caring for their garden. When they were tired, they rested in the shade and ate some of the fresh vegetables.

"Yum," said Daniel. "I'm glad we have food to eat."

"I'm glad that God plans for food," said Father.

"Thank you, God, for our food," said Father and Daniel.

Prepare

for the Story

a **Welcome Each Child**
Do this as each child enters the room.

Stoop to the child's eye level and welcome each child by name. If you are teaching this lesson on Thanksgiving weekend, you may have some visitors, and for sure you will be missing some of your regulars.

Say to each child: "Thank you for coming to church today."

Be prepared to involve children in an interesting or comforting activity.

b **Explore Food Cards**
Do this in the Discovery Center.

Gather two or three children. Point out the cards that have pictures of food glued to them. Look at the cards and help the children identify each food item.

Say: "Have you ever eaten broccoli? Yum, I like ice cream. I'm so glad that God plans good food for us to eat."

c **Enjoy Books and Puzzles**
Do this in the Discovery Center.

Gather two or three children. Invite the children to enjoy looking at books or working simple puzzles about food.

Read the books to them and talk to the children as they work.

d **Make Food Plates**
Do this in the Conversation Center.

Gather two or three children. Give each child a paper plate. Let the children choose pre-cut food pictures to glue to their plates.

As the children work, talk about the foods pictured and whether the children have eaten them and like to eat them.

Print around the edge or on the back of each plate: "Thank you, God, for food."

Tell

the Story

a **Tell the Bible Story**
Do this in the Storytelling Center.

Gather two or three children together. Tell the Bible story, using the storytelling figures (figures 21, 22).

Open a Bible and **say** the Bible verse. Invite the children to repeat the verse with you: "I will sing praise to God."

b **Retell the Bible Story**
Do this in the Storytelling Center.

Retell the Bible story, this time encouraging the children to act out the motions with you as you tell it: cultivating and weeding the garden, being tired, sitting down, eating, and bowing heads to thank God for the food.

c **Sing a Song**
Do this in the Storytelling Center.

Sing "I Will Sing My Praise to God" (CD, Songbook). It is sung to the tune of "London Bridge."

I will sing my praise to God,
Praise to God, praise to God.
I will sing my praise to God,
Praise forever.

3 Connect
with the Story

a Enjoy Fruit Color Cutouts
Do this in the Discovery Center.

Gather two or three children. Display the fruit color cutouts (Activity Pak—p. 20). Talk with the children about the different fruits, their names, and their colors. Say the following poem for the children:

(*Hold up each fruit as you name it.*)
Apples are red and sometimes yellow.
Bananas are yellow too.
Oranges are orange and pears are green,
And grapes are sometimes blue.

(*Place each fruit in the basket as you name it.*)
Red and yellow and orange and green,
Mixed with dark, dark blue,
Placed in a basket make a gift:
A fruit basket for you.

b Tell Another Story
Do this in the Storytelling Center.

Megan liked going to the grocery store with her father. She could see lots of fruit while sitting in the grocery cart. There were red and yellow apples, yellow bananas, and oranges that were bright orange, just like their name. She also saw different kinds of grapes—red, green, and dark, dark blue.

"I'm glad God planned for good fruit for us to eat," said Dad as he put the fruit in their basket.

When they got home, Megan and Dad ate a big red apple. "Thank you, God, for good fruit to eat," prayed Dad.

c Play Grocery Store
Do this in the Family Living Center.

Set out common grocery items on a shelf or countertop in your Family Living Center. If you have a toy grocery shopping cart or a basket, let the children put all of the boxes and cans in their cart or basket, then take them out and put them back on the shelf.

While the children are playing, talk to them about the foods they select.

4 Celebrate
the Story

a Enjoy Music
Do this in the Storytelling Center.
Sing "Show How Much God Loves Us" (Songbook, CD).

Sing other praise songs, using rhythm instruments as accompaniment.

b Make Yogurt Pudding
Do this in the Conversation Center.

Let the children help you empty the yogurt into a large bowl. Let each child have a turn to stir as you add banana slices and optional sweetening.

Give each child a small amount of the pudding in a paper cup.

As the children enjoy this snack, **pray**: "I will sing praise to you, God. I will sing praise to you."

c Say Goodbye
Recall today's Bible story. Have the children say or sing the Bible verse with you.

Say: "I am thankful (*name one of the children*) came to church today." Repeat this for each child in the class.

Pray: "Thank you, God, for good food. We will sing praise to you."

Be sure to have a teacher or a helper at the door to ensure that anxious children do not leave until someone comes for them.

Tell parents about today's Bible story. Make sure that each child has today's Bible Story Picture Card. Show the parents the "Nurturing Your Child's Faith" section of the card.

Tell parents about the things the children did in class today. Be sure the children take home their food plates.

Tip
If the children have enjoyed some of the games or pictures from the Activity Pak, store them for use later in the year. matching hearts game cards may be stored in a plastic bag. The "Boaz Shares" activity may be stored in the check boxes.

Look Back
What did you do in class today to help the children think about their favorite foods?

Did each child have an opportunity to express happiness and thanksgiving to God today? How?

Did the children sing, move their bodies, pray, and say the Bible verse or some of the words with you?

Look Ahead
This session marks the end of the fall quarter. Plan your lessons so that you teach Session 18, "Jesus is Born," on the Sunday before Christmas.

One of the most important things we do as teachers is to show children how great God's love is for them.

Bible Verse:
You will name him Jesus.
(Luke 1:31)

Resources:
Bible
CD
patterns (pages 238-239, 241)
Activity Pak (Winter) page 5 (figures 1,2)
Songbook
Bible Story Picture Cards

Supplies:
sandbox (see p. 234)
toy creche figures
sand toys
building blocks
construction paper
crayons or markers
glue or tape
CD player
three or four pictures from magazines showing people helping one another
Christmas tree cut from green construction paper
teacher scissors
(optional: stickers, small artificial Christmas tree, paper punch and yarn)

Mary Is Told About Jesus..............

Enter the Bible Story

Read Luke 1:26-38: We begin Advent with the story of Mary and her encounter with the angel, who tells her of the upcoming birth of Mary's son. Mary was probably in many ways like other women her age in Nazareth. She was a poor, young woman preparing for one of the most important events of her life—the day when she would legally be married to Joseph. Little did Mary know that her hopes and dreams would be dramatically altered after the incredible message was delivered by the angel, Gabriel. Why did God choose an unknown peasant to be the mother of God's Son? The Scriptures do not offer us any concrete details regarding Mary's childhood or her moral or religious training. But we do clearly read in the Scriptures Mary's answer to Gabriel's incredible news: "Here am I, the servant of the Lord; let it be with me according to your word" (Luke 1:38). Somewhere in Mary's childhood, a seed was sown and nurtured. Mary's faith was firmly rooted in trusting God and in believing the wonders of God.

Think About It: Nothing is so powerful as the reality of this message: "God loves you!" The more one says it, the more one believes it. The more one believes it, the more one desires to live it. The more one attempts to live it, the more real God's grace, joy, and peace become. Reflect on these questions as you prepare to tell the story and then help the children retell the story: In what ways have you experienced God's love? God's presence? How will you express this understanding to the children today? How will you encourage the children to say, "I will help God"?

Through the Week: The last words that Gabriel speaks to Mary are, "For nothing will be impossible with God." (Luke 1:37) What impossible things has God done in your life? You may have thought it impossible that you could teach toddlers for this long. Reflect on these things and prepare for the impossible things God will continue to accomplish in your life.

Pray: Thank you, God, for using me to bring about your kingdom on earth. Help me prepare myself for your instruction. Amen.

The Story and Young Children

Many times we educators ask ourselves: "How can I possibly teach this story to a young child?" By using this curriculum resource, you are setting up the classroom so that the classroom itself becomes the curriculum. That's right, the room becomes the curriculum. The resource materials and manipulatives placed in each center by the teacher assist in relating the story or reinforcing the story. The young child can begin to understand God's love by experiencing God's love in action. It is the loving caregiver who attends to the child's emotional and physical needs, expressing this awesome message: *God loves you.*

Room Setup: Locate a creche for your room that the children can play with. Place the figures of Mary and the angel in the sandbox or the Discovery Center. Leave the remaining figures put away for later. Place a paper Christmas tree in the Family Living Center.

Learning Centers

Work with two or three children at a time in each learning center.

Conversation Center

You will need: teacher scissors, ornament patterns (pp. 238–239, 241), crayons or markers, three or four pictures cut from magazines showing people helping one another (optional: stickers).

Get ready: Use the patterns to cut ornaments from different colors of construction paper. Cut pictures of people helping one another from magazines. Include a picture of a child helping another person.

- Make Ornaments, Activity 1d
- Talk About Helpers, Activity 3a

Storytelling Center

You will need: Activity Pak—p. 5 (figures 1, 2), Bible, CD, CD player, Activity Pak Songbook.

Get ready: Prepare storytelling figures. (See Activity Pak—p. 2).

- Tell a Bible Story, Activity 2a
- Retell the Bible Story, Activity 2b
- Sing a Song, Activity 2c
- Tell Another Story, Activity 3b
- Enjoy Music, Activity 4a

Discovery Center

You will need: a sandbox (see p. 234), sand toys, crèche figures of Mary and the angel, blocks to build Mary a house.

Get ready: If you do not use the sandbox, place Mary and the angel pieces in this center. You will add pieces to the crèche each week.

- Play With Sand, Activity 1c

Family Living Center

You will need: a Christmas tree cut from green construction paper taped to the wall, ornaments from Activity 1d, glue or tape (optional: artificial tree, paper punch and yarn).

- Decorate a Christmas Tree, Activity 4b

Building Center

You will need: building blocks

Get ready: Provide enough blocks for toddlers to share. Use wooden unit blocks or large cardboard or plastic blocks.

Mary Is Told About Jesus

One day God sent an angel to tell Mary some very good news.
"God loves you, Mary!" the angel said. "You will be a mommy. You are going to have a baby boy. God wants you to name the baby Jesus. He will be God's Son."
"I will help God!" Mary said. "I will do what God wants me to do."
Mary loved God and wanted to be God's helper.

Prepare

for the Story

a **Welcome Each Child**
Do this as each child enters the room.

Have the CD playing as the children enter. Stoop to the children's eye level and welcome each child by name.

Say to each child: "Hello, God loves (*name*)."

b **Experience Love**
Prepare the child for today's story by relating God's love. Put the children on your lap, or hug them, or pat them on the back.

As you are showing this love and attention, call each child by name twice and **say**: "God loves you." For example, "Sarah, Sarah, God loves you!"

c **Play With Sand**
Do this in the Discovery Center.

Gather two or three children. Let them explore the sand, teaching them to keep the sand inside the sandbox.

Use the blocks to build a house and place the toy woman (Mary) beside it.

Say: "Here is a house for the woman." Talk about what she would need in her house." Notice the angel in the sandbox.

Say: "Look, there's an angel. Today we will hear a story about this woman and the angel."

d **Make Ornaments**
Do this in the Conversation Center.

Gather two or three children. Allow the children to choose one of the precut shapes (pp. 238–239, 241) to decorate.

Talk about the shape they chose: "Oh, you chose a blue bell, David. Why did you choose that?" "I like the purple star you chose, Alicia." Let the children decorate the ornaments with the markers or crayons. Or let the children use stickers for decoration.

If you are using an artificial tree instead of a paper one, use the paper punch and yarn to make hangers for the ornaments.

Collect the ornaments for use later, making sure that each child's name is on his or her ornament.

Tell

the Story

a **Tell the Bible Story**
Do this in the Storytelling Center.

Gather two or three children. Tell the children the Bible story, using the storytelling figures (figures 1, 2) at appropriate times.

Open the Bible and **say** the Bible verse: "You will name him Jesus." Ask the children to repeat the verse with you.

b **Retell the Bible Story**
Do this in the Storytelling Center.

Gather two or three children. Use the following action verse:

God loved Mary very much.
(*Cross arms over your chest.*)
God sent an angel to give Mary good news.
(*Flap arms like a Christmas angel.*)

The angel said, "You will be a mommy."
(*Pretend to rock a baby.*)
Mary said, "I will help God."
(*Hold out hands with palms raised.*)

c **Sing a Song**
Do this in the Storytelling Center.

Gather two or three children. Play "An Angel Told Mary" (CD, Activity Pak Songbook) for the children. Have the children play the song again and clap every time they hear the words *good news*.

Play the song a third time and sing along. (Setting the CD player on "repeat" allows you to repeat the song several times without touching the player.)

3 Connect
with the Story

a **Talk About Helpers**
Do this in the Conversation Center.

Gather two or three children. Show the children the pictures you cut out of magazines. Ask the children to describe what is happening in each picture. Encourage them to notice that people are helping one another.

Say: "This person is helping God by (*putting a bandage on the hurt, giving food to a hungry person, helping Daddy feed a pet*). You can help God too. Say this with me: 'I can help God, too!'" Then clap your hands together one time. Repeat.

Make a game out of the chant. **Say:** "Julie can help God too! (*clap*). Matt can help God too!" (*clap*)

b **Tell Another Story**
Do this in the Storytelling Center.

"Katie, my love, it's time to decorate the Christmas tree," Mommy called.

Katie ran to see the beautiful tree. What a big tree it was! And there were lots and lots of Christmas ornaments. It would take a long time to put the ornaments on that tree.

Mommy needed Katie's help. And Katie needed Mommy's help. So Mommy and Katie helped each other put all the Christmas ornaments on the tree. They had so much fun together.

c **Play "Will You Help Me?"**
Tell each child that Mary loved God and that Mary was God's helper. God needs other helpers as well.

Ask each child to help clean up by putting away one toy or manipulative. Gently tell and show the child where to place it.

After any attempt **say**: "What a good helper! Thank you!" Then sing "Will You Help Me?" (CD, Activity Pak Songbook) to the tune of "Are You Sleeping?"

Will you help me? Will you help me?
(*name of child*), (*name of child*)?
Put the toys away now,
Put the toys away now.
Thank you, (*name of child*),
Thank you, (*name of child*).

4 Celebrate
the Story

a **Enjoy Music**
Do this in the Storytelling Center.

Sing "An Angel Told Mary" and "Mary Had a Baby" (CD, Activity Pak Songbook). Sing other favorites that you have learned this year.

b **Decorate a Christmas Tree**
Do this in the Family Living Center.

Gather two or three children. **Say:** "Look, today we have a tree and lots and lots of pretty things to put on our tree."

Count the ornaments with the children to be placed on the tree. **Say:** "Christmas is the birthday of Jesus. It is a happy time when we remember that God loves us."

Help each child use tape or glue to place his or her ornament on the tree. Tell the children that you are going to leave the tree up until Christmas is over.

c **Say Goodbye**
Recall today's Bible story, encouraging children to say the Bible verse with you.

Say: "I am glad that (*name one of the children*) is a helper." Repeat this for each child in the class.

Pray: "Thank you, God, for Mary and the angel. We will be helpers too."

Be sure to have a teacher or helper at the door to ensure that anxious children do not leave until someone comes for them. Tell parents about today's Bible story and make sure that each child has today's Bible Story Picture Card.

Show the parents the "Nurturing Your Child's Faith" section of the card. Point out to parents the Christmas tree that the class made.

Tip
Make the stories more personal. Substitute your name and that of the children in the contemporary stories.

Look Back
What went especially well today? What things would you change about the lesson?

Did each child have a chance to hear the story today? Did each child get an experience at helping another?

Were there any children who could not find anything interesting to do? What could you provide for that child next week?

Look Ahead
Remember that for some of your children, this will be the first Christmas that they remember. They may not understand what all of the hubbub is about, but you may be sure they are aware of the hubbub. Plan ahead for excited children who may be a bit crankier than usual, or who may cry more easily or be more easily distracted.

Session

16

Luke 2:4-5

We need to help our children realize the true meaning of Christmas, not the commercial aspects.

Bible Verse:
You will name him Jesus.
(Luke 1:31)

Resources:
Bible
CD
patterns (pp. 238–241)
Activity Pak (Winter)
    page 5 (figures 1, 3, 5)
    Songbook
Bible Story Picture Cards

Supplies:
several small suitcases
dress-up clothes
sandbox (see p. 234)
sand toys
toy creche figures (Mary,
    Joseph, and donkey)
construction paper
crayons or markers
glue sticks
CD player
teacher scissors
stapler and staples
dolls and baby items
strips of red and green
    paper
Christmas stickers
Christmas tree from last
    week
building blocks
(optional: paper punch
    and yarn)

Mary and Joseph Get Ready................

Enter the Bible Story

Read Luke 2:4-5: Mary and Joseph had to take a long trip by official decree just as Jesus was ready to be born. They lived in Nazareth, which was some ninety miles north of Bethlehem. But the Roman ruler of the time decreed that everyone should go back to the town of each person's ancestors. Joseph was descended from King David. If you will remember, David was from Bethlehem (as was Naomi and Ruth). Therefore, the two had to go back to a town where they had never lived before. Travel would have been hard, particularly for a pregnant woman. It probably took weeks to make the journey as they traveled by day and rested in friendly homes along the way by night.

Think About It: Getting ready for Christmas! This phrase both delights and frightens me. I love the pretty decorations, and the parties, and the pure excitement, especially in children's faces. I do not like looking for the perfect gift for the hard-to-buy-for relative; the malls; any store of any size; and the greediness of children as they make out their long lists for Santa. Reflect on the following questions as you prepare to tell the story: What are you doing to get ready for Christmas? How are you keeping focused on "The Reason for the Season"? How can you help your children know that Christmas is a time for love, peace, and goodwill?

Through the Week: Focus on the things that you can do to simplify your life this Christmas. Could you give gifts to mission projects in lieu of gifts to relatives who already have too much? Could you host a cookie exchange so that you and your friends could make one recipe of cookies and still have an assortment for holiday entertaining? Could you forego the turkey in favor of an already cooked ham?

Pray: Dear God, please help me stay focused on you in this busy, busy season. Give me the peace I need to continue to spread your love to all whom I meet.

The Story and Young Children

The children are noticing the hustle and bustle of the season. They probably already have a tree up in their homes and may be spending more evenings than they would like with a babysitter, while their parents go to parties and to do shopping. They see the growing mound of presents under the tree and cannot understand their parents' admonitions to wait.

Toddlers and two-year-olds do not understand the concept of geography and therefore will not really understand about traveling from Nazareth to Bethlehem. However, they do know how to get ready for something. And they can know that Bethlehem is a special place, because Jesus was born there.

Room Setup: Make sure the Christmas tree that you made last week is still up. Put out more ornaments for those who were absent last week and for those who would like to make another one this week. Put Mary, Joseph, and the donkey figures from your creche in the sandbox or in the Discovery Center for the children to play with.

Learning Centers

Work with two or three children at a time in each learning center.

Conversation Center

You will need: patterns (pp. 238-239, 241), teacher scissors, stapler and staples, construction paper (brightly colored and gray and brown), crayons or markers, glue sticks, red and green paper strips (two by twelve inches), Christmas stickers (optional: paper punch and yarn, if you have an artificial tree).

Get ready: Cut brightly colored construction paper into ornament shapes (pp. 238–239, 241). Cut the donkey ears and headband (p. 240) from brown or gray construction paper, one set for each child

- Make Ornaments, Activity 1c
- Make Donkey Ears, Activity 3a
- Make Decorations, Activity 4b

Family Living Center

You will need: a few small suitcases and dress-up clothes, dolls and baby items.

- Play "Going on a Trip," Activity 1d
- Play With Dolls, Activity 3d

Discovery Center

You will need: a sandbox (see p. 234); several sand toys; Mary, Joseph, and donkey figures from a Nativity set.

- Play With Sand, Activity 1b

Building Center

Provide enough blocks for toddlers to share. You may use wooden unit blocks or large cardboard or plastic blocks.

Storytelling Center

You will need: Activity Pak—p. 5 (figures 1, 3, 5), CD, CD player, Songbook, Bible.

Get ready: Prepare storytelling figures (see Activity Pak—p. 2).

- Tell the Bible Story, Activity 2a
- Sing a Song, Activity 2b
- Retell the Bible Story, Activity 2c
- Do a Donkey Dance, Activity 3b
- Tell Another Story, Activity 3c
- Enjoy Music, Activity 4a

Mary and Joseph Get Ready

"Come, Mary," said Joseph. "We must go to Bethlehem. We must get ready for the trip."

"And we must get ready for our baby," said Mary. Mary and Joseph loaded the donkey with food and water and soft cloths for the baby. Mary got on the donkey to ride. Joseph walked beside her. They started down the road to Bethlehem.

"Do you remember what the angel said?" asked Mary.

"Yes," said Joseph. "Our baby is special because he is the Son of God. We are to name him Jesus."

"His name will be Jesus," said Mary.

# 1 Prepare

for the Story

a   Welcome Each Child
Do this as each child enters.

Stoop to the children's eye level and welcome each child by name.

Say to each child: "I am so happy you have come to church today."

Be prepared to involve children in an interesting or comforting activity.

b   Play With Sand
Do this in the Discovery Center.

Place Mary, Joseph, and the donkey from a creche scene in the sandbox. These can be used to retell the story later, but just let the children enjoy playing with them for now.

Encourage the children to play with the sand. Talk with them about walking in sand.

Say: "I wonder what it would feel like if we had to walk a long, long way in the sand."

c   Make Ornaments
Do this in the Conversation Center.

Repeat this activity from last week, especially if you have some children who were absent.

Gather two or three children. Allow the children to choose one of the precut shapes to decorate. Talk about the shapes they chose.

Let the children decorate the ornaments with the markers or crayons. When finished, allow the child to place the ornament on the tree in the Family Living Center.

d   Play "Going on a Trip"
Do this in the Family Living Center.

Allow the children to play as if they are preparing to go on a trip. Talk about the things they would need to put in their suitcase if they were going a long way away.

2 Tell

the Story

a   Tell the Bible Story
Do this in the Storytelling Center.

Gather two or three children.

Say: "A long time ago there were no cars to take us places when we went on a trip. Mary and Joseph had to use this donkey to help them go on a trip." Hold up the donkey.

Tell the Bible story, using the storytelling figures (figures 10, 12, 13) at the appropriate times.

Open a Bible and say the Bible verse. Encourage the children to **say** the Bible verse with you: "You will name him Jesus."

Pray: "Thank you, God, for Jesus. Amen."

b   Sing a Song
Do this in the Storytelling Center.

With the children, sing the verse about Joseph in "An Angel Told Mary" (Activity Pak Songbook, CD). Have the children clap their hands whenever they sing the words *good news.*

c   Retell the Bible Story
Do this in the Storytelling Center.

Gather one or two children. Use the following action verse:

Clippity clop, clippity clop.
(*Pat hands on your lap.*)
Joseph brought the donkey to Mary.
(*Pantomime.*)

Clippity clop, clippity clop.
(*Pat hands on your lap.*)
Mary put the things they needed for
    their trip on the donkey.
(*Pantomime.*)

Clippity clop, clippity clop.
(*Pat hands on your lap.*)
Mary and Joseph and the donkey walked
    down the road to Bethlehem.
(*Pantomime.*)

Clippity clop, clippity clop.
(*Pat hands on your lap.*)
Mary and Joseph were ready for Jesus.
(*Fold hands in lap.*)

Connect

with the Story

a **Make Donkey Ears**

Do this in the Conversation Center.

Gather two or three children.

Let the children decorate their donkey ears with crayons or markers. Staple the ears onto the headband and staple the headband together. Make sure that the prongs of the staples face away from the children's heads.

Encourage the children to wear their donkey ears.

b **Do a Donkey Dance**

Do this in the Storytelling Center.

Gather two or three children. **Say:** "Let's pretend to be the donkey taking Mary and Joseph to Bethlehem."

Say the poem below. Have the children move like donkeys on the first three lines of the poem and fall down on the last line.

Repeat as long as the children show interest.

Little donkey going to Bethlehem,
How will you go to town?
I'll clip, clip, clop. I'll clip, clip, clop,
And then I'll sit right down!

From from BibleZone® 2, Preschool; © Abingdon Press.

c **Tell Another Story**

Do this in the Storytelling Center.

Substitute the names of your children in the story, especially if one of your children is about to have a new baby in his or her family.

Aimee's mommy is going to have a new baby. Aimee helped her mommy and daddy get ready. They got Aimee's old cradle out of the attic. It was too small for Aimee. Mommy made new covers for the cradle. Aimee had her own blanket for her big bed.

Granny brought a new baby swing. It was too little for Aimee! Aunt Julie brought over some diapers. Aimee did not need diapers! She wore big girl panties. Aimee and her family had fun getting ready for the new baby.

d **Play With Dolls**

Do this in the Family Living Center.

Allow the children to play with dolls in the Family Living Center.

Talk with the children about babies: "What things do you need to be ready for a new baby? What do you do when a baby is crying? What do you do when a baby is hungry? How do you get a baby to go to sleep?"

Celebrate

the Story

a **Enjoy Music**

Do this in the Storytelling Center.

Sing the action song "This Is the Way We Trim Our Tree" (CD, Activity Pak Songbook). Use the recorded stanzas and the optional stanzas. Then let the children help you make up additional verses. Sing other songs that you have learned in Sunday school.

b **Make Decorations**

Do this in the Conversation Center.

Give each child a strip of paper and some Christmas stickers. Let the children decorate their strips with stickers. When they finish, take their strips and make a circle out of them, stapling them together. Join all the circles together in a chain to hang on the wall.

c **Say Goodbye**

Recall today's Bible story. Have the children say the Bible verse with you.

Say: "I am glad (*name a child*) helped get our room ready for Christmas today." Repeat for each child. **Pray:** "Thank you, God, for Jesus. We are ready for him to come."

Have a teacher or helper at the door to ensure that anxious children do not leave until someone comes for them. Tell parents about today's Bible story and make sure that each child has today's Bible Story Picture Card.

Show parents the "Nurturing Your Child's Faith" section of the card. Point out to parents the Christmas tree and the chain decoration that the class made. Let the children take home their donkey ears.

Tip

Make the stories more personal. Substitute your name and that of the children in the contemporary stories.

Look Back

Did all of the children experience the Bible story today? Do they know what the name of the new baby will be?

Today we wanted children to get a sense of getting ready for something to happen. Do you think the children experienced that sense of preparation?

Look Ahead

Next week you will be using wheat stalks. These can be obtained from any place that sells silk or dried flowers. You also will be making a straw bed for a baby. Read ahead to make sure you have the supplies you need.

71

Mary and Joseph got ready for the baby to be born. We can get ready for Christmas.

Bible Verse:
You will name him Jesus.
(Luke 1:31)

Resources:
Bible
CD
Activity Pak (Winter)
  pages 5–8 (figures
  1–3, 5–6)
  Songbook
Bible Story Picture Cards

Supplies:
CD player
sandbox (see p. 234)
sand toys
creche figures (Mary,
  Joseph, angel, stable,
  animals)
tempera paint (one color)
paper
wheat stalks
coverups
baby dolls and baby items
small box, (big enough
  to put a baby doll
  inside)
baby blankets
hay, straw, or shredded
  paper
building blocks
toy farm animals
bulletin board or
  clothesline and
  clothespins

Mary and Joseph Look for a Place to Stay...........................

Enter the Bible Story

Read Luke 2:6-7: Travelers in Jesus' day usually took lodging in the homes of strangers along the way. Apparently there was no one willing to take in a man and his wife, who was on the verge of giving birth. Bethlehem was on the caravan route from Jerusalem to Egypt. The inn would have been a stopping place for the caravans. There would have been small rooms for wealthy persons to sleep, but most people would simply sleep in the courtyard. The stable could have been in a corner of the courtyard. Or, many caves around Bethlehem were used as stables. So Jesus could have been born in a cave, which would have given the little family more privacy and would make more sense for the shepherds to be the first to greet the newborn child.

Think About It: Things don't always work out as planned, do they? Mary and Joseph must have been sure they would find some place to stay while in Bethlehem, but they wound up in a stable. The irony does not escape the Gospel writer: The Savior of the World, the Prince of Peace, the Son of God, was born not in a palace, but in a lowly stable. If you have ever been on a working farm, or been to a state or county fair, you know what stables smell like. How do you think Mary must have felt as she saw the stable and realized that her baby would be born in the smelly hay, far away from her home and family? How must Joseph have felt when a stable was the only thing he could provide for his wife? What does it mean for us that the Savior of us all took human form and was born in a place that many of us would hesitate to spend time in, much less stay overnight?

Through the Week: Probably many things in your life right now are not "going according to plan." What kind of lemonade can you make with the lemons you have received? Remember that God uses us as we are, not as we wish we were.

Pray: Thank you, God, that you thought so much of us that you took human form as Jesus, who was born like the least and the lowliest of us all.

The Story and Young Children

This story has been romanticized to the point that often young children think of it as normal for a baby to be born in a stable. Help your children realize that being born in a stable was a "silly" place for a baby to be born. This will help them remember the story and will prepare them to realize the irony of the situation once they are mature enough.

Room Setup: Put the stable and the animals in the sandbox with Mary, Joseph, and the angel for the children to play with. Prepare the Conversation Center for painting with straw. Gather shredded paper to make straw for the manger.

Learning Centers

Work with two or three children at a time in each learning center.

Conversation Center

This should be a table around which you may gather the children. Sit down with the children and engage them in conversation.

You will need: tempera paint (one color), paper, wheat stalks (can be purchased at a craft store), short-sleeved adult shirts, bulletin board or clothesline and clothespins.

• Paint With Straw, Activity 1d

Discovery Center

You will need: a sandbox (see session 4), sand toys; hay, straw, or shredded paper; blanket; small box big enough to put a baby doll in; creche figures (Mary, Joseph, angel, stable, and animals, except camels and sheep).

• Play With Sand, Activity 1b
• Make a Straw Bed for a Baby, Activity 3a

Family Living Center

You will need: baby dolls and baby items.

• Play With Dolls, Activity 1c

Building Center

Provide enough blocks for toddlers to share. You may use wooden unit blocks or large cardboard or plastic blocks.

You will need: blocks, toy farm animals, shredded paper.

• Build a Stable, Activity 3b

Storytelling Center

This should be an open area where you may gather children for storytelling, or to listen and respond to music. It would be helpful to have this center on a carpeted area.

You will need: Activity Pak—pp. 5-8 (figures 1-3, 5-6), CD, CD player, Activity Pak Songbook, Bible.

Get ready: Prepare storytelling figures (see Activity Pak—p. 2).

• Tell the Bible Story, Activity 2a
• Retell the Bible Story, Activity 2b
• Sing a Song, Activity 2c
• Tell Another Story, Activity 3c
• Enjoy Music, Activity 4a

Mary and Joseph Look for a Place to Stay

Mary and Joseph and the donkey finally got to Bethlehem. They had had a long trip, and they were tired. But they could not find a place to stay! A man told them they could stay in the stable with the cows, and they went there.

"Joseph," said Mary, "this will be fine. I am glad to have a warm and dry place to stay for my baby to be born."

"I wish we had a better place for you," Joseph said. "But this will be a good place. We will be safe here."

Mary and Joseph were glad to have a place to rest.

 **Prepare**

for the Story

 Welcome Each Child

Do this as each child enters the classroom.

Stoop to the children's eye level and welcome each child by name. **Say** to each child: "I am so happy to see you today." Be prepared to involve children in an interesting or comforting activity.

Play With Sand

Do this in the Discovery Center.

Let the children play in the sandbox, taking care that they keep the sand *in* the sandbox. Encourage them to tell the story of Mary and Joseph going to Bethlehem, using the figures from a Nativity set.

Say: "I wonder what this building is? There are animals here. Our story today will tell us where Mary and Joseph stayed in Bethlehem."

Play With Dolls

Do this in the Family Living Center.

Allow the children to play with dolls in the Family Living Center. Engage the children in conversation.

Ask: "What things do you need to be ready for a new baby? What do you do when a baby is crying? What do you do when a baby is hungry? How do you get a baby to go to sleep?"

Paint With Straw

Do this in the Conversation Center.

Gather two or three children. Protect their clothing from the paint by putting an adult, short-sleeved shirt on them, buttoned in the back.

Hold up a bundle of wheat stalks and **say**: "This is a sheaf of wheat." Move the sheaf through the air.

Say: "What sound do you hear?" Separate the stalks and give one to each child. Have the children examine the stalks. Notice how dry they are and how they tickle your skin when you gently draw it across your cheek or arm. Notice the seed head and the long fingers of chaff that grow off the seed head.

Say: "This is what the cows eat." Hold the stalk by the straw end and carefully dip the chaff into paint and move it across the sheet of paper. Help the children paint with their wheat stalk.

When each child is finished, put his or her name on the paper and hang it on the wall or on your clothesline to dry.

 Tell

the Story

 Tell the Bible Story

Do this in the Storytelling Center.

Gather two or three children. Recall the stories of the previous two weeks, using the angel storytelling figure (figure 2) if desired. Tell today's story, using the storytelling figures (figures 1, 3, 5, 6) as appropriate.

Open a Bible and **say** the Bible verse: "You will name him Jesus." Encourage the children to say the verse with you.

Pray: "Dear God, thank you that Mary and Joseph found a warm and dry place to stay to get ready for their baby."

 Retell the Bible Story

Do this in the Storytelling Center.

Use the action verse "Mary and Joseph Look for a Place to Stay" (Songbook) to retell the Bible story.

 Sing a Song

Do this in the Storytelling Center.

Sing "An Angel Told Mary" (CD, Songbook).

Have the children clap their hands whenever they sing the words *good news*.

3 Connect
with the Story

a | Make a Straw Bed for a Baby
Do this in the Discovery Center.

Gather two or three children. Tell them that you need to get a bed ready for baby Jesus. Ask the children to fill the box with hay, straw, or shredded paper.

Let the children feel the hay with their hands. **Say:** "I don't think we should lay a baby on this! Let's put down a soft blanket." Gently smooth a blanket on top of the hay. Let the children feel the blanket.

Say: "There, that's better." Place the box in a special place, ready for the baby.

b | Build a Stable
Do this in the Building Center.

Gather two or three children. Use the blocks and animals to build a stable such a where Joseph and Mary might have stayed.

Make stalls for the various animals. Build a manger to hold the "hay" (shredded paper). Let the animals eat from the manger. Build another manger to make a bed for the baby.

c | Tell Another Story
Do this in the Storytelling Center.

"It's time to get ready," said Mrs. Adams. "We are going to have a snack." Jason and Shaquille and Janet knew what to do. They cleaned off the table and helped put napkins at each place for a snack.

"It's time to get ready," said Mr. Dustin. "We are going to play some music." Anna and Kate and Sam knew what to do. They came to the big carpet and got some instruments out of the big box.

"It's time to get ready," said Miss Lauren. "We are going to go outside." Sabrina and Thompson and Ethan knew what to do. They went to the cubbies and got their coats and hats.

"It's time to get ready," said Mr. Steve. "We are going to have a story." Robert and Kevin and Lisa knew what to do. They went to the big carpet and sat down quietly.

"I am so glad that you know how to get ready!" said Mrs. Adams.

4 Celebrate
the Story

a | Enjoy Music
Do this in the Storytelling Center.

Sing "This Is the Way We Trim the Tree" with motions (CD, Songbook).

Sing "An Angel Told Mary" (CD, Songbook), clapping when you sing the words *good news*. Sing other favorite songs you enjoy and the children know.

b | Take a Walk

Walk through your church building to see how the church is getting ready for Christmas. Are there decorations on the doors? Is there a special tree in the fellowship hall? Is the sanctuary decorated?

Ask the children to look for signs of Christmas as you walk.

c | Say Goodbye

Recall today's Bible story. Have the children say or sing the Bible verse with you.

Say: "I am glad (*name a child*) came to church today." Repeat this for each child in the class. **Pray:** "Thank you, God, for our church. We are happy to come to church."

Have a teacher or helper at the door to ensure that anxious children do not leave until someone comes for them. Tell parents about today's Bible story. Make sure that each child has today's Bible Story Picture Card.

Show the parents the "Nurturing Your Child's Faith" section of the card. Point out to parents the manger bed that the class made. Be sure the children take home their straw paintings.

Tip
Make the stories more personal. Substitute your name and that of the children in the contemporary stories.

Look Back
Did the children have joyful experiences in class today? Were some children's experiences not so joyful?

How can these children be helped to be happy at church in the next session?

Did the children experience the sense of getting ready for something?

What have the children taught you?

Look Ahead
Next week we will celebrate Jesus' birth. There is far too much in the lesson for one class to do. Pick and choose among the activities to suit your class. Prepare to have fun with the children, not to have the session be a chore.

Luke 2:6-7

We celebrate the birth of children, and especially remember the birth of Jesus, God's Son.

Bible Verse:
You will name him Jesus.
(Luke 1:31)

Resources:
Bible
CD
Activity Pak (Winter)
 page 3 ("Jesus Is Born" picture)
 pages 9–10 (Christmas matching game)
 pages 5, 8
 (figures 3, 4, 7)
 Songbook
Bible Story Picture Cards

Supplies:
CD player
sandbox (see p. 234)
sand toys
creche figures (baby Jesus, Mary, Joseph, angel, stable, animals except camels and sheep)
lunch-size paper bags
tempera paint
small paper plates
paper towels
Christmas cookie cutters
coverups (short-sleeved adult shirts that button down the front)
newspaper
manger children made last week
round coffee filters
watercolor markers
peg-type clothespins
yarn
baby dolls and baby items
special birthday snack
napkins
fine-tipped permanent marker
building blocks

Jesus Is Born..........

Enter the Bible Story

Read Luke 2:6-7: The Bible story for today tells the story of the birth of Jesus Christ. In the story the term "firstborn" indicates other sons may have been born later. "Swaddling cloths" were long strips of cloth that were used to wrap infants so tightly that their arms and legs could not move. It was believed that this wrapping was necessary for arms and legs to grow straight and strong. Several times a day the cloth would have been loosened and the baby cleaned, but for the first few months, a child would have been tightly bound most of the time.

Think About It: The birth of Jesus Christ! This story is so familiar that we run the risk of forgetting just what a remarkable story it was. Imagine, the Creator of the Universe, the Great God of Heaven, the God who brought the Hebrew people out of Egypt, this God chose to become human! What does it mean to you that God would take on the vulnerability of a small child in order to experience all that we as human beings experience? Is it easier to believe that God knows what you are going through if you know that God, as Jesus, experienced it? We have been preparing for this event for weeks. How will you help children experience this celebration as one which many people have waited and prepared for?

Pray: Thank you, God, that you came as a human child to understand us and to show us how to live. Amen.

The Story and Young Children

Obviously, the whole concept of "the Word being made flesh" is too complicated for young children. Most adults do not understand it fully. But children can understand the excitement of the birth of a baby. So far this year, you have told stories of the birth of Moses and Obed. Be sure to emphasize that this birth is different. While Moses and Obed had families that were very happy when they were born, the birth of Jesus caused all creation to rejoice. The birth of Jesus caused angel choirs to appear and a new star to come into the heavens, signaling the wise men to begin their journey. Jesus was born to show us how very much God loves us.

Room Setup: Set up the Nativity scene with Mary, Joseph, and the baby in the sandbox. Place a baby doll in the manger that the children made last week. Set up the Conversation Center with art supplies that you will need. Prepare for a happy birthday celebration at the end of class today.

Learning Centers

Work with two or three children at a time in each learning center.

Conversation Center

This should be a table around which you may gather the children. Sit down with the children and engage them in conversation.

You will need: lunch-size paper bags, tempera paint, small paper plates, paper towels, Christmas cookie cutters, coverups (short-sleeved adult shirts that button down the front), newspaper, round coffee filters, watercolor markers, peg-type clothespins (available at most craft stores), yarn, a special snack that the children would associate with a birthday party, napkins, fine-tipped permanent marker.

Get ready: Draw a face on the clothespin with a fine-tipped permanent marker.

- Make Gift Bags, Activity 1c
- Make an Ornament, Activity 2c
- Have a Birthday Snack, Activity 4b

Family Living Center

This would include a toy kitchen set and props appropriate to the lesson.

You will need: dolls and baby items.

- Play With Dolls, Activity 3a

Discovery Center

You will need: Activity Pak—pp. 9-10 (Christmas matching game); sandbox (see p. 234), sand toys, creche figures (baby Jesus, Mary, Joseph, angel, stable, animals except camels and sheep).

- Play With Sand, Activity 1b
- Play a Matching Game, Activity 3b

Building Center

Provide enough blocks for toddlers to share. You may use wooden unit blocks or large cardboard or plastic blocks.

Storytelling Center

You will need: Activity Pak—p. 3 ("Jesus Is Born" picture), pp. 5-8 (figures 3, 4, 7), baby doll, the manger the children made last week, CD, CD player, Activity Pak Songbook, Bible.

Get ready: Prepare storytelling figures (see Activity Pak—p. 2).

- Tell the Bible Story, Activity 2a
- Retell the Bible Story, Activity 2b
- Tell Another Story, Activity 3c
- Enjoy Music, Activity 4a

Jesus Is Born

At last everything was ready for Mary's new baby boy. The stable was warm and dry. The hay was sweet and clean.

Mary and Joseph were ready.

When the baby was born, Mary washed him and wrapped him in soft cloths. She fed the baby and held him while he gently fell asleep.

A star was shining in the sky overhead. The cows were eating their dinner. Joseph watched over Mary and the new baby.

Joseph and Mary remembered what the angels told them. They named their new baby Jesus.

1 Prepare

for the Story

a **Welcome Each Child**

Do this as each child enters the classroom.

Stoop to the child's eye level; welcome each child by name. Point out the baby in the manger that the children made last week, or the baby in the Nativity set.

b **Play With Sand**

Do this in the Discovery Center.

Let the children play in the sandbox, taking care that they keep the sand *in* the sandbox. Help them tell the story of Mary and Joseph going to Bethlehem. They should be familiar enough with the story to tell it themselves.

Point out that this week we have a baby in the sandbox. Ask the children if they remember what the baby's name is.

c **Make Gift Bags**

Do this in the Conversation Center.

Cover the table with newspaper. Set out several paper plates with folded paper towels on top of them. Pour tempera paint onto the paper towels until the towels are soaked. Place a different cookie cutter on each paper plate.

Gather two or three children. Protect their clothing by having each child wear a coverup. Put each child's name on the bottom of a paper bag.

Give each child her or his paper bag (folded flat). Have the children lay the bags down on the newspaper with the folded part on the bottom. (You should not be able to see the child's name on the bottom of the bag.)

Give each child one of the cookie cutters that you have set on each tempera-soaked paper towel. Allow each child to use it as a stamp on his or her paper sack. After the children have made two or three imprints, give them a different cookie cutter with a different color of paint.

Allow the bag to dry after each child has used several cutters with two or three different colors.

2 Tell

the Story

a **Tell the Bible Story**

Do this in the Storytelling Center.

Gather two or three children. Recall the stories that you have told over the past three weeks, particularly if any of the children have been absent.

Show the children the "Jesus Is Born" picture (Activity Pak—p. 3). Ask the children to describe what they see in the picture. Tell the Bible story, using the storytelling figures (figures 3, 4, 7).

Open a Bible and **say** the verse; "You shall name him Jesus." Have the children say the verse with you. **Pray**: "Thank you, God, for baby Jesus."

b **Retell the Bible Story**

Do this in the Storytelling Center.

Gather two or three children. Pretend to rock a baby while listening to "Sleep, Baby Jesus" (CD, Songbook). When the baby is asleep, put the baby in the manger. Then **say**: "Oh, no, the baby is awake!"

Let one of the children rock the baby and listen to the song again. Repeat as long as the children are interested.

c **Make an Ornament**

Do this in the Conversation Center.

Gather two or three children. Give each child a round coffee filter and watercolor markers. Let each child decorate his or her "blanket" with the markers. Show the children how to "dot" on the filters with the markers.

When the children have decorated their blanket, show them how to fold the blanket around their baby (the clothespin). Wrap yarn around the blanket to hold it in place. Tie the yarn in a knot on the back of each ornament. Form a loop that can be used to hang the ornament on a tree.

While the children work, talk about how Mary must have cared for baby Jesus, wrapping him in soft cloths.

3 Connect
with the Story

a Play With Dolls
Do this in the Family Living Center.

Allow the children to play with dolls in the Family Living Center.

Engage the children in conversation. **Ask:** "What do you do when a baby is crying? What do you do when a baby is hungry? How do you get a baby to go to sleep?"

b Play a Matching Game
Do this in the Discovery Center.

Gather two or three children. Spread the Christmas matching cards in front of them. (Activity Pak—pp. 9–10). Show the children the picture of the star.

Ask: "Do you know what this is? That's right, it's a star. Can you find another star like this one on the big card? There it is! Let's put this star on the other star."

Repeat with each of the six pictures.

c Tell Another Story
Do this in the Storytelling Center.

Nathan was excited! He ran into the living room. There, underneath the Christmas tree, were lots of presents!

"This is a very special day, Nathan," Mommy said. "It is the birthday of Jesus. We give gifts to each other to celebrate that Jesus was born."

"When we open the presents, we remember that God loves us and that we love each other," Daddy said.

Mommy and Daddy and Nathan thanked God for the presents. They thanked God for loving them. They thanked God for Jesus.

Nathan was glad that it was Jesus' birthday.

4 Celebrate
the Story

a Enjoy Music
Do this in the Storytelling Center.

Gather two or three children. Sing "Away in a Manger" (CD, Songbook), using the motions indicated in the Songbook.

Sing other songs that you have learned.

b Have a Birthday Snack
Do this in the Conversation Center.

Gather the children together. **Say:** "Today we are celebrating Jesus' birthday. When you celebrate a birthday, you have a party!"

Provide a birthday party snack such as cupcakes. If desired, place a candle on one of the cupcakes. Sing "Happy Birthday to Jesus." Enjoy your snack.

c Say Goodbye
Recall today's Bible story, encouraging children to say or sing the Bible verse with you.

Say: "I am glad (*name one of the children*) came to church today." Repeat this for each child in the class." **Pray:** "Thank you, God, for our church. We are happy to come to church."

Be sure to have a teacher or helper at the door to ensure that anxious children do not leave until someone comes for them. Tell parents about today's Bible story and make sure that each child has today's Bible Story Picture Card.

Show the parents the "Nurturing Your Child's Faith" section of the card. Be sure the children take home their ornaments and gift bags.

Tip
Make the stories more personal. Substitute your name and that of the children in the contemporary stories.

Look Back
What feelings did the children express today?

Did the children feel the excitement of Jesus being born to Mary?

What is it you now know about the story and about the students that you did not know before this session?

What did you do that was good or that would work again?

What could you change about the lesson to make it better?

Look Ahead
Read the plan for the next session and begin to prepare yourself during the week with prayer and gathering resources.

Pray for God's help in creating a safe, happy place where the children can discover that God loves them.

Pray for each child by name. Also pray for the child's parents.

The Shepherds See Baby Jesus.......

We can share the Good News that Jesus is born.

Bible Verse:
You will name him Jesus.
(Luke 1:31)

Resources:
Bible
CD
sheep pattern (p. 236)
Activity Pak (Winter)
    pages 5–8 (figures 2–4, 7, 9)
    pages 9–10 (Christmas matching game)
    Songbook
Bible Story Picture Cards

Supplies:
sandbox (see p. 234)
Nativity set with baby Jesus
glue
small paper cups
cotton balls.
Christmas cards (fronts only)
construction paper
tempera paint
sponges cut into Christmas shapes
small plastic or paper plates
coverups
CD player
instruments
blocks and toy sheep (or farm animals)
blue and green construction paper or cloth
permanent felt-tip marker
teacher scissors
bulletin board or clothesline and clothespins
baby dolls and doll items

Enter the Bible Story

Read Luke 2:8-20: The Bible story for today tells the story of the shepherds hearing about the birth of Jesus. Sheep were kept out in the open between March and December. The shepherds had to stay out with them to keep them safe. So the shepherds rarely made it back into town, living instead a nomadic life for the duration of the warm weather. Only during the coldest months did the shepherds and the sheep come back to civilization for protection.

Think About It: The birth announcement of the Son of God did not go out to kings and emperors, not even leading townspeople. No, the first to hear of Jesus' birth were the dirty, smelly shepherds that lived out in the fields with the sheep. Reflect on the following questions as you prepare to tell the story and to help the children retell the story: Why did God choose to reveal the birth of Jesus to these shepherds? How has God been revealed to you? Why were the shepherds afraid? What does Christ's birth mean to you personally?

Through the Week: The Bible states that the shepherds "glorified and praised God for all the things that they had heard and seen" (Luke 2:20). Think of things this week that you have seen and heard God do. Praise God for these things. List different ways to encounter the story throughout the week.

Pray: Thank you, God, for the good news of Jesus' birth. Thank you that you do not always choose the wise and powerful to reveal yourself. Amen.

The Story and Young Children

Children can understand simple stories. The story of the birth of Jesus and the shepherds is so simply written that they too can enjoy the excitement of the account. The children can hear that Jesus was so special that God sent angels to announce his birth to the shepherds. They can know that Christmas is a time for celebration, happiness, and praising God.

Room Setup: Place the Nativity set in the sandbox. Place the teaching picture, "Jesus is Born" (Activity Pak—p. 3), in the storytelling center. Photocopy page 236 for each child.

Learning Centers

Work with two or three children at a time in each learning center.

Conversation Center

You will need: sheep pattern (page 236), glue, small paper cups, cotton balls, construction paper, thick tempera paint, sponges, small plastic or paper plates, coverups, permanent felt-tip marker, teacher scissors.

Get ready: Make a copy of the sheep pattern for each child. Pour glue into small cups. Cut sponges into Christmas shapes about two inches in size. Print "Good News! Jesus Is Born!" in the center of several sheets of construction paper.

- Make Sheep, Activity 1e
- Make Good News Cards, Activity 3a

Discovery Center

You will need: Activity Pak—pp. 9–10 (Christmas matching game), sandbox (see p. 234), sand toys, Nativity set complete with baby Jesus, old Christmas cards (fronts only), bulletin board or clothesline and clothespins.

- Play With Sand, Activity 1b
- Play a Matching Game, Activity 1d
- Look at Christmas Cards, Activity 3b

Family Living Center

You will need: baby dolls and doll items.

- Play With Dolls, Activity 1c

Building Center

You will need: blocks, toy sheep, blue and green construction paper or cloth.

- Play With Toy Sheep, Activity 4b

Storytelling Center

You will need: CD, CD player, instruments, Activity Pak—pp. 5, 8 (figures 2–4, 7, 9), Activity Pak Songbook, Bible.

Get ready: Prepare storytelling figures (see Activity Pak—p. 2).

- Tell the Bible Story, Activity 2a
- Sing a Song, Activity 2b
- Retell the Bible Story, Activity 2c
- Tell Another Story, Activity 3c
- Enjoy Music, Activity 4a

Shepherds See Baby Jesus

One night there were some shepherds watching their sheep. It was nighttime, and everything was quiet.

All of a sudden an angel stood in front of the shepherds. The shepherds were afraid.

The angel said, "Don't be afraid, shepherds. I have good news! Baby Jesus has been born in Bethlehem. Go and see!"

The shepherds ran to Bethlehem and found Mary and Joseph and the baby. They were so happy. They told their friends and praised God.

 **Prepare**

for the Story

a   Welcome Each Child
Do this as each child enters the room.
Stoop to the children's eye level and welcome each child by name. Be prepared to involve children in an interesting or comforting activity.

b   Play With Sand
Do this in the Discovery Center.
Gather one or two children. **Say** to each child: "I have good news! Baby Jesus is born in Bethlehem! Come and see!"
Show the children the Nativity set in the sandbox and encourage them to play with the figures, retelling the stories that they have heard.

c   Play With Dolls
Do this in the Family Living Center.
Invite the children to take care of dolls in the Family Living Center.

 Play a Matching Game
Do this in the Discovery Center.
Gather two or three children. Show the children the star from the Christmas matching game (Activity Pak—pp. 9–10).
Ask: "Do you know what this is? That's right—it's a star. Can you find another star like this one on the big card? There it is! Let's put this star on the other star." Repeat with each of the six pictures.

e   Make Sheep
Do this in the Conversation Center.
Gather two or three children. Give each child a copy of the sheep template (p. 236) and several cotton balls.
Show each child how to dip the cotton ball into the glue and then stick it on the paper. Allow the children to fill in the outline of their sheep with cotton.
Say: "Today we will hear a story about some people who took care of sheep."

 Tell

the Story

a   Tell the Bible Story
Do this in the Storytelling Center.
Gather two or three children. Recall the Christmas stories that you have told over the past weeks.
Tell the Bible story, using the storytelling figures (figures 2-4, 7, 9) as appropriate.
Open a Bible and **say** the Bible verse: "You will name him Jesus."
Encourage the children to say the verse with you.

b   Sing a Song
Do this in the Storytelling Center.
Sing "An Angel Told Mary" (CD), adding the third verse.
Have the children clap twice whenever they sing the words *good news*.

c   Retell the Bible Story
Do this in the Storytelling Center.
Use the action verse with the children:

Shepherds were watching their sheep.
(*Make sheep noises.*)
All of a sudden
(*Whisper and lean forward.*)
An angel appeared!
(*Hold out hands wide and speak loudly.*)
The shepherds were afraid.
(*Make scared motions.*)
The angel said, "Do not be afraid."
(*Shake head.*)
"I have good news."
(*Smile and clap hands on "good news."*)
"Jesus is born in Bethlehem, go see!"
(*Point away.*)
The shepherds ran to Bethlehem.
(*Make running motions.*)
They found Mary and Joseph with baby Jesus.
(*Rock a baby.*)

3 Connect
with the Story

a Make Good News Cards
Do this in the Conversation Center.

Gather two or three children. Protect their clothing by putting adult shirts on them, buttoned in the back.

Give each child a piece of construction paper, a plate with paint in it, and a sponge. Show the children how to dip the sponge into the paint and press the sponge on the paper several times to make a design. Encourage the children to print on the edge of the paper around the words.

Say: "Often when a baby is born, the parents are so excited that they send announcements to all their friends. We can take these cards with us and give them to people to tell them that Jesus was born!"

b Look at Christmas Cards
Do this in the Discovery Center.

Place several Christmas cards in a basket or box, or hang them on a clothesline. Encourage the children to identify the pictures on the cards.

Say: "What is this picture, Amy? Yes, it is an angel! Do you remember what the angel did?" Talk about the pictures, helping children remember the details of the Christmas story.

c Tell Another Story
Do this in the Storytelling Center.

"Good news," said Josh as he ran into the Sunday school room.

"What is your news?" asked Mr. Martin.

"Grammy is coming to see me, and she is coming on an airplane!"

"Wow!" said Mr. Martin. "That is good news. And when we have good news, we want to tell everyone about it. Let's go tell everyone!"

"Children," said Mr. Martin, "Josh has good news. His grammy is coming to see him on an airplane!"

Josh was happy that his Grammy was coming and that he could tell his friends about it.

4 Celebrate
the Story

a Enjoy Music
Do this in the Storytelling Center.

Gather two or three children. Enjoy listening to Christmas music (CD).

Let the children play the instruments as you listen. Sing the songs (Songbook, CD) that you have learned the past few weeks

b Play With Toy Sheep
Do this in the Building Center.

Gather two or three children. Talk to the children about what it takes to take care of sheep. Encourage the children to build a pen for the sheep. Give the children a blue piece of paper or cloth and tell them to provide water for the sheep to drink. Give each of the children a green piece of paper or cloth and tell them to provide grass for the sheep to eat.

c Say Goodbye
Recall today's Bible story. Encourage the children to say the Bible verse with you.

Say: "Good news! (*Name one of the children*) came to church today!" Repeat this for each child in the class.

Pray: "Thank you, God, for baby Jesus. Help us to tell everyone the good news that he was born."

Be sure to have a teacher or helper at the door to ensure that anxious children do not leave until someone comes for them.

Tell parents about today's Bible story and make sure that each child has today's Bible Story Picture Card.

Show the parents the "Nurturing Your Child's Faith" section of the card. Be sure the children take home their sheep and their Good News Cards.

Tip
Make the stories more personal. Substitute your name and that of the children in the contemporary stories.

Look Back
What feelings did the children express today?

Did the children feel the excitement of the shepherds seeing the angels and Jesus?

What do you know now about the story and the students that you did not know before this session?

What did you do that was good or that would work again?

What could you change about the lesson to make it better?

Look Ahead
Next week, as you tell the story of the wise men from the East, you will do a lot with stars and star shapes. You will also need to wrap several gift boxes to use in the Blocks Center. Consider wrapping the boxes with pretty plastic adhesive paper to make them more durable and to discourage the children from unwrapping them.

We respond to God's gift with gifts of our own.

Bible Verse:
You will name him Jesus.
(Luke 1:31)

Resources:
Bible
CD
star pattern (page 238)
Activity Pak (Winter)
   pages 5, 8, 17
   (figures 3, 4, 10–13)
   page 3
   pages 9–10 (Christmas
   matching game)
   Songbook
Bible Story Picture Cards

Supplies:
star stickers
clear water or soda bottle
water
star-shaped confetti
   (found in card shops)
glue
gift boxes
newspaper
9-by-12-inch pieces of
   posterboard
matte knife
masking tape
white paper
tempera paint
chunky paintbrushes
coverups
CD player
black construction paper
crayons or markers
cardboard or construction
   paper
teacher scissors
toys (one per child)
scarfs or lightweight cloth
   strips

Wise Men See Baby Jesus.............

Enter the Bible Story

Read Matthew 2:11: The Bible story for today tells the story of the wise men bringing their gifts to young Jesus. By the time the wise men found Jesus, he was no longer an infant. Some Bible scholars believe that Jesus was approximately two years old. The wise men had been studying the skies and observed an unexplained star. They interpreted this sign as an indication that the King of the Jews was born. When they found Jesus with Mary and Joseph, the Bible gave no indication that they were doubtful about Jesus' kingship. Surely they must have noted the humble surroundings. Yet they responded with faith and worship. There was no question for them that Jesus was indeed the King of the Jews.

Think About It: Jesus' birth is one of the most well-known stories of the Bible. What a difference Jesus' birth made to the world! Even though we do not know the exact date of his birth, time is marked by his coming. For those who were watching, the birth of Jesus was not a surprise. (Read also about Simeon and Anna in Luke 2:25-38.) Think about how the wise men responded when they saw Jesus. How do you respond to Jesus? What signs of Jesus' coming were apparent to the people in the first century? What signs of Jesus' presence do you see today?

Through the Week: The wise men brought gifts to Jesus. Think about the gifts that you can give to Jesus. Do you have the gift of hospitality—to help make people feel comfortable and at home? Do you have the gift of laughter when things get tense? Do you have the gift of tears to share with friends who are mourning? Make a list of the gifts that you can offer Jesus.

Pray: Thank you, God, for the good news of Jesus' birth. Thank you for revealing yourself to those who seek you. Amen.

The Story and Young Children

Stories teach many things to children. The story of the birth of Jesus and the wise men can continue the Christmas story for the children. They will know that we can celebrate Jesus' birth all year long. The story of the wise men holds a very special message for children and adults of all ages—that Jesus is worthy of our worship and that we can bring gifts to Jesus. We may not have the gold, frankincense, and myrrh, but we can give ourselves to Jesus. The children can know that they can give gifts to others.

Room Setup: Have the Nativity set in the sandbox. Place the teaching picture, "Jesus is Born" (Activity Pak—p. 3), in the Storytelling Center. Prepare star stencils for painting and gift boxes for the Building Center. Make a large star for the "Follow the Star" game.

Learning Centers

Work with two or three children at a time in each learning center.

Conversation Center

You will need: star stencils (posterboard, matte knife), masking tape, white paper, tempera paint, chunky paintbrushes, coverups, crayons or markers, black construction paper, newspaper.

Get ready: Trace the star pattern (p. 238) onto pieces of posterboard. You will need one stencil for each child. Cut out the star with a matte knife. Cover the table with newspaper. Tape a piece of paper on the newspaper and tape the stencil on top of the paper.

- Paint With Star Stencils, Activity 1d
- Make Gifts, Activity 4b

Discovery Center

You will need: star-shaped confetti, clear water or soda bottle, water, glue, Activity Pak—pp. 9-10 (Christmas matching game).

Get ready: Fill plastic bottle with water. Add star confetti. Put glue in the bottle cap and screw on. Allow the glue to dry overnight.

- Play With a Star Bottle, Activity 1b
- Play a Matching Game, Activity 3c

Family Living Center

Include gifts for your Christmas tree.

Building Center

You will need: gift boxes, newspaper, masking tape.

Get ready: Stuff each each gift box with newspaper and tape closed.

- Play With Gift Boxes, Activity 1c

Storytelling Center

You will need: star pattern (p. 238); Activity Pak—pp. 5, 8, 17 (figures 3, 4, 10-13); Bible; large cardboard or construction paper; CD, CD player, Activity Pak Songbook; scarfs or lightweight cloth strips; toys (one per child)

Get ready: Using the star pattern, cut a star from construction paper. Prepare storytelling figures (see Activity Pak—p. 2).

- Tell the Bible Story, Activity 2a
- Retell the Bible Story, Activity 2b
- Sing a Song, Activity 2c
- Play Follow the Star, Activity 3a
- Tell Another Story, Activity 3b
- Enjoy Music, Activity 4a

Wise Men See Baby Jesus

A long time ago there were some wise men who looked at the stars every night. One night they saw an unusual star. What did this mean? A king had been born!

"Let's go find the new king so we can give him gifts," said one of the wise men.

They looked up in the sky and followed the star. The star led them to a house. Inside they found Mary, Joseph, and Jesus.

The wise men were very happy they found Jesus. They gave him gifts.

1 Prepare

for the Story

a Welcome Each Child
Do this as each child enters the room.

Stoop to the child's eye level and welcome each child by name. Give each child a star sticker to place on her or his hand or clothing.

Say: "We are wearing a star to remind us that Jesus is born. God sent a star in the sky to tell the whole world about Jesus' birth."

Be prepared to involve children in an interesting or comforting activity.

b Play With a Star Bottle
Do this in the Discovery Center.

Gather two or three children. Let the children play with the bottle filled with water and confetti, noticing how the stars float through the water.

c Play With Gift Boxes
Do this in the Building Center.

Let the children stack the boxes on top of one another. See how high they can build a tower of boxes. Can they build a bridge with boxes?

Remember that the children have just learned that gift boxes often hold surprises. Assure them that the boxes are empty and do not need to be opened.

d Paint With Star Stencils
Do this in the Conversation Center.

Gather two or three children. Protect their clothing by having them wear coverups.

Give each child a paintbrush and some paint. Let the child paint the paper and the stencil that you have cut from posterboard.

When finished, remove the stencil. You should have a rough star shape for each child.

2 Tell

the Story

a Tell the Bible Story
Do this in the Storytelling Center.

Gather two or three children. Tell the children the Bible story, using the storytelling figures (3, 4, 10-13) at the appropriate times.

Open a Bible and **say** the Bible verse: "You will name him Jesus." Invite the children to say the Bible verse with you.

b Retell the Bible Story
Do this in the Storytelling Center.

Gather two or three children. Use the following action verse:

Wise men were watching the stars.
(*Look up at the sky.*)
One night they saw a special star.
(*Point to the sky.*)
"I see a star! Let's go find the new king!"
(*Hold hands out to side.*)

They followed the star.
(*Pat your legs to indicate walking.*)
They followed a long, long, time.
(*Continue to pat legs.*)
The star stopped above a house.
(*Stop patting.*)
The wise men knocked.
(*Make knocking sounds.*)
Mary opened the door.
(*Pretend to open door.*)
When they saw the child, they gave him gifts.
(*Pretend to give gifts.*)
They worshiped the new king.
(*Kneel and bow head.*)

c Sing a Song
Do this in the Storytelling Center.

Sing "Twinkle, Twinkle, Shining Star" (CD, Songbook) while holding fingers high in the air.

3 Connect
with the Story

a Play "Follow the Star"
Do this in the Storytelling Center.

Designate one child to be young Jesus. Have her or him sit in a designated place. Give other children toys from the room to serve as gifts.

Hold the star you cut from cardboard or construction paper above your head. Lead the children around the room until you reach the child pretending to be Jesus. Have the children give the toys to "Jesus." Repeat the game, using different children to portray Jesus.

b Tell Another Story
Do this in the Storytelling Center.

Jonathan came into the Sunday school room. He went up to Miss Jenny.

"I have a gift," said Jonathan.

Miss Jenny asked to see Jonathan's gift. He showed her a shiny coin.

"Did your mommy give you a gift for Jesus?" asked Miss Jenny.

"Yes," said Jonathan.

"Let's put your gift in the offering plate," said Miss Jenny. "Jesus can use your gift to help people."

Jonathan was glad to put his coin in the offering plate.

c Play a Matching Game
Do this in the Discovery Center.

Gather two or three children. Show the children the picture of the star from the Christmas matching game (Activity Pak— pp. 9-10).

Ask: "Do you know what this is? That's right, it's a star. Can you find another star like this one on the big card? There it is! Let's put this star on the other star."

Repeat with each of the six pictures.

4 Celebrate
the Story

a Enjoy Music
Do this in the Storytelling Center.

Play Christmas music on the CD, inviting the children to dance with the scarfs or cloth strips.

Sing songs that the children have enjoyed over the past few weeks (Songbook, CD).

b Make Gifts
Do this in the Conversation Center.

Gather two or three children. Give each child a piece of white paper and invite him or her to make a picture that will be a gift for someone he or she knows.

When the children have finished their pictures, glue them onto the black construction paper to frame them. Ask each child who he or she drew a picture for.

Across the top of each picture, write "To: (*name the picture is for*)" and "From: (*name of child*)."

c Say Goodbye
Recall today's Bible story, encouraging children to say the Bible verse with you.

Say: "I am glad (*name one of the children*) came to church today." Repeat this for each child in the class.

Pray: "Thank you, God, for the gift of Jesus."

Be sure to have a teacher or helper at the door to ensure that anxious children do not leave until someone comes for them. Tell parents about today's Bible story and make sure that each child has today's Bible Story Picture Card.

Show the parents the "Nurturing Your Child's Faith" section of the card.

Be sure the children take home their stars and their picture gifts.

Tip
While making the star stencils, *do not* leave the knife where children can get to it.

Look Back
What feelings did the children express today?

Did the children feel the excitement of the wise men finding Jesus?

What is it you now know about the story and about the students that you did not know before this session?

What did you do that was good or that would work again?

What could you change about the lesson to make it better?

Look Ahead
Next week, we will learn about Jesus' family. Try to get family information on all of your children. Who lives in their house with them?

Pray for each child by name. Also pray for the child's family.

**Mark 6:3
and Luke 4:22**

Jesus lived in a
family, and we live
in families too.

Bible Verse:
Jesus grew both in
body and in
wisdom.
(Luke 2:52, *Good
News Bible*)

Resources:
Bible
CD
Activity Pak (Winter)
  pages 5, 17
  (figures 1, 3, 14)
  page 16 (patterns)
  page 21 ("Many Kinds
  of Families" picture)
  Songbook
Bible Story Picture Cards

Supplies:
dolls
doll care items
doll furniture
dress-up clothes.
picture books showing
  family activities
puzzles showing family
  members
colored construction
paper
white or manila paper
crayons or markers
glue
teacher scissors
CD player
wooden and plastic
  family figures or craft
  stick people figures
(optional: felt-tip marker,
  large cardboard box)

Jesus Lived in a Family...............

Enter the Bible Story

Read Mark 6:3 and Luke 4:22: The Scriptures record very little about Jesus' childhood or family life. The verses listed give us an indirect picture of Jesus' family. Today's story about Jesus speaking in the synagogue to the wonder of his hearers is found not only in today's Mark and Luke passages but also in Matthew 13:55 as well. Jesus' hearers were amazed by his knowledge and wisdom and cannot believe that the hometown boy whose family they knew could have this kind of power or speak these gracious words. "Isn't this the brother of James?" they ask. "Isn't this the carpenter Jesus?" It is interesting to note that Mark 6:3 is the only information we have about Jesus' occupation as a carpenter prior to his ministry.

Think About It: According to Mark, Jesus' family grew large after that first Christmas. Mark lists four brothers and an indeterminate number of sisters. Reflect on the following questions as you prepare to help children know that Jesus lived in a family that God planned for him: How do you think Jesus related to his younger siblings? We know today that the oldest children in families often become achievers and leaders and that they frequently take on the role of parent surrogate in the family. Do you think Jesus' birth position had any effect on the person that Jesus became? Think about your own family of origin. Did you have any siblings? What was your own birth position? Do you think that these things have affected you as an adult? In what ways? Think about the children you are teaching. What do you know about their family lives? How do you think their lives at home are affecting who they are?

Through the Week: The family and tribe were important in the history of the Hebrew people. They were a people of large and complex family connections. Give thanks to God for your own family connections, whether they are complex or relatively simple. Ask for God's help in juggling your own family responsibilities.

Pray: Thank you, God, for my family. I pray especially for (*name members with special needs at this time or family relationships that may need strengthening or healing*).

The Story and Young Children

Children can know that God plans for many kinds of families, including the family that cared for Jesus. They can explore ways that Jesus' family cared for him. The Bible passage from Mark for today refers to the brothers and sisters of Jesus and gives us an implied picture of Jesus' large family. As we help children in this session understand that Jesus had a loving family to care for him, it will be helpful to simplify the facts by referring only to Mary and Joseph and Jesus in the years before Jesus' siblings were born. As children think about the family that cared for Jesus, they will begin to explore their own families. It will be helpful to you to know all that you can about the background of the children you teach. In smaller churches you may already know a great deal about the children's families. Some churches or classes have parents of young children routinely fill out information sheets that are available to teachers. This is especially important as you move into the next session entitled "I Live in a Family."

Learning Centers

Work with two or three children at a time in each learning center.

Conversation Center

You will need: Activity Pak—p. 16 (family patterns), colored construction paper, white or manila paper, crayons or markers, glue, teacher scissors, CD, CD player, Activity Pak Songbook.

Get ready: Using the family patterns, cut from construction paper two adult figures and one child figure for each child in your class. Use a variety of colors.

• Make Jesus' Family Pictures, Activity 3a

Building Center

You will need: Activity Pak—pp. 5, 17 (figures 1, 3, 14) (optional: large cardboard box).

• Build Jesus' House, Activity 4b

Family Living Center

This would include a toy kitchen set and props appropriate to the lesson.

You will need: dolls, doll care items, doll furniture, dress-up clothes.

• Enjoy Family Play, Activity 1c

Discovery Center

You will need: Activity Pak—p. 21 ("Many Kinds of Families" picture), books and puzzles showing family activities (optional: wooden or plastic family figures or craft stick people figures, felt-tip marker).

• Enjoy Books and Puzzles, Activity 1b
• Look at a Poster, Activity 1d

Storytelling Center

You will need: Activity Pak—pp. 5, 17 (figures 1, 3, 14), Bible, CD, CD player, Activity Pak Songbook.

Get ready: Prepare storytelling figures (see Activity Pak—p. 2).

• Tell the Bible Story, Activity 2a
• Retell the Bible Story, Activity 2b
• Sing a Song, Activity 2c
• Tell Another Story, Activity 3b
• Use a Fingerplay, Activity 3c
• Enjoy Music, Activity 4a

Jesus and His Family

When Jesus was a little boy, Mary and Joseph took care of him in many ways. They gave him clothes to wear and food to eat. They gave him hugs.

"I love you," they told him.

When Jesus was a little boy, he helped his family in many ways.

"I'll help you carry the water," he said to Mary as they walked from the well.

"I'll sweep the wood scraps," he told Joseph as he worked with Joseph making things from wood.

Jesus was glad to have a loving family and to be able to help them.

Prepare

for the Story

a **Welcome Each Child**
Do this as each child enters the room.

Stoop to the children's eye level and welcome each child by name. **Say** to each child: "I am glad you are here, (*name of child*)." Be prepared to involve the children in an interesting or comforting activity.

b **Enjoy Books and Puzzles**
Do this in the Conversation Center.

Let the children enjoy looking at books or working puzzles about family activities. Help them tell about what they see pictured in the books and puzzles.

c **Enjoy Family Play**
Do this in the Family Living Center.

Help the children think about how everyone lives in a family as they enjoy family play, taking care of dolls or pretending to be parents and children themselves. Tell them that today they will hear a story about Jesus' family.

d **Look at a Poster**
Do this in the Discovery Center.

Gather two or three children. **Say** to children: "Here is a picture of many different families" (Activity Pak—p. 21).

Invite the children to look at the poster with you and talk about what they see. Help them pick out the mothers, fathers, children, and grandparents in the families. Tell the children that the families are different, but that all of them are families.

Point out Jesus' family on the poster. Tell the children that today they will hear a story about Jesus' family.

Option: Display the poster over a low table. Place wooden, plastic, or craft stick family figures on the table. Let older children pick out family figures to match the people in each family pictured on the poster.

Say: "This family has a mother and a little girl. Can you find a mother and a little girl on the table?" Simple craft stick figures may be made by drawing a "smiley" face on one end of a craft stick with a marker.

Use wide sticks (tongue depressor size) for adults and small sticks (popsicle size) for children. Or cut sticks in half and smooth edges with a file to make child-sized figures.

Tell

the Story

a **Tell the Bible Story**
Do this in the Storytelling Center.

Gather two or three children. **Say**: "I know a story about Jesus' family." Tell the Bible story, using the storytelling figures (figures 1, 3, 14) appropriately.

Open a Bible and **say**: "The Bible tells us about Jesus' family. Today's verse is, 'Jesus grew both in body and wisdom.' Families help us grow by taking care of us."

Pray: Thank you, God, for families."

b **Retell the Bible Story**
Do this in the Storytelling Center.

Retell the Bible story, acting out the things that young Jesus did to help. Add

activities such as rolling up his sleeping mat in the morning, helping Mary carry clothes to the roof to wash, stirring a pot of cooking beans for Mary, and collecting leftover wood scraps in a special basket so that Joseph could use them later.

Let the children act out all of these helping activities as you tell the story.

c **Sing a Song**
Do this in the Storytelling Center.

Sing "Jesus Had a Family" (Songbook, CD). Then sing the song using each of the children's names. For example, "Leticia has a family, family, family. Leticia has a family, they love her very much."

# Connect

with the Story

a **Make Jesus' Family Pictures**
Do this in the Conversation Center.

Gather two or three children. Give each child a sheet of white or manila paper and let the children decorate their papers with crayons or markers. Let each child choose a Mary, Joseph, and Jesus figure (Activity Pak—p. 16) to glue to the decorated paper with white glue.

Remember today's story about Jesus' family. Sing "Jesus Had a Family" (Songbook, CD) as the children work.

b **Tell Another Story**
Do this in the Storytelling Center.

Carlos lives with his sister, Maria, and his mother and father on a ranch, where they have many horses. Carlos and Maria like to ride the horses and help to feed them. Carlos and Maria and Mother and Father are a family.

Mommy works hard at the office all day while Jan plays with her friends at day care. In the evening they get to eat together and talk about what happened that day. After dinner Mommy tucks Jan into bed with a hug. Mommy and Jan are a family.

Robert lives above the city in a tall apartment house. Daddy works all day driving a bus, and Granny takes care of Robert. Robert helps Granny make bread for supper. After supper Daddy reads Robert a story. Robert and Daddy and Granny are a family too.

c **Use a Fingerplay**
Do this in the Storytelling Center.

Gather two or three children. Hold up a finger to represent each family member, starting with the "mother thumb." Cradle family member fingers in the other hand as you say the last line.

Here is the mother,
(*Hold up thumb.*)
Here is the father,
(*Add pointer finger.*)
Here is the brother tall.
(*Add middle finger.*)
Here is the sister,
(*Add ring finger.*)
Here is the baby,
(*Add pinkie.*)
Oh, how we love them all.
(*Cradle all in opposite hand.*)

Celebrate

the Story

a **Enjoy Music**
Do this in the Storytelling Center.

Sing "Jesus Had a Family" (Songbook, CD). Then listen to "Jesus Grew" (CD, Songbook).

Play the song again, this time singing along. Sing the song the third time, adding the motions from the Activity Pak Songbook.

b **Build Jesus' House**
Do this in the Building Center.

Invite the children to build houses where Jesus lived with his family.

Or make a simple Bible-times house out of a cardboard box, and have the children build walkways and fences about the house, moving the figures (Activity Pak—pp. 5-6, 17-18) to retell the story.

c **Say Goodbye**
Recall today's Bible story. Encourage the children to say the Bible verse with you.

Say: "Jesus had a family to care for him, and we all have families to care for us. I am glad (*name one of the children*) has a family." Repeat this for each child in the class.

Pray: "Thank you, God, for our families. We are happy that you plan for families."

Have a teacher or helper at the door to ensure that anxious children do not leave until someone comes for them. Tell parents about today's Bible story. Make sure that each child has today's Bible Story Picture Card. Show parents the "Nurturing Your Child's Faith" section of the card. Be sure the children take home their Jesus' Family pictures.

Tip
Make the stories more personal. Substitute your name and that of the children in the contemporary stories.

Look Back
Did each child have a chance to hear today's Bible story?

Are there any children who regularly do not hear the story? Is there an alternative way to involve these children in the story?

What do you know now about the story and the students that you did not know before this session?

Look Ahead
The next session is really the second part of today's session. It is entitled "I Live in a Family" and carries over ideas about Jesus' family more directly into the children's own experiences.

An optional activity for the next session involves the children bringing pictures of their own families to class. You will need to inform families before the next session if you wish to do this.

Mark 6:3
and Luke 4:22

Jesus lived in a
family, and I live in
a family too.

Bible Verse:
Jesus grew both in
body and in
wisdom.
(Luke 2:52, *Good
News Bible*)

Resources:
Bibles
CD
Activity Pak (Winter)
    pages 5, 17
    (figures 1, 3, 14)
    page 21 ("Many Kinds
    of Families" picture)
    Songbook
Bible Story Picture Cards

Supplies:
dolls, doll care items
posterboard or bulletin
    board
books showing family
    activities
puzzles showing family
    members
Bible-times dress-up
    clothes
cardboard or posterboard
white or manila paper
masking tape
tempera paint
sponge
shallow container
small paintbrush
fine-tip permanent marker
coverups
CD player
blocks
plastic, wooden, or craft
    stick family figures
doll furniture
doll house
toy cars, trucks, boats
family photos the children
    brought from home

I Live in a Family....

Enter the Bible Story

Read Mark 6:3 and Luke 4:22: The Scriptures record very little about Jesus' childhood or family life. The verses listed above give us an indirect picture of Jesus' family.

Think About It: Review "Enter the Bible Story" in the previous session. In preparation for that session, you thought about your own family of origin and how you were affected by your position in the birth order. If you have children, grandchildren, nieces, or nephews, think about how their relationships with other family members affect their lives. What do we expect from the oldest children in a family? Do we expect something different from the youngest child? What about a middle child or children? What happens to them, and what feelings about themselves do they acquire because of their place in the birth order? Where do the children you teach fit into their families? Who are only children? youngest children? oldest children? What results of these relationships do you see as you work with the children?

Through the Week: Review ideas and activities from the previous session. Think about favorite activities from the last session that the children may wish to repeat.

Pray: Thank you, God, for families who care for us. Help me to know the best ways to relate to the families of the children I teach. Give me wisdom to work together with them to nurture their children in the Christian faith and to help the children come to know you.

The Story and Young Children

Children can know that God plans for families, including the family that cared for Jesus. They can become aware that they live in a family who cares for them, just as Jesus did.

Because children in this age group are generally lacking in verbal skills, it will be helpful to acquire information about their families from an information sheet or from talking to parents, as was suggested in the last session. (It is often difficult to know if "Mac" is a brother, an uncle, or the dog!) If children bring family photos for a project today, ask parents as they arrive about the people pictured.

Learning Centers

Work with two or three children at a time in each learning center.

Conversation Center

You will need: books showing family activities, white or manila paper, posterboard or cardboard, masking tape, tempera paint, sponge, shallow container, small paintbrush, fine-tip permanent marker, coverups.

Get ready: Pour paint into a shallow container.

- Make Fingerprint Families, Activity 3a

Discovery Center

You will need: Activity Pak—p. 21 ("Many Kinds of Families" picture) or family pictures from home; puzzles showing family members.

- Learn About Different Families, Activity 1b
- Enjoy Books and Puzzles, Activity 1c

Family Living Center

You will need: dolls, doll care items, doll furniture, dress-up clothes.

- Enjoy Family Play, Activity 1d

Building Center

You will need: blocks; plastic, wooden, or craft stick family figures from previous sessions; doll furniture, doll house; toy cars, trucks, boats.

- Build a Family House, Activity 4b

Storytelling Center

You will need: Activity Pak—pp. 5, 17 (figures 1, 3, 14); CD, CD player, Activity Pak Songbook; Bible.

Get ready: Prepare storytelling figures (see Activity Pak—p. 2).

- Tell the Bible Story, Activity 2a
- Retell the Bible Story, Activity 2b
- Tell Another Story, Activity 3b
- Sing a Song, Activity 3c
- Enjoy Music, Activity 4a

Jesus' Family Shows Care

"Oww! Oww!" called Jesus as he came running home. He had skinned his knee playing with his friends.

"Come here," said his mother, Mary. "I'll make your knee feel better." Mary bathed Jesus' knee with cool water.

"It's time for supper," said Mary. She placed meat and beans in a big bowl. She broke off pieces of freshly baked bread.

Jesus and Mary and Joseph sat around the fire and ate supper. Joseph told stories after supper. Soon the sun went down. Mary and Joseph and Jesus hugged each other and watched the twinkling stars.

Jesus' knee felt much better now. He was glad he had a family to care for him.

 Prepare

for the Story

a **Welcome Each Child**
Do this as each child enters the room.

Stoop to the children's eye level and welcome each child by name.

Say to each child: "Here is (*name of child*). I'm happy to see you today." If the children brought family snapshots, let them help you tape the photos to a posterboard or bulletin board.

Be prepared to involve children in an interesting or comforting activity.

b **Learn About Different Families**
Do this in the Discovery Center.

Gather two or three children. Encourage the children to talk about their own families and the families of classroom friends as they add to and look at the family photos they have brought.

If no one brought photos, have the "Many Kinds of Families" picture (Activity Pak—p. 21) in the center for the children to look at.

c **Enjoy Books and Puzzles**
Do this in the Discovery Center.

Let the children enjoy looking at books or working puzzles about family activities.

Help the children tell about what they see pictured in the books and puzzles.

d **Enjoy Family Play**
Do this in the Family Living Center.

As the children enjoy family play, taking care of dolls or pretending to be parents and children themselves, help them think about how everyone lives in a family.

Tell the children that today they will hear another story about Jesus' family.

Tell

the Story

a **Tell the Bible Story**
Do this in the Storytelling Center.
Gather two or three children.

Say: "Last week we heard a story about Jesus' family. Today I know another story about Jesus' family."

Tell the Bible story, using the storytelling figures (figures 1, 3, 14) appropriately.

Open a Bible and **say:** "Do you remember the Bible verse we heard last time? Help me say it again: 'Jesus grew both in body and in wisdom.' Families help us grow by taking care of us."

Pray: "Thank you, God, for families."

b **Retell the Bible Story**
Do this in the Storytelling Center.

Retell the story, this time letting the children act out the story as you tell it.

With this age group, acting out a story does not involve assigning roles for them to play. Instead, involve all of the children in the same action at the same time.

For example, everyone says "Oww!" and has a skinned knee; everyone acts out bathing a knee; everyone puts meat and beans into a bowl; and so forth. Do the action first yourself, and have the children follow your lead.

 Connect
with the Story

a Make Fingerprint Families
Do this in the Conversation Center.

Gather two or three children. Protect their clothing with coverups.

Using the small paintbrush, paint each child's thumb. Let the child press the thumb onto the paper the correct number of times for the adults in her or his family.

Repeat the process using an index finger for each child in the family.

Write "(*name of child*)'s Family" across the top of the paper. If known, write the name of each family member underneath each print.

Add a smiley face and stick arms and legs to each one with a marker, if you wish.

Then give each child a piece of cardboard or posterboard. Let the child press all fingers to the paint-soaked sponge in the container.

The children may decorate their cardboard or posterboard by "bouncing" their painted fingers on it. When the prints have dried, use masking tape to mount the fingerprint family picture on the decorated cardboard.

If you do not have information about all the members of a child's family, and the child cannot tell you, just include what you do know. Does the child's mother bring the child to class? You can at least make a picture of the mother and child and caption it "James and his Mother."

b Tell Another Story
Do this in the Storytelling Center.

Jump! Jump! Jump! Claria was jumping up and down on the sidewalk.

"Oh! Oh! Oh!" Claria fell down and scraped her elbow.

"I'll make your elbow feel better," said Mother. She cleaned it and put a bandage on it. "It's time for dinner," said Mother.

Claria helped Mother put chicken and fruit salad on the table.

After dinner, Father read to Claria from her favorite books. Then Mother and Father and Claria went to the porch to look at the moon and the stars.

Claria's elbow felt much better now. She was glad she had a family to take care of her.

c Sing a Song
Do this in the Storytelling Center

Gather two or three children. Sing "It's So Nice to Have a Mommy" (Songbook, CD). Change or omit words or verses depending on the family situations of the children.

4 Celebrate
the Story

a Enjoy Music
Do this in the Storytelling Center.

Sing "Jesus Had a Family" and "Jesus Grew" (Songbook, CD). Repeat the fingerplay from Session 21 (page 91).

Sing "It's So Nice to Have a Mommy" (Songbook, CD).

b Build a Family House
Do this in the Building Center.

Gather two or three children. Let the children use blocks to build a house and furniture.

Let the children use the toys to play "family."

c Say Goodbye
Recall today's Bible story. Have the children say the Bible verse with you. **Say:** "I am glad (*name a child*) came to church today." Repeat for each child in the class.

Pray: "Thank you, God, for (*name of child*)'s family." Repeat for each member of the class.

Have a teacher or helper at the door to ensure that anxious children do not leave until someone comes for them. Tell parents about today's Bible story. Make sure that each child has today's Bible Story Picture Card.

Show the parents the "Nurturing Your Child's Faith" section of the card. Be sure the children take home their Fingerprint Families.

Tip
If you do not have handwashing facilities readily available, place a dishpan partially filled with warm, soapy water in the Conversation Center and provide a big towel for drying wet hands.

Look Back
As you have helped children know about Jesus' family and explore their own families, what have you learned about the children and the families from which they come?

Look Ahead
Today's session grew directly out of the previous session. The next four sessions will follow the same pattern.

Session 23 examines the fact that Jesus was a baby, and Session 24 will help the children understand that they were once babies as well. Session 25 will explore the fact that Jesus grew, and Session 26 will help the children see that they grow too.

As you look ahead toward the coming sessions, remember that families, babyhood, and growth are all part of God's plan and that Jesus experienced these things just as we do.

Jesus was once a tiny, helpless baby.

Bible Verse:
Jesus grew both in body and in wisdom.
(Luke 2:52, *Good News Bible*)

Resources:
Bible
CD
Activity Pak (Winter)
    pages 5-8
    (figures 4 and 8)
    pages 19 and 20 (baby things game)
    Songbook
Bible Story Picture Cards

Supplies:
play dough
play dough toys
baby dolls
baby items
small dishpan
liquid soap
water
washcloths
towels
· baby blanket
cloth strips (such as gauze strips)
manger (see Session 17) or baby bed
CD player
tempera paint (one or two colors)
fat paintbrushes
newspaper
baby powder
books and puzzles about babies
blocks
coverups
masking tape

Jesus Is a Baby........

Enter the Bible Story

Read Luke 2:7, 12: Although at first glance it may seem like we are revisiting the Christmas story, this Scripture is really setting us up for the next three sessions on growing from a baby to a child. The action of "swaddling" a newborn (see Session 18) makes an infant even more dependent than newborns are today. Today we encourage infants to begin to hold up their head, roll over, and sit up. But not when Jesus was a baby. Mary would have rubbed the newborn Jesus with salt and then placed him in the middle of a square of soft cloth. Then she would have carefully folded the cloth around him and wrapped bands (often decorated with embroidery) around him, making his arms and legs perfectly straight. She would loosen the bands several times a day and rub Jesus' skin with olive oil and dust him with powdered myrtle.

Think About It: What is more touching than a baby? Most of us melt at the sight of a tiny baby and wonder how something as small as a newborn could ever be quite so perfect, complete with tiny fingers and toes and ears and nose. New parents are often aware of the utter helplessness of their child. Newborns literally need to be brought to the breast or bottle for sustenance—they cannot get there on their own. Without adult help, babies would quickly die. Reflect on the following questions as you prepare to tell the Bible story this week: Why is it important to spend time reflecting on the Son of God as a helpless infant? When have you felt helpless and dependent? On whom can you depend when you need help?

Through the Week: Read Job 38 and 39. Marvel again at the great power of God and the love that God feels for us.

Pray: Dear God, when I feel helpless and needy, remind me that you are there and will take care of the universe.

The Story and Young Children

Young children love babies. Bring a baby into a room full of young children, and the children flock around, wanting to touch and see. They are fascinated by the fact that babies cannot walk, talk, eat by themselves, and are utterly helpless. Toddlers and two-year-olds, on the other hand, feel in charge of the world, being proud of each accomplishment. Indeed, it is hard for young children to admit that they are dependent on anyone. "Let me do it!" is their battle cry.

Room Setup: Cover the Conversation Center table with several layers of newspaper, taping down each sheet. Put a baby doll in the Storytelling Center.

Learning Centers

Work with two or three children at a time in each learning center.

Conversation Center

This should be a table around which you may gather the children. Sit down with the children and engage them in conversation.

You will need: play dough, play dough toys, coverups, masking tape, tempera paint (one or two colors), fat paintbrushes, newspaper, baby powder.

Get ready: Make play dough (see p. 232). For the painting activity, cover the table with several layers of newspaper. Mix a handful of baby powder into the tempera paint to give it a nice smell and an interesting texture.

- Play With Play Dough, Activity 1b
- Paint With Baby Powder Paint, Activity 3a

Building Center

You will need: blocks.

- Play With Blocks, Activity 3c

Discovery Center

You will need: Activity Pak—pp. 19-20 (baby things game); books and puzzles about babies.

- Play a Game, Activity 1d
- Enjoy Books and Puzzles, Activity 4b

Family Living Center

This would include a toy kitchen set and props appropriate to the lesson.

You will need: baby dolls, baby items, small dishpan partially filled with warm soapy water, washcloths, and towels.

- Take Care of Baby Dolls, Activity 1c

Storytelling Center

This should be an open area where you may gather children for storytelling, or to listen and respond to music. It would be helpful to have this center on a carpeted area.

You will need: Activity Pak—pp. 5–8 (figures 4 and 8), baby doll, baby blanket, cloth strips (such as gauze strips), manger the children made in Session 17 or baby bed, CD, CD player, Activity Pak Songbook, Bible.

Get ready: Prepare storytelling figures (see Activity Pak—p. 2).

- Tell the Bible Story, Activity 2a
- Retell the Bible Story, Activity 2b
- Rock the Baby, Activity 2c
- Tell Another Story, Activity 3b
- Enjoy Music, Activity 4a

Jesus Was a Baby

Mary hummed softly as she took care of her baby, Jesus. She fed him and burped him. She loosened the cloth around him and cleaned him. She rubbed oil on his skin. Then she wrapped him back up and rocked him back and forth until he went to sleep.

Mary was so happy to have a baby. She thanked God for baby Jesus.

1 Prepare

for the Story

a Welcome Each Child

Do this as each child enters the room.

Stoop to the child's eye level and welcome each child by name.

Say to each child: "(*Name of child*), I am so happy you have come to church today."

Be prepared to involve children in an interesting or comforting activity.

b Play With Play Dough

Do this in the Conversation Center.

Gather two or three children. Sit with the children at a low table as they enjoy manipulating the play dough.

You can provide round blocks or toy rolling pins for smoothing dough or items with which children may make interesting prints in the dough.

As you and the children work with the dough, **say:** "I am glad we can play with play dough. Babies can't play with play dough, can they?"

c Take Care of Baby Dolls

Do this in the Family Living Center.

Let the children play with dolls in the Family Living Center. Talk with the children as they play. Allow the children one at a time to bathe the babies in the soapy water.

You may wish to put an apron on the children to minimize the amount of water that gets on their clothes.

d Play a Game

Do this in the Discovery Center.

Gather two or three children. Show them the pictures from the baby things game (Activity Pak—pp. 19 and 20).

Say: "Here's a bottle. Do babies use the bottle, or do big boys and girls?" Repeat with each card, sorting the cards into two piles.

Be aware that if you have young two-year-olds, some of them may still be using a pacifier, bottle, or diapers, so remember that there are no right or wrong answers in this game.

2 Tell

the Story

a Tell the Bible Story

Do this in the Storytelling Center.

Gather two or three children. Tell the Bible story, using the storytelling figures (figures 4, 8) as appropriate.

Open a Bible and **say:** "Jesus was a baby. But the Bible tells us he grew up. Do you remember the Bible verse from last week? 'Jesus grew both in body and in wisdom.'" Encourage the children to say the verse with you.

Pray: "Dear God, we are glad that you planned for babies and for people to take care of them."

b Retell the Bible Story

Do this in the Storytelling Center.

Retell the Bible story, this time acting out the actions of Mary with the baby doll. (Even though it is not biblically correct to feed the baby with a bottle, for modesty's sake you may wish to do so.)

Repeat the story, letting each of the children act out the story.

c Rock the Baby

Do this in the Storytelling Center.

Gather two or three children. Pretend to rock the baby while listening to "Sleep, Baby Jesus" (Songbook, CD).

When the baby is asleep, lay the baby in the manger or bed. Then **say:** "Oh no, the baby is awake!" Let one of the children rock the baby and listen to the song again.

Repeat as long as the children are interested.

3 Connect
with the Story

a Paint With Baby Powder Paint
Do this in the Conversation Center.

Gather one or two children. Put coverups on them to protect their clothing. Let the children paint with the paint and baby powder mixture directly on the newspaper—they don't mind the printing.

When all of the children have had a turn, pick up the newspaper piece by piece and hang it to dry. If you have a large group, you may want to take off one layer of newspaper after several children have painted, to reveal a fresh supply of paper.

Remember, the value of art at this age is the creating and not the finished product. Let the children paint, and don't worry too much about whether they stay on one piece of paper or not. Just keep the paint on the table.

When done, be sure to have enough pieces for every child to take one home. If necessary, cut larger pieces of paper in two.

b Tell Another Story
Do this in the Storytelling Center.

Baby Carlos woke up and began to cry. Papa picked him up and soothed him. He changed the baby's diaper and put sweet-smelling powder all over his body.

Then Papa gave baby Carlos a bottle and rocked him in the big rocking chair until he fell asleep. Papa thanked God for baby Carlos.

c Play With Blocks
Do this in the Building Center.

Gather two or three children. Help them to stack one block on top of another to make a tower. **Say:** "Babies can't build with blocks. But we can build a tall tower." Count the blocks as you stack them and then knock them down.

Be sure to monitor so that the children do not knock down one another's towers.

4 Celebrate
the Story

a Enjoy Music
Do this in the Storytelling Center.

Sing "Jesus had a Family" and "Jesus Grew" (Songbook, CD), using the motions in the Songbook.

Sing other favorite songs that the children love. Remember that young children have little sense of seasons and like to sing songs such as "Jingle Bells" all year round.

b Enjoy Books and Puzzles
Do this in the Discovery Center.

Encourage the children to play with simple puzzles about babies and to look at books about baby life.

c Say Goodbye

Recall today's Bible story, encouraging children to say the Bible verse with you.

Say: "I am glad (*name one of the children*) that you are not a baby, because then you couldn't be in my class." Repeat this for each child in the class.

Pray: "Thank you, God, for babies. Help us to know how to take care of them."

Be sure to have a teacher or helper at the door to ensure that anxious children do not leave until someone comes for them. Tell parents about today's Bible story and make sure that each child has today's Bible Story Picture Card.

Show the parents the "Nurturing Your Child's Faith" section of the card.

Let the children take their paintings home if they are dry enough.

Tip
Make the stories more personal. Substitute your name and that of the children in the contemporary stories.

Look Back
What feelings did the children express today? Do they remember the stories of Jesus as a baby that you have told over the past month, or did you find yourself repeating them?

Were the children proud of their own accomplishments as bigger boys and girls, without being scornful of babies?

What did you do that you would like to repeat next week?

What would you do differently?

Look Ahead
Next week you will be repeating many of the activities from this week as you explore what it means to be a baby.

Children at this age thrive on repetition, so don't be afraid to repeat a favorite activity. Also remember that you have fourteen lessons in this quarter, and probably only thirteen weeks in which to do them. Plan to combine a couple of lessons.

Luke 2:7, 12

Once we were all babies, but we grew.

Bible Verse:
Jesus grew both in body and in wisdom.
(Luke 2:52, *Good News Bible*)

Resources:
Bible
CD
Activity Pak (Winter)
    pages 5–8
    (figures 4 and 8)
    pages 19 and 20
    (baby things game)
    Songbook
Bible Story Picture Cards

Supplies:
play dough
play dough toys
baby dolls
baby items
small dishpan
mild soap
water
washcloths
towels
baby blanket
cloth strips (such as
    gauze strips)
CD player
food coloring
heavy white paper towels
eye droppers or cotton
    swabs
newspaper
muffin tin or plastic ice
    cube tray
books and puzzles about
    babies
blocks

I Was a Baby............

Enter the Bible Story

Read Luke 2:7, 12: The Scripture reminds us that Jesus became just as human as we are. He was a baby, and we were once babies too. Many of us have an idealized view of Jesus as a baby. We cannot imagine that Jesus ever cried or was demanding in any way. And yet, how could Jesus understand us completely if he had not gone through life as a full human being? When Jesus was hungry, or tired, or soiled, as all babies are, he must have used the only means of communication that he had—crying.

Think About It: Babies are sweet, but they can be downright annoying at times. Their helplessness, which is so touching, is also draining on those of us who care for them. It is no coincidence that among childcare professionals, those who care for infants and young toddlers burn out at a faster pace than those who care for older preschoolers. Reflect on the following questions as you prepare to retell this week's Bible story: When have you been annoyed at a child because he or she is so demanding of your time and energy? When have you been tempted to tell him or her to just go away and watch a video or something? Think of your own prayer life. When have you behaved as an annoying infant, demanding that God recognize that you are the center of the universe?

Through the Week: As you encounter demanding people this week—both children and adults—try to put yourself in their shoes. When have you behaved in the same manner?

Pray: Dear God, help me to recognize the immaturity in myself when I demand to be the center of your attention. Give me the patience to work with those who demand so much of me. Amen.

The Story and Young Children

Toddlers and two-year-olds love little babies—at least until they start drawing attention away from them. If your children welcome a new baby into their family, be prepared for some regression of toilet training, thumb sucking, whining, and general immaturity. This is perfectly normal. Children still need to know that they are very important in the lives of those who love them. They do not always understand that parents have enough love for more than one child at a time.

Room Setup: Cover the Conversation Center table with newspaper. Place the baby things game (Activity Pak—p. 19 and 20) in the Discovery Center and a baby doll in the Storytelling Center.

Learning Centers

Conversation Center

You will need: play dough, play dough toys, heavy white paper towels, eye droppers or cotton swabs, food coloring, muffin tin or ice tray.

Get ready: Prepare play dough (see page 232). For the painting activity, cover the work space with newspaper. Put food coloring in several sections of the muffin tin or ice tray.

- Play With Play Dough, Activity 1b
- Make a Baby Blanket, Activity 3a

Discovery Center

You will need: Activity Pak—pp. 19 and 20 (baby things game), books and puzzles about babies.

- Play a Game, Activity 1d
- Enjoy Books and Puzzles, Activity 4b

Building Center

Provide enough blocks for toddlers to share.

- Play With Blocks, Activity 3c

Family Living Center

This would include a toy kitchen set and props appropriate to the lesson.

You will need: baby dolls, baby items, small dishpan, mild soap, water, washcloths, towels.

- Take Care of Baby Dolls, Activity 1c

Storytelling Center

You will need: Activity Pak—pp. 5–8 (figures 4, 8), baby doll, baby blanket, cloth strips (such as gauze strips), CD, CD player, Activity Pak Songbook, Bible.

Get ready: Prepare storytelling figures (see Activity Pak—p. 2).

- Tell the Bible Story, Activity 2a
- Retell the Bible Story, Activity 2b
- Sing a Song, Activity 2c
- Tell Another Story, Activity 3b
- Enjoy Music, Activity 4a

Jesus Cried

"Waah! Waah!" Jesus cried. Mary came running to pick up baby Jesus.

"Oh, no," she said. "I think the baby is hungry." So she sat and fed baby Jesus.

"Waah! Waah!" Jesus cried. Mary held baby Jesus close.

"Oh, no," she said. "I think the baby is dirty." So she unwrapped Jesus and washed and powdered him.

"Waah! Waah!" Jesus cried. Mary picked Jesus up again.

"Oh, no," she said. "I think it is time for a nap." So she rocked and held baby Jesus until he fell asleep.

1 Prepare

for the Story

a Welcome Each Child

Do this as each child enters the room.

Stoop to the child's eye level and welcome each child by name. **Say** to each child: "I am so happy you have come to church today."

Be prepared to involve children in an interesting or comforting activity.

b Play With Play Dough

Do this in the Conversation Center.

Gather two or three children. Sit with the children at a low table as they enjoy manipulating the play dough.

Provide round blocks or toy rolling pins for smoothing dough or items with which the children can make interesting prints in the dough.

As you work with the dough, **say:** "I am glad we can play with play dough. Babies can't play with play dough, can they?"

c Take Care of Baby Dolls

Do this in the Family Living Center.

Allow the children to play with dolls. Engage the children in conversation.

Allow the children one at a time to bathe the babies in the soapy water. Let the older children wash the baby clothes in the water and hang them up to dry on a clothesline.

You may wish to put an apron on each child to minimize the amount of water that gets on his or her clothes.

d Play a Game

Do this in the Discovery Center.

Gather two or three children. By now they should be able to remember the baby things game (Activity Pak—pp. 19 and 20) and how to play it.

See if the children remember the game without instruction from you. (Identify each card and let the children determine if the item is used by babies or big girls and boys.)

2 Tell

the Story

a Tell the Bible Story

Do this in the Storytelling Center.

Gather two or three children. Tell the Bible story, using the storytelling figures (figures 4, 8) as appropriate.

Open a Bible and **say:** "Jesus was a baby, just like you were a baby. But Jesus grew up, just like you are growing up. Do you remember our Bible verse? 'Jesus grew in both body and wisdom.'" Encourage the children to say the verse with you.

Pray: "Dear God, we are glad that we can help to take care of babies."

b Retell the Bible Story

Do this in the Storytelling Center.

Retell the Bible story, this time acting out the actions of Mary with the baby doll. (Even though it is not Biblically correct to feed the baby with a bottle, for modesty's sake you may wish to do so.)

Repeat the story, letting each of the children act out the story.

c Sing a Song

Do this in the Storytelling Center.

Gather two or three children. Sing "It's So Nice to Have a Mommy" (Songbook, CD) to the tune of "Did You Ever See a Lassie?"

You may change or omit words or verses, depending on the family situations of the children.

3 Connect
with the Story

a Make a Baby Blanket
Do this in the Conversation Center.

Gather two or three children. Show them how to draw up some food coloring into an eye dropper and drip it onto a paper towel. Watch as the colors spread and intermingle.

When there are several colors on the towel, hang it up to dry.

Option: With younger children, you may wish to use cotton swabs for transferring the food coloring to the towel. This activity also works by folding the paper towel and dipping it into the color, although it is not as dramatic as watching the colors spread.

b Tell Another Story
Do this in the Storytelling Center.

"Waah!" "Waah!" cried baby Justin. Grammy came running to see what was the matter.

"Are you hungry?" asked Grammy, holding a bottle to his lips.

"Waah! Waah!" cried baby Justin.

"No, you're not hungry. Do you need your diaper changed?" asked Grammy, checking under his nightgown.

"Waah! Waah!" cried baby Justin.

"No, your diaper is dry," Grammy said. "Whatever could be the matter?"

"Waah! Waah!" cried baby Justin.

Grammy had an idea. She picked Justin up and held him close.

"Coo! Coo!" gurgled baby Justin.

"Now I know what you want. You want to be held!" said Grammy.

c Play With Blocks
Do this in the Building Center.

Gather two or three children. Help them stack one block on top of another to make a tower.

Say: "Babies can't build with blocks. But we can build a tall tower." Count the blocks as you stack them and then knock them down.

Be sure to monitor so that children do not knock down one another's towers.

4 Celebrate
the Story

a Enjoy Music
Do this in the Storytelling Center.

Sing "Jesus Had a Family" and "Jesus Grew" (Songbook, CD), using the motions in the Songbook. Sing other favorite songs that the children love.

b Enjoy Books and Puzzles
Do this in the Discovery Center.

Encourage the children to play with simple puzzles about babies and to look at books about baby life.

c Say Goodbye

Recall today's Bible story, encouraging the children to say the Bible verse with you. Especially note children who have a baby in their home.

Say: "I am glad (*name one of the children*) came to church today." Repeat this for each child in the class.

Pray: "Thank you, God, for babies. Help us to take care of them."

Be sure to have a teacher or helper at the door to match children with their caregivers.

Tell parents about today's Bible story and make sure that each child has today's Bible Story Picture Card.

Show the parents the "Nurturing Your Child's Faith" section of the card. Be sure the children take home their baby blankets.

Tip
Make the stories more personal. Substitute your name and that of the children in the contemporary stories.

Look Back
We have done a lot of talking about babies for the past two weeks. What emotions did the children experience as they talked about their experiences with babies?

What have you learned about the children during this lesson?

Look Ahead
The next two sessions focus on Jesus growing. Because children of this age thrive on repetition of favorite activities, read both sessions and pick the better activities for your class.

Plan on doing the same activity over several weeks until the children lose interest.

Once the children stop wanting to do a particular activity, eliminate it for a few weeks. When you re-introduce it after a hiatus, it will almost be like a brand new activity for them.

Jesus grew and changed as he became older.

Bible Verse:
Jesus grew both in body and in wisdom.
(Luke 2:52, *Good News Bible*)

Resources:
Bible
CD
Activity Pak (Winter)
 page 19 (baby things game)
 page 23 ("Jesus Growing' book")
 Songbook
Bible Story Picture Cards

Supplies:
baby clothes and shoes
baby dolls
baby care items
toddler dolls
masking tape
magazine pictures of babies and young children
clear self-adhesive paper
books and puzzles about babies and young children growing
blocks
CD player
teacher scissors
(optional: wax paper)

Look! Jesus Is Growing...............

Enter the Bible Story

Read Luke 2:40, 52: These verses, which state simply that Jesus grew, along with the story of Jesus staying behind in the Temple at the age of twelve, are all that we know about the childhood of Jesus. This session and the one following are based on the verses about Jesus' growth.

Think About It: These passages from the Bible describe the whole range of Jesus' growth and development. Consider the following: We are told that Jesus grew in wisdom, that he grew intellectually. How do we stimulate the children we teach to ask questions and to learn? We are told that Jesus grew in years; he grew physically. Is it apparent that the physical needs of the children we teach, the needs for good food, sleep, and exercise, are being met? We are told that Jesus grew "in human favor." He grew appropriately emotionally and socially. He related well to others. Are the children we teach learning to relate to their friends in our class? In what ways can we help them learn social skills? We are also told that Jesus grew in divine favor. He grew spiritually in his relationship with God. How are we helping the children in our class grow in faith? Are we living our own faith with them so that they can experience God's love from us?

Through the Week: Toddlers and two-year-olds have had only a brief amount of time in which to experience growing. Think of all the things that they can do now that they were not able to do when they were babies. How can you share these accomplishments with them in class?

Pray: Thank you, God, for your plan for growing. Help us to know the best ways to be part of your plan for the growth of the children we teach. Help us to be aware that we continue to grow too, and that the children teach us as well.

The Story and Young Children

Children can hear that Jesus grew, just as God planned. They can explore the ways in which God plans for everyone, including Jesus, to grow. Observe the physical development of the children in your class. Who is not able to run or climb or use large muscles well? Whose fine motor skills for holding a marker or paintbrush are developing? Observe the intellectual development of the children. We need to let children learn at their own pace, providing an accepting climate in which they feel free to try. Observe the social and emotional development of the children. Are they beginning to help each other? To wait for a turn? Observe the faith development of the children. Are they learning trust as you meet their needs? The trust that they learn now lays the foundation for later trust in God.

Room Setup: Set aside an area of your room for active play today. Provide rocking, climbing, or riding equipment that encourages children to use their large muscles.

Learning Centers

Conversation Center

You will need: clear self-adhesive paper, masking tape, pictures cut from magazines of babies and young children, teacher scissors (optional: wax paper).

Get ready: Tape a large piece of self-adhesive paper (sticky side up) to the table or wall. (To keep the paper smooth as you remove the backing, first fold down the backing on the top two corners of the paper. Tape those securely. Then remove the backing and tape the bottom corners.) Cut pictures of babies and children from magazines.

• Make a Baby and Child Collage, Activity 3a

Storytelling Center

This should be an open area where you may gather children for storytelling, or to listen and respond to music. It would be helpful to have this center on a carpeted area.

You will need: Activity Pak—p. 23 ("Jesus Growing" book), CD, CD player, Activity Pak Songbook, Bible.

Get ready: Prepare storytelling figures (see Activity Pak—p. 2).

• Tell the Bible Story, Activity 2a
• Retell the Bible Story, Activity 2b

• Say an Action Verse, Activity 2c
• Tell Another Story, Activity 3c
• Say an Action Verse, Activity 3d
• Enjoy Music, Activity 4a

Discovery Center

You will need: Activity Pak—p. 19 (baby things game), baby clothes and shoes, books and puzzles about babies and about young children growing.

• Examine Baby Clothes, Activity 1b
• Play a Game, Activity 1c
• Enjoy Books and Puzzles, Activity 4b

Building Center

You will need: blocks.

• Play With Blocks, Activity 3b

Family Living Center

You will need: baby dolls, baby care items, toddler dolls (if possible).

• Play With Dolls, Activity 1d

Jesus Is Growing

"Waah, waah," cried baby Jesus. Mary rocked him quietly back to sleep.

"I like the stars," said the little boy Jesus to his father, Joseph.

"I can help sweep for you," said the big boy Jesus in his father's carpenter shop.

"Love one another," said the grownup Jesus to his friends.

1 Prepare

for the Story

a Welcome Each Child

Do this as the child enters the room.

Stoop to the children's eye level and welcome each child by name. As each child enters, notice one way that she or he is growing.

b Examine Baby Clothes

Do this in the Discovery Center.

Display baby clothes and shoes on a low table.

Encourage the children to examine and talk about the clothes: "Who wears these clothes? Did you wear clothes like this when you were a baby? Do they fit you now? (*Let them try.*) Why don't they fit you? How have you changed?"

Talk with the children about how they have changed and grown.

c Play a Game

Do this in the Discovery Center.

Gather two or three children. Show them the pictures from the baby things game (Activity Pak—p. 19).

Say: "Here's a bottle. Do babies use the bottle, or do big boys and girls?" Repeat with each card, sorting the cards into two piles.

Be aware that if you have young two-year-olds, some of them will still be using a pacifier, bottle, or diapers, so remember that there are no right or wrong answers in this game.

d Play With Dolls

Do this in the Family Living Center.

Encourage the children to play with the dolls. Talk about the differences in the baby doll and the toddler doll, if you have access to a toddler doll. (*The toddler doll wears shoes as if for walking*). What can the toddler do that the baby cannot?

2 Tell

the Story

a Tell the Bible Story

Do this in the Storytelling Center.

Gather two or three children. Show them the "Jesus Growing" book (Activity Pak—p. 23).

Read the captions to the children and talk about what they see in each picture. How does Jesus change? Remember, young children may not be able to discern that the baby, the little boy, the big boy, and the adult are all the same individual.) Talk about what the individuals in each picture do that is different from the picture before.

Open a Bible and **say**: "The Bible says, 'Jesus grew.'" Invite the children to repeat the verse with you.

Pray: "We are glad, God, that Jesus grew and that we are growing too."

b Retell the Bible Story

Do this in the Storytelling Center.

Encourage the children to act out the story after you finish telling it. As you read the first page, let the children pretend to cry. As you read the second page, have them point up in the air at the stars. As you read the third page, imitate sweeping the floor. As you read the fourth page, ask the children to give each other hugs.

c Say an Action Verse

Do this in the Storytelling Center.

Gather two or three children. Help them do the motions to the following action verse:

Little Jesus, sleep in your bed,
Sleep in your bed all day.
(*Lie down on the floor.*)
Soon you will learn to sit up straight,
(*Sit up.*)
Then learn to crawl away.
(*Crawl around.*)
Next you will learn to stand up tall,
(*Stand up.*)
Then take steps, one and two.
(*Take two steps.*)
Soon you'll be walking everywhere,
Just as grownups do.
(*March in place.*)

3 Connect

with the Story

a Make a Baby and Child Collage

Do this in the Conversation Center.

Gather two or three children. Encourage them to take one of the magazine pictures and place it on the self-adhesive paper. The children will delight in touching the back of the paper.

Once all the children have had an opportunity to place pictures on the adhesive paper, cover the paper with another piece of adhesive paper or with waxed paper. Cut the collage into pieces for the children to take home.

While the children work, **say**: "Look at the baby picture Kashonda found! Timothy found a picture of a big boy!"

b Play With Blocks

Do this in the Building Center.

As the children play with blocks, point out to them that they could not pile the blocks like that or build such a straight road when they were little babies.

Tell them that they are growing and learning new things, just as Jesus did in today's story.

c Tell Another Story

Do this in the Storytelling Center.

Penny was unhappy. She wanted to play with her baby brother, Bryan, but Bryan was asleep. "Bryan is always sleeping!" she said to her mother.

"When you were a baby, you slept all of the time too," Mother said. "But you stay awake more now that you are a big girl. You will go to school like your sister when you get bigger. God plans for children to start out as babies and grow and grow."

Penny liked God's plan for growing.

d Say an Action Verse

Do this in the Storytelling Center.

Gather two or three children. Do these motions: On lines one and two, stoop and curl into a ball. On lines three and four, uncurl slowly, stand, and stretch your arms high.

Now I'm tiny.
Now I'm small.
Now I'm growing
Tall, tall, tall.

Tip
Make the stories more personal. Substitute your name and that of the children in the contemporary stories.

Look Back
What did the children learn about growing today? Did each child have a chance to hear that Jesus grew?

Think back over the sessions you have been teaching. What signs of growth have you observed in the children? What growth have you experienced yourself?

Look Ahead
The next session grows directly out of this session. Plan to use some of the favorite activities again to help the children feel secure.

Find ways to point out to the children how they are growing.

4 Celebrate

the Story

a Enjoy Music

Do this in the Storytelling Center.

Gather two or three children. Recall today's Bible story and verse. Listen to "Child Jesus Song" (Songbook, CD) with the children, patting your legs along with the rhythm. Say the words with the children while patting your legs. Then play the CD again and sing along with the music.

Sing "Growing in a Family" with the children, encouraging them to dance to the music.

b Enjoy Books and Puzzles

Do this in the Discovery Center.

Gather two or three children. Help them put together puzzles.

Point out that babies can't do puzzles, but that big children can.

Read a book together. Remind the children that babies cannot turn pages like they can.

c Say Goodbye

Recall today's Bible story. Encourage the children to say the Bible verse with you. **Say**: "I am glad, (*name one of the children*), that you are growing and that you came to church today." Repeat this for each child in the class.

Pray: "Thank you, God, that we are growing. We are glad for your plan for growing."

Be sure to have a teacher or helper at the door to match children with their caregivers. Tell parents about today's Bible story and make sure that each child has today's Bible Story Picture Card. Show the parents the "Nurturing Your Child's Faith" section of the card. Be sure the children take home their collages.

All children grow
and develop, just as
Jesus did.

Bible Verse:
Jesus grew both in
body and in
wisdom.
(Luke 2:52, *Good
News Bible*)

Resources:
Bible
CD
Activity Pak (Winter)
    page 8 (figure 10)
    page 11 (growth chart)
    Songbook
Bible Story Picture Cards

Supplies:
three boxes
pictures of babies,
    children, and adults
cardboard or tagboard
colored markers
ruler or straight edge
climbing or rocking
    equipment such as a
    slide or rocking boat
    or large box
manila paper
powdered tempera paint
water
small paintbrushes or
    cotton swabs
coverups

building blocks

Look! I Am Growing............

Enter the Bible Story

Read Luke 2:40, 52: The Bible passages for this session are the same as for the previous session. Read them again as you prepare to teach. We are forced to imagine what Jesus must have been like as a child, since we have no textual information. We believe, as Christians, that Jesus was fully human along with being fully divine, so he must have gone through the same emotional struggles that we have gone through in growing. We know that Jesus got angry, and sad, and frustrated as an adult, so we can be fairly sure that he felt those emotions as a child as well. This should give us hope, as emotional beings ourselves, that Jesus fully understands us and can advocate for us with God.

Think About It: Review "Enter the Bible Story" in the previous session. Think again about the questions posed there. Remember that children grow at different rates from one another. Be aware that children grow in spurts, sometimes gaining inches rapidly, other times suddenly understanding a concept or overcoming behavior that has been a problem to the group.

Through the Week: Take some time during the week to think about each child in your class. What are evidences of the child's growth? In what areas is help needed? How can you contribute to the growth process for that particular child? Pray for each child.

Pray: Give me wisdom, God, to know how to encourage children's questions and explorations. Give me patience, God, to help the children learn caring, sharing ways. Give me an accepting heart in order that I may help the children learn to accept each other. Help me to be aware of your love for me, God, that I may be able to model that love for the children. Amen.

The Story and Young Children

Children can know that God plans for us to grow in many different ways. They can become aware of ways in which they are growing. Toddlers and two-year-olds are working hard at being independent. The word *no*, a frequent visitor to the vocabulary of two-year-olds, is an attempt to push against authority, to establish a being different from the all-powerful parent or adult figure. You may notice two-year-olds saying no at the same time they are doing what you asked them to do.

Room Setup: Place the growth chart (Activity Pak—p. 11) on the wall. Cover a table with several thicknesses of newspaper. Set up an active play area with climbing or rocking equipment.

Learning Centers

Conversation Center

You will need: pictures of babies, children and adults; three boxes large enough to hold the pictures; cardboard or tagboard, manila paper; powdered tempera paint; water; small paintbrushes or cotton swabs; coverups.

Get ready: Cut pictures of babies, children, and adults from magazines. Mount the pictures on construction paper or tagboard. Cover the table with several thicknesses of newspaper to absorb extra water.

- Sort Pictures, Activity 1b
- Make Powder Paint Pictures, Activity 4b

Family Living Center

This would include a toy kitchen set and props appropriate to the lesson.

Building Center

Provide enough blocks for toddlers to share. You may use wooden unit blocks or large cardboard or plastic blocks.

Storytelling Center

You will need: Bible; Activity Pak—p. 8 (figure 10); climbing or rocking equipment such as a slide, or rocking boat, large box or carton through which the children may crawl; CD, CD player, Activity Pak Songbook.

Get ready: Prepare storytelling figures (see Activity Pak—p. 2).

- Tell the Bible Story, Activity 2a
- Retell the Bible Story, Activity 2b
- Say an Action Verse, Activity 2c
- Enjoy Active Play, Activity 3a
- Sing a Song, Activity 3b
- Tell Another Story, Activity 3c
- Enjoy Music, Activity 4a

Discovery Center

You will need: Activity Pak—p. 11 (growth chart), colored markers, ruler or straight edge.

- Measure Children, Activity 1c

How Jesus Grew

When Jesus was a little boy, he ate good food and liked to run and play. The Bible says that Jesus grew taller and stronger.

When Jesus was a little boy, he liked to learn new things. He watched the stars move and the olive trees grow. The Bible says that Jesus grew by knowing more and more.

When Jesus was a little boy, he learned to share and wait for his turn. The Bible says that Jesus grew by learning to be kind.

When Jesus was a little boy, he listened when others told about God. The Bible says Jesus grew by learning more and more about God.

1 Prepare

for the Story

a Welcome Each Child

Do this as each child enters the room.

Stoop to the child's eye level and welcome each child by name. **Say** to each child: "I am so happy you have come to church today."

Be prepared to involve children in an interesting or comforting activity.

b Sort Pictures

Do this in the Conversation Center.

Gather two or three children. Let the children look at and talk about the pictures.

Notice the differences and the similarities in the pictures. Do all of the pictures show a nose? Do all of the pictures show hair? Older children can sort the pictures into three groups: babies, children, and adults.

Provide three boxes. Glue a picture to the outside of the box to show which group goes into which box.

As the children enjoy this activity, talk with them about how God plans for us to grow from babies to children to adults.

c Measure Children

Do this in the Discovery Center.

Gather two or three children. Let each child back up to the growth chart (Activity Pak—p. 11). Use the straight edge to help you mark the child's height on the chart.

When you have marked the child's height, ask the child to turn around and see how tall he or she is.

Say: "Michael, you are growing!" Write the child's name next to his or her mark.

Some children may be hesitant to let you measure them. They may become more comfortable after watching other children be measured.

Toddlers and two-year-olds may already have absorbed the cultural idea that "bigger is better." It is important not to compare children's heights with each other. Some children are short, and some are tall, but all are *growing*!!

2 Tell

the Story

a Tell the Bible Story

Do this in the Storytelling Center.

Gather two or three children. Show the storytelling figure of Jesus as a child (figure 10).

Remind the children that Jesus was once a child just as they are and that he grew in many ways, just as they are growing.

Tell the story, "How Jesus Grew." Open a Bible and **say**: "The Bible says, 'Jesus grew both in body and in wisdom.'" Invite the children to repeat the verse with you.

Pray: "We are glad, God, that Jesus grew. We are glad that we grow too."

b Retell the Bible Story

Do this in the Storytelling Center.

Say the first line: "When Jesus was a little boy . . ." Stop and invite the children to repeat the line with you.

Continue to involve children in repeating this line with you whenever it

occurs in the story, as well as the line, "The Bible says . . ."

c Say an Action Verse

Do this in the Storytelling Center.

Gather two or three children. Help them do the motions from last week:

Little Jesus, sleep in your bed,
Sleep in your bed all day.
(*Lie down on the floor.*)
Soon you will learn to sit up straight,
(*Sit up.*)
Then learn to crawl away.
(*Crawl around.*)
Next you will learn to stand up tall,
(*Stand up.*)
Then take steps, one and two.
(*Take two steps.*)
Soon you'll be walking everywhere,
Just as grownups do.
(*March in place.*)

3 Connect
with the Story

a Enjoy Active Play
Do this in the Storytelling Center.

Let the children enjoy climbing, sliding, crawling, or rocking with large motor equipment. Tell the children that they are growing and can now do these things that they could not do when they were babies.

b Sing a Song
Do this in the Storytelling Center.

Gather two or three children. Sing "I Am Growing" (CD) to the tune of "London Bridge." Do the motions described.

Add the other verses as suggested in the Songbook.

c Tell Another Story
Do this in the Storytelling Center.

Gilbert was growing. His daddy said, "You are getting so tall!"

Gilbert was learning to work puzzles. His teacher said, "You know so many things."

Gilbert let his sister Selena play with his truck. His aunt said, "You are learning to share."

Gilbert heard a Bible story when he went to bed. His mother said, "You are learning about God."

Gilbert prayed: "Thank you, God, that I am growing."

4 Celebrate
the Story

a Enjoy Music
Do this in the Storytelling Center.

Gather two or three children. Encourage the children to sing along with the CD—especially the "Child Jesus Song" and "Growing in a Family" (Songbook, CD).

Do the action verses "Little Baby Jesus" and "Now I'm Tiny" from previous weeks.

b Make Powder Paint Pictures
Do this in the Conversation Center.

Gather one or two children. Protect their clothing by putting a short-sleeved adult shirt on them, buttoned down the back. Push up long sleeves.

Place a piece of manila paper on the table and sprinkle it lightly with powdered paint. Let the children dip their brushes or cotton swabs into water and paint on the sprinkled paper.

Say: "I am glad you have grown big enough to make these pretty pictures."

c Say Goodbye
Recall today's Bible story, encouraging the children to say or sing the Bible verse with you.

Say: "I am glad that (*name one of the children*) is growing." Repeat this for each child in the class.

Pray: "Thank you, God, for your plan for growing."

Be sure to have a teacher or helper at the door to ensure that anxious children do not leave until someone comes for them. Tell parents about today's Bible story and make sure that each child has today's Bible Story Picture Card.

Show the parents the "Nurturing Your Child's Faith" section of the card.

Be sure the children take home their Powder Paint Pictures.

Tip
Make the stories more personal. Substitute your name and that of the children in the contemporary stories.

Look Back
How did the children learn today about God's plan for growing?

How did they become aware or were reminded of how they are growing?

How did you help children become more independent today?

What did they learn about relating to others?

Look Ahead
The next two sessions will examine the only other information from the Bible that we have about Jesus' childhood.

Make sure that you are planning ahead for the correct number of lessons before Easter, and combining lessons so that you are at the proper place in the teacher guide during Lent.

Jesus and his family worshiped God by going to the Temple. We worship God by going to church.

Bible Verse:
Jesus grew both in body and in wisdom.
(Luke 2:52, *Good News Bible*)

Resources:
Bible
CD
Activity Pak (Winter)
    pages 5, 17
    (figures 1, 3, 5, 15)
    page 22 ("Jesus Takes
    a Trip" picture)
    page 15 (suitcase
    pattern)
    Songbook
Bible Story Picture Cards

Supplies:
glue
pictures of clothing cut
    from catalogs
small paper cups
blocks
toy airplanes, toy cars,
    toy trains
small suitcases
dress-up clothes
sandbox (see p. 234)
sand toys
toy figures
books, puzzles about
    transportation
CD player

Jesus Takes a Trip................

Enter the Bible Story

Read Luke 2:41-42: The Bible story for today tells the story of Jesus traveling to Jerusalem with his family for Passover. Jewish law required that males attend the feasts of Passover, Pentecost, and Tabernacles (Exodus 23:14-17, Deuteronomy 16:16). At the age of twelve a Jewish boy was to observe all of the requirements of the law. So while Jesus must have gone to Jerusalem in earlier years, this was the first year he was legally required to observe the feast. The trip would have covered approximately seventy miles and would have taken several days. For protection, the family would have formed a caravan with many other families, traveling in a great big community. It must have been a festive time for all.

Think About It: This story recalls an important event in Jesus' life. Going to Jerusalem for Passover must have been a high point in every Hebrew family's year. Reflect on the following questions as you prepare to tell the story and to help children retell the story: What are the annual events in your life by which you mark time? Is your life marked by a school calendar? a fiscal year? birthdays and anniversaries? What are the special days in the church year that are important to you? Pentecost? Ash Wednesday? Christmas? Easter? All Saints? How can you make special days come alive for the children you teach?

Through the Week: Recall events in your life that have brought you closer to God. How did these events reveal God to you? What made them different?

Pray: Thank you, God, for the festivals and celebrations that remind us of you and your great love for us. Thank you for the journeys on which you take us. Thank you for guiding us on our way. Amen.

The Story and Young Children

Toddlers and two-year-olds do not understand the concept of "last week," much less the concept of Passover and what it must have meant to the young Jesus. But they can understand taking trips. To a toddler, taking a trip is a magical experience. Imagine, you step into an automobile, and after you wake up from a nap, you are in a totally different place. When my son was two years old, we took a trip on a train. Whenever he heard the whistle blow, he would run to the window and look for the "choo choo." He was distressed that he could not see it. He never did figure out that we were actually *on* the "choo choo."

Room Setup: Set up a sandbox with toy people. Put transportation toys in the Building Center and suitcases and dress-up clothes in the Family Living Center.

Learning Centers

Conversation Center

Sit down and talk with the children.

You will need: Activity Pak—p. 15, pictures of clothing cut from catalogs, glue, small paper cups.

Get ready: Make a copy of the suitcase pattern for each child.

- Make Suitcases, Activity 4b

Building Center

Provide enough blocks for toddlers to share. You may use wooden unit blocks or large cardboard or plastic blocks.

You will need: blocks, toy airplanes, toy cars, toy trains.

- Play With Transportation Toys, Activity 3a

Discovery Center

You will need: a sandbox (see p. 234), sand toys, toy figures to represent people, books and puzzles about transportation.

- Play With Sand, Activity 1c
- Use Books and Puzzles, Activity 3b

Family Living Center

This would include a toy kitchen set and props appropriate to the lesson.

You will need: a few small suitcases and dress-up clothes.

- Get Ready for a Trip, Activity 1b

Storytelling Center

This should be an open area where you may gather children for storytelling, or to listen and respond to music. It would be helpful to have this center on a carpeted area.

You will need: Activity Pak—p. 22 ("Jesus Takes a Trip") and pp. 5, 17 (figures 1, 3, 5, 15); CD, CD player, Activity Pak Songbook; Bible.

Get ready: Prepare storytelling figures (see Activity Pak—p. 2).

- Tell the Bible Story, Activity 2a
- Retell the Bible Story, Activity 2b
- Tell Another Story, Activity 3c
- Enjoy Music, Activity 4a

Jesus Takes a Trip

Jesus was excited! He was going on a trip to Jerusalem. It would take several days. He helped his mother and father get ready to travel.

Jesus' friends were going on the trip with him. They would walk together. They would sing special songs, and they would eat special food. They would worship God together.

Jesus was glad for his family and friends. And he was glad to worship God.

1 Prepare

for the Story

a Welcome Each Child

Do this as each child enters the room.

Stoop to the children's eye level and welcome each child by name.

Say to each child: "I am so happy you have come to church today." Be prepared to involve children in an interesting or comforting activity.

b Get Ready for a Trip

Do this in the Family Living Center.

Allow the children to play as if they are preparing to go on a trip. Talk about the things they would need to put in their suitcases if they were going a long way away.

Play With Sand

Do this in the Discovery Center.

Gather two or three children. Let them explore the sand, teaching them to keep the sand inside the sandbox.

Show the children the toy figures.

Say: Let's pretend these people are going on a trip. They have to walk a l-o-o-n-n-g way." Have the figures walk across the sandbox.

2 Tell

the Story

a Tell the Bible Story

Do this in the Storytelling Center.

Gather two or three children. Look at the "Jesus Takes a Trip" picture (Activity Pak—p. 22). Notice Jesus and the members of his family. Notice the donkey loaded with supplies. Ask the children what they think the donkey is carrying.

Tell the Bible story, using the storytelling figures (1, 3, 5, 15). Open a Bible and **ask** the children: "Do you remember our Bible verse? 'Jesus grew both in body and in wisdom.'" Invite the children to repeat the verse with you

Pray: "Thank you, God, for Jesus. Amen."

b Retell the Bible Story

Do this in the Storytelling Center.

Gather two or three children. Do a version of "Going on a Bear Hunt" with the children. Pat your legs in a steady rhythm.

Keep the rhythm going while you tell the story, unless you are doing another motion.

Going to Jerusalem, going to Jerusalem. Oh, look! (*Shade your eyes as if you see something a long way off.*)
There are rocks in the road. Let's walk through. (*Stand up. Pretend to walk over sharp rocks.*) Ouch, ouch, ouch, ouch!

Going to Jerusalem, going to Jerusalem. Oh, look! (*Shade your eyes as if you see something a long way off.*)
There's hot sand in the desert. Let's walk through. (*Stand up and pretend to walk on hot sand.*) Hot, hot, hot, hot.

Going to Jerusalem, going to Jerusalem. Oh, look! (*Shade your eyes as if you see something a long way off.*)
There's some very tall grass. Let's walk through. (*Stand up and pretend to part the grass.*) Swish, swish, swish, swish.

Going to Jerusalem, going to Jerusalem. Oh, look! (*Shade your eyes as if you see something a long way off.*)
There's a big river. Let's swim across. (*Swim with your arms.*)

Going to Jerusalem, going to Jerusalem. Oh, look! (*Shade your eyes as if you see something a long way off.*)
Jerusalem is on top of a mountain. Let's climb up. (*Move fist over fist.*)

We got to Jerusalem! Hooray! (*Jump up and down and clap.*)

3 Connect

with the Story

a Play With Transportation Toys
Do this in the Building Center.

Gather two or three children. Talk to the children as they play with the toys.

Ask: Have you ever been on a plane? a train? a boat?

b Use Books and Puzzles
Do this in the Discovery Center.

Enjoy books and puzzles that show various forms of transportation.

Talk to the children as they work the puzzles: "What is that, Paige? An airplane? What sound does it make? Where does it go?"

c Tell Another Story
Do this in the Storytelling Center.

Eliza was going on a trip. She got together everything she would need.

She got her pajamas and her toothbrush. She got her favorite sleeping blanket and some clean clothes. She got some crackers and cheese, in case she got hungry.

She even got a pillow so she could sleep on the train.

Eliza was happy to go on a trip.

4 Celebrate

the Story

a Enjoy Music
Do this in the Storytelling Center.

Sing "Jesus Took a Trip" (Songbook, CD) to the tune of "Mary Had a Little Lamb." Enjoy other action songs.

Sing other songs that the children enjoy, allowing the children to dance to the music.

b Make Suitcases
Do this in the Conversation Center.

Gather two or three children. Give each child a suitcase (Activity Pak—p. 15).

Show the children how to "touch" the glue and then "touch" their paper to put a small amount of glue on the suitcase.

Then let the children "pack" articles of clothing in their suitcase by making a collage of the pictures that you cut out ahead of time.

c Say Goodbye

Recall today's Bible story, encouraging the children to say or sing the Bible verse with you.

Say: "I am glad (*name one of the children*) came to church today." Repeat this for each child in the class. **Pray**: "Thank you, God, for trips."

Be sure to have a teacher or helper at the door to match children with their caregivers.

Tell parents about today's Bible story and make sure that each child has today's Bible Story Picture Card. Show the parents the "Nurturing Your Child's Faith" section of the card.

Be sure the children take home their suitcase pictures.

Tip
Make the stories more personal. Substitute your name and that of the children in the contemporary stories.

Look Back
What feelings did the children express today?

What is it you know about this story and about your students that you did not know before this session?

What did you do that was good or that would work again?

What could you change about the lesson to make it better?

Look Ahead
Next week is a continuation of this week's lesson. Plan to use some of the same activities that you used this week.

Pray for God's help in creating a safe, happy place for the children to learn that God loves them.

Jesus learned about God, and we can learn about God.

Bible Verse:
Jesus grew both in body and in wisdom.
(Luke 2:52, *Good News Bible*)

Resources:
Bible
CD
Activity Pak (Winter)
   pages 5, 17
   figures (1, 3, 15, 16)
   page 22 ("Jesus Takes
   a Trip" and "Jesus and
   the Teachers" pictures)
   Songbook
Bible Story Picture Cards

Supplies:
paper
rubber cement
watercolor paints
water
fat paintbrushes
coverups
blocks
toy airplanes, toy cars,
   toy trains
simple puzzle
a few small suitcases
dress-up clothes
sandbox (see p. 234)
sand toys
toy figures
CD player

Jesus Stays Behind...........................

Enter the Bible Story

Read Luke 2:43-51: The Bible story for today tells the story of Jesus and his family at the end of the trip to Jerusalem for Passover. Those who made pilgrimages to Jerusalem usually did so in caravans. The women and children would always travel separately from the men. This is why a whole day went by before Jesus' parents knew he was missing. Joseph assumed he was with the women and children, and Mary, knowing that Jesus would have been considered a man, thought he was traveling with the rest of the men.

Think About It: This story sends chills down the spine of any parents who have ever lost sight of their child in a public place. Imagine not knowing where your child is for three whole days! Never mind that in the Hebrew culture, he was considered an adult, or that the world (in some ways) was a lot safer in the first century than it is now. What do you think Mary and Joseph felt after finding their son in the Temple? What do you think the teachers felt, listening to a twelve-year-old's questions? Are there other times in Jesus' life when he only listened and asked questions?

Through the Week: Try to imagine your students at twelve years of age. Which of them will be astounding their confirmation class teachers with their insights? Which will be more intent on getting laughs? Pray for each of your students by name that they may, like Jesus, will grow in body, mind, and spirit.

Pray: Dear God, you have given me so much responsibility in taking care of these precious two-year-olds. Guide me as I learn from them how to be your child. Amen.

The Story and Young Children

Toddlers are truly not aware that other people have feelings. In fact, when an adult they know gets angry, or begins to cry, it is very upsetting to them. So your students will not understand that Mary and Joseph were upset when Jesus stayed behind. Nor will they think it is anything special that adults were astonished by what this twelve-year-old boy was saying. After all, adults are astonished by toddlers all the time. What they will understand is that when we are lost, the people who love us will look for us, even if we do not know we are lost. We can never get too far away for the ones who love us to stop loving us and looking for us.

Room Setup: Set up a sandbox again this week. Invite a pastor or adult church leader to visit the class.

Learning Centers

Work with two or three children at a time in each learning center.

Conversation Center

This should be a table around which you may gather the children. Sit down with the children and engage them in conversation.

You will need: paper, rubber cement, watercolors and water, fat paintbrushes, coverups.

Get ready: Use rubber cement to paint simple shapes on pieces of paper.

• Make Surprise Pictures, Activity 3a

Storytelling Center

You will need: Activity Pak—p. 22 ("Jesus Takes a Trip" and "Jesus and the Teachers" pictures) and pp. 5, 17 (figures 1, 3, 15, 16); CD, CD player, Activity Pak Songbook, Bible.

Get ready: Prepare storytelling figures (see Activity Pak—p. 2).

• Tell the Bible Story, Activity 2a
• Retell the Bible Story, Activity 2b
• Enjoy Music, Activity 4a
• Visit With a Pastor, Activity 4b

Family Living Center

You will need: a few small suitcases and dress-up clothes.

• Get Ready for a Trip, Activity 1b

Discovery Center

You will need: a sandbox (see instructions on p. 234), sand toys, and toy figures to represent people going on a trip; simple puzzle.

Get ready: Gather two or three children. Let them explore the sand, teaching them to keep the sand inside the sandbox.

• Play With Sand, Activity 1c
• Look For Puzzle Pieces, Activity 3b

Building Center

You will need: blocks; toy cars, trucks, planes, and boats.

• Build the Temple, Activity 2c
• Play With Transportation Toys, Activity 3c

Jesus Stays Behind

"Where is Jesus?" asked Mary.
"Where is Jesus?" asked Joseph.
Mary and Joseph were going home from Jerusalem and could not find Jesus.
They looked and looked and looked and finally found him. He was in the Temple talking to the teachers!
Mary and Joseph were glad to find Jesus. They loved him very much.
Jesus went home with Mary and Joseph. He knew he would come back to the Temple someday.

117

1 Prepare

for the Story

a **Welcome Each Child**
Do this as each child enters the room.

Stoop to the children's eye level and welcome each child by name.

Say to each child: "I am so happy you have come to church today."

Be prepared to involve children in an interesting or comforting activity.

b **Get Ready for a Trip**
Do this in the Family Living Center.

Allow the children to play with the suitcases and dress-up clothes as if they are preparing to go on a trip.

Talk about the things they would need to put in their suitcase if they were going a long way away.

c **Play With Sand**
Do this in the Discovery Center

Gather two or three children. Let them explore the sand, teaching them to keep the sand inside the sandbox. Show the children the toy figures.

Say: "Let's pretend these people are going on a trip. They have to walk a l-o-o-n-n-g way." Have the figures walk across the sandbox.

2 Tell

the Story

a **Tell the Bible Story**
Do this in the Storytelling Center.

Gather two or three children. Recall last week's story—where Jesus and his family took a long trip to Jerusalem. **Say:** "Let me tell you a story of what happened when it was time to go home." Tell the Bible story, using the storytelling figures (figures 1, 3, 15, 16).

Open a Bible and **ask** the children: "Do you remember our Bible verse? 'Jesus grew both in body and in wisdom.'" Invite the children to repeat the verse with you.

Pray: "Thank you, God, for Jesus. Amen."

b **Retell the Bible Story**
Do this in the Storytelling Center.

Place the "Jesus and the Teachers" teaching picture (Activity Pak—p. 22) where the children can see it. Then do the following echo pantomime:

"Jesus! Jesus! Where are you, Jesus?" called Mary. (*Cup hands around mouth.*)

"Jesus! Jesus! Where are you, Jesus?" called Joseph. (*Cup hands around mouth.*)

Mary and Joseph could not find Jesus. (*Hold palms up beside shoulders and shake head.*)

Mary looked in the tent. "Jesus, are you there?" (*Bend over and pretend to pull aside tent flap.*)

Jesus was not in the tent. (*Shake your head.*)

Joseph saw some boys running.

"Jesus, are you there?" (*Run in place.*)

Jesus was not with the other boys. (*Shake head.*)

Mary and Joseph walked back to Jerusalem. (*Walk in place.*)

They looked in the market. (*Shade your eyes as if looking for something.*)

Jesus was not there. (*Shake your head.*)

They looked in the street. (*Shade your eyes as if looking for something.*)

Jesus was not there. (*Shake your head.*)

They looked in the Temple. (*Shade your eyes as if looking for something.*)

There was Jesus! (*Nod your head and point to the picture.*)

He was talking to the teachers. (*Nod head.*)

Mary and Joseph were happy to find Jesus. (*Hug yourself.*)

 Build the Temple
Do this in the Building Center.

As the children play, encourage them to build a temple like Jesus visited.

 **Connect**

with the Story

 Make Surprise Pictures
Do this in the Conversation Center.

Paint simple shapes on pieces of paper ahead of time with the rubber cement. Allow the cement to dry.

Gather two or three children. Protect their clothing by placing adult-sized shirts on them, buttoned down the back.

Say: "Mary and Joseph were looking for Jesus and couldn't find him. But he wasn't hiding; he was in plain sight. There is a surprise on this paper. It's not hiding, either. Let's look for a surprise on this piece of paper."

Invite the children to paint with watercolors on the paper. Notice the surprise.

When the paint is dry, peel off the rubber cement.

b **Look for Puzzle Pieces**
Do this in the Discovery Center.

Before class, scatter pieces of a puzzle around the center. Gather two or three children.

Say: "Oh, no, the pieces of this puzzle are lost! Can you help me find them?"

When the children have found all of the pieces, put the puzzle together and celebrate. Don't be surprised if the children want you to scatter the pieces again.

c **Play With Transportation Toys**
Do this in the Building Center.

Gather two or three children. Talk to the children as they play with the toys. Remind the children that Jesus was on a trip when his parents could not find him. Have they ever been separated from their parents?

Celebrate

the Story

 Enjoy Music
Do this in the Storytelling Center.

Sing "Jesus Took a Trip" (Songbook, CD) to the tune of "Mary Had a Little Lamb." Enjoy action songs.

Sing other songs that the children enjoy, allowing the children to dance to the music.

 Visit With a Pastor
Do this in the Storytelling Center.

Ask your pastor or another church leader ahead of time to come and talk to the children. Remind the children that Jesus was asking questions of the teachers in the Temple and that we can ask questions of the leaders in our church.

 Say Goodbye
Recall today's Bible story, encouraging children to say the Bible verse with you.

Say: "I am glad (*name one of the children*) came to church today. I hope you ask lots of questions."

Pray: "Thank you, God, for our church. And thank you for our parents who do not go home without us."

Be sure to have a teacher or helper at the door to ensure that anxious children do not leave until someone comes for them.

Tell parents about today's Bible story and make sure that each child has today's Bible Story Picture Card. Show the parents the "Nurturing Your Child's Faith" section of the card.

Be sure the children take home their Surprise Pictures.

Tip
Make the stories more personal. Substitute your name and that of the children in the contemporary stories.

Look Back
What emotions did the children express today? Did all of the children have a chance to hear the Bible story?

What have you learned today about God? about your students? about yourself?

What activities went especially well today? Which ones have you learned never to repeat?

What could you change about the lesson to make it better?

Look Ahead
This is the last lesson in the winter quarter. Look ahead and plan to teach Session 41 on Palm Sunday and Session 42 on Easter.

Arrange the other lessons in the spring quarter around these two weeks. Some of the lessons will come before Easter, and some may happen after Easter so that you begin Session 43 on the first Sunday in June.

Session

29

Matthew 4:18-20

Jesus asked Peter and Andrew to follow him. We can follow Jesus too.

Bible Verse:
Jesus said, "Follow me." (Matthew 4:19, adapted)

Resources:
Bible
CD
Activity Pak (Spring)
page 5 (figures 1, 3, 4)
page 9 (fish game)
Songbook
Bible Story Picture Cards

Supplies:
light blue paper
small plates
sponges (cut into fish shapes)
tempera paint
spring-type clothespins
short-sleeved adult shirts that button down the front
rocking boat or large cardboard box
fishing nets
CD player
large plastic tub or several dishpans
water
items for water play (funnels, scoops, small containers)
floating items (corks, toy boats)
towels
blocks
teacher scissors
(optional: fish stickers)

Jesus Said, "Follow Me"...........

Enter the Bible Story

Read Matthew 4:18-20: This passage recounts the story of Jesus calling Simon, later called Peter, and his brother Andrew.

Think About It: Jesus called the disciples in many ways. Some he called from their nets at the seaside. Some he called from their places of business. Some he called down out of a tree. And some he picked up from the dirt of the street and said, "Go and sin no more." But no matter from where he called them, the message was always the same: "Follow me." Reflect on the following questions this week as you prepare to tell your children the simple message Jesus taught his disciples. Where has Jesus called you to go? Have you been called to make decisions you did not want to make or go places that you did not want to go? Given a toddler's limited abilities, what could Jesus possibly be calling your students to do? What is the value in teaching this lesson to toddlers and two-year-olds?

Through the Week: The old story, "In His Steps," recalls the tale of a group of people who took seriously the question, "What would Jesus do?" More recently, the WWJD bracelets call us to consider this question. This week, as a spiritual discipline, ask yourself this question before every decision you make. Does it make a difference in your life?

Pray: Dear God, thank you for Jesus, who calls me to follow your way. Help me to hear the call clearly, and give me the courage to respond. Amen.

The Story and Young Children

Toddlers are learning independence, so following directions can sometimes be challenging to them. Indeed, sometimes teachers of toddlers feel that they are herding sheep or dealing with stubborn mules. Even so, toddlers also thrive on adult approval. They truly do want adults to like them. When trying to get your students to follow directions, keep the following in mind: Never laugh when they do the opposite of what you tell them to, even when it is very funny. Children of this age love to play games with adults and will continue the behavior if they think it is a game. Give only one direction at a time, and make sure the child is listening when you give the direction. Sometimes it is helpful to put your hand on their forehead or chin and make sure they are looking at you when you tell them what you want them to do. Toddlers respond much better if your tone of voice is one of playfulness rather than authoritarian ordering. Remember that they like to play games.

Learning Centers

Conversation Center

You will need: light blue paper, small plates, sponges, teacher scissors, tempera paint, spring-type clothespins, short-sleeved adult shirts that button down the front (optional: fish stickers).

Get ready: Cut sponges into fish shapes. Rinse sponges in water and squeeze out all the water, leaving the sponges slightly damp. Clip a spring-type clothespin on the top of each sponge, creating a handle for each sponge. Pour tempera paint into small plates.

- Sponge Paint Fish, Activity 1c

Discovery Center

You will need: large plastic tub or several dishpans, water, items for water play (funnels, scoops, small containers), floating items (corks, toy boats), towels, Activity Pak—p. 9 (fish game).

- Play With Water, Activity 1b
- Play a Game, Activity 3b

Family Living Center

This would include a toy kitchen set and props appropriate to the lesson.

- Play House, Activity 3c

Building Center

Provide enough blocks for toddlers to share. You may use wooden unit blocks or large cardboard or plastic blocks.

You will need: blocks.

- Play With Blocks, Activity 3a

Storytelling Center

This should be an open area where you may gather children for storytelling, or to listen and respond to music. It would be helpful to have this center on a carpeted area.

You will need: Activity Pak—p. 5 (figures 1, 3, 4), rocking boat or large cardboard box, fishing nets, CD, CD player, Songbook, Bible.

- Tell the Bible Story, Activity 2a
- Retell the Bible Story, Activity 2b
- Sing a Song, Activity 2c
- Enjoy Music, Activity 4a

Follow Me

Jesus saw Peter and Andrew in a boat. They were fishing.
Jesus said, "Follow me."
Peter and Andrew got out of the boat and followed Jesus.
They were glad that Jesus had chosen them to help him.

Prepare
for the Story

a **Welcome Each Child**
Do this as each child enters the room.

Have the CD playing as the children arrive. Stoop to the children's eye level and welcome each child by name.

Say to each child: "I am so happy you have come to church today."

Be prepared to involve children in an interesting or comforting activity.

b **Play With Water**
Do this in the Discovery Center.

Gather one or two children. Encourage the children to play in the water with the items you have provided.

Tell them that today they will hear a story about some fishermen.

c **Sponge Paint Fish**
Do this in the Conversation Center.

Gather two or three children. Put a short-sleeved shirt buttoned down the back on the children.

Give each child a piece of blue paper. Encourage the children to use the sponges to stamp fish on the blue paper.

As an option purchase fish stickers and let the children stick them on blue paper.

Tell
the Story

a **Tell the Bible Story**
Do this in the Storytelling Center.

Gather two or three children. **Say:** "Jesus wanted some helpers to go with him. Let me tell you a story about when he asked two brothers to help him."

Tell the Bible story using the storytelling figures (figures 1, 3, 4) at appropriate times. Open a Bible and **say** the Bible verse: "Jesus said, 'Follow me.'" Encourage the children to say the Bible verse with you.

Pray: "Thank you, God, for helpers."

b **Retell the Bible Story**
Do this in the Storytelling Center.

Gather two or three children. Ask the children to get into the boat (or cardboard box). Tell them to pretend to be fishing.

If you have a fishing net (often available at party supply stores), show the children how to throw the net out and pull it back in. Then stand up and **say:** "I am Jesus. Follow me!" Tell the children to throw down the net and get out of the boat and follow you.

Lead the children around the room and back to the boat. Repeat as long as the children have interest.

If you have older two-year-olds, let the children pretend to be Jesus and call their friends to follow them.

c **Sing a Song**
Do this in the Storytelling Center.

Gather two or three children. Play "Follow Me" (Songbook, CD). Encourage the children to move their bodies to the music.

Play the song again, and invite the children to follow you around the room while you wave your arms and step in time to the music. Hold your hands high, shake your hands, and ask the children to follow you again as you sing the song. Hold your arms straight out and pretend to be an airplane as you lead the children around the area.

Make up lots of motions and encourage the children to follow your lead.

3 Connect
with the Story

a Play With Blocks
Do this in the Building Center.

Gather one or two children. Ask the children to follow your directions.

Place one block beside another block and invite the children to mimic your action. Place a block on top of another and invite them to do it as well.

Say: "Jesus asked Peter and Andrew to follow him—to do what he told them to do. Peter and Andrew are good followers. I am glad that you are good followers too."

b Play a Game
Do this in the Discovery Center.

Gather two or three children. Place the fish game pictures (Activity Pak—p. 9) on the table or carpet in front of them.

Say: "Look at this pretty fish. Can you find another fish that looks just like it?"

Remind the children that Peter and Andrew were fishermen. Wonder aloud if the fish you are playing with look like the ones they were catching.

Older children can play this matching game: Divide up the cards between the children. Allow them to place the cards face up. Ask one child to place a card in the middle. Invite the child who has a matching fish card to place it on top. Then tell the second child to put one card in the middle. Whoever has a matching card can play next.

Play until all the cards are matched or the children get tired of the game.

c Play House
Do this in the Family Living Center.

While the children play, remind them of the story of Jesus and Peter and Andrew.

Say: "Jesus told Peter and Andrew to follow him. Jesus wants us to follow him too. One way we can follow Jesus is by listening to our mommies and daddies and by doing what they say."

As the children play, encourage one of them to be a parental figure and give the others guidance. Encourage the children to listen to the directions the parental figure gives them.

4 Celebrate
the Story

a Enjoy Music
Do this in the Storytelling Center.

Enjoy songs where the children need to follow direction, such as "If You're Happy and You Know It" or "Having Fun Today" (Songbook, CD).

Say: "Peter and Andrew could listen and follow direction. We can listen and follow direction too." Sing "Follow Me" (Songbook, CD) and encourage the children to imitate your actions. Sing other songs the children have learned this year.

b Clean Up
Gather two or three children. **Say:** "Jesus wants us to follow him. One way we can follow Jesus is by cleaning up our messes."

Make a game out of cleaning up. Ahead of time mark toy shelves with pictures so the children can easily see where the toys belong. Avoid saying, "(*Child's name*), please pick up this toy." This could get you

into a power struggle. Rather, **say:** "I need someone to pick up this toy. Who could that someone be?" This will allow the children to volunteer to clean up.

Then, if you heap lots of genuine praise on the volunteer, the children will be running to help clean up and get the individual attention.

c Say Goodbye
Recall today's Bible story. Encourage the children to say or sing the Bible verse with you. **Say:** "I'm glad that (*name of child*) is a follower." Repeat this for each child in the class. **Pray:** "Thank you, God, for followers."

Have a teacher or helper at the door to match the children with their caregivers. Tell parents about today's Bible story and make sure that each child has today's Bible Story Picture Card. Show parents the "Nurturing Your Child's Faith" section of the card. Be sure the children take home their fish pictures.

Tip
Cleanup is easier when the children know where to put things away. Teach the children where toys and books belong.

Look Back
What activities went particularly well today? With what activities did you or the children have trouble? What activities will you want to repeat next week?

Did all of the children have a chance to experience the Bible story this week? Can the children retell the story?

Look Ahead
Count ahead and make sure that you have scheduled your Palm Sunday lesson on Palm Sunday and your Easter lesson on Easter. Arrange the other lessons around these two Sundays. Note that you will need to combine one or two lessons in order to cover all of the material within three months.

Jesus asked James and John to follow him. We can follow Jesus too.

Bible Verse:
Jesus said, "Follow me." (Matthew 4:9, adapted)

Resources:
Bible
CD
page 242 (helper badge pattern)
Activity Pak (Spring)
    page 5 (figures 2-5)
    page 9 (fish game)
    Songbook
Bible Story Picture Cards

Supplies:
CD player
markers or crayons
teacher scissors
tape
building blocks
toy boats
large piece of blue fabric
rocking boat or large
    cardboard box
toy kitchen set
dress-up clothes
chairs
large plastic tub or
    several dishpans
water
items for water play
    (funnels, scoops, small
    containers)
floating items (corks, toy
    boats, small sieves, or
    strawberry baskets that
    can scoop things out of
    the water)
towels
(optional: construction
    paper, fishing nets)

Jesus Said, "Follow Me"

Enter the Bible Story

Read Matthew 4:21-22: The story from last week continues with Jesus calling the sons of Zebedee: James and his brother John. Nothing much is said about Zebedee's reaction to his son's leaving him, but it must be presumed that the loss of two healthy young men would have been a blow to the family business.

Think About It: In this passage Jesus called two brothers to leave their father and their nets and to follow him, which they willingly did. But sometimes we focus on James and John and forget the father, left alone with the nets and the work. Reflect on the following questions as you prepare to teach your students to follow Jesus this week. How do you think that Zebedee must have felt as he watched his sons walk away from their work to follow an itinerant rabbi? Could he have been jealous that his sons were getting to go off and follow this charismatic fellow, while he had to stay with the family business? Or would he have been proud to see his sons enter the work of bringing about the kingdom of God? Obviously, if everyone simply followed Jesus around, listening to his teachings, the villages would starve. So the work of fishing was important. But it certainly was not as glamorous as following Jesus. Just as obviously, the work of teaching two-year-olds is not nearly as glamorous as preaching, or ministering to people in the hospital, or singing solos in the choir. Do you ever wish Jesus would lead you into some more visible calling, where you might receive more praise? As you read and contemplate this story, what word is God giving you?

Through the Week: Make a list of the things you do that bring about the kingdom of God. Do you stop to listen to a neighbor whose tales you have heard a hundred times, but who just needs someone to listen? Are you courteous to the clerks and other customers in the grocery store? Do you yield the right of way to the confused person who is in the wrong lane? How do these activities bring about the kingdom of God?

Pray: Dear God, I thank you for the opportunity to spread your love about in my community. Give me the patience and the sense of humor I need to show others your love. Amen.

The Story and Young Children

Follow the leader is a favorite game of young children. They willingly play along whenever an adult says, "Can you do this?" Imitation of adults is big at this age. It is important that you begin to teach children to take consequences for their actions. Whoever gets toys off the shelf should put them back so that later we know where to find them. "Lisa, are you finished with the blocks? Let's see if we can find the right spot for them on the shelf." Encourage the children to notice when they make a mess and to help clean it up. "Oh, dear, Justin, you just spilled your juice. Let's get some paper towels and clean it up." Avoid telling the children to do something and not helping them do it. Remember that they are imitating and may not understand directions unless you show them what to do.

Learning Centers

Conversation Center

You will need: copies of p. 242 for each child, markers or crayons, teacher scissors, tape (optional: construction paper).

Get ready: Photocopy p. 242. Decide if the children will make headbands.

- Make Helper Badges, Activity 3a

Building Center

You will need: building blocks, toy boats, large piece of blue fabric.

Get ready: Provide enough blocks for toddlers to share.

- Play With Blocks, Activity 1c

Family Living Center

You will need: toy kitchen set, dress-up clothes, chairs.

Get ready: Have items on hand so the children can pretend to play house.

- Play House, Activity 3c

Storytelling Center

You will need: Activity Pak—p. 5 (figures 2–5); rocking boat or large cardboard box that children can climb in and out of; CD and CD player, Songbook, Bible (optional: fishing nets).

Get ready: Prepare storytelling figures (see Activity Pak—p. 2).

- Tell the Bible Story, Activity 2a
- Retell the Bible Story, Activity 2b
- Sing a Song, Activity 2c
- Enjoy Music, Activity 4a

Discovery Center

You will need: Activity Pak—p. 9 (fish game); large plastic tub or several dishpans; water; items for water play such as funnels, scoops, small containers; floating items such as corks and toy boats; small sieves or strawberry baskets that can be used to scoop things out of the water; towels.

Get ready: See p. 234 for instructions on setting up the water play activity.

- Play With Water, Activity 1b
- Play a Game, Activity 3b

Follow Me

Jesus saw James and John with their nets. They were fishing.

Jesus said to John and James, "Follow me."

James and John dropped their nets and went with Jesus. They were glad Jesus had chosen them to be his helpers.

1 Prepare
for the Story

a Welcome Each Child
Do this as each child enters.

Have the CD playing as the children arrive. Stoop to the children's eye level and welcome each child by name. **Say** to each child: "I am so happy you have come to church today."

Be prepared to involve children in an interesting or comforting activity.

b Play With Water
Do this in the Discovery Center.

Gather one or two children. Encourage the children to play in the water with the items you have provided. Show the children how to use a sieve or a strawberry basket to scoop things out of the water.

Say: "This is one way that people can get fish out of the water." Tell the children that today they will hear a story about some more fishermen.

c Play With Blocks
Do this in the Building Center

Gather two or three children. Spread out the blue fabric and tell the children that this is a big lake. Let the children put the boats on the lake.

Tell the children that today they will hear a story about some boats on a lake.

2 Tell
the Story

a Tell the Bible Story
Do this in the Storytelling Center.

Gather two or three children. **Say**: "Last week we heard about when Jesus called Peter and Andrew to help him. But Jesus wanted some more helpers to go with him. Let me tell you a story about when he asked two more brothers to help him."

Tell the Bible story using the storytelling figures (figures 2–5) at appropriate times.

Open a Bible and **say** the Bible verse: "Jesus said, 'Follow me.'" Encourage the children to say the Bible verse with you.

Pray: "Thank you, God, for helpers."

b Retell the Bible Story
Do this in the Storytelling Center.

Gather two or three children. Ask the children to get into the boat. If they were present last week, they will remember this game and join in happily. Tell them to pretend to be fishing.

If you have a fishing net (often available at party supply stores), show the children how to throw the net out and pull it back in. Then stand up and **say**: "I am Jesus. Follow me!"

Tell the children to throw down the net and get out of the boat and follow you. Lead the children around the room and back to the boat. Repeat as long as the children have interest.

If you have older two-year-olds, let the children pretend to be Jesus and call their friends to follow them.

c Sing a Song
Do this in the Storytelling Center.

Gather two or three children. Play "Follow Me" (Songbook, CD). Encourage the children to move their bodies to the music.

Play the song again, and invite the children to follow you around the room while you wave your arms and step in time to the music.

Hold your hands high, shake your hands, and ask the children to follow you again as you sing the song. Hold your arms straight out and pretend to be an airplane as you lead the children around the area.

Make up lots of motions and encourage the children to follow your lead.

3 Connect
with the Story

a Make Helper Badges
Do this in the Conversation Center.

Give each child a copy of the helper badge pattern (p. 242). Let the children decorate it with markers or crayons. When each child has finished, cut out his or her badge. Tape it to the child's clothing. **Say:** "This badge will tell everyone you are one of Jesus' helpers." Or make headbands out of construction paper and tape the badge to the headband to make a helper hat.

b Play a Game
Do this in the Discovery Center.

Gather two or three children. Place the fish game pictures (Activity Pak—p. 9) on the table or carpet in front of them. **Say:** "Look at this pretty fish. Can you find another fish that looks just like it?"

Remind the children that Peter and Andrew were fishermen. Wonder aloud if the fish you are playing with look like the ones they were catching.

If you have older children, teach them a game with the cards. Divide up the cards between the children and allow them to lay them flat. (This is not a strategy game where you must keep your cards hidden.)

Ask one child to place a card in the middle. Invite the child who has a matching card to place it on top of the fish. Then have the second child put one of his or her cards in the middle. Whoever has a matching card can play next. Play until all the cards are matched or the children get tired of the game.

c Play House
Do this in the Family Living Center.

While the children play, remind them of the story of Jesus, Peter, and Andrew. **Say:** "Jesus told James and John to follow him. Jesus wants us to follow him too. One way we can follow Jesus is by listening to our mommies and daddys and doing what they say."

As the children play, encourage one of them to be a parental figure and to give the others guidance. Encourage the children to listen to the directions the parental figure gives them.

4 Celebrate
the Story

a Enjoy Music
Do this in the Storytelling Center.

Enjoy songs where the children need to follow direction, such as "If You're Happy and You Know It" or "Having Fun Today" (Songbook, CD). **Say:** "James and John could listen and follow direction. We can listen and follow direction too."

Sing "Follow Me" (Songbook, CD). Encourage the children to imitate your actions. Sing other songs that the children have learned this year.

b Clean Up
Gather two or three children. **Say:** "Jesus wants us to follow him. One way we can follow Jesus is by cleaning up our messes." Make a game out of cleaning up. Ahead of time mark toy shelves with pictures so that the children can easily see where toys belong. Avoid saying, "(*Child's name*), please pick up this toy." This could get you into a power struggle. Rather, **say:** "I need someone to pick up this toy. Who could that someone be?" This will allow the children to volunteer to clean up. Then, if you heap lots of genuine praise on the volunteer, children will be running to help clean up and get the individual attention.

c Say Goodbye
Recall today's Bible story. Have the children say or sing the Bible verse with you.

Say: "I'm glad that (*child's name*) is a follower." Repeat for each child in the class.

Pray: "Thank you, God, for followers."

Have a teacher or helper at the door to match children with caregivers. Tell parents about today's Bible story and make sure that each child has today's Bible Story Picture Card. Show parents the "Nurturing Your Child's Faith" section of the card.

Have the children take home their helper badges.

Tip
Cover the fish game with clear self-adhesive paper, or have it laminated for durability.

Look Back
What activities went particularly well today?

With what activities did you or the children have trouble?

What activities will you want to repeat next week?

Did all of the children have a chance to experience the Bible story this week?

Can the children retell the story?

Look Ahead
Count ahead and make sure that you have scheduled your Palm Sunday lesson on Palm Sunday and your Easter lesson on Easter. Arrange the other lessons around these two Sundays. Note that you will need to combine one or two lessons in order to cover all of the material within three months.

Jesus loves little children and told the grownups they should be more like them.

Bible Verse:
Jesus said, "Let the little children come to me." (Mark 10:14, adapted)

Resources:
Bibles
CD
Activity Pak (Spring)
    pages 5, 8
    (figures 1, 3, 4, 6, 7)
    page 3 ("Jesus and the Children" picture)
    Songbook
Bible Story Picture Cards

Supplies:
paper
glue
3- to 5-ounce paper cups
pictures of children cut from magazines
play dough
gingerbread people cookie cutters
old curriculum pictures of Jesus and the children, mounted on construction paper and cut in half
building blocks
CD player
storybook
several dolls
large bowl of soapy water
straws

Let the Children Come.......

Enter the Bible Story

Read Mark 10:13-16: Jesus rebukes those who would hold children back from coming to see him. He also affirms that children have an easier time entering the kingdom of God than many adults do.

Think About It: In Jesus' day children had few rights. Mortality rates were high, and children could not contribute much to family enterprises. And yet children were also highly prized. One of the first commandments given to humankind was to "be fruitful and multiply" (Genesis 1:28). Children were always the property of the man who fathered them. But no man would have taken an interest in their well being. That was women's work.

Of course, Jesus had a way of turning everything upside down. He said that children, rather than being a nuisance, were an example to adults as to how to live before God. He told adults to become more childlike, more trusting, more full of wonder, more innocent, more able to forgive. Jesus valued children and blessed them.

Let's face it. Toddlers are demanding and selfish. They always demand to be the center of attention. And when we would really like to be engaging in deep conversation about important subjects, toddlers only want their nose wiped or their diapers changed. It is easy to sympathize with the disciples who wanted the children to just go away. Reflect on the following questions this week as you prepare to tell this story and to help the children retell the story. What is your honest reaction when you are on a plane or a train, ready to take a trip, and a school group of young children climb aboard and sit near you? Have you ever been trying to listen to a sermon, or a concert, or a movie, and had a noisy child near you? What would Jesus say to you in your annoyance? How could it help us enter the kingdom of God to become like a little child?

Through the Week: Get a brand new set of crayons and some manila paper. Draw a picture and smell the crayons. Then go blow bubbles outside in the wind. Notice how wonderful the bubbles look in the sunshine. Splash in a puddle, or slide down a hill on a snow sled. Play with children and forget about grownup worries, even if for just an hour.

Pray: Dear God, thank you that I never grow too old to be childlike. Help me remember the wonder of being a child and to use that wonder to worship you. Amen.

The Story and Young Children

Children are naturally friendly to those who want them around. (Aren't we all?) They would have responded to Jesus' smile and to his tone of voice. They must have known instinctively that Jesus loved them. We can imagine that his face softened and broke into a smile when he saw young children.

Do your students know how much you love them? Practice "brightening" when you see them. Break out into a smile and let your eyes show interest in them. When you greet them, let your excitement at seeing them show in your face and voice. Respond to them with a pat on the back or a big hug. Tell them you love them by having the room set up with interesting activities when they arrive.

Learning Centers

Conversation Center

This should be a table around which you may gather the children and engage them in conversation.

You will need: paper, glue, small paper cups, pictures of children cut from magazines, marker; play dough and gingerbread people cookie cutters.

Get ready: Purchase play dough, or make your own (see p. 232). Cut pictures of children from magazines.

- Make a Collage, Activity 1b
- Play With Play Dough, Activity 3a

Building Center

Provide enough blocks for toddlers to share. You may use wooden unit blocks or large cardboard or plastic blocks.

You will need: building blocks.

- Play With Blocks, Activity 3c

Family Living Center

This would include a toy kitchen set and props appropriate to the lesson.

You will need: storybook, several dolls.

- Read a Book, Activity 3b

Storytelling Center

This should be an open area where you may gather children for storytelling, or to listen and respond to music. It would be helpful to have this center on a carpeted area.

You will need: Activity Pak—pp. 5, 8 (figures 1, 3, 4, 6, 7), p. 3 ("Jesus and the Children" picture); CD, CD player, Songbook; Bible.

- Tell the Bible Story, Activity 2a
- Retell the Bible Story, Activity 2b
- Sing a Song, Activity 2c
- Enjoy Music, Activity 4a

Discovery Center

You will need: large bowl of soapy water, straws; old curriculum pictures of Jesus and the children, construction paper, glue.

Get ready: Mount on cardboard pictures of Jesus and the children. Cut the pictures in half.

- Blow Bubbles, Activity 1c
- Play With Puzzles, Activity 4b

Let the Children Come

Many people wanted to see Jesus.
Some children wanted to see Jesus too.
But Jesus' helpers told the children to go away.
"No, no, no!" Jesus said. "Let the children to me. I want to see the children. God loves little children."

# **1 Prepare**

for the Story

a **Welcome Each Child**

Do this as each child enters.

Have the CD playing as the children arrive. Stoop to the children's eye level and welcome each child by name.

Say to each child: "I am so happy you have come to church today."

Be prepared to involve children in an interesting or comforting activity.

b **Make a Collage**

Do this in the Conversation Center.

Gather two or three children. Give each child a piece of paper. Put the glue in small paper cups. Show each child how to "touch" the glue with his or her finger and then "touch" the paper to place a small amount of glue on it.

Let the children choose pictures from those you cut out before class. Help the children place a picture of a child on each dot of glue to make a collage of children. Write across the top of the collage, "Jesus Loves the Children."

c **Blow Bubbles**

Do this in the Discovery Center.

Gather two or three children. Give each child a straw. Show the children how to blow air through the straw onto their hands.

When the children get the hang of blowing through the straw, let them blow into the bowl of soapy water. What a wonderful surprise! The bubbles come up to the top of the bowl and mound over.

If the children forget and suck on their straw, a small amount of soapy water won't hurt them. But if they keep sucking and get some in their stomach, it could give them an upset stomach. Close adult supervision of this activity is necessary.

2 Tell

the Story

a **Tell the Bible Story**

Do this in the Storytelling Center.

Gather two or three children. **Say:** "Jesus loved being with children. But sometimes his helpers thought children were in the way. Let me tell you a story about Jesus and some children."

Tell the Bible story, using the storytelling figures (figures 1, 3, 4, 6, 7) at appropriate times.

Open a Bible and **say** the Bible verse: "Jesus said, 'Let the little children come to me.'" Encourage the children to say the Bible verse with you.

Pray: "Thank you, God, for children."

b **Retell the Bible Story**

Do this in the Storytelling Center.

Gather two or three children. Show the children the picture of Jesus and the children (Activity Pak—p. 3). Notice the children with Jesus.

Make up stories about each child. **Say:** "This girl's name is Sarah. She likes to look at pretty flowers. Jesus loves Sarah." Or, "This baby's name is Jacob. He cries a lot. Jesus loves Jacob."

Continue by putting your finger on the nose of each of your children. **Say:** "This boy's name is Zachary. He likes to play with the blocks. Jesus loves Zachary."

c **Sing a Song**

Do this in the Storytelling Center.

Gather two or three children. Play "Let the Children Come To Me" (Songbook) to the tune of "London Bridge." Encourage the children to move their bodies to the music. Play the song again and invite the children to sing along.

Make a game out of the song by gathering the children in your arms while singing the song. When you finish singing, let the children stand up. When you begin singing again, encourage them to come running to you to be gathered onto your lap.

3 Connect
with the Story

a **Play With Play Dough**
Do this in the Conversation Center.

Ahead of time, make play dough according to the recipe on p. 232. Or use purchased play dough.

Gather one or two children. Play with the play dough. Encourage the children to roll out or pat the dough until it is flat. Then encourage them to cut out children by using the cookie cutter.

Say: "Let's make lots of children, because Jesus wanted lots of children to come to him."

b **Read a Book**
Do this in the Family Living Center.

Gather two or three children and several dolls around you for a story time.

Tell the children that Jesus liked to tell stories to children. Read or tell a story to the children and the dolls.

If you have older children, encourage them to read a story to the dolls.

c **Play With Blocks**
Do this in the Building Center.

As the children play with the blocks, get down and play with them.

Say: "I like to play with children. Jesus liked to play with children too."

4 Celebrate
the Story

a **Enjoy Music**
Do this in the Storytelling Center.

Teach the children "Jesus Loves Me" (CD, Songbook). Remember that because your children are toddlers, this may be the first time they hear this song. Sing other songs that the children have learned this year.

b **Play With Puzzles**
Do this in the Discovery Center.

Gather two or three children. Show them the picture halves that you made by mounting pictures of children on posterboard and cutting them in half. Invite the children to find the other half of each picture and to match them up. When the picture is whole, talk about the pictures. Encourage the children to repeat the Bible verse for today.

c **Say Goodbye**

Recall today's Bible story, encouraging the children to say or sing the Bible verse with you.

Say: "Jesus loves little children. Jesus loves (*name of child*)." Repeat this for each child in the class.

Pray: "Thank you, God, for Jesus."

Be sure to have a teacher or helper at the door to match children with their caregivers.

Tell parents about today's Bible story and make sure that each child has today's Bible Story Picture Card. Show parents the "Nurturing Your Child's Faith" section of the card.

Be sure the children take home their collages.

Tip
Ask parents to help you gather pictures for collages, or look through old curriculum for puzzles. Use the form on p. 254.

Look Back
What activities went particularly well today? With what activities did you or the children have trouble? What activities will you want to repeat next week?

Did all of the children have a chance to experience the Bible story this week?

Can the children retell the story?

Look Ahead
Count ahead and make sure that you have scheduled your Palm Sunday lesson on Palm Sunday and your Easter lesson on Easter. Arrange the other lessons around these two Sundays. Note that you will need to combine one or two lessons in order to cover all of the material within three months

Jesus teaches us about God. We can learn about God.

Bible Verse:
Jesus said, "Love one another." (John 15:12, adapted)

Resources:
Bible
CD
Activity Pak (Spring)
   pages 5, 8
   (figures 1–4, 6–9)
   page 23-24 ("Jesus Teaching" book)
   Songbook
Bible Story Picture Cards

Supplies:
several simple puzzles
paper
paintbrushes
tempera paint
short-sleeved adult shirts that button down the front
newspaper
building blocks
CD player
crepe paper streamers
toy dishes

Jesus Teaches..........

Enter the Bible Story

Read Matthew 5:1-2: When Jesus saw the crowds of people who were following him, he began to teach them about God.

Think About It: When Jesus saw the enormous crowds following him, he drew his disciples to a mountainside and sat down. At first glance one would not think very much about the fact that Jesus sat down, but in that day, Jewish rabbis usually sat down when they taught. So Jesus was following this tradition, or maybe he was offering more than a tradition. The act of sitting down indicates that the teacher is willing to share more of herself or himself with a child. It is a significant change in body posture from the usual standing posture. It puts the teacher's eyes nearer to the level of the child's eyes. It tells the child that he or she is important.

Think about the relationship between you and your best friend. How do you feel when your friend sits down and talks with you face to face? How will your students feel this week when you sit with them? Even though this passage is recorded near the beginning of Jesus' ministry, large crowds of people had begun to notice and to follow him. The disciples who followed Jesus noticed the popularity and charisma of Jesus. Perhaps this man would become famous and bring them great fame. Jesus must have known their thoughts. He sat down with his disciples and gave them the beatitudes, Matthew 5:1-12, where Jesus described the traits he is seeking in his followers.

Through the Week: Practice getting on the same level as anyone you talk to. If talking to a child, kneel or sit on the ground. If talking to someone sitting down, be sure to sit down as well. Really look each person in the eye, and help him or her know that you feel that person is special enough to take up your time.

Pray: Dear God, thank you for loving me enough to become human and to come down on my level. Help me to treat all people that I meet with dignity and love. Amen.

The Story and Young Children

Remember that for toddlers and two-year-olds the room itself is the teacher. The children will learn by manipulating the activities that you have prepared for them. As they play in the Family Living Center, they are trying to sort out what it means to live in a family. As they manipulate the blocks, they are gaining important lessons in physics and engineering. Unless there is a solid foundation on which to build a tower, the tower will fall down.

The role of the teacher with young children is to create an appropriate and safe learning environment for them. It is best if your room is structured in such a way that you do not have to say, "No, don't do that!" too often. If you have a piano, keep it closed unless you want the children to play on it. Keep toys and supplies that you do not wish them to play with behind closed doors or remove them from the room. Careful attention to structure will make the learning session more enjoyable for both you and the child.

Learning Centers

Work with two or three children at a time in each learning center.

Conversation Center

This should be a table around which you may gather the children and engage them in conversation.

You will need: paper, paintbrushes, tempera paint, short-sleeved adult shirts that button down the front, newspaper or plastic tablecloth.

Get ready: Cover the table with several layers of newspaper. Prepare paint and brushes for use.

• Paint With a Brush, Activity 3b

Building Center

Provide enough blocks for toddlers to share. You may use wooden unit blocks or large cardboard or plastic blocks.

You will need: building blocks.

• Play With Blocks, Activity 2d

Discovery Center

You will need: several simple puzzles.

• Play With Puzzles, Activity 1c

Storytelling Center

This should be an open area where you may gather children for storytelling, or to listen and respond to music. It would be helpful to have this center on a carpeted area.

You will need: Activity Pak—pp. 5, 8 (figures 1-4, 6-9); pp. 23-24 ("Jesus Teaching" book); CD and CD player; Songbook; Bible; crepe paper streamers.

Get ready: Prepare storytelling figures (see Activity Pak—p. 2).

• Tell the Bible Story, Activity 2a
• Retell the Bible Story, Activity 2b
• Sing a Song, Activity 2c
• Play Follow the Leader, Activity 3a
• Play a Game, Activity 3c
• Enjoy Music, Activity 4a

Family Living Center

This would include a toy kitchen set and props appropriate to the lesson.

You will need: toy dishes.

Get ready: Put out empty dishes. In order to foster imagination do not use plastic food.

• Feed the Hungry, Activity 1b

Jesus Was a Teacher

Jesus went about telling all the people about God. He told the people that God loved them. The people liked to hear Jesus. They followed Jesus wherever he went.

When Jesus saw all the people, he sat down to teach them. He said, "God loves you. I love you. Love one another."

Jesus was a good teacher.

Prepare
for the Story

a Welcome Each Child
Do this as each child enters.

Have the CD playing as the children arrive. Stoop to the children's eye level and welcome each child by name.

Say to each child: "I am so happy you have come to church today."

Be prepared to involve children in an interesting or comforting activity.

b Feed the Hungry
Do this in the Family Living Center.

Gather two or three children. **Say:** "I'm hungry! Will you feed me?" Ask a child to give you a plate. Pretend there is something good on the plate, such as macaroni and cheese, or pizza. **Say:** "Thank you for my pizza. What would you like me to give you?"

c Play With Puzzles
Do this in the Discovery Center

Gather two or three children. Show them the puzzles. Take the pieces out and show each child how to put them back in the puzzle.

Say: "Look, I am teaching you how to play with the puzzles. Can you teach Lisa?"

Tell
the Story

a Tell the Bible Story
Do this in the Storytelling Center.

Gather two or three children. **Say:** "Let me tell you another story about Jesus." Tell the Bible story, using the storytelling figures (figures 1–4, 6–9) at appropriate times.

Open a Bible and **say** the Bible verse: "Jesus said, 'Love one another.'" Encourage the children to say the Bible verse with you. Ask the children if they remember anything else that Jesus said.

Pray: "Thank you, God, for teachers."

b Retell the Bible Story
Do this in the Storytelling Center.

Assemble the "Jesus Teaching" book (Activity Pak—pp. 23–24) by removing the page from the Activity Pak and folding it in half. Gather two or three children.

Read the book to the children, pointing out the details in the pictures. Encourage the children to say, "Love one another" with you.

c Sing a Song
Do this in the Storytelling Center.

Gather two or three children. Play "Love One Another" (Songbook, CD). Encourage the children to move their bodies to the music.

Play the song again, and invite the children to dance to the music.

d Play With Blocks
Do this in the Building Center

Gather two or three children. Encourage the children to make a chair for Jesus, the teacher, to sit down on. Use the storytelling figures to retell the story with blocks.

Make block seats for the disciples and the children to sit on. Repeat the Bible verse: "Jesus said, 'Love one another.'"

3 Connect

with the Story

a Play Follow the Leader
Do this in the Storytelling Center.

Gather one or two children. **Say:** "Let's play follow the leader. Will you step, step, step, with me? Good stepping. Now do as I do. Little girl, little girl, turn around. (*Turn around.*) Little girl, little girl, touch the ground. (*Touch the ground.*) Little girl, little girl, that will do. (*Sit down.*) Little girl, little girl, God bless you! (*Smile.*)" Repeat with the next child, changing gender as necessary.

b Paint With a Brush
Do this in the Conversation Center.

Gather two or three children. Protect their clothing by putting a shirt on them, buttoned down the back.

Protect the table by covering it with newspaper or a plastic tablecloth. Give each child a piece of paper. **Say:** "I am going to teach you to paint." Demonstrate how to make long strokes with the brush. Notice what happens when there is a lot of paint on the brush and what happens when there is not much paint on the brush. Look at the patterns when you dab an almost dry brush onto the paper with short strokes. **Say:** "Jesus taught by showing people what to do. Jesus loved everyone, and wants us to love one another."

c Play a Game
Do this in the Storytelling Center.

Gather two or three children. Say the following action verse. This game will be similar to "Ring Around the Rosie".

Jesus walked around and around.
(*Hold hands and move in a circle.*)
The people followed around and around.
(*Hold hands and move in a circle.*)
Then Jesus stopped, and he sat down.
(*Drop hands and sit down.*)
"Love one another!"
(*Hold hands up high.*)

4 Celebrate

the Story

a Enjoy Music
Do this in the Storytelling Center.

Give each child a crepe paper streamer. Play "Love One Another" (Songbook, CD) and encourage the children to move their streamers in time with the music. Let the children dance around the area while waving their streamers. Notice the wonderful sound the streamers make.

Sing "Follow Me" (Songbook, CD) and encourage the children to imitate your actions. Sing other songs that the children have learned this year.

b Follow Jesus

Remember that Jesus taught by example. As children play today, look for opportunities to reinforce what Jesus taught. When a child cries, **say:** "Oh look, you fell down and hurt your arm. Let me look at it. Let's rock together. Jesus would help others when they were hurt." Or when children are arguing over a toy, **say:** "Let's take turns. I will play with you for a minute. Here's another dinosaur. Jesus would teach people how to share."

c Say Goodbye

Recall today's Bible story, encouraging children to say or sing the Bible verse with you.

Say: "Jesus said to love one another. I love (*name of child*)." Repeat this for each child in the class.

Pray: "Thank you, God, for Jesus."

Be sure to have a teacher or helper at the door to match children with their caregivers.

Tell parents about today's Bible story and make sure that each child has today's Bible Story Picture Card. Show parents the "Nurturing Your Child's Faith" section of the card.

Be sure the children take home their paintings.

Tip
Repeating the Bible verse again and again will help the children remember it. Work it into your conversation often.

Look Back
What activities went particularly well today? With what activities did you or the children have trouble? What activities will you want to repeat next week?

Did all of the children have a chance to experience the Bible story this week?

Can the children retell the story?

Look Ahead
Count ahead and make sure that you have scheduled your Palm Sunday lesson on Palm Sunday and your Easter lesson on Easter. Arrange the other lessons around these two Sundays. Note that you will need to combine one or two lessons in order to cover all of the material within three months.

Jesus helped people just as they were.

Bible Verse:
Jesus said, "Love one another." (John 15:12, adapted)

Resources:
Bible
CD
Activity Pak (Spring)
 pages 5, 16
 (figures 2, 10–13)
 Songbook
Bible Story Picture Cards

Supplies:
crayons or markers
several round containers
 such as oatmeal
 boxes or coffee cans
paper cut to fit around
 the containers
small pebbles or jingle
 bells
several simple puzzles
short-sleeved adult shirts
 that button down the
 front
long sheet of butcher
 paper
fingerpaint (see p. 233)
building blocks
stuffed animals
dolls
CD player
instruments
soapy water
dishrags
(optional: doll clothes,
 clothesline and
 clothespins)

Jesus Helps People...........................

Enter the Bible Story

Read Matthew 9:35: Jesus not only sat on a mountaintop, dispensing his wisdom, but he also came down into the villages and towns, spreading the word of God wherever he went.

Think About It: Jesus cared for individuals in his ministry. He looked at people and knew their individual needs. He did not have a "cookie cutter" ministry for all people. Reflect on the following questions as you prepare to teach your individual children this week: In what ways are your children alike? How do you consistently deal with them? How do you set up behavior guidelines that do not vary from child to child? In what ways are your children different? How do you vary your approach when encouraging children to listen to a story or to participate in an art activity? When we read about him in the Bible, we find Jesus ministering to many, many people. He ministered to others by serving them. He put people before things. He was more interested in the relationships he made than with entertaining people. He may have had many conversations about things, funny and serious, but he put people first. Jesus purely offered himself and used whatever he had on hand to help others better understand God. And he did all of this without suggesting that his deeds would lead to any earthly reward.

Through the Week: Read Matthew 9:35-38. It is easy to get overwhelmed with the needs of the world. Focus on the needs of your class, or perhaps on the needs of one of your children. Perhaps the best way to meet their needs is to simply play with them and tell them again and again how much God loves them.

Pray: Dear God, you know me inside and out. You know how many hairs are on my head and what my good intentions are. Thank you for loving me just as I am. Help me to love others in the same way. Amen.

The Story and Young Children

What does it mean to start where the learner is and then proceed? First you pray for God's help and guidance. Then you give time and attention to a child, playing with the child. Notice what activities seem to draw the child's attention. If a child is totally engrossed in an activity, do not make him or her move on to another one just because "it is time." Let the child take his or her own time. Likewise, sometimes a child is not interested in doing anything. It may be that he is tired or just in need of some extra "lap time." I have spent many sessions with a child on my lap, reading books, talking to other children, or playing with blocks. And I have had my share of children fall asleep in a book center filled with pillows. Knowing what a child is capable of at any given time takes a fair amount of intuition and observation over the long haul. Keep mental or physical notes on each child and develop a relationship with parents so that you will know the best way to lead each individual child.

Learning Centers

Conversation Center

You will need: several round containers (with lids) such as oatmeal boxes or coffee cans; paper cut to fit around the containers; crayons or markers, tape, small pebbles or jingle bells, short-sleeved adult shirts that button down the front; long sheet of butcher paper, fingerpaint (see p. 233).

Get ready: Cut paper to fit around the containers.

- Make Toys, Activity 1c
- Make a Helper Painting, Activity 3c

Building Center

You will need: building blocks, stuffed animals, dolls.

Get ready: Provide enough blocks for toddlers to share.

- Play With Blocks, Activity 3a

Discovery Center

You will need: several simple puzzles.

Get ready: Take pieces out of several puzzles.

- Play With Puzzles, Activity 3b

Storytelling Center

This should be an open area where you may gather children for storytelling, or to listen and respond to music. It would be helpful to have this center on a carpeted area.

You will need: Bible; Activity Pak—pp. 5, 16, (figures 2, 10-13); CD and CD player; Songbook; instruments.

Get ready: Prepare storytelling figures (see Activity Pak—p. 2).

- Tell the Bible Story, Activity 2a
- Play a Game, Activity 2b
- Retell the Bible Story, Activity 2c
- Enjoy Music, Activity 4a

Family Living Center

You will need: soapy water, dishrags (optional: doll clothes, clothesline and clothespins).

Get ready: Fill dishpans with a couple of inches of soapy water.

- Help Clean the House, Activity 1b

Jesus Helps People

Jesus loved all the people. Whenever he met new people, he would help them.

If they were sick, he made them feel better.

If they could not see, he fixed their eyes so they could see.

If they could not walk, he fixed their legs so they could walk.

If they were sad, he told them God loved them and made them happy.

Jesus helped people wherever he went.

1 Prepare

for the Story

a Welcome Each Child

Do this as each child enters.

Have the CD playing as children arrive.

Stoop to the children's eye level and welcome each child by name.

Say to each child: "I am so happy you have come to church today."

Be prepared to involve children in an interesting or comforting activity.

b Help Clean the House

Do this in the Family Living Center.

Gather two or three children. Help the children clean the items in the Family Living Center. They may wash the dishes and wipe the furniture with a damp rag.

Make sure that the teacher wrings the rag out before giving it to the child. You may even wash doll clothes and hang them on a clothesline.

As the children work, thank them for helping one another.

c Make Toys

Do this in the Conversation Center.

Gather two or three children. Let each child scribble on paper. Help the child put a handful of pebbles or jingle bells inside a round container.

Tape the scribble picture around the container. Encourage the child to roll his or her container on the floor to see what kind of sound it makes.

2 Tell

the Story

a Tell the Bible Story

Do this in the Storytelling Center.

Gather two or three children. **Say:** "Let me tell you another story about Jesus." (Show figure 2.) Put figures 10 and 12 on the flannelboard, replacing them with figures 11 and 13 as you tell the story.

Open a Bible and **say** the Bible verse: "Jesus said, 'Love one another.'" Encourage the children to say the Bible verse with you.

See if the children remember anything else Jesus said.

Pray: "Thank you, God, for helpers."

b Play a Game

Do this in the Storytelling Center.

Gather two or three children. Say the following action verse. This game will be similar to "Ring Around the Rosie."

Jesus walked around and around.
(*Hold hands and move in a circle.*)
The people followed around and around.
(*Hold hands and move in a circle.*)
Then Jesus stopped, and he sat down.
(*Drop hands and sit down.*)

"Love one another!"
(*Hold hands up high.*)

c Retell the Bible Story

Do this in the Storytelling Center.

Gather two or three children. Use the following action verse.

Jesus loved everyone.
(*Cross arms over your chest.*)
He was God's helper.
(*Put your thumbs up.*)
When Jesus saw a man who could not see,
(*Cover eyes with hands.*)
He helped him see again.
(*Remove hands.*)
When Jesus saw a man who could not walk,
(*Put both hands on legs.*)
He helped him walk again.
(*Remove hands and walk in place.*)
When Jesus saw a woman who was sad,
(*Put on a sad face.*)
He made her happy.
(*Smile.*)
Jesus said, "Love one another."
(*Cross arms over your chest.*)

3 Connect
with the Story

a Play With Blocks
Do this in the Building Center.

Gather one or two children. **Say:** "These animals and dolls need a home. We can help them! Can you build them a house with rooms for all of them?"

Encourage the children to build a house for the toys. Thank them for helping the toys.

b Play With Puzzles
Do this in the Discovery Center.

Gather two or three children. Show them the puzzles. Take the pieces out. **Say:** "Oh no! Who can help me get the puzzle pieces back in the puzzle?"

Let the children help you. Praise the children for being good helpers.

c Make a Helper Painting
Do this in the Conversation Center.

Ahead of time, tape the butcher paper to the table. Gather two or three children. Pour a "blob" of fingerpaint in front of each child. Encourage each child to spread the paint around.

As new children come up to paint, put a "blob" in a clean space on the paper. **Say:** "Look, we are helping to make a big painting. Everyone is helping."

When all the children have had a chance to fingerpaint, hang the picture on the wall for decoration.

4 Celebrate
the Story

a Enjoy Music
Do this in the Storytelling Center.

Sing "Jesus Loves Me" and "Love One Another" (Songbook, CD). Encourage the children to play instruments as accompaniment. Sing other songs that the children have learned this year.

b Clean Up

Gather two or three children. **Say:** "Jesus wants us to help others. One way we can help is by cleaning up our messes."

Make a game out of cleaning up. Ahead of time mark toy shelves with pictures so that the children can easily see where toys belong. Avoid saying, "(*Child's name*), please pick up this toy." This could get you into a power struggle. Rather, **say:** "I need someone to pick up this toy. Who could that someone be?" This will allow children to volunteer to clean up.

Then, if you heap lots of genuine praise on the volunteer, children will be running to help clean up and get the individual attention.

c Say Goodbye

Recall today's Bible story, encouraging children to say or sing the Bible verse with you.

Say: "I'm glad that (*name of child*) is a helper." Repeat this for each child in the class.

Pray: "Thank you, God, for helpers."

Be sure to have a teacher or helper at the door to match children with their caregivers.

Tell parents about today's Bible story and make sure that each child has today's Bible Story Picture Card. Show parents the "Nurturing Your Child's Faith" section of the card.

Point out the helper painting to the parents.

Tip
Help children begin to memorize Bible verses by repeating them again and again. Most of the verses this spring begin with "Jesus said . . ." Help the children hear the many things that Jesus said.

Look Back
What activities went particularly well today? With what activities did you or the children have trouble? What activities will you want to repeat next week?

Did all of the children have a chance to experience the Bible story this week?

Can the children retell the story?

Look Ahead
Count ahead and make sure that you have scheduled your Palm Sunday lesson on Palm Sunday and your Easter lesson on Easter. Arrange the other lessons around these two Sundays. Note that you will need to combine one or two lessons in order to cover all of the material within three months.

Luke 18:1

Jesus wants us to talk to God by praying.

Bible Verse:
Jesus said to always pray.
(Luke 18:1, *Good News Bible*, adapted)

Resources:
Bible
CD
Activity Pak (Spring)
  pages 5, 8
  (figures 1, 3, 4, 6–9)
  page 11 (Jesus
  Praying" picture)
  Songbook
Bible Story Picture Cards

Supplies:
play dough (see p. 232)
several simple puzzles
CD player
paper
tempera paint
paintbrush
pan of warm soapy water
building blocks
instruments
dolls
simple snack food
napkins
cups

Jesus Said, "Always Pray".............

Enter the Bible Story

Read Luke 18:1: As his disciples faced hard times, Jesus reminded them to pray always and to not lose heart.

Think About It: Why would Jesus say, "Always pray?" Why would God want you to *always pray*? Does this sound too pious? too intimate? too painful? Now, we all know that prayer requires focusing on God. Focusing requires concentration, and that takes time. Who has time anymore? In this day and age no one has time to stop and be still for prayers every waking minute. So many of us are desperate to be closer to God. And yet we're not. We continue in the same old routines. Reflect on the following as you prepare to teach your children this week: Does one need to stop and be still to pray? Is prayer a posture, an attitude, and/or a relationship? How will you actively and quietly teach prayerful attitudes to the young child? Jesus said, "Always pray," and then went on to tell the parable of the persistent widow. She went before an uncaring judge who didn't fear God and begged that she be treated fairly. After many requests were made, the judge finally saw to it that the widow received justice. The widow persisted, and the unloving judge granted justice. Think of how much more our loving, caring God will bring justice to the attentive heart. Read the parable of the persistent widow, Luke 18:1-8.

Through the Week: Look through the psalms and find a prayer that expresses your thoughts and feelings. Or use the prayer in today's lesson. Learn your prayer and hide it in your heart. Pray it.

Pray: Dear God, I ask only one thing: Let me live in your house every day of my life, to see how wonderful you are and to pray in your temple. Amen. (Psalm 27:4, paraphrased)

The Story and Young Children

A two-year-old is a bundle of energy: walking, climbing, and exploring. It can be difficult to entice the child to sit still for prayer. But you're up to the challenge, aren't you? The tender young child's spirit is open, accepting, and searching for something to love and adore. Show your children what prayer is. Who will teach them if you don't?

Here's the real challenge! Remember even the two-year-old needs both quiet and active periods throughout his or her waking day. Put on your observation cap and reel up that antenna. As you perceive the child's spirit to be receptive, teach that child. One child may be quiet and responsive; while another may be active and responsive. What would really happen if you just jumped in and worked with each child individually?

Learning Centers

Work with two or three children at a time in each learning center.

Conversation Center

You will need: play dough (see p. 232), newspaper, marker, paper, tempera paint, paintbrush, pan of warm soapy water, simple snack food, napkins, cups.

Get ready: Make or buy play dough.

- Play With Play Dough, Activity 1c
- Make Handprint Paintings, Activity 3c
- Have a Snack, Activity 4b

Discovery Center

You will need: several simple puzzles.

- Play With Puzzles, Activity 3b

Building Center

You will need: building blocks.

Get ready: Provide enough blocks for toddlers to share.

- Play With Blocks, Activity 1b

Storytelling Center

This should be an open area where you may gather children for storytelling, or to listen and respond to music. It would be helpful to have this center on a carpeted area.

You will need: Activity Pak—pp. 5 and 8 (figures 1, 3, 4, 6-9), p. 11 ("Jesus Praying" picture); CD and CD player; Songbook; Bible; instruments.

Get ready: Prepare storytelling figures (see Activity Pak—p. 2).

- Tell the Bible Story, Activity 2a
- Listen to a Prayer Song, Activity 2b
- Retell the Bible Story, Activity 2c
- Sing a Song, Activity 3a
- Enjoy Music, Activity 4a

Family Living Center

You will need: dolls.

- Play With Dolls, Activity 1d

Jesus Teaches About Prayer

Jesus told all the people that God loves them. Jesus loved God. He talked to God every day.

Talking to God is called praying.

Jesus told all of the people to pray. He said to pray all the time.

1 Prepare

for the Story

a Welcome Each Child
Do this as each child enters.

Have the CD playing as children arrive. Stoop to the children's eye level and welcome each child by name.

Say to each child: "I am so happy you have come to church today."

Be prepared to involve children in an interesting or comforting activity.

b Play With Blocks
Do this in the Building Center

Encourage the children to have fun with the blocks. As they work, **say:** "I am so happy for blocks. I want to pray. Thank you, God, for blocks. Amen."

c Play With Play Dough
Do this in the Conversation Center.

Prepare play dough ahead of time using the recipe on page 232. Or purchase prepared play dough.

Let the children manipulate play dough as they desire. If you want, provide cookie cutters or round blocks for rolling the dough. As you work, **say:** "I am so happy for play dough. I want to pray. Thank you, God, for play dough. Amen."

d Play With Dolls
Do this in the Family Living Center.

As the children play with the various dolls in the Family Living Center, offer a prayer thanking God for all the wonderful toys that you have.

2 Tell

the Story

a Tell the Bible Story
Do this in the Storytelling Center.

Gather two or three children. **Say:** "Jesus' helpers had many questions. Let me tell you a story about when they asked Jesus about talking to God." Tell the Bible story, using the storytelling figures (figures 1, 3, 4, 6–9) at appropriate times.

Open a Bible and **say** the Bible verse: "Jesus said to always pray." Encourage the children to say the Bible verse with you. Ask the children if they remember anything else that Jesus said.

Pray: "Thank you, God, for everything."

b Listen to a Prayer Song
Do this in the Storytelling Center.

Play "Prayer Song" (Songbook, CD) while the children have their eyes closed and their hands folded.

c Retell the Bible Story
Do this in the Storytelling Center.

Gather two or three children. Look at the picture of Jesus praying (Activity Pak— p. 11). How do we know he is praying? (Most likely the children *don't* know, so you will have to tell them how *you* know he is praying. **Say:** "Jesus told his friends to pray. Let's pray together." Do the following finger play:

Open and shut, open and shut,
(*Open fingers wide and then close into a fist.*)
Put your hands away.
(*Put hands in your lap.*)
Open and shut, open and shut,
(*Open fingers wide and then close into a fist.*)
Now it's time to pray.
(*Fold hands together as for prayer.*)

Pray: "Thank you, God, for Jesus. Amen."

 **Connect**

with the Story

a **Sing a Song**

Do this in the Storytelling Center.

Sing the following song to the tune of "This is the Way."

This is the way we fold our hands
Fold our hands, fold our hands.
This is the way we fold our hands,
To pray to God.
This is the way we bow our heads
Bow our heads, bow our heads.
This is the way we bow our heads,
To pray to God.
This is the way we close our eyes,
Close our eyes, close our eyes.
This is the way we close our eyes
To pray to God.

b **Play With Puzzles**

Do this in the Discovery Center.

Gather two or three children. Show them the puzzles. Take the pieces out. **Say:**

"Oh no! Who can help me get the puzzle pieces back in the puzzle?" Let the children help you.

Praise the children for being good helpers. **Say:** "I am so happy to have such wonderful helpers. I want to thank God for my helpers." Bow your head and fold your hands. **Say:** "Thank you, God, for (*child's name*) and (*child's name*)."

c **Make Handprint Paintings**

Do this in the Conversation Center.

Protect the table top by covering it with newspaper. Ask the children to come to you one at a time. Use the paintbrush to brush paint on their hands.

Guide the children in placing their hands on a piece of paper. You may choose to place the handprints on top of one another. Across the top of the paper write, "We Fold Our Hands to Pray."

 Celebrate

the Story

a **Enjoy Music**

Do this in the Storytelling Center.

Sing "Jesus Loves Me" and "Love One Another" (Songbook, CD). Encourage the children to play instruments as accompaniment. Sing other songs that the children have learned this year.

b **Have a Snack**

Do this in the Conversation Center.

Gather two or three children. Have them help you set the table for a snack. Make sure they wash their hands first. The children may be able to set out napkins or cups. Praise the children for their help.

Before you serve the snack, ask each child to pray with you. **Say:** "Let's pray. I'll say the words first. Thank you, God, for our food. Now you say the words. Thank you, God, for our food. Amen."

c **Say Goodbye**

Recall today's Bible story, encouraging children to say the Bible verse with you.

Say: "I'm glad that (*name of child*) is a helper." Repeat this for each child in the class.

Pray: "Thank you, God, for (*name of child*)."

Be sure to have a teacher or helper at the door to match children with their caregivers.

Tell parents about today's Bible story and make sure that each child has today's Bible Story Picture Card. Show parents the "Nurturing Your Child's Faith" section of the card.

Be sure the children take home their Handprint Pictures.

Tip

Use prayer often when you work with children. Modeling is the best way to teach young children about prayer.

Look Back

What activities went particularly well today? With what activities did you or the children have trouble? What activities will you want to repeat next week?

Did all of the children have a chance to experience the Bible story this week?

Can the children retell the story?

Look Ahead

Count ahead and make sure that you have scheduled your Palm Sunday lesson on Palm Sunday and your Easter lesson on Easter. Arrange the other lessons around these two Sundays. Note that you will need to cover all of the materials within three months.

143

Jesus taught his friends how to talk to God in prayer.

Bible Verse:
Jesus said to always pray. (Luke 18:1, *Good News Bible*, adapted)

Resources:
Bible
CD
Activity Pak (Spring)
    pages 5, 8
    (figures 1, 3, 4, 6–9)
    page 11 ("Jesus Praying" picture)
    Songbook
Bible Story Picture Cards

Supplies:
several simple puzzles
CD player
glue
3- to 5-ounce paper cups
pictures cut from a magazine
paper
marker
simple snack
napkins
cups
building blocks
grocery items
favorite toy or stuffed animal

Teach Us to Pray..........................

Enter the Bible Story

Read Luke 11:1-2: While Jesus exhorted his disciples to pray, they confessed their own insecurities in prayer and begged Jesus to teach them how, just as John the Baptizer had done.

Think About It: The Lord's Prayer is the model prayer that Jesus taught his disciples. It begins with praise to God, putting God first. When we focus on God first, we open our minds, hearts, souls, and strength to God's authority and power. Only after we give God first place can we put everything else in the proper perspective. If God does not come first, our prayer lists may quickly resemble our grocery lists. The Lord's Prayer then beckons God to establish God's kingdom on earth as it is in heaven. Jesus said the kingdom of heaven is both now and at hand, meaning God's kingdom is shown through our present relationship with Jesus Christ and it is also our future hope in heaven.

Psalm 9:10 says, "And those who know your name put their trust in you, for you, O LORD, have not forsaken those who seek you." A person's name in Hebrew has a greater meaning than simply the name by which a person is called. The name means the whole character of the person as known. When we say, "hallowed be your name," we mean we joyfully put our trust in God, the one we know has never and will never abandon us.

Through the Week: Write a prayer in your own words. Use five or six words. Tell the children that you wrote a prayer just for them. Pray it. Then observe how God uses your prayer. Observe any differences in the atmosphere of your classroom after you prayed? in the children? in you?

Pray: Dear God, let your name be held in reverence and let your kingdom come. Amen.

The Story and Young Children

In a classroom that uses learning centers, the child initiates the learning activity by naturally playing and exploring the activities that the teacher sets up. The teacher fully participates with the child—working, playing, and responding. The teacher lovingly responds and verbalizes what is happening. The child learns more about prayer, play, decision-making, and problem-solving than when the teacher initiates the learning activity.

Learning Centers

Work with two or three children at a time in each learning center.

Conversation Center

You will need: paper, glue, small paper cups, pictures cut from a magazine, marker, simple snack, napkins, cups.

Get ready: Gather the children around a table and sit down with them; engage them in conversation. Cut pictures out of magazines of things the children might want to thank God for.

- Make a Prayer Collage, Activity 3c
- Have a Snack, Activity 4b

Building Center

Provide enough blocks for toddlers to share. You may use wooden unit blocks or large cardboard or plastic blocks.

Family Living Center

You will need: grocery store items (see session 9).

Get ready: Prepare and set out items for a pretend grocery store.

- Play Grocery Store, Activity 1d

Storytelling Center

This should be an open area where you may gather children for storytelling, or to listen and respond to music. It would be helpful to have this center on a carpeted area.

You will need: CD and CD player, Songbook; Activity Pak—pp. 5, 8 (figures 1, 3, 4, 6-9); p. 11 (Jesus praying picture); favorite toy or stuffed animal.

Get ready: Prepare storytelling figures (see Activity Pak—p. 2).

- Welcome a Visitor, Activity 1c
- Tell the Bible Story, Activity 2a
- Retell the Bible Story, Activity 2b
- Listen to a Prayer Song, Activity 2c
- Sing a Song, Activity 3a
- Enjoy Music, Activity 4a

Discovery Center

You will need: several simple puzzles.

Get ready: Set out puzzles.

- Play With Puzzles, Activity 3b

Teach Us to Pray

Jesus told the people that God loved them. The people listened to Jesus.

Jesus said to pray. But the people said, "We don't know how to pray."

So Jesus told them how to pray. He said, "When you pray, say, 'Dear God, you are great. Thank you for loving me. Amen.'"

1 Prepare

for the Story

a Welcome Each Child
Do this as each child enters.

Have the CD playing as children arrive.

Stoop to the children's eye level and welcome each child by name.

Say to each child: "I am so happy you have come to church today."

Be prepared to involve children in an interesting or comforting activity.

b Prayers of Thanksgiving
This can be done in any center.

As the children play with toys this week, offer up prayers of thanksgiving for each toy, much as you did last week.

Encourage the children to pray with you. **Say:** "God, you are great. Thank you for this (*name of toy*). Amen."

c Welcome a Visitor
Do this in the Storytelling Center.

Invite your pastor to visit the classroom this week. Have the pastor hold a toy or stuffed animal that the children enjoy.

As the children wander over to the pastor, ask her or him to chat with them.

Ask the pastor to bless each child by placing his or her hand on the child's head and **saying**: "God bless you."

d Play Grocery Store
Do this in the Family Living Center.

Invite the children to play grocery store this week. Be sure to thank God for all the wonderful food.

2 Tell

the Story

a Tell the Bible Story
Do this in the Storytelling Center.

Gather two or three children. **Say:** "Jesus' helpers asked many questions. Let me tell you a story about when they asked Jesus for help." Tell the Bible story, using the storytelling figures (figures 1, 3, 4, 6–9) at appropriate times.

Open a Bible and **say** the Bible verse: "Jesus said to always pray." Encourage the children to say the Bible verse with you. Ask the children if they remember anything else Jesus said.

Pray: "Thank you, God, for everything."

b Retell the Bible Story
Do this in the Storytelling Center.

Gather two or three children. Look at the picture of Jesus praying (Activity Pak—p. 11). How do we know he is praying? (Most likely the children *don't* know, so you will have to tell them how *you* know he is praying.)

Say: "Jesus told his friends to pray. Let's pray together."

Do the following fingerplay:

Open and shut, open and shut,
(*Open fingers wide and then close into a fist.*)
Put your hands away.
(*Put hands in your lap.*)
Open and shut, open and shut,
(*Open fingers wide and then close into a fist.*)
Now it's time to pray.
(*Fold hands together as if in prayer.*)

Pray: "Thank you, God, for Jesus."

c Listen to a Prayer Song
Do this in the Storytelling Center.

Play "Prayer Song" (Songbook, CD) while the children have their eyes closed and their hands folded.

3 Connect
with the Story

a Sing a Song
Do this in the Storytelling Center.

Sing the following song to the tune of "This is the Way."

This is the way we fold our hands,
Fold our hands, fold our hands.
This is the way we fold our hands
To pray to God.
This is the way we bow our heads,
Bow our heads, bow our heads.
This is the way we bow our heads
To pray to God
This is the way we close our eyes, close
Our eyes, close our eyes.
This is the way we close our eyes
To pray to God.

b Play With Puzzles
Do this in the Discovery Center.

Gather two or three children. Show them the puzzles. Take the pieces out. **Say:**

"Oh no! Who can help me get the puzzle pieces back in the puzzle?" Let the children help you. Praise the children for being good helpers.

Say: "I am so happy to have such wonderful helpers. I want to thank God for my helpers." Bow your head and fold your hands. **Say:** "Thank you, God, for (*child's name*) and (*child's name*)."

c Make a Prayer Collage
Do this in the Conversation Center.

Give each child a piece of paper. Write along the top of the paper "I Thank God For:"

Pour a small amount of glue in the paper cups. Show the children how to "touch" the glue and then "touch" the paper to place a small amount of glue on it. Invite the children to glue pictures of things they would like to thank God for onto their paper.

4 Celebrate
the Story

a Enjoy Music
Do this in the Storytelling Center.

Sing "Jesus Loves Me" and "Love One Another" (Songbook, CD). Encourage the children to play instruments as accompaniment. Sing other songs that the children have learned this year.

b Have a Snack
Do this in the Conversation Center.

Gather two or three children. Have them help you set the table for a snack. Make sure they wash their hands first. The children may be able to set out napkins or cups. Praise the children for their help.

Before you serve the snack, ask each child to pray with you. **Say:** "Let's pray. I'll say the words first. Thank you, God, for our food. Now you say the words: Thank you, God, for our food. Amen."

c Say Goodbye
Recall today's Bible story, encouraging children to say or sing the Bible verse with you.

Say: "I'm glad that (*name of child*) is a helper." Repeat this for each child in the class.

Pray: "Thank you, God, for (*name of child*)."

Be sure to have a teacher or helper at the door to match children with their caregivers.

Tell parents about today's Bible story and make sure that each child has today's Bible Story Picture Card. Show parents the "Nurturing Your Child's Faith" section of the card.

Show parents the Prayer Collage and encourage them to pray at home with their child.

Tip
Continue to model prayer as you work with the children in each center.

Look Back
What activities went particularly well today?

With what activities did you or the children have trouble? What activities will you want to repeat next week?

Did all of the children have a chance to experience the Bible story this week? Can the children retell the Bible story?

Look Ahead
Count ahead and make sure that you have scheduled your Palm Sunday lesson on Palm Sunday and your Easter lesson on Easter. Arrange the other lessons around these two Sundays. Note that you will need to combine one or two lessons in order to cover all of the material within three months.

God loves us and looks for us when we go away.

Bible Verse:
Jesus said, "Follow me." (Matthew 4:19, adapted)

Resources:
Bible
CD
sheep patterns (p. 236)
Activity Pak (Spring)
    page 17
    (figures 15–18)
    Songbook
Bible Story Picture Cards

Supplies:
glue
3- to 5-oz. paper cups
cotton balls
large building blocks
identical items to hide
    around the room,
    such as blocks or
    pieces of a
    manipulative toy
CD player
toy pets (dogs, cats,
    birds) and items to
    take care of them,
    such as feeding
    dishes, pet beds,
    grooming brushes,
    and so forth
soft items such as
    cotton balls, fabric
    scraps, loosely wound
    yarn, terry cloth towel

God Loves You..

Enter the Bible Story

Read Luke 15:3-10: When the Pharisees and the scribes complained that Jesus welcomed and ate with sinners, Jesus answered them with the two parables recorded in these verses.

Think About It: The parables of the lost sheep and the lost coin illustrate for us God's seeking love. Just as the woman rejoiced when she found her coin and the shepherd rejoiced when he found his sheep, God rejoices when we are found after wandering away. Reflect on the following questions as you prepare to tell these stories and to help the children retell them: Look back on your own life. In what ways has God sought you? Are there particular events or people through which you have clearly felt the love of God? What opportunities have you had to show God's seeking love to others? In what ways can you show that love to the children in your class?

Shepherds and sheep are mentioned often in the Bible. Shepherding was a major occupation in Bible times. In the Old Testament the leaders of God's people were often referred to as shepherds. Shepherd and sheep imagery continued into New Testament times and was used by Jesus himself. The parable of the lost coin is found only in Luke. Some scholars notice that Luke is more likely to include stories about women and to include stories where a woman can be used to represent God.

Through the Week: Check your library for "The Runaway Bunny" by Margaret Wise Brown. Remember that no matter where we go, God will look for us and find us and welcome us home.

Pray: Thank you, God, for your seeking, rejoicing love. Thank you for moving in my life through events and other people. Use me to show your love to others, especially those I teach.

The Story and Young Children

Young children can hear that God loves them, but to a toddler, God is a totally abstract concept that has no real meaning. Young children experience God's love through God's representatives—their parents and the adults whom they encounter in God's house. In other words you represent God to a young child. Children who feel loved and accepted by adults when they are young have an easy time believing that God loves them when they are older. Children who do not learn to trust adults when they are young have a difficult time trusting in God when they reach adolescence. Never doubt that what you are doing is important!

Learning Centers

Work with two or three children at a time in each learning center.

Conversation Center

You will need: sheep pattern (page 236), glue, small paper cups, cotton balls, CD and CD player, Activity Pak Songbook.

Get ready: Photocopy the sheep pattern (p. 236), one for each child. Gather the children around a table and sit down with them; engage them in conversation.

• Make Sheep, Activity 3c

Building Center

You will need: large building blocks.

Get ready: Provide enough blocks for toddlers to share.

• Pretend to Be Sheep, Activity 3b

Discovery Center

You will need: several soft items such as cotton balls, fabric scraps, loosely wound yarn, terry cloth towel.

Get ready: Place items on a low table.

• Touch Softies, Activity 1b

Family Living Center

You will need: toy pets (dogs, cats, birds) and things to take care of them, such as feeding dishes, pet beds, grooming brushes, and so forth.

Get ready: Set the pet items within easy reach of the children.

• Care for Pets, Activity 4b

Storytelling Center

You will need: identical items to hide around the room, such as blocks or pieces of a manipulative toy; Activity Pak—p. 17 (figures 15–18); CD and CD player, Songbook; Bible.

Get ready: Prepare storytelling figures (see Activity Pak—p. 2).

• Play a Lost and Found Game, Activity 1c
• Tell the Bible Story, Activity 2a
• Sing a Song, Activity 2b
• Tell Another Bible Story, Activity 2c
• Sing a Song, Activity 3a
• Enjoy Music, Activity 4a

The Lost Sheep

The shepherd counted the sheep. "Oh, no!" he said. "One of my sheep is not here!" He went looking for the lost sheep. He looked under the bushes. He looked behind the rocks. He looked in the grass field. He looked beside the river. Where was the sheep?

"Baah! Baah!" He heard the sheep. He looked into the valley. There was the sheep with her foot caught on a tree. The shepherd picked up the sheep and took her back home.

He called his friends. He said, "I am so happy! One of my sheep was lost, and I found her!"

1 Prepare

....

for the Story

a **Welcome Each Child**

Do this as each child enters.

Have the CD playing as children arrive.

Stoop to the children's eye level and welcome each child by name.

Say to each child: "I am so happy you have come to church today."

Be prepared to involve children in an interesting or comforting activity.

b **Touch Softies**

Do this in the Discovery Center.

Gather two or three children. Encourage the children to touch the items you have placed on the table.

Talk about the items and encourage the children to notice how soft they are.

Contrast this with the top of the table. Press the child's finger onto the table top and **say**: "hard." Then touch the soft items and **say**: "soft."

Be aware that children of this age are just learning the words *soft* and *hard*.

c **Play a Lost and Found Game**

Do this in the Storytelling Center.

Hide items around the room. Gather two or three children. Show the children a block. **Say**: "I lost a block that looks just like this. Can you help me find it?"

Accompany the children while they look for the block. When you find the block, celebrate by **saying**: "Hooray! We found the block! (or other toy)."

2 Tell

....

the Story

a **Tell the Bible Story**

Do this in the Storytelling Center.

Gather two or three children. **Say:** "Today I want to tell you a story that Jesus told." Tell the Bible story, using the storytelling figures (figures 15–16) at appropriate times.

Open a Bible and **say** the Bible verse: "Jesus said, 'Follow me.'" Encourage the children to say the Bible verse with you. Invite the children to remember other things that Jesus said.

Pray: "Thank you, God, for people who love us."

b **Sing a Song**

Do this in the Storytelling Center.

Say: "The shepherd loved his sheep and the woman loved her coin enough to look for them when they were lost. God loves us like that."

Play "Show How Much God Loves Us" (Songbook, CD). Add the suggested verses.

c **Tell Another Bible Story**

Do this in the Storytelling Center.

Gather two or three children. **Say:** "Let me tell you another story that Jesus told." Tell the story, using the storytelling figures (figures 17–18) at appropriate times.

Once there was a woman. She had lost a piece of money. She was very sad because she needed the money to get some food. She looked under the table. It was not there! She looked behind the chair. It was not there! She looked under the bed. It was not there! She looked behind the water jar. There it was! The woman was so happy, she ran to tell her friends that she had found her lost coin.

3 Connect

with the Story

a | Sing a Song
Do this in the Storytelling Center.

Sing the following song to the tune of "Twinkle, Twinkle, Little Star."

"Bah, bah, bah, bah," goes the sheep.
"Bah, bah," 'til he falls asleep.
When he wakes another day,
"Bah, bah, bah," is what he'll say.
"Bah, bah, bah, bah," goes the sheep.
"Bah, bah," 'til he falls asleep.

b | Pretend to Be Sheep
Do this in the Building Center.

Gather two or three children. Let the children help build a sheepfold by making a circle of large blocks with an opening on one side for a door. Tell the children that sheep like to follow one another.

Let the children pretend to be sheep, crawling follow-the-leader style about the room, going into the sheepfold, and lying down to sleep. Then pretend it is morning and have the sheep wake up and start again.

c | Make Sheep
Do this in the Conversation Center.

Gather two or three children. Give each child a copy of the sheep template (p. 236) and several cotton balls.

Show the children how to dip the cotton ball into the glue and then stick it on the paper. Allow the children to fill the outline of the sheep with cotton.

While the children work, sing "The Bah Bah Song" (Songbook, CD).

4 Celebrate

the Story

a | Enjoy Music
Do this in the Storytelling Center.

Sing "Jesus Loves Me" and "Love One Another." Also sing "Show How Much God Loves Us" and "The Bah Bah Song" (Songbook CD).

Sing other songs that the children have learned this year. If you wish, let the children accompany themselves with instruments.

b | Care for Pets
Do this in the Family Living Center.

As the children play in the Family Living Center, invite them to care for the pets they find there.

Engage the children in conversation about how to care for pets: What do they like to eat? Where do they like to sleep?

c | Say Goodbye
Recall today's Bible story, encouraging children to say or sing the Bible verse with you.

Say: "I'm glad that God loves (*name of child*)." Repeat this for each child in the class.

Pray: "Thank you, God, for (*name of child*)."

Be sure to have a teacher or helper at the door to match children with their caregivers.

Tell parents about today's Bible story and make sure that each child has today's Bible Story Picture Card. Show parents the "Nurturing Your Child's Faith" section of the card.

Be sure the children take home their Sheep Pictures.

Tip
When asking toddlers to look for something, remember to always show them an identical item to the "lost" item. Toddlers do not always have the vocabulary to understand spoken directions without a visual clue to back them up.

Look Back
What activities went particularly well today? With what activities did you or the children have trouble?

What activities will you want to repeat next week?

Did all of the children have a chance to experience the Bible stories this week? Can the children retell the stories?

Look Ahead
Count ahead and make sure that you have scheduled your Palm Sunday lesson on Palm Sunday and your Easter lesson on Easter. Arrange the other lessons around these two Sundays. Note that you will need to combine one or two lessons in order to cover all of the material within three months.

Session

John 13:34

Jesus wants us to love others, just as he loves us.

Bible Verse:
Jesus said, "Love one another." (John 15:12, adapted)

Resources:
Bible
CD
heart pattern (page 235)
Activity Pak (Spring)
  pages 5, 8
  (figures 1, 3, 4, 6–9)
Songbook
Bible Story Picture Cards

Supplies:
play dough
CD player
heart-shaped cookie
  cutters
construction paper
small squares of tissue
  paper
small paper cups
building blocks
toy cars, trucks, trains,
  or boats
dolls and items to take
  care of them
heart shapes cut from
  material scraps of
  different textures such
  as felt, velvet,
  corduroy, dotted
  swiss, satin, and
  posterboard
glue
teacher scissors

Love One Another...........

Enter the Bible Story

Read John 13:34: Jesus gave a new commandment to his disciples: that they love one another, just as he loved them.

Think About It: Jesus' commandment to his followers to love others continues down through the generations of Jesus' followers to us today. Reflect on the following questions as you prepare to teach this lesson: How do others know that you are a follower of Jesus? Is the love of others apparent in the way you live your life? In what ways do you express this love? Teaching young children is one way that you express love and show yourself to be a follower of Jesus. What opportunities do you have in the classroom to show love? Are there particular children who are in special need of your love?

John 13 and the following chapters record the events and Jesus' words during his last hours with his disciples. It seems to have been a time of great confusion for the disciples. They often did not seem to understand what Jesus was saying. They asked him a number of questions. They did not even seem to understand when Jesus indicated that Judas would betray him and then sent him out to do it quickly. But Jesus' command to his disciples to love one another did not bring questions. It was a clear statement: "I have loved you, and you, in like manner, are to love others. Others will know you are my followers by your love."

Through the Week: We are in the midst of three sessions emphasizing love. In the previous session children heard that God loves them. In both this session and the next, we will be helping children understand that Jesus loves his friends and that we too should love others. Target specific ways that you wish to show love to your students and specific behaviors that you want your students to use to show love.

Pray: Dear God, help me remember to show love to others as Jesus did. Let me be a witness to my faith by acting in loving ways. Let my relationships with the children I teach reflect your love that Jesus showed to us.

The Story and Young Children

Young children learn to show love in many ways. We teach them to give hugs and kisses, and we guide them in not hurting others. When a child inadvertently hurts another, teach him or her to say, "I'm sorry" and either give a hug or a pat on the back. Be alert for aggressive behavior such as biting, which usually occurs when a child cannot figure out any other way of expressing frustration and anger. Encourage the children to use words such as "No" or "I don't like that!" instead of hitting or biting.

By now the children have heard several references to Jesus and what he wants us to do; saying that Jesus wants us to love each other is starting to make some sense. Talk to the children about what it means to love one another.

Learning Centers

Work with two or three children at a time in each learning center.

Conversation Center

You will need: play dough, heart-shaped cookie cutters; construction paper, heart pattern (p. 235), small squares of tissue paper, glue, small paper cups.

Get ready: Photocopy the heart pattern (p. 235) onto construction paper.

- Play With Play Dough, Activity 1c
- Make Heart Pictures, Activity 4b

Building Center

You will need: building blocks; toy cars, trucks, trains, or boats.

Get ready: Provide enough blocks for toddlers to share.

- Travel to Show Love, Activity 3c

Storytelling Center

This should be an open area where you may gather children for storytelling, or to listen and respond to music. It would be helpful to have this center on a carpeted area.

You will need: Activity Pak—pp. 5, 8 (figures 1, 3, 4, 6–9); CD and CD player, Songbook; Bible.

Get ready: Prepare storytelling figures (see Activity Pak—p. 2).

- Tell the Bible Story, Activity 2a
- Sing a Song, Activity 2b
- Retell the Bible Story, Activity 2c
- Sing a Song, Activity 3b
- Enjoy Music, Activity 4a

Family Living Center

You will need: dolls and items to take care of them.

- Show Love to Dolls, Activity 3a

Discovery Center

You will need: heart shapes cut from material scraps of different textures such as felt, velvet, corduroy, dotted swiss, satin, and posterboard; glue; teacher scissors.

Get ready: Cut out heart shapes from material scraps of different textures such as felt, velvet, corduroy, dotted swiss, and satin. Glue the heart shapes to a piece of posterboard.

- Feel Textured Hearts, Activity 1b

Love One Another

Jesus was with his friends.
"I have something important to tell you," Jesus said. "I love you very much. I want you to love one another like I love you. When people see you showing love to one another, they will know that you are my friends."

1 Prepare

for the Story

a Welcome Each Child

Do this as each child enters.

Have the CD playing as the children arrive. Stoop to the children's eye level and welcome each child by name.

Say to each child: "I am so happy you have come to church today."

Be prepared to involve children in an interesting or comforting activity.

b Feel Textured Hearts

Do this in the Discovery Center.

Ahead of time glue the heart shapes you have cut out to a piece of posterboard.

Gather two or three children. Let the children explore the textures of the hearts. Give them words to describe the various textures (smooth, soft, bumpy). If you have older children, you may wish to make matching cards with the textured hearts. Ask the children to match the hearts by feeling them.

c Play With Play Dough

Do this in the Conversation Center.

Prepare play dough ahead of time using the recipe on page 232. Or purchase prepared play dough.

Let the children manipulate play dough as they desire. Provide heart-shaped cookie cutters and round blocks for rolling the dough. Tell the children that heart shapes remind us that we are loved and that Jesus wants us to love each other.

2 Tell

the Story

a Tell the Bible Story

Do this in the Storytelling Center.

Gather two or three children. **Say:** "Let me tell you another story about Jesus." Tell the Bible story, using the storytelling figures (figures 1, 3, 4, 6–9) at appropriate times.

Open a Bible and **say** the Bible verse: "Jesus said, 'Love one another.'" Encourage the children to say the Bible verse with you.

Pray: "Thank you, God, for people who love us."

b Sing a Song

Do this in the Storytelling Center.

Gather two or three children. Play "Love One Another" (Songbook, CD). Encourage the children to dance to the music. Repeat the song and invite the children to sing along.

c Retell the Bible Story

Do this in the Storytelling Center.

Use the following litany, encouraging the children to say: "Love one another.".

Jesus said to Peter: "Love one another."
Jesus said to Andrew: "Love one another."
Jesus said to James: "Love one another."
Jesus said to John: "Love one another."
Jesus said to Mary: "Love one another."
Jesus said to Martha: "Love one another."

You may wish to continue the litany with the names of your children.

3 Connect
with the Story

a **Show Love to Dolls**
Do this in the Family Living Center.

As children play in the Family Living Center with the dolls, engage them in conversation.

Say: "It looks like you love that doll an awful lot. You are taking good care of him."

b **Sing a Song**
Do this in the Storytelling Center.

Sing the following song to the tune of "This Is the Way."

I can show love to everyone,
Everyone, everyone.
I can show love to everyone
With a great big smile. (*Smile.*)
I can show love to everyone,

Everyone, everyone.
I can show love to everyone
With a great big hug. (*Hug each other.*)

c **Travel to Show Love**
Do this in the Building Center.

Invite the children to build block roads on which to play with the cars and trucks. Invite them to build block railroad tracks for the train.

As the children play with the transportation toys, **say:** "Let's pretend we are going to show love to others. How shall we go?"

If the children choose a car, for example, help them make the car move across the room and pretend to tell someone that they are loved.

4 Celebrate
the Story

a **Enjoy Music**
Do this in the Storytelling Center.

Sing "Jesus Loves Me" and "Love One Another." Also sing "Show How Much God Loves Us" and "The Bah Bah Song" (Songbook, CD). Sing other songs that the children have learned this year.

b **Make Heart Pictures**
Do this in the Conversation Center.

Use the heart pattern (see p. 235) to place a heart in the center of a piece of construction paper. Many copy machines will allow you to run construction paper through them.

Pour a small amount of glue in the bottom of paper cups.

Gather two or three children. Give each child a piece of paper with a heart drawn on it. Show the children how to crumple a square of tissue paper, dip it in glue, and place it on the heart. Encourage the children to place the tissue inside the heart, but do not be upset if they ignore the heart template.

When the children have decorated their heart with crumpled tissue paper, tell them to give their picture to someone whom they love.

c **Say Goodbye**

Recall today's Bible story, encouraging children to say or sing the Bible verse with you.

Say: "I'm glad that God loves (*name of child*). I love you too." Repeat this for each child in the class.

Pray: "Thank you, God, for (*name of child*)."

Be sure to have a teacher or helper at the door to match children with their caregivers.

Tell parents about today's Bible story and make sure that each child has today's Bible Story Picture Card. Show parents the "Nurturing Your Child's Faith" section of the card. Be sure the children take home their Heart Pictures.

Session

38

John 13:34

Jesus wants us to love others, just as he loves us.

Bible Verse:
Jesus said, "Love one another." (John 15:12, adapted)

Resources:
Bible
CD
Activity Pak (Spring)
    pages 5, 8
    (figures 2–4, 6–9)
    Songbook
Bible Story Picture Cards

Supplies:
play dough
CD player
heart-shaped cookie
    cutters
paper plates
black marker
paper punch
colored yarn
crayons or markers
dolls and items to take
    care of them
heart shapes cut from
    scraps of different
    textures, such as felt,
    velvet, corduroy,
    dotted swiss, satin,
    and posterboard
building blocks
toy cars, trucks, trains,
    or boats
glue
teacher scissors

Love One Another.................

Enter the Bible Story

Read John 13:34: Jesus' commandment to his disciples to love one another was given to them at the last meal they had together. Jesus told them that their love for one another would be the sign to others that they were his disciples.

Think About It: Review the "Think About It" section in the previous session. Think again about the questions posed there. Think about special children in your class who may need extra love and understanding. What are their specific needs? What are some particular ways in which you can meet their needs? The Bible story for today is a continuation of last week's lesson. It tells about Jesus' friends following his commandment to show love to others. Loving activities include the followers of Jesus sharing food together (Acts 6:1-6) and Peter healing the lame man at the gate (Acts 3:1-10). Read these passages in Acts as you prepare for this session.

Through the Week: Think of ways that young children show love to others—by helping, by giving, by showing care and kindness to others, and by beginning to learn to share. Plan to incorporate opportunities for children to help, give, care, share, and show kindness during this session.

Pray: Dear God, help me to be aware of the special needs for love that children in my class may have. Help me to show my love by meeting their needs. Give me wisdom and understanding that I may plan opportunities for the children to show love to others.

The Story and Young Children

Children learn about God's love from adults in their lives. Parents, teachers, and other caregivers model God's love for children. If children are fortunate, even the youngest ones will arrive at church carrying an experience of God's love in their hearts and heads.

Children who are not so fortunate may have little experience of love or may not have received the seeking, accepting, joyful love that is like God's. This makes it all the more important that we as teachers act in kind, caring, and understanding ways with the children. Our class may be one of the few places where they can come to know what God's love is like.

156

Learning Centers

Work with two or three children at a time in each learning center.

Conversation Center

You will need: play dough, heart-shaped cookie cutters; paper plates, black marker, paper punch, colored yarn, crayons or markers.

Get ready: Gather the children around a table and sit down with them; engage them in conversation.

- Play With Play Dough, Activity 1c
- Color the Bible Verse, Activity 4b

Building Center

You will need: building blocks; toy cars, trucks, trains, or boats.

Get ready: Provide enough blocks for toddlers to share.

- Travel to Show Love, Activity 3c

Family Living Center

You will need: dolls and items to take care of them.

Get ready: Provide plenty of toys to share.

- Show Love to Dolls, Activity 3a

Storytelling Center

You will need: Activity Pak—pp. 5, 8 (figures 2-4, 6-9); CD and CD player, Songbook; Bible.

Get ready: Prepare storytelling figures (see Activity Pak—p. 2).

- Tell the Bible Story, Activity 2a
- Sing a Song, Activity 2b
- Retell the Bible Story, Activity 2c
- Sing a Song, Activity 3b
- Enjoy Music, Activity 4a

Discovery Center

You will need: heart shapes cut from material scraps of different textures, such as felt, velvet, corduroy, dotted swiss, satin, and posterboard; glue; teacher scissors.

Get ready: Cut out heart shapes from material scraps of different textures, such as felt, velvet, corduroy, dotted swiss, and satin. Glue the heart shapes to a piece of posterboard.

- Feel Textured Hearts, Activity 1b

Love One Another

"Love one another," said Jesus.
Jesus' friends gave food to people who were hungry.
"Love one another," said Jesus.
Jesus' friends helped people who were sick.
"Love one another," said Jesus.
Everyone who saw Jesus' friends knew that they loved one another.

 Prepare
for the Story

a **Welcome Each Child**
Do this as each child enters.

Have the CD playing as children arrive.

Stoop to the children's eye level and welcome each child by name.

Say to each child: "I am so happy you have come to church today."

Be prepared to involve children in an interesting or comforting activity.

b **Feel Textured Hearts**
Do this in the Discovery Center.

Ahead of time, cut out heart shapes and glue the heart shapes to the piece of posterboard.

Gather two or three children. Let the children explore the textures of the hearts.

Give them words to describe the textures (smooth, soft, bumpy). If you have older children, make matching cards with the textured hearts. Ask the children to match the hearts by feeling them.

c **Play With Play Dough**
Do this in the Conversation Center.

Prepare play dough ahead of time, using the recipe on page 232. Or purchase prepared play dough.

Let the children manipulate the play dough. Provide heart-shaped cookie cutters and round blocks for rolling the dough.

Remind the children that heart shapes remind us that we are loved and that Jesus wants us to love each other.

Tell
the Story

a **Tell the Bible Story**
Do this in the Storytelling Center.

Gather two or three children. **Say:** "Let me tell you another story about Jesus and his helpers." Tell the Bible story, using the storytelling figures (figures 2-4, 6-9) at appropriate times.

Open a Bible and **say** the Bible verse: "Jesus said, 'Love one another.'" Encourage the children to say the Bible verse with you. Invite the children to remember other things that Jesus said.

Pray: "Thank you, God, for people who love us."

b **Sing a Song**
Do this in the Storytelling Center.

Gather two or three children. Play "Love One Another" (Songbook, CD). Encourage the children to dance to the music.

Repeat the song and invite the children to sing along.

c **Retell the Bible Story**
Do this in the Storytelling Center.

Use the following litany, encouraging the children to **say:** "Love one another."

Jesus said to Peter: "Love one another."
Jesus said to Andrew: "Love one another."
Jesus said to James: "Love one another."
Jesus said to John: "Love one another."
Jesus said to Mary: "Love one another."
Jesus said to Martha: "Love one another."

Use the children's names in the litany and respond by singing "Love one another."

 **Connect**

....

with the Story

a **Show Love to Dolls**
Do this in the Family Living Center.

As the children play in the Family Living Center with the dolls, engage them in conversation.

Say: "It looks like you love that doll an awful lot. You are taking good care of him."

b **Sing a Song**
Do this in the Storytelling Center.

Sing the following song to the tune of "This Is the Way."

I can show love to everyone,
Everyone, everyone.
I can show love to everyone
With a great big smile. (*Smile.*)
I can show love to everyone,
Everyone, everyone.

I can show love to everyone
With a great big hug.
(*Hug each other.*)

c **Travel to Show Love**
Do this in the Building Center.

Invite the children to build block roads on which to play with the cars and trucks. Invite them to build block railroad tracks for the train.

As the children play with the transportation toys, **say:** "Let's pretend we are going to show love to others. How shall we go?"

If the children choose a car, for example, help them make the car move across the room and pretend to tell someone that they are loved.

4 Celebrate

....

the Story

a **Enjoy Music**
Do this in the Storytelling Center.

Sing "Jesus Loves Me" and "Love One Another." Also sing "Show How Much God Loves Us" and "The Bah Bah Song" (Songbook, CD).

Sing other songs that the children have learned this year.

 Color the Bible Verse
Do this in the Conversation Center.

Gather two or three children. Give each child a paper plate on which you have written with a black marker, "Love one another."

Invite the children to color on their paper plate. When they have finished, punch two holes in the top of the plate and thread yarn through them to provide a hanger for their Bible verse.

c **Say Goodbye**
Recall today's Bible story, encouraging children to say or sing the Bible verse with you.

Say: "I'm glad that God loves (*name of child*). I love you too." Repeat this for each child in the class.

Pray: "Thank you, God, for (*name of child*)."

Be sure to have a teacher or helper at the door to match children with their caregivers.

Tell parents about today's Bible story and make sure that each child has today's Bible Story Picture Card. Show parents the "Nurturing Your Child's Faith" section of the card.

Be sure the children take home their decorated Bible verse.

Tip
If you have kept Activity Pak items from past quarters, you may wish to use the matching hearts game from the Fall Activity Pak in this session.

Look Back
What activities went particularly well today? With what activities did you or the children have trouble?

What activities will you want to repeat next week?

Did all of the children have a chance to experience the Bible story this week? Can the children retell the story?

Look Ahead
Count ahead and make sure that you have scheduled your Palm Sunday lesson on Palm Sunday and your Easter lesson on Easter. Arrange the other lessons around these two Sundays. Note that you will need to combine one or two lessons in order to cover all of the material within three months.

Jesus wants us to love everyone— even those who do not look or act like us.

Bible Verse:
Jesus said, "Love one another." (John 15:12, adapted)

Resources:
Bible
CD
Activity Pak (Spring)
    pages 20, 21
    (figures 19–24)
    Songbook
Bible Story Picture Cards

Supplies:
CD player
four-inch circles cut from self-adhesive paper
stickers
several simple puzzles
shaving cream
damp towels
building blocks
stuffed animals
dolls
soapy water
dishrags

Be a Neighbor ....

Enter the Bible Story

Read Luke 10:25-37: The familiar story of the Good Samaritan reminds us that God does not set boundaries on who can be a disciple.

Think About It: How many times do we read about Jesus answering a question with another question or a story? In this account by Luke, a lawyer tried to test Jesus. "What shall I do to inherit eternal life?" asked the lawyer. Reflect on the following questions as you prepare to tell the story and to help the children retell the story: How would you answer the lawyer's question? What do you think the lawyer felt when he heard Jesus' answer? How do you respond when you see someone in need?

In Luke 9:52-56 we hear an account of Jesus being rejected by the Samaritans. The disciples John and James wanted to command fire to come down from heaven and consume the Samaritans. We also know from our study of the Bible that Samaritans were considered outsiders by the Hebrews and that the term "Good Samaritan" would have been an oxymoron. In the parable for today Jesus possibly was making a point to the disciples as well as to the lawyer. Jesus always responded in kindness to those in need. His anger only seems to be toward those who know what God commands but do not do it. This is a story about "doing." Read Matthew 25:31-46 and James 1:22-27 for further study.

Through the Week: In our culture it would be dangerous for us to stop to help a supposedly injured man beside the road. It is often foolish for us to give money to anyone who asks for it. Nevertheless, we are called to help. What are some safe ways that we can respond to other's needs? Could we use our cell phone to call for help and stay in sight of the injured man until help arrives? Could we pass out fast food gift certificates instead of cash to those who claim to be hungry?

Pray: Dear God, thank you for the story of the Good Samaritan. Thank you that you have shown us how to love our neighbors, no matter what their race, age, or gender. Help us to work toward a time when all people are recognized as your children. Amen.

The Story and Young Children

Children are fortunate in that they do not yet notice differences in people that would make them dislike someone because of skin color, language, or social status. They trust everyone until they have been proved untrustworthy. It may be hard for them to understand the antipathy that Jesus' friends felt toward Samaritans.

Perhaps that is why Jesus says that unless we become as a little child, we cannot enter the kingdom of God. The story of the Good Samaritan holds a special message for children and adults of all ages: It is important to not only speak of love but also to show love to all humankind.

Learning Centers

Work with two or three children at a time in each learning center.

Conversation Center

You will need: four-inch circles cut from self-adhesive paper, stickers, shaving cream, damp towels.

Get ready: Cut four-inch circles from self-adhesive paper.

- Make Helper Badges, Activity 1c
- Fingerpaint With Shaving Cream, Activity 3c

Building Center

You will need: building blocks, stuffed animals, dolls.

Get ready: Provide enough blocks for toddlers to share.

- Play With Blocks, Activity 3a

Discovery Center

You will need: several simple puzzles.

- Play With Puzzles, Activity 3b

Storytelling Center

This should be an open area where you may gather children for storytelling, or to listen and respond to music. It would be helpful to have this center on a carpeted area.

You will need: Activity Pak—pp. 20, 21 (figures 19–24); Songbook; CD and CD player; Bible.

Get ready: Prepare storytelling figures (see Activity Pak—p. 2).

- Tell the Bible Story, Activity 2a
- Dance and Sing, Activity 2b
- Retell the Bible Story, Activity 2c
- Enjoy Music, Activity 4a

Family Living Center

You will need: soapy water, dishrags.

Get ready: Wet several rags with soapy water and wring them out. Let the children play with the dampened rags.

- Help Clean House, Activity 1b

The Good Samaritan

One day a man was walking down the road. Some bad men stopped him and pushed him down and took his things. Then they ran away.

"Help me," the man cried out to the people walking by. But no one stopped to help him. They were too busy.

But then a Samaritan came by. He stopped to help the man. He helped the man up and took care of him.

Jesus said we should be like the Samaritan.

1 Prepare
for the Story

a Welcome Each Child
Do this as each child enters.

Have the CD playing as children arrive.

Stoop to the child's eye level and welcome each child by name.

Say to each child: "I am so happy you have come to church today."

Be prepared to involve children in an interesting or comforting activity.

b Help Clean House
Do this in the Family Living Center.

Gather two or three children. Help the children clean the items in the Family Living Center. They may wash the dishes and wipe the furniture with a damp rag.

As the children work, thank them for helping each other.

c Make Helper Badges
Do this in the Conversation Center.

Gather two or three children. Tell them that today we are going to be good helpers, so we need to wear a badge.

Let the children place stickers on the self-adhesive paper circles. When they finish, remove the paper backing from the self-adhesive paper and place the badge on the child's clothing.

Do not be surprised if the badges do not stay on long. Toddlers love to take sticky things off of their clothing and put them back on.

If the children lose their badges, quietly put them away and give the badges to the children as they go home.

2 Tell
the Story

a Tell the Bible Story
Do this in the Storytelling Center.

Gather two or three children. Tell the children that a Samaritan was a person who looked and acted different. **Say:** "Let me tell you a story that Jesus told." Tell the Bible story, using the storytelling figures (figures 19–24) at appropriate times.

Open a Bible and **say** the Bible verse: "Jesus said, 'Love one another.'" Encourage the children to say the Bible verse with you.

Pray: "Thank you, God, for people who love us."

b Dance and Sing
Do this in the Storytelling Center.

Gather two or three children. Play "Love One Another" (Songbook, CD).

Encourage the children to dance to the music. Repeat the song and invite the children to sing along.

c Retell the Bible Story
Do this in the Storytelling Center.

One day a man was walking down the road. (*Make walking motions.*)

Some bad people came and pushed him down and took away his things! (*Pretend to cry.*)

He cried out, "Help me!" but the people were too busy. (*Stick your nose up in the air and turn your head.*)

But a Samaritan came by. (*Make walking motions.*)

He stopped. (*Stop motions.*)

And he immediately helped the man. (*Pretend to reach down to a person.*)

He helped the man up and took him to a place to stay and get all better. (*Make walking motions.*)

The Samaritan loved his neighbor. (*Hug yourself.*)

# Connect

with the Story

a Play With Blocks

Do this in the Building Center.

Gather one or two children. **Say:** "These animals and dolls need a home. Can you build them a house with rooms for all of them?"

Encourage the children to build a house for the toys. Talk about how to show love for the toys by helping them have a nice place to live. How else can we show love to the toys? Could we make them some food? Could we pretend they are crying and comfort them? Thank them for helping the toys.

b Play With Puzzles

Do this in the Discovery Center.

Gather two or three children. Show them the puzzles. Take the pieces out.

Say: "Oh no! Who can help me get the puzzle pieces back in the puzzle?"

Let the children help you. Praise the children for being good helpers.

c Fingerpaint With Shaving Cream

Do this in the Conversation Center.

Encourage the children to clean off the tops of tables by squirting a bit of shaving cream on the table and letting the children fingerpaint. Wipe with a damp rag.

Celebrate

the Story

a Enjoy Music

Do this in the Storytelling Center.

Sing "Jesus Loves Me" and "Love One Another" (Songbook, CD). Encourage the children to play instruments as accompaniment.

Sing other songs that the children have learned this year.

b Clean Up

Do this in any center.

Gather two or three children. **Say:** "Jesus wants us to love others. One way we can show our love is by cleaning up our messes."

Make a game out of cleaning up. Ahead of time mark toy shelves with pictures so that the children can easily see where toys belong.

Avoid saying, "(*Child's name*), please pick up this toy." This could get you into a power struggle. Rather, **say:** "I need someone to pick up this toy. Who could that someone be?" This will allow children to volunteer to clean up.

c Say Goodbye

Recall today's Bible story, encouraging the children to say or sing the Bible verse with you.

Say: "I'm glad that God loves (*name of child*). I love you too." Repeat this for each child in the class.

Pray: "Thank you, God, for people who love us."

Be sure to have a teacher or helper at the door to match children with their caregivers.

Tell parents about today's Bible story and make sure that each child has today's Bible Story Picture Card. Show parents the "Nurturing Your Child's Faith" section of the card.

Show the parents how clean the Family Living Center and the Conversation Center are. Be sure the children take home their sticker pictures.

Tip

It is never too soon to teach children to clean up their own messes. It just takes a lot of patience. Keep the child focused on one task at a time: "Ginger, pick up the toy. Now, Ginger, put the toy on the shelf. Now you may come have a snack."

Look Back

What activities went particularly well today? With what activities did you or the children have trouble?

What activities will you want to repeat next?

Did all of the children have a chance to experience the Bible story this week? Can the children retell the story?

Look Ahead

Count ahead and make sure that you have scheduled your Palm Sunday lesson on Palm Sunday and your Easter lesson on Easter. Arrange the other lessons around these two Sundays. Note that you will need to combine one or two lessons in order to cover all of the material within three months.

Jesus loves us just as we are.

Bible Verse:
Jesus said, "Love one another." (John 15:12, adapted)

Resources:
Bible
CD
Activity Pak (Spring)
   pages 5, 21
   (figures 2, 25, 26)
   page 23 ("Jesus
   Teaching" book)
   Songbook
Bible Story Picture Cards

Supplies:
play dough
CD player
colored or printed self-adhesive paper cut into 9-by-12-inch pieces
scraps of construction paper
clear self-adhesive paper
masking tape
several simple puzzles
heart-shaped cookie cutters
building blocks
(optional: toy dishes and food, storybook about Jesus)

God Gives Us Friends.............................

Enter the Bible Story

Read Luke 10:38-42: The story of Mary and Martha reminds us that all of us are valued and that all of our work is important.

Think About It: Mary and Martha. Two sisters who loved Jesus. But what different ways they showed that love! Martha showed her love in the more traditional way of women, by providing food and hospitality for her guest. Mary showed her love by sitting and listening intently to the teachings of Jesus. When Martha asked Jesus to rebuke her sister for her non-womanly ways, Jesus surprised everyone by taking up for Mary, even though there is no evidence that he did not appreciate what Martha was doing. Reflect on the following questions as you prepare to tell the story and to help children retell the story: What issues connect your life with the story? How do you show your love for Jesus? Do you feel that your way of showing love is valued? Have you been impatient with those who would sit around and think deep thoughts when there were chores to be done? Have those who could only see the daily chores and not see beyond them to the bigger picture irritated you? Try to picture this story from both sisters' points of view.

Mary and Martha lived in Bethany, which was on the eastern slope of the Mount of Olives. Bethany was about two miles from Jerusalem. Martha may have been the older of the two, because verse 38 states that Martha welcomed Jesus into "her home." Possibly as the older sister she felt a necessity for serving. Whatever the reason, Jesus saw that Martha was worried and concerned about many things. Jesus gently reminded Martha of what is most important. And yet, one of the foundations of Hebrew culture is that of hospitality. Surely it is expected that a host will do whatever it takes to serve her guests. Perhaps Martha was more concerned about appearances than about listening to Jesus.

Through the Week: As you go about your daily tasks this week, try to schedule time for sitting and meditating on God. Do not let your life get so busy with the mundane that you no longer have time for God.

Pray: Dear God, thank you for sending Jesus to visit with us. Help us to see our tasks and our responses in the light of your love. Amen.

The Story and Young Children

Children do not understand the concept of setting priorities—to them the top priority is placed on whatever catches their ear or eye at the moment. Nevertheless, they do understand that Jesus wants to be with friends and talk to them. In some ways this story affirms again the need to be like children. When it is time to be with Jesus, daily chores do not matter.

Learning Centers

Work with two or three children at a time in each learning center.

Conversation Center

You will need: colored or printed self-adhesive paper cut into 9-by-12-inch pieces; scraps of construction paper; clear self-adhesive paper; masking tape; play dough, heart-shaped cookie cutters.

Get ready: Tape the adhesive paper, sticky side up, to the table. Prepare play dough (see p. 232) or purchase prepared dough.

- Make Placemats, Activity 1c
- Play With Play Dough, Activity 4b

Building Center

You will need: building blocks.

Get ready: Provide enough blocks for toddlers to share.

Discovery Center

You will need: several simple puzzles; Activity Pak—pp. 23 and 24 ("Jesus Teaching" book) or another storybook about Jesus.

- Read a Book, Activity 3b
- Play With Puzzles, Activity 3c

Storytelling Center

This should be an open area where you may gather children for storytelling, or to listen and respond to music. It would be helpful to have this center on a carpeted area.

You will need: Bible; Activity Pak—pp. 5, 21 (figures 2, 25, 26); Songbook, CD and CD player.

Get ready: Prepare storytelling figures (see Activity Pak—p. 2).

- Tell the Bible Story, Activity 2a
- Dance and Sing, Activity 2b
- Retell the Bible Story, Activity 2c
- Play a Game, Activity 3a
- Enjoy Music, Activity 4a

Family Living Center

You will need: optional: toy dishes and food.

Get ready: Set up this center as a restaurant.

- Play Restaurant, Activity 1b

Mary and Martha

Mary and Martha were excited. Jesus was coming to their house. They cleaned the house and made some food. When Jesus came, Mary sat down, but Martha kept cooking and cleaning, cooking and cleaning.

"Jesus," said Martha, "make Mary come and help me."

"It's OK, Martha," said Jesus. "What Mary is doing is good. Come and sit down with us."

1 Prepare

for the Story

a Welcome Each Child
Do this as each child enters.

Have the CD playing as children arrive.

Stoop to the children's eye level and welcome each child by name.

Say to each child: "I am so happy you have come to church today."

Be prepared to involve children in an interesting or comforting activity.

b Play Restaurant
Do this in the Family Living Center.

Encourage the children to play as if they were eating in a restaurant. You may wish to put flowers on the table, although most two-year-olds would not notice floral arrangements when they eat out.

Sit at the table and **say:** "Would you bring me a hamburger?" Encourage the child to go get a plate with a pretend hamburger on it.

When they bring it to you, **say:** "Thank you," and give them some pretend money.

You do not have to use toy money, food, or even plates for this game. The children can imagine everything—even the table.

c Make Placemats
Do this in the Conversation Center.

Ahead of time, tape the colored or printed self-adhesive paper to the table, sticky side up.

To do this easily, fold back the paper from the top two corners of the self-adhesive paper. Tape these corners to the table. Then pull off the paper backing and tape the bottom two corners to the table.

Gather two or three children. Let the children put scraps of paper on the sticky side of the self-adhesive paper. When they are finished, cover the top of the placemat with clear self-adhesive paper.

2 Tell

the Story

a Tell the Bible Story
Do this in the Storytelling Center.

Gather two or three children. **Say:** "Let me tell you another story about Jesus and his friends." Tell the Bible story, using the storytelling figures (figures 2, 25, 26) at appropriate times.

Open a Bible and say the Bible verse: "Jesus said, 'Love one another.'" Encourage the children to say the Bible verse with you. Invite the children to remember other things that Jesus said.

Pray: "Thank you, God, for helpers."

b Dance and Sing
Do this in the Storytelling Center.

Gather two or three children. Play "A Friend Loves at All Times" (Songbook, CD). Encourage the children to dance to the music. With older children, encourage them to sing along with the music.

c Retell the Bible Story
Do this in the Storytelling Center.

Gather two or three children. Tell the following story with motions.

"Martha! Martha! Jesus is coming to our house!" said Mary. (*Wave hands in the air.*)

Martha was excited. She cooked (*Pretend to stir a pot.*) and cleaned. (*Pretend to sweep the floor.*)

But Martha was not happy. (*Put hands on hips and frown.*)

"Jesus," said Martha, "Mary is not helping me." (*Shake finger.*) "Make her help me!"

Jesus said, "Martha, do not be sad. Mary is doing good. I love Mary, and I love you too."

It is good to listen to Jesus. (*Put hands behind ears.*)

3 Connect
with the Story

a Play a Game
Do this in the Storytelling Center.

Gather two or three children. Say the following action verse.

This game will be similar to "Ring Around the Rosie."

Jesus walked around and around.
(*Hold hands and move in a circle.*)
The people followed around and around.
(*Hold hands and move in a circle.*)
Then Jesus stopped, and he sat down.
(*Drop hands and sit down.*)
"Love one another!"
(*Hold hands up high.*)

b Read a Book
Do this in the Discovery Center.

Remind the children that Jesus said it was good to sit and listen. Read the "Jesus Teaching" book (Activity Pak—pp. 23-24) or another storybook from your library about Jesus.

c Play With Puzzles
Do this in the Discovery Center.

Gather two or three children. Show them the puzzles. Take the pieces out and show the child how to put them back in the puzzle.

Say: "Look, I am helping you play with the puzzles. Can you help your friend Shelby?"

4 Celebrate
the Story

a Enjoy Music
Do this in the Storytelling Center.

Sing "Jesus Loves Me" and "Love One Another." Also sing "Show How Much God Loves Us" and "A Friend Loves at All Times" (Songbook, CD).

Sing other songs that the children have learned this year.

b Play With Play Dough
Do this in the Conversation Center.

Let the children manipulate play dough, as they desire. Provide heart-shaped cookie cutters and round blocks for rolling the dough.

Remind the children that heart shapes remind us that we are loved and that Jesus wants us to love each other.

c Say Goodbye
Recall today's Bible story, encouraging the children to say or sing the Bible verse with you.

Say: "I'm glad that God loves (*name of child*). I love you too." Repeat this for each child in the class.

Pray: "Thank you, God, for (*name of child*)."

Be sure to have a teacher or helper at the door to match children with their caregivers.

Tell parents about today's Bible story and make sure that each child has today's Bible Story Picture Card. Show parents the "Nurturing Your Child's Faith" section of the card.

Be sure the children take home their place mats.

Tip
Be sure that you are showing love and acceptance to all children. While it is tempting to praise only those children who sit quietly, find things to praise in the child who is a bundle of energy at all times.

Look Back
What activities went particularly well today? With what activities did you or the children have trouble?

What activities will you want to repeat next week?

Did all of the children have a chance to experience the Bible story this week? Can the children retell the story?

Look Ahead
This lesson is probably occurring at the end of the spring quarter. Be sure to save favorite games and activities from the Activity Pak for use this summer.

The people were happy to see Jesus in Jerusalem.

Bible Verse:
Jesus said, "Follow me." (Matthew 4:19, adapted)

Resources:
Bible
CD
donkey ears pattern (page 240)
Activity Pak (Spring) page 4 ("Palm Sunday" picture) Songbook
Bible Story Picture Cards

Supplies:
CD player
brown or gray construction paper
teacher scissors
stapler
crayons
two or three palm branches
masking tape
newsprint
simple snack
cups and napkins
building blocks
toy donkey
leaves from a tree
scraps of cloth
dress-up clothes
(optional: palm plant)

Palm Sunday..........

Enter the Bible Story

Read Matthew 21:9: The triumphal entry of Jesus into Jerusalem stands in shocking irony to the events of Holy Week.

Think About It: Everyone loves a parade—especially one in honor of a well-loved hero. The people of the first century were no exception. Many had heard tales of this rabbi who healed illnesses, calmed storms, and preached common sense rather than legalism. The people at the time were looking for a military leader who would free them from the oppressive yoke of the Roman Empire. They saw their salvation in an itinerant rabbi from Galilee who, they thought, had come to set them free from oppression. Reflect on the following questions as you prepare to tell this story to the children and to help the children retell the story: Who are the heroes of today—the ones who you believe will make the world a better place for you and your children? Have you ever supported a candidate for public office only to find after that person was elected that he or she did not live up to your expectations?

The account of Jesus riding into Jerusalem on a donkey is reminiscent of a similar account of Judas Maccabeus riding into Jerusalem after ridding Judea from foreign oppression less than two hundred years before the time of Jesus. So it is no wonder that the people, who would know the story of the Maccabees, mistook Jesus for a military hero. The cry "Hosanna" means "save us." It is clear that the people expected Jesus to give orders for a rebellion to rid Jerusalem of Roman rule. But Jesus always seems to turn everything on its head. His kingdom is not one of military might, but one of peace and love.

Through the Week: This is Holy Week. Spend some time each day in prayer and meditation. Read the Gospel of Mark and remember the events of the last week of Jesus' life. If possible, attend a Maundy Thursday service and a Good Friday service. Without these services the joy of Easter morning is not quite as dramatic.

Pray: Dear God, thank you for giving us leaders. When they do not do what we want, give us understanding so that we may determine whether they are true leaders that will bring about your kingdom. When they do not live up to our expectations, help us to see them as the human beings they are. Amen.

The Story and Young Children

Children love celebrations. Even when they do not understand all of the symbolism, or know to anticipate the treachery of the coming week, they can get caught up in the excitement of the waving palm branches and the shouts of "Hosanna."

The children you teach probably will not remember this story until the next Palm Sunday, since this is not a story that is repeated often. But you will introduce them to the concept of waving palm branches, and you will introduce them to the word *hosanna*, so when they hear the story again, they will know they have heard this before.

Learning Centers

Work with two or three children at a time in each learning center.

Conversation Center

You will need: donkey ears pattern (page 240), brown or gray construction paper, teacher scissors, stapler, two or three palm branches, masking tape, newsprint, crayons; simple snack, cups and napkins.

Get ready: Gather the children around a table and sit down with them; engage them in conversation. Tape the palm leaves to the table and tape paper on top of them for the rubbings. Photocopy the donkey ears pattern (page 240) onto brown or gray construction paper.

- Make Donkey Ears, Activity 1b
- Make Palm Leaf Rubbings, Activity 3c
- Have a Snack, Activity 4b

Building Center

You will need: building blocks, toy donkey, leaves from a tree, scraps of cloth.

Get ready: Provide enough blocks for toddlers to share.

- Play With Blocks, Activity 3b

Family Living Center

Include a toy kitchen set and props to play house.

Storytelling Center

This should be an open area where you may gather children for storytelling, or to listen and respond to music.

You will need: Bible; Activity Pak—p. 4 ("Palm Sunday" picture); CD and CD player, Songbook; dress-up clothes, palm branches, donkey ears made earlier.

- Tell the Bible Story, Activity 2a
- Retell the Bible Story, Activity 2b
- Sing a Song, Activity 2c
- Do a Donkey Dance, Activity 3a
- Enjoy Music, Activity 4a

Discovery Center

You will need: palm branches or a palm plant.

- Examine Palm Branches, Activity 1c

A Happy Walk

Jesus and his friends were going into Jerusalem. Jesus rode on a donkey.

When the people heard that Jesus was coming, they got excited. They went to the road and put their coats on it. They took palm branches off the trees and waved them. They said, "Hosanna! Hosanna!"

Jesus and his friends waved at the crowd. They were glad to see so many people in Jerusalem.

1 Prepare

for the Story

a Welcome Each Child
Do this as each child enters.

Have the CD playing as children arrive.

Stoop to the children's eye level and welcome each child by name.

Say to each child: "I am so happy you have come to church today."

Be prepared to involve children in an interesting or comforting activity.

b Make Donkey Ears
Do this in the Conversation Center.

Cut out the ears and headband ahead of time. Gather two or three children. Let the children decorate their donkey ears with crayons.

Staple the ears onto the headband and staple the headband together. Make sure that the prongs of the staples face away from the children's heads.

Encourage the children to wear their donkey ears.

c Examine Palm Branches
Do this in the Discovery Center.

Gather two or three children. Let the children touch the palm branches. Notice how smooth the tops of the leaves feel.

Touch the spine of the leaf and feel the "bump" as you run your hand across it.

If you are using a plant, make sure the children know not to take a branch off of a living tree. This will be tempting if the children see palm branches in other parts of the room.

Say: "God told us to take care of living plants."

If you have individual palm branches, let the children wave them in the air. What sound do they make when you wave them fast? What sound do they make when you shake them? What sound do they make when you move them slowly?

Invite the children to use the branches as a fan to cool a friend, being careful not to touch their friends with the branches.

2 Tell

the Story

a Tell the Bible Story
Do this in the Storytelling Center.

Gather two or three children. Show the children the "Palm Sunday" picture (Activity Pak—p. 4). Notice the details in the picture and talk about them.

Say: "Let me tell you another story about Jesus and his friends." Tell the Bible story.

Open a Bible and **say** the Bible verse: "Jesus said, 'Follow me.'" Encourage the children to say the Bible verse with you. Encourage the children to remember other things that Jesus said.

Pray: "Thank you, God, for people who love us."

b Retell the Bible Story
Do this in the Storytelling Center.

Gather two or three children. Act out the Bible story. Let the children put the clothing on the floor and walk on it. Show them how to wave the palm branches and say, "Hosanna!"

Make a game out of picking up the clothing that is behind the children and putting it in front of them to step on it.

c Sing a Song
Do this in the Storytelling Center.

Gather two or three children. Play "Hosanna" (Songbook, CD). Help the children sing, "Hosanna" when they hear it.

Play the song several times and let the children march around the room waving their palm branches and singing, "Hosanna!"

3 Connect
with the Story

a **Do a Donkey Dance**
Do this in the Storytelling Center.

Say: "Let's pretend to be the donkey taking Jesus into Jerusalem." Let the children wear the donkey ears they made earlier. Say the poem below. Have the children move like donkeys on the first three lines of the poem. Let the children fall down on the last line. Repeat as long as the children show interest.

> Little donkey going to Jerusalem,
> How will you go to town?
> I'll clip, clip, clop. I'll clip, clip, clop.
> And then I'll sit right down.

(Adapted from BibleZone 2: Preschool; © 1997 Abingdon Press.)

b **Play With Blocks**
Do this in the Building Center.

Gather two or three children. **Say:** "Let's pretend we are in Jerusalem."

Help the children build Jerusalem with blocks. Then have the donkey move toward Jerusalem.

Invite the children to place the leaves and the scraps of cloth on the floor in front of the donkey.

Sing "Hosanna" (Songbook, CD) as you play.

c **Make Palm Leaf Rubbings**
Do this in the Conversation Center.

Gather two or three children. Give each child a crayon. Show the child how to rub on the newsprint to reveal the shape of the leaf.

Help the child press hard enough while coloring to get a good rubbing.

4 Celebrate
the Story

a **Enjoy Music**

Have a Palm Sunday parade. If you used palm branches in the Discovery Center, get them for the parade. Also gather the dress-up clothes you used in "Retell the Bible Story."

Play "Hosanna!" (Songbook, CD). March around the room as you lead the children in singing the song. Some children may want to wear their donkey ears.

Sing other praise songs that the children have learned this year.

b **Have a Snack**
Do this in the Conversation Center.

Tell the children that when Jesus got to Jerusalem, he had a special meal with his friends. We can eat special meals with our friends.

As you serve the snack, **say:** "Whenever we eat with our friends, we can remember Jesus and how he ate with his friends."

c **Say Goodbye**

Recall today's Bible story, encouraging children to say or sing the Bible verse with you.

Say: "I'm glad that God loves (*name of child*). I love you too." Repeat this for each child in the class.

Pray: "Thank you, God, for (*name of child*)."

Be sure to have a teacher or helper at the door to match children with their caregivers.

Tell parents about today's Bible story and make sure that each child has today's Bible Story Picture Card. Show parents the "Nurturing Your Child's Faith" section of the card.

Be sure the children take home their palm leaf rubbings and their donkey ears.

Tip
Toddlers are apt to get excited when given palm branches. If a child gets too rowdy with the branch, firmly remove the branch from his or her hand and say, "Let's look at our friends. How do you see them handling the branches? Is anyone else hitting his or her friends with the branches? What do you think you should do with the branch?"

Look Back
What activities went particularly well today? With what activities did you or the children have trouble?

What activities will you want to repeat next week?

Did all of the children have a chance to experience the Bible story this week? Can the children retell the story?

Look Ahead
Next week is Easter. Prepare for extra children and for children who have had candy before they arrive. Have plenty of activities to keep your group active.

Easter is when the church celebrates the fact that Jesus is alive.

Bible Verse:
Jesus said, "Love one another." (John 15:12, adapted)

Resources:
Bible
CD
Activity Pak (Spring) page 12 (Easter montage)
Songbook
Bible Story Picture Cards

Supplies:
CD player
building blocks
large white paper towels
food coloring in squeeze bottles or eye droppers
peg-type clothespins or green chenille sticks
silk or plastic flowers
flowerpots'
plastic foam
plastic Easter eggs of different colors (two or three of each color)
one basket or bowl for each color of egg
large cardboard box
instruments

"I Have Seen Jesus!".............

Enter the Bible Story

Read John 20:1-18: Alleluia! Christ is risen! Christ is risen indeed! The resurrection story forms the very foundation of the Christian faith.

Think About It: If you have been following the events of Holy Week, especially the betrayal of Judas, the denial of Peter, and the horrific crucifixion on the cross, the joy of Easter is especially acute. Earlier in the twentieth century Easter was the time when there were dramatic changes in dress. White shoes and gloves would appear, and Easter bonnets would bloom like flower gardens. Some churches today do not have flowers in their sanctuary during the season of Lent, so to make a more visible difference in the sanctuary on Easter morning. Others do not have Easter egg hunts until Sunday morning to impress on the children that the time for celebration does not begin until Easter. Reflect on the following questions as you prepare for Sunday school this week: What differences will you make in your life now that it is Easter season? Will those who know you sense a difference as you move from Lent to Easter?

Scholars believe that Jesus was crucified on a Friday about noon and that he died around 3:00 p.m. Crucified criminals usually were simply thrown into a ditch nearby, but Joseph of Arimathea asked for and received permission to bury Jesus in a newly hewn tomb in his garden. But time was of the essence. No work could be done after sundown on Friday due to sabbath law. The body could not lie unburied over the sabbath, so Jesus was hastily wrapped in linen and placed in the tomb without the proper preparation. As soon as it was possible, which would have been dawn on Sunday, the women went to the tomb to prepare the body for a proper burial.

Through the Week: Read the resurrection stories in all of the Gospels. Even though each one varies on details, what are the common elements in each story?

Pray: Dear God, fill me with the joy and wonder of Easter. Help me to live each day secure in the knowledge that Jesus is alive. Amen.

The Story and Young Children

Young children do not understand the concept of death, much less resurrection. But they do know that something is different about today. Some of them will have received Easter baskets before they came to church, and they may already be suffering from a sugar high. Others will have fancy new clothes. Be prepared for the children to react to the excitement around them with signs of distress—additional crying or aggression, or the inability to sit still for very long. These are all normal behaviors for children who are faced with excitement that they do not understand.

Learning Centers

Work with two or three children at a time in each learning center.

Conversation Center

You will need: large white paper towels, food coloring in squeeze bottles or eye droppers, peg-type clothespins or green chenille sticks.

Get ready: Gather the children around a table and sit down with them; engage them in conversation.

- Make Butterflies, Activity 3a

Building Center

You will need: building blocks.

Get ready: Provide enough blocks for toddlers to share.

- Play With Blocks, Activity 3b

Discovery Center

You will need: plastic Easter eggs in different colors (two or three of each color) and one basket or bowl for each color; real or silk spring flowers for the children to examine.

- Match Easter Eggs, Activity 1b
- Examine Spring Flowers, Activity 1c
- Look for Signs of Spring, Activity 2d

Storytelling Center

This should be an open area where you may gather children for storytelling, or to listen and respond to music. It would be helpful to have this center on a carpeted area.

You will need: Activity Pak—p. 12 (Easter montage); Bible; CD and CD player, Songbook; large cardboard box; instruments.

Get ready: Prepare storytelling figures (see Activity Pak—p. 2).

- Tell the Bible Story, Activity 2a
- Retell the Bible Story, Activity 2b
- Sing and Dance, Activity 2c
- Enjoy Music, Activity 4a

Family Living Center

You will need: silk or plastic flowers, flowerpots, plastic foam.

Get ready: Put pieces of plastic foam in several pots. Make sure it is easy for toddlers to push the flowers into the foam and to take them out.

- Plant Flowers, Activity 3c

Happy Easter

Mary was sad. Her friend Jesus had died. She was going to see his body.

But when she got to the place where she had left him, he was not there! Where was Jesus?

Mary saw an angel. The angel said, "Do not be sad. Jesus is not dead. He is alive!"

"Jesus is alive!" Mary ran to tell her friends. "Jesus is alive! He is not dead!"

1 Prepare
for the Story

a Welcome Each Child
Do this as each child enters.

Have the CD playing as children arrive.

Stoop to the children's eye level and welcome each child by name.

Say to each child: "I am so happy you have come to church today."

Be prepared to involve children in an interesting or comforting activity.

b Match Easter Eggs
Do this in the Discovery Center.

Gather two or three children. Show the children the eggs. If you have older children, name the colors of Easter eggs. Try to sort the eggs into colors.

Say: "Look, here is a purple egg. I will put it in this basket. Can you find an egg that matches it? No, that egg is red. It goes in this basket. Which one matches the purple one. Yes! You found the purple one! Now let's find one to match this red one."

c Examine Spring Flowers
Do this in the Discovery Center.

Gather two or three children. Examine the flowers you have collected.

Ask the children if they have ever seen these before. Look at the different colors and see if the children can name the colors.

Say: "Whenever we see these flowers, we know that Easter is near."

2 Tell
the Story

a Tell the Bible Story
Do this in the Storytelling Center.

Gather two or three children. Show the children the Easter montage (Activity Pak—p. 12). Notice the details and talk about them.

Say: "Let me tell you a very important story about Jesus." Tell the Bible story.

Open a Bible and **say** the Bible verse: "Jesus said, 'Love one another.'" Encourage the children to say the Bible verse with you. Invite the children to remember other things that Jesus said.

Pray: "Thank you, God, for Jesus."

b Retell the Bible Story
Do this in the Storytelling Center.

Gather two or three children. **Say:** "Let's pretend to be Mary going to see Jesus." Walk slowly toward the box, pretending to cry. Look inside the empty box.

Say: "Where is Jesus? He is not here! He is alive!" Go running away from the box to tell others that Jesus is alive.

c Sing and Dance
Do this in the Storytelling Center.

Gather two or three children. Play "Happy Easter" (Songbook, CD). Encourage the children to dance to the music.

Say: "When we are happy, we dance!" Dance joyfully to the Easter music.

As the children become familiar with the song, encourage them to sing along.

d Look for Signs of Spring
Do this in the Discovery Center.

If you have a window in your classroom low enough for children to see out, and if your view is an appropriate one for today's session, let the children look out the window to find signs of spring.

Point out signs such as new leaves on trees or fresh grass.

3 Connect
with the Story

a **Make Butterflies**
Do this in the Conversation Center.

Gather two or three children. Give each child a paper towel. Show the children how to drop food coloring onto the paper towel. Watch as the color spreads in the towel.

When the child has put several drops of color on the towel, **say:** "Let's make a butterfly! Watch this." Gather the center of the paper towel in the clothespin. If you want, draw a face on the top of the clothespin. Or fold the chenille stick in half and gather the center of the towel in the fold.

Twist the top of the chenille stick to form antenna.

b **Play With Blocks**
Do this in the Building Center.

While the children play in this center, show them how to build a tomb out of blocks and put one block in front of the tomb.

Say: "Let's look for Jesus in the tomb."

Move the block to show the empty tomb. **Say:** "He is not here! He is alive!"

c **Plant Flowers**
Do this in the Family Living Center.

Have an assortment of artificial spring flowers available for "planting." Show the children how to push the stem of the flower into the plastic foam and make the plant stand up.

Allow the children to pull the plant out and replant it. The benefit of this exercise is the putting in and the taking out of the flower—not the finished product. Let the children experiment.

4 Celebrate
the Story

a **Enjoy Music**
Do this in the Storytelling Center.

Sing "Happy Easter" and "Jesus Loves Me" (Songbook, CD). Encourage the children to play instruments as accompaniment. Sing other songs that the children have learned this year.

b **Have an Egg Hunt**

If the weather and your location are appropriate, take the children outside for an Easter egg hunt. You may use plastic eggs, filled or unfilled. Let the children enjoy picking up the eggs, putting them in the basket, and then getting them out of the basket again.

While you are outside, notice all the signs of God's love around you. Give thanks to God for the blessings you can see. Spread a blanket and have a simple snack outdoors.

c **Say Goodbye**

Recall today's Bible story, encouraging children to say or sing the Bible verse with you.

Say: "I'm glad that God loves (*name of child*). I love you too." Repeat this for each child in the class.

Pray: "Thank you, God, for (*name of child*)."

Be sure to have a teacher or helper at the door to match children with their caregivers.

Tell parents about today's Bible story and make sure that each child has today's Bible Story Picture Card. Show parents the "Nurturing Your Child's Faith" section of the card.

Be sure the children take home their butterflies.

Tip
Because this story has so many concepts that toddlers will not understand, do not focus on the story, but on the signs of new life that you see.

Look Back
What activities went particularly well today? With what activities did you or the children have trouble?

What activities will you want to repeat next week?

Look Ahead
Go back and schedule the sessions you skipped in order to use this session on Easter. Remember that you probably have one too many sessions for the quarter and will need to leave one out or combine two.

God made the light, which does many things.

Bible Verse:
We give thanks to you, O God.
(Psalm 75:1a)

Resources:
Bible
CD
Activity Pak (Summer)
    page 9 (figure 1)
    page 2 ("Light Does Many Things" picture)
    Songbook
Bible Story Picture Cards

Supplies:
CD player
building blocks
play dough (see p. 232) and items used with play dough
construction paper
glue
3 5-ounce paper cups
reflecting materials such as foil pieces, gold braid or ribbon, one-inch sequins, sparkly stickers
plastic, wooden, or craft stick figures
large lightweight blanket
flashlight
large sheets of paper
markers
items used to pretend daytime and nighttime activities
flannelboard or bulletin board
(optional: color matching toy)

God Created Light ·······························

Enter the Bible Story

Read Genesis 1:1-3: In the first verses of the Book of Genesis, God begins to bring order out of chaos. The very first thing God created was light. This formed the basis for the increasingly complex created order that was to follow.

Think About It: As you think about God's creation of the sun that holds our earth in orbit, and the light from it that supports life on this planet, consider the following: What sort of God is able to bring light from the original void? What knowledge and power must God have to be able to scatter the stars in the heavens and the planets around them? As we look at God's awesome creative activity, we see a portrait of the Hebrew and Christian God who is all-powerful and all-knowing. What does it mean to you personally to worship a God who has such power?

Genesis means "beginning" (literally, "in the beginning"). The Book of Genesis tells of a number of beginnings: our earth and the cosmos, humankind, sin, and God's plan for God's people. Originally the first five books of the Hebrew Scripture had no individual titles but were all part of the books of the law for the Hebrew people. This book of Law is referred to as the Torah. The books tell the story of that people. They describe how the Hebrews came to be and how God was active in their history. Genesis should, therefore, be seen in the context of the whole of those first five books.

Through the Week: This is the first session of the Creation unit. Think about ways in which young children experience the creative activity of God. Consider learning activities in which children can use all of their senses to see, hear, smell, taste, and feel God's creation.

Pray: Creator God, I stand in awe of the greatness of your vast work. I stand in humility when I remember that, with all of your power, you desire to come personally into my life and into the lives of the children I teach. Help me keep both your powerful and the personal images before me as I prepare for this session.

The Story and Young Children

This is the first session of a Creation unit that spans the next three months. The only Bible story for the entire summer is that of Genesis 1, although other stories will be introduced. But this will be a highly enjoyable unit for you to teach. Young children love to create. And young children love to explore creation. Be prepared for a really fun summer!

Also, if your church is like many churches, attendance will be sporadic this summer. Because of this, and because the Bible story is the same all summer, glance through the activities in the rest of this book. They are all interchangeable. Pick out some of your favorite activities and introduce them in this lesson. Repeat them weekly as long as there is interest. (Less work for you!) When you notice that the children are no longer interested in an activity, choose another one. Repetition is the name of the game for toddlers. The refrain of many toddlers is, "Again! Again!" Enjoy your summer.

Learning Centers

Work with two or three children at a time in each learning center.

Conversation Center

You will need: play dough (see p. 232) and items used with play dough; construction paper; glue, small paper cups; reflecting materials such as foil pieces, gold braid or ribbon, large (one-inch) sequins, sparkly stickers.

Get ready: Prepare play dough (p. 232) or use purchased dough.

- Play With Play Dough, Activity 1d
- Make Sparkle Banners, Activity 3a

Building Center

You will need: building blocks; plastic, wooden, or craft stick figures.

Get ready: Provide enough blocks for toddlers to share.

- Play With Blocks, Activity 3b

Family Living Center

You will need: props for things to do in daytime (eat, mow grass) and nighttime (pajamas, pillow, and blanket)

- Play Day and Night, Activity 3c

Storytelling Center

This should be an open area where you may gather children for storytelling, or to listen and respond to music.

You will need: Bible; Activity Pak—p. 9 (figure 1); large lightweight blanket; flashlight; large sheets of paper; markers; CD and CD player, Activity Pak Songbook; flannelboard or bulletin board.

Get ready: Prepare storytelling figures (see Activity Pak—p. 2).

- Tell the Bible Story, Activity 2a
- Retell the Bible Story, Activity 2b
- Use an Action Verse, Activity 2c
- Explore Shadows, Activity 3d
- Enjoy Music, Activity 4a

Discovery Center

You will need: squares of different colors of construction paper, two squares per color (optional: a color matching toy); Activity Pak—p. 3 (Light Does Many Things)

Get ready: Prepare matching color cards. Place the poster on the wall or bulletin board.

- Match Colors, Activity 1b
- Look at a Poster, Activity 1c

God Made Day and Night

When God made the world, everything was gray. You could not tell when it was time to go to bed and when it was time to get up. Everything looked the same.

So God said, "This is not good!" And God made daytime and nighttime. When it was day, it was time to play and to eat and to work. When it was night, it was time to sleep and to rest.

And God said, "This is very, very good!"

 **Prepare**

for the Story

a Welcome Each Child

Do this as each child enters.

Have the CD playing as children arrive. Stoop to the children's eye level and welcome each child by name.

Say to each child: "I am so happy you have come to church today." Be prepared to involve children in an interesting or comforting activity.

b Match Colors

Do this in the Discovery Center.

Gather two or three children. Show the children the colored squares or the pieces of the toy. Older children will be able to name the colors. Help younger children by giving them the color names.

The children will enjoy exploring a toy with pieces of matching color. They can often see that one color matches another without being able to name the color.

c Look at a Picture

Do this in the Discovery Center

Gather two or three children. As the children look at the "Light Does Many Things" picture (Activity Pak—p. 3), invite conversation about what they see there. What is the sun doing in each picture?

Help younger children with words. Tell the children that God plans for the sun and the light.

d Play With Play Dough

Do this in the Conversation Center

Encourage the children to manipulate the dough in rhythm with the music of the CD.

Provide round blocks or rolling pins for smoothing dough, or provide items with which the children can make interesting prints in the dough.

 Tell

the Story

a Tell the Bible Story

Do this in the Storytelling Center.

Gather two or three children. Show the children the figure of the sun (figure 1).

Say: "Did you know that one time there was no light at all? I think I would have been scared. Let me tell you about when God made the light."

Tell the Bible story. Show the picture of the sun and place it on a flannelboard or bulletin board.

Open a Bible and **say** the Bible verse: "We give thanks to you, O God." Encourage the children to say the Bible verse with you.

Pray: "Thank you, God, for light. Amen."

b Retell the Bible Story

Do this in the Storytelling Center.

Gather two or three children. **Say:** "Let's see what it was like before there was light."

Gather the children under the blanket.

Say: "And God said, 'Let there be light.'" Throw the blanket off. Repeat as long as the children show interest.

Be aware of children who may be afraid of the dark. Do not keep the blanket over these children very long. Let them see how much fun it is to throw the blanket off and say "Let there be light."

c Use an Action Verse

Do this in the Storytelling Center.

Gather two or three children. Begin to teach the action verse "God Planned for Light," which is printed in the Activity Pak Songbook. Every two weeks add another verse.

3 Connect
with the Story

a Make Sparkle Banners
Do this in the Conversation Center.

Gather two or three children. Give each child a piece of construction paper. Pour glue into small paper cups. Show each child how to "touch" the glue with his or her finger and then "touch" the paper to transfer the glue.

Help the children glue the sparkly material to their construction paper. Notice how the light makes the items shine and sparkle. The children may move their banners about in direct sunlight, if possible, to see extra reflections and glitter.

Do not use sequins or gummed stars with younger children. Never use glitter with this age group, as it is an eye hazard.

b Play With Blocks
Do this in the Building Center.

As the children play with blocks, encourage pretending day or night activities with the people figures.

Make a block bed for the people to sleep in at night. Make a church for the people to walk to in the daytime.

c Play Day and Night
Do this in the Family Living Center.

As the children play, encourage them to pretend daytime and nighttime activities.

Say: "Now let's pretend it is nighttime. What do we do now? Look! The sun came up! It's morning! What do we do now?"

d Explore Shadows
Do this in the Storytelling Center or outdoors.

Gather two or three children. Let the children explore shadows outdoors, in the light from a bright window, or in the beam of a flashlight. Show them their shadows and how the shadows move when they move.

Place a large sheet of paper in the light on the floor or ground. Draw around each child's shadow or the shadow of the child's hand. (The children may color these later.)

If you are outdoors, point out shadows of nearby objects such as trees or a fence. Tell the children that when something blocks light, it makes a shadow.

4 Celebrate
the Story

a Enjoy Music
Do this in the Storytelling Center.

Gather two or three children. Play "This Little Light of Mine" (Activity Pak Songbook, CD). Encourage the children to dance to the music.

Show the children how to hold up their index fingers as they dance. Encourage the children to sing along with the music.

b Enjoy Light
Choose from the following light activities:

Walk to the sanctuary to look at light coming through stained-glass or tinted windows.

Use a prism outdoors or in a sunny window. Hold the prism in the sun and rotate it until a spectrum can be seen.

c Say Goodbye
Recall today's Bible story. Have the children say the Bible verse with you.

Say: "We enjoyed God's gift of light today. (*Child's name*) saw her shadow." Repeat each child's name and mention a light-exploring activity in which he or she took part.

Pray: "Thank you, God, for light."

Be sure to have a teacher or helper at the door to match children with their caregivers.

Tell parents about today's Bible story and make sure that each child has today's Bible Story Picture Card. Show parents the "Nurturing Your Child's Faith" section of the card.

Be sure the children take home their Sparkle Banners.

Tip
Toddlers and two-year-olds have little sense of time, and days of the week do not mean much to them. Avoid saying, "The first day, God made light; the second day, God made earth, water and sky," and so on. It is enough for the children to hear that God made all things.

Look Back
What activities went particularly well today? With what activities did you or the children have trouble?

What activities will you want to repeat next week?

Look Ahead
Because of sporadic attendance in the summer months and the fact that the whole summer centers around creation, you will want to read ahead. It is highly recommended that you use all of the session plans.

Using these Bible stories will ensure that the children hear all of the Creation story. But you will want to substitute activities from the sessions you do not use for those in which your children have no interest, or which are not practical for your use (for example, going outside).

Psalm 75:1

We praise God for light and for all that it does.

Bible Verse:
We give thanks to you, O God.
Psalm 75:1

Resources:
Bible
CD
Activity Pak (Summer)
  page 9 (figure 1)
  page 3 ("Light Does
  Many Things" picture)
  page 5 (day/night
  sorting cards)
  Songbook
Bible Story Picture Cards

Supplies:
CD player
play dough and items to
  use with play dough
building blocks
clear plastic soda bottles
cellophane paper in
  many colors
glue
small paper cups
plastic, wooden, or craft
  stick people figures
large lightweight blanket
two boxes or baskets
shoebox with lid
small toy
props for things to do in
  daytime and nighttime
teacher scissors
large box
heavy fabric
flashlight
(optional: clear tape,
  utility knife)

Thank You, God, for Light.........

Enter the Bible Story

Read Psalm 75:1: Psalm 75 seems to have been part of a ritual. The first verse of the psalm expresses gratitude for God's great deeds.

Think About It: Light is an important theological concept as well as a physical one. Jesus said, "I am the light of the world. Whoever follows me will never walk in darkness but will have the light of life" (John 8:12). He also said, "You are the light of the world" (Matthew 5:14). When we cannot see the light, we are often frightened. Many times children (and sometimes adults) ask for a night light to sleep with. Light keeps us from stepping on things that might injure us. Light helps to keep us safe from obstacles in our path. Light informs us of our surroundings. How do you interpret the phrase, "You are the light of the world"? Remembering that young children do not understand abstract concepts like this, how are you going to present this information to your students this week?

Psalm 75 is one of the Psalms known as "liturgies," words spoken as part of a ritual gathering. Not much is known about these rituals, but this psalm was probably part of a new year's festival. It was a time when the people renewed their covenant with God, telling of God's wonderful past deeds and looking forward to a future relationship with God.

Through the Week: Notice how often you are out in natural light during a normal day. Studies have shown that people who live in artificial light need supplements of vitamin D, which occurs naturally in sunlight. What are other ways you depend on light?

Pray: Dear God, you have truly been a light to me. Thank you for sending the light in your Son. Help me to be a light to all those I touch this week. Amen.

The Story and Young Children

Children enjoy learning about God's plan for light. As children explore God's creation, they should have opportunities to do it firsthand, out of doors, if it is at all possible. Several activities in the last session and this one can be done outdoors. If you do not have a safe place in which children can be outside, the next best experience with light would be in a window with direct sun. Of course, God plans for *all* light, even that which humankind causes to come from bulbs or flashlights. (It's still God's particle-and-wave light.)

Learning Centers

Conversation Center

You will need: play dough and items to use with play dough; clear plastic soda bottles, cellophane paper in many colors; glue, small paper cups (optional: clear tape).

Get ready: Cut cellophane into small squares.

- Play With Play Dough, Activity 1d
- Make Light Catchers, Activity 3a

Building Center

You will need: building blocks; plastic, wooden, or craft stick people figures.

Get ready: Provide enough blocks for toddlers to share.

- Play With Blocks, Activity 3d

Family Living Center

You will need: props for things to do in daytime (eat, mow grass) and nighttime (pajamas, pillow, blanket).

- Play Day and Night, Activity 3c

Storytelling Center

You will need: Bible, Activity Pak—p. 9 (figure 1); Activity Pak Songbook, CD and CD player; large lightweight blanket; large box, teacher scissors, heavy fabric, flashlight (optional: utility knife).

Get ready: Cut a door in a large box.

- Tell the Bible Story, Activity 2a
- Retell the Bible Story, Activity 2b
- Use an Action Verse, Activity 2c
- Explore a Dark Box, Activity 3b
- Enjoy Music, Activity 4a

Discovery Center

You will need: Activity Pak—pp. 5 (day/night sorting cards) and 3 (Light Does Many Things picture); two boxes or baskets; shoebox with lid, small toy, teacher scissors.

Get ready: Cut a small hole in the side of a shoebox.

- Play a Game, Activity 1b
- Look at a Poster, Activity 1c
- Enjoy Light, Activity 4b

Thank You, God, for Day

Martha sat with her family after supper.

"It's been a good day," said Father. "I worked in the garden. Soon we will have beans to eat."

"It's been a good day for me too," said Mother. "I talked to my friends while I washed the clothes."

"I had fun today," said Martha. "My friends and I played with a ball."

"I am glad for daytime," said Father.

"Me too," said Martha.

Martha and her family prayed together. "Thank you, God, for daytime."

 **Prepare**

for the Story

a **Welcome Each Child**
Do this as each child enters.

Have the CD playing as children arrive.

Stoop to the children's eye level and welcome each child by name.

Say to each child: "I am so happy you have come to church today."

Be prepared to involve children in an interesting or comforting activity.

b **Play a Game**
Do this in the Discovery Center.

Gather two or three children. Show the children the day/night sorting cards (Activity Pak—p. 5).

Ask: "Do we do this in the daytime or the nighttime? OK, let's put all of the daytime cards in this box (or basket). How about the next one? Where does it go?"

c **Look at a Picture**
Do this in the Discovery Center.

Gather two or three children. As the children look at the "Light Does Many Things" picture (Activity Pak—p. 3), talk about what they see there: What is the sun doing in each picture? Help younger children with words.

Tell the children that God plans for the sun and the light.

Pray: "Thank you, God, for light."

d **Play With Play Dough**
Do this in the Conversation Center.

Encourage the children to manipulate the dough in rhythm with the music of the CD. Provide round blocks or rolling pins for smoothing dough, or provide items with which the children can make interesting prints in the dough.

 Tell

the Story

a **Tell the Bible Story**
Do this in the Storytelling Center.

Gather two or three children. If needed, repeat last week's Bible story. Then tell the story for this week.

Open a Bible and **say** the Bible verse: "We give thanks to you, O God." Encourage the children to say the Bible verse with you.

This week before you say the prayer, encourage the children to say the prayer with you. Put up the picture of the sun from last week (figure 1) as you say the prayer.

Pray: "Thank you, God, for light. Amen."

b **Retell the Bible Story**
Do this in the Storytelling Center.

Gather two or three children. **Say:** "Let's see what it was like before there was light."

Gather the children under the blanket. **Say:** "And God said, 'Let there be light.'" Throw the blanket off. Repeat as long as the children have interest.

Be aware of children who may be afraid of the dark. Do not keep the blanket over these children very long. Let them see how much fun it is to throw the blanket off and **say:** "Let there be light."

c **Use an Action Verse**
Do this in the Storytelling Center.

Gather two or three children. Begin to teach the action verse "God Planned for Light," which is printed in the Activity Pak Songbook. Every two weeks add another verse.

3 Connect
with the Story

a **Make Light Catchers**
Do this in the Conversation Center.

Gather two or three children. Give each child a soda bottle and several cellophane squares. Pour glue into small paper cups. Have the children "touch" the glue with their finger and then "touch" the paper to transfer the glue. Or attach the squares with clear tape.

Help the children glue cellophane to their soda bottle. Notice how light shines through colored cellophane. If desired, hang or place your bottles in a sunny window.

b **Explore a Dark Box**
Do this in the Storytelling Center.

Gather two or three children. Cut a door in the box large enough for a teacher to crawl into. Tape heavy fabric across the door.

Get into the box with a child. Pull the fabric curtain over the door. Is it dark? What can you see? Is it hard to see without light? Where can you see the most light in the dark box? Around the curtain? Why?

Turn on the flashlight. What can you see now? Why?

Hold the mirror so that it reflects the flashlight beam inside the box. Let the child move the mirror about to move the reflection. **Say:** "It's fun to play with light."

c **Play Day and Night**
Do this in the Family Living Center.

As the children play, encourage them to pretend daytime and nighttime activities. **Say:** "Now let's pretend it is nighttime. What do we do now? Look! The sun came up! It's morning! What do we do now?"

d **Play With Blocks**
Do this in the Building Center.

As the children play with blocks, encourage pretending day or night activities with the people figures. Make a block bed for the people to sleep in at night. Make a church for the people to walk to in the daytime.

4 Celebrate
the Story

a **Enjoy Music**
Do this in the Storytelling Center.

Gather two or three children. Play "This Little Light of Mine" (Activity Pak Songbook, CD). Encourage the children to dance to the music. Show the children how to hold up their index fingers as they dance. Encourage the children to sing along with the music.

Play the Bible verse song, "We Give Thanks" (Activity Pak Songbook, CD). Sing the song and add verses that are appropriate to this week (see the Activity Pak Songbook).

b **Enjoy Light**
Do this in the Discovery Center.

Place a hole in the side of a shoebox with a lid. Place a small toy inside the box.

Let the children observe how they can see the toy through the hole when the lid is off and the light can enter the box. They will see that when the lid is in place and

light cannot enter the box, they cannot see the toy.

c **Say Goodbye**

Recall today's Bible story. Have the children say the Bible verse with you.

Say: "We enjoyed God's gift of light today. (*Child's name*) saw her shadow." Repeat each child's name and mention a light-exploring activity in which he or she took part.

Pray: "Thank you, God, for light."

Be sure to have a teacher or helper at the door to match children with their caregivers.

Tell parents about today's Bible story. Make sure that each child has today's Bible Story Picture Card. Show parents the "Nurturing Your Child's Faith" section of the card.

Have the children take home their Sparkle Banners.

Tip
Make the stories more personal. Substitute your name and that of the children in the contemporary stories.

Look Back
What activities went particularly well today? With what activities did you or the children have trouble?

What activities will you want to repeat next week?

Did all of the children have a chance to experience the Bible story this week? Can the children retell the story?

Look Ahead
Because of sporadic attendance in the summer months and the fact that the whole summer centers around Creation, you will want to read ahead. It is highly recommended that you use all of the odd numbered session plans. Using these Bible stories will ensure that the children hear all of the Creation story. But you will want to substitute activities from the sessions you do not use for those in which your children have no interest, or which are not practical for your use (for example, going outside).

God made the world we live on.

Bible Verse:
We give thanks to you, O God.
(Psalm 75:1)

Resources:
Bible
CD
Activity Pak (Summer)
  page 9 (figures 1–4)
  page 21 ("God Made
  the Earth, the Sea,
  and the Sky" picture)
  Songbook
Bible Story Picture Cards

Supplies:
paper
water play items (see
  p. 234)
building blocks
water
toy boats and/or fish
small suitcases
CD player
glue in squirt bottles
sand
baking sheets or trays
  with rims
cotton balls
construction paper
large piece of blue fabric
dishpan with a mixture
  of sand and water
clear two-liter plastic
  bottle
glitter or confetti
collection of rocks
large sock or cloth bag
(optional: glue that is not
  water soluble)

God Created Sky, Earth, and Seas.......

Enter the Bible Story

Read Genesis 1:6-10: After light was created, God separated the sky and the earth and the water.

Think About It: God continued to create order out of chaos. When you are faced with a big mess, what is the first thing you do? There is no right or wrong answer to this question. Some of us start by making a list of tasks. Some of us just pick up whatever is closest and deal with it first. I love to sort things into piles. What is your style? According to the first chapter of Genesis, God created the sky, earth, and seas out of what was already there. Later, the plants and animals and people seem to come from God's word alone. How is this different from the second story of creation in Genesis 2? Remember that when the Bible was first written down, there was no concept of a spherical earth. The ancients believed that the earth was a platform of dirt that was held up on pillars above a watery abyss. This is why if you dig a hole deep enough, you will find water. There was also a "bowl" called "sky" that was placed upside down on top of the earth. This held at bay the waters that were above the earth. Sometimes God would open the "windows" of the sky, and rain would fall until God closed the windows again. With this interpretation in mind read Genesis 7:11 and see how the great flood came about.

Through the Week: Spend some time digging in dirt this week. What does it smell like? What does it feel like? Is it hard? crumbly? moist? full of clay? Imagine your students looking at dirt for the first time. What will fascinate them about playing in dirt?

Pray: Thank you, God, for giving me children to work with. Help me to accept them as they are. Help me to recognize where they are, and show me what I need to do to help them grow from here. Amen.

The Story and Young Children

One of the characteristics of a two-year-old is curiosity. Walking a child through a park can be as frustrating as walking an unleashed puppy. Many toddlers notice tiny details in their world and are impatient to examine every minute characteristic of materials placed in front of them. Children will love this week's session, particularly if they get to experiment with water. As you plan for this week, you might wish to tell parents to dress their children in clothing that can withstand a little mess. Or be sure to provide coverups for messier activities. Allow lots of time for independent exploration. This is not a session to be rushed through.

Learning Centers

Conversation Center

This should be a table around which you may gather the children. Sit down with the children and engage them in conversation.

You will need: paper, glue in squirt bottles, sand, baking sheets or trays with rims, cotton balls, construction paper.

- Make Sand Pictures, Activity 1c
- Make Cotton Ball Clouds, Activity 3a

Building Center

You will need: blocks; toy boats and/or fish, large piece of blue fabric.

- Play With Blocks, Activity 3b

Storytelling Center

You will need: Activity Pak—pp. 9 (figures 1–4) and 21 ("God Made the Earth, the Sea, and the Sky" teaching picture); dishpan with a mixture of sand and water; CD, CD player, Activity Pak Songbook; Bible.

Get ready: Experiment with sand and water to find the best mixture. It should be mostly sand, but when you push the sand to one side, the water should pool on the other.

- Tell the Bible Story, Activity 2a
- Retell the Bible Story, Activity 2b
- Use an Action Verse, Activity 2c
- Enjoy Music, Activity 4a

Family Living Center

You will need: a toy kitchen set and props appropriate to the lesson.

Discovery Center

You will need: items for water table activities (see p. 234), clear two-liter plastic soda bottle, glitter or confetti, water, collection of rocks; large sock or cloth bag (optional: glue that is not water-soluble).

Get ready: Gather rocks with many different characteristics—bumpy, shiny, and dull. Gather as many colors as you can find.

- Play With Water, Activity 1b
- Play With a Water Bottle, Activity 3c
- Look at Rocks, Activity 4b

God Created the Sky, the Earth, and the Sea

When God made the world, everything was icky, sticky mud. There was no place to walk and no place for plants to grow. There was no place to swim and no place to get a drink of water.

Everything was icky, sticky mud.

So God said, "This is not good!"

God pushed all the dirt to one side and pushed all the water to the other. There, that was better. Now you could walk on the dirt and swim in the water. The plants could grow on the dirt, and the fish could live in the water.

God said, "This is very, very good!"

1 Prepare

for the Story

a Welcome Each Child

Have the CD playing as the children arrive. Stoop to the child's eye level and welcome each child by name.

Say to each child: "I am so happy you have come to church today." Be prepared to involve the children in an interesting or comforting activity.

b Play With Water

Do this in the Discovery Center.

Let the children play in the water. Notice how the water pours through funnels and squirts from meat basters. See what things float in the water and what things sink.

c Make Sand Pictures

Do this in the Conversation Center.

Gather two or three children. Give each child a piece of paper and a bottle of glue. Put the piece of paper on a baking sheet or a tray that has a rim.

Let the children squirt glue in a design onto their papers. Help the children sprinkle sand on top of the glue.

If the glue is not too thick, you may pick up the picture immediately and shake the excess sand back into the tray. If the glue is very thick, you may wish to let it dry before picking up the picture.

2 Tell

the Story

a Tell the Bible Story

Do this in the Storytelling Center.

Gather two or three children. If needed, repeat last week's Bible story. Then tell the story for this week, showing the pictures of the sky, the earth and the sea (figures 2–4) at the appropriate time.

Open a Bible and **say** the Bible verse: "We give thanks to you, O God." Encourage the children to say the Bible verse with you.

This week before you say the prayer, encourage the children to say the prayer with you. Put up the picture of the sun from last week (figure 1) as you say the prayer. Then add the pictures from this week as you continue the prayer. **Pray:**

Thank you, God, for light.
Thank you, God, for sky.
Thank you, God, for dirt.
Thank you, God, for water. Amen.

b Retell the Bible Story

Do this in the Storytelling Center.

Gather two or three children. Show the children the teaching picture called "God Made the Earth, the Sea, and the Sky" (Activity Pak—p. 21).

Say: "Let me show you how God made the dirt and the water."

Tell the story again, but this time when you tell how God pushed the dirt, push the sand to one side, letting the water drain to the other side.

Let the children experiment with the sand to see if they can make a pool of water and some fairly sturdy damp sand.

If you are able to be outside this summer, this activity would be best done outside.

c Use an Action Verse

Do this in the Storytelling Center.

Gather two or three children. Say the action verse, "God Planned For Light," adding the second verse (Activity Pak Songbook).

3 Connect
with the Story

 a **Make Cotton Ball Clouds**
Do this in the Conversation Center.

Give each child a piece of construction paper. Show the children how to pull apart cotton balls to make them more fluffy.

Encourage the children to glue the cotton balls onto their pieces of construction paper however they wish.

Tell the children that the cotton balls on their papers can be pretend clouds. Remind the children that God created the sky.

b **Play With Blocks**
Do this in the Building Center.

As the children play with blocks, spread out the blue fabric and pretend that it is a large lake. Play with the boats and the fish.

Encourage conversation as you play:

What can you do in the water? What can you do on the land?

c **Play With a Water Bottle**
Do this in the Discovery Center.

Ahead of time, pour the glitter or confetti into the bottle and fill it with water. Securely screw the lid on. You may wish to pour some non-water soluble glue into the cap before screwing it on.

Let the children play with the water bottle. Notice that if you shake the bottle, the glitter or confetti seems to fill the bottle.

Or you can gently pour the glitter or confetti from the bottom to the top of the bottle by moving it very slowly.

Do not expose children directly to glitter. Glitter is hazardous to young children's eyes.

4 Celebrate
the Story

a **Enjoy Music**
Do this in the Storytelling Center.

Gather two or three children. Play the Bible verse song, "We Give Thanks" (Songbook, CD).

Sing the song and add verses that are appropriate to this week.

Sing other songs that the children have enjoyed in Sunday school this year. If desired, add instruments.

 b **Look at Rocks**
Do this in the Discovery Center.

Gather two or three children. Examine the rocks. Encourage the children to talk about the rocks and their characteristics.

Put the rocks inside a large sock or a cloth bag and see if children can find "the smooth one" or "the bumpy one" by touch alone.

c **Say Goodbye**

Recall today's Bible story. Encourage the children to say the Bible verse with you.

Say: "We enjoyed God's gift of sky, dirt and water today. (*Child's name*) played in the water." Repeat each child's name and mention an activity in which he or she took part.

Pray: "Thank you, God, for sky, earth, and water."

Be sure to have a teacher or helper at the door to match children with their caregivers.

Tell parents about today's Bible story and make sure that each child has today's Bible Story Picture Card. Show parents the "Nurturing Your Child's Faith" section of the card.

Be sure the children take home their cloud pictures.

Tip
Remember that for young children the process of creating art is much more important than the actual finished product. There is no right or wrong way to do an art project.

Look Back
What activities went particularly well today? With what activities did you or the children have trouble? What activities will you want to repeat next week?

Did all of the children have a chance to experience the Bible story this week? Can the children retell the story?

Look Ahead
Because of sporadic attendance in the summer months and the fact that the whole summer centers around creation, you will want to read ahead.

It is highly recommended that you use all of the odd-numbered session plans. Using these Bible stories will ensure that the children hear all of the Creation story. But you will want to substitute activities from the sessions you do not use for those in which your children have no interest, or which are not practical for your use (for example, going outside).

We praise God for the world.

Bible Verse:
We give thanks to you, O God.
(Psalm 75:1a)

Resources:
Bible
CD
Activity Pak (Summer)
    page 9 (figures 1–4)
    page 21 ("God Made
    the Earth, the Sky, and
    the Sea" picture)
    Songbook
Bible Picture Story Cards

Supplies:
CD player
building blocks
blue fingerpaint
fingerpaint paper
short-sleeved adult
    shirts that button
    down the front
toy boats and/or fish
large piece of blue
    fabric
water table activities
    (see page 234)
clear two-liter plastic
    soda bottle
glitter or confetti
water
collection of rocks
manila paper
powdered paint
paintbrushes or cotton
    swabs
scarfs or streamers
(optional: glue that is not
    water-soluble)

Thank You, God, for Earth, Sky, and Seas ....

Enter the Bible Story

Read Psalm 75:1a: This psalm reminds us to give thanks to God for the world in which we live.

Think About It: The earth, the sky, and the seas form the foundation of everything that God created. Out of the earth sprang the plants, which are watered by the seas and protected by the sky. The animals and people are dependent upon all three for sustenance. Reflect on the following questions as you prepare to teach this week: What images come to you as you think of the sky? clouds? sunsets? rain or snow? How do you see God in the sky? What images come to you when you dig in the dirt? How do you see God in ordinary dirt? What images come to you as you imagine the seashore? How do you see God in the sea?

  If you have not done so, read the "Enter the Bible Story" section of last week's lesson for an explanation of this section of the creation story. Separation of elements and assigning each a place is foundational to creating order from chaos. We thank God that we live in a world that has a natural order, even if, with our dams, roads, and dikes, we try to control it even further.

Through the Week: Spend time this week noticing water. Approximately how much water do you use daily for drinking, bathing, and cooking? How about watering gardens or flushing your toilet? It has been said that one of the major accomplishments of the twentieth century was the water treatment plant.

Pray: Thank you, God, for giving me the basics I need for life. I have air to breathe, water to drink, and land on which to stand. Help me to be grateful for the simple things. Amen.

The Story and Young Children

  Even toddlers who live close to an ocean may not have yet experienced the vastness of the sea. Toddlers tend to keep their area of focus small and often do not notice things that are far away. Nevertheless, this is the year in which this opening of the world begins. Point out to the children the clouds in the sky. If you are fortunate enough to live in a setting with wide vistas, show the children the vastness of the earth.

  Recognize that children delight in small things. Have dirt available for touching, digging, and piling. Play with water and notice how it runs through a funnel or squirts out from a meat baster. Praise God for the wonders of nature.

Learning Centers

Work with two or three children at a time in each learning center.

Conversation Center

You will need: manila paper, powdered paint, paintbrushes or cotton swabs, water, blue fingerpaint, paper, short-sleeved adult shirts that button down the front.

- Paint With Water, Activity 1c
- Fingerpaint, Activity 3a

Building Center

You will need: building blocks, toy boats and/or fish, large piece of blue fabric.

- Play With Blocks, Activity 3b

Storytelling Center

This should be an open area where you may gather children for storytelling, or to listen and respond to music. It would be helpful to have this center on a carpeted area.

You will need: Activity Pak—pp. 9 (figures 1–4) and 21 ("God Made the Earth, the Sky, and the Sea" teaching picture); CD and CD player, Activity Pak Songbook; Bible; scarfs or streamers.

- Tell the Bible Story, Activity 2a
- Retell the Bible Story, Activity 2b
- Use an Action Verse, Activity 2c
- Enjoy Music, Activity 4a

Family Living Center

You will need: a toy kitchen set and props appropriate to this lesson.

Discovery Center

You will need: water play items (see p. 234); clear two-liter plastic soda bottle, glitter or confetti, water; collection of rocks (optional: glue that is not water-soluble).

Get ready: Gather rocks with many different characteristics: smooth, bumpy, shiny, and dull. Gather as many colors as you can find.

- Play With Water, Activity 1b
- Play With a Water Bottle, Activity 3c
- Look at Rocks, Activity 4b

Thank You, God, for Earth, Sky, and Seas

Jonathan and his daddy went to the lake. They sat down on the grass and felt the warm sun on their faces. They went wading in the shallow water. They looked for fish under the rocks. They made mud pies along the shore.

That night, before Jonathan went to sleep, he and his daddy prayed.

"Thank you, God, for the water in the lake, and for the grass on the shore, and for the sun in the sky, and for the fish in the water, and for the mud to play with," they said. "Thank you, God, for everything. Amen."

1 Prepare
for the Story

a Welcome Each Child

Do this as each child enters.

Have the CD playing as children arrive.

Stoop to the children's eye level and welcome each child by name. **Say** to each child: "I am so happy you have come to church today."

b Play With Water

Do this in the Discovery Center.

Let the children play in the water. Point out how the water pours through funnels and squirts from meat basters. See what things float in the water and what things sink.

c Paint With Water

Do this in the Conversation Center.

Gather two or three children. Protect their clothing by putting a short-sleeved adult shirt on them, buttoned down the back.

Place a piece of manila paper on the table and sprinkle it lightly with powdered paint.

Let the children dip their paintbrushes or cotton swabs into water and "paint" on the sprinkled paper.

2 Tell

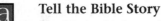

the Story

a Tell the Bible Story

Do this in the Storytelling Center.

Gather two or three children. If needed, repeat last week's Bible story.

Look at the "God Made the Earth, the Sky, and the Sea" picture (Activity Pak—p. 21) and notice the detail. Can the children find the sky? Can the children find the water? the dirt (or rocks)? Is all of the sky the same? Is all of the water the same? Then tell the story for this week.

Open a Bible and **say** the Bible verse: "We give thanks to you, O God." Encourage the children to say the Bible verse with you.

This week before you say the prayer, encourage the children to say the prayer with you. Put up the picture of the sun from last week (figure 1) as you say the prayer. Then add the pictures from this week (figures 2–4) as you continue the prayer. **Pray:**

Thank you, God, for light.
Thank you, God, for sky.
Thank you, God, for dirt.
Thank you, God, for water. Amen.

b Retell the Bible Story

Do this in the Storytelling Center.

Gather two or three children. Tell the story and use the motions. Encourage the children to do the motions with you.

Jonathan and his daddy went to the lake. (*Walk in place.*)

They sat down on the grass (*Sit down and pat the ground.*) and felt the warm sun on their faces. (*Smooth your hands on your face.*)

They went wading in the shallow water. (*Wiggle your feet as if splashing.*)

They looked for fish under the rocks. (*Pretend to look under a rock.*)

They made mud pies along the shore. (*Pat hands together.*)

That night Jonathan and his daddy prayed. (*Fold hands.*) They said, "Thank you, God for everything. Amen."

c Use an Action Verse

Do this in the Storytelling Center.

Gather two or three children. Say the action verse, "God Planned for Light" (Activity Pak Songbook). Use the first two verses.

 **Connect**

. . . .

with the Story

a Fingerpaint

Do this in the Conversation Center.

Gather two or three children. Protect clothing by putting a shirt on each child, buttoned down the back.

Give each child a piece of fingerpaint paper and a blob of fingerpaint. As the children paint, talk with them about water.

b Play With Blocks

Do this in the Building Center.

As the children play with blocks, spread out the blue fabric and pretend that it is a large lake. Play with the boats and the fish.

Encourage conversation as you play: What can you do in the water? What can you do on the land?

c Play With a Water Bottle

Do this in the Discovery Center.

Ahead of time, pour glitter or confetti into the bottle and fill it with water. Securely screw the lid on. You may wish to pour some glue that is not water-soluble into the cap before screwing it on.

Let the children play with the water bottle. Notice that if you shake the bottle, the glitter or confetti seems to fill the bottle.

Or you can gently pour the glitter or confetti from the bottom to the top of the bottle by moving it very slowly.

Celebrate

. . . .

the Story

a Enjoy Music

Do this in the Storytelling Center.

Gather two or three children. Play the Bible verse song, "We Give Thanks" (Activity Pak Songbook, CD).

Sing the song and add verses that are appropriate to this week.

Give the children scarfs or streamers and let them dance to "Happy Music" (Activity Pak Songbook, CD).

Sing other songs that the children enjoy.

b Look at Rocks

Do this in the Discovery Center.

Gather two or three children. Examine the rock that you have collected. Encourage the children to talk about the rocks and their characteristics.

Put the rocks inside a large sock or a cloth bag and see if children can find "the smooth one" or "the bumpy one" by touch alone.

c Say Goodbye

Recall today's Bible story, encouraging the children to say the Bible verse with you.

Say: "We enjoyed God's gift of sky, dirt, and water today. (*Child's name*) played in the water." Repeat each child's name and mention an activity in which he or she took part.

Pray: "Thank you, God, for sky, dirt, and water."

Be sure to have a teacher or helper at the door to match children with their caregivers.

Tell parents about today's Bible story and make sure that each child has today's Bible Story Picture Card. Show parents the "Nurturing Your Child's Faith" section of the card.

Be sure the children take home their fingerpainting or water painting.

Tip

Parents may wonder what you are teaching, since nonverbal toddlers cannot tell their parents about the lesson. Try to arrange your room so that it is obvious what the focus of the lesson is, and point out to parents the Bible verse that you are learning this summer.

Look Back

What activities went particularly well today? With what activities did you or the children have trouble?

What activities will you want to repeat next week?

Did all of the children have a chance to experience water today? Can they remember who made the water?

Look Ahead

Next week we will talk about plants. Look over the lesson and get any necessary supplies.

God made a wide
variety of plants.

Bible Verse:
We give thanks to
you, O God.
(Psalm 75:1a)

Resources:
Bible
CD
Activity Pak (Summer)
   page 9 (figures 1–5)
   page 16 (fruits and
    vegetables puzzles)
   page 22 ("God Made
    Plants" picture)
   Songbook
Bible Story Picture Cards

Supplies:
CD player
building blocks
green tempera paint
paper
big chunky paintbrush
several large leaves
short-sleeved adult
   shirts that button
   down the front
fruits and vegetables
   for a snack
toy trees and flowers
planter or dishpan
   filled with dirt or sand
silk flowers and plants
several different plants
collection of leaves, cut
   flowers, vegetables,
   and fruits
clear plastic cups
stickers
paper towels
large soup beans such
   as lima beans
water
napkins

God Created Plants

Enter the Bible Story

Read Genesis 1:11-12: The Bible story for today focuses on the creation of plant life. Once the water, earth, and sky were separated, plant life could flourish, as it still does today.

Think About It: Without plant life, life as we know it would be impossible. We are dependent on plants to create the air we breathe and the food we eat. Plants, in turn, are dependent on the sun for growth. Can you imagine a world without plants? Think of an office building or apartment building completely devoid of plant life. Imagine a new subdivision that has been cleared of all plant life and contains only streets and houses. How would it differ from the place where you work or live?

While plants have many things in common with one another, there is also a great variety in plant life. Some plants can exist on very little water, and some grow underwater. Some plant flourish in full sunlight, and others need the dark of caves for life. Some plants are so large they cannot be ignored, and others can only be seen with a microscope. Plants are also tenacious. Many a parking lot has been destroyed by plants that, against all odds, push through the asphalt. Some plants, like kudzu in the southern United States, resist all efforts at eradication.

Through the Week: Spend some time exploring the plant world. Visit a public park or garden. Stop by a professional nursery. Can you find two plants that are exactly alike? Locate two or three plants that you have never seen before.

Pray: We are truly thankful, O God, for the many varieties of plants you created. From the smallest fungus to the largest tree, your creation is wonderful. Help us enjoy and appreciate it.

The Story and Young Children

Young children cannot understand the scientific concepts behind creation, but they can daily see those things that God has created. Toddlers are still a couple of years from understanding that a seed may be planted and watered and will grow into a plant, but they can wonder and marvel at the plant itself. We can remind children that God made the plants. We can tell the children that what God created is good. As we continue the creation story, we see anew how God created the world for use by humankind. When we look at God's creation, we cannot help but see God's wisdom and love.

Learning Centers

Work with two or three children at a time in each learning center.

Conversation Center

You will need: green tempera paint and paper, big chunky paintbrush, several large leaves, short-sleeved adult shirts that button down the front, fruits and vegetables for a snack, napkins.

Get ready: Pour green tempera paint into small paper cups.

- Paint Leaves, Activity 3a
- Enjoy a Snack, Activity 4b

Discovery Center

You will need: several different plants; collection of leaves, cut flowers, vegetables, and fruits; Activity Pak—p. 16 (fruits and vegetables puzzles); clear plastic cups; stickers; paper towels; large soup beans such as lima beans; water.

Get ready: Make sure you do not have any plants that may be toxic to young children. Separate the fruits and vegetables puzzles.

- Play With Puzzles, Activity 1b
- Examine Plants, Activity 1c
- Plant a Seed, Activity 3c

Family Living Center

You will need: silk or plastic plants.

Get ready: Include silk or plastic plants as the children play house.

Building Center

You will need: building blocks, toy trees and flowers.

Get ready: Set out several toy trees and flowers.

- Play With Blocks, Activity 3b

Storytelling Center

You will need: Bible; Activity Pak—p. 9 (figures 1-5) and p. 22 ("God Made Plants" teaching picture); CD and CD player; Songbook; planter or dishpan filled with dirt or sand; silk or plastic flowers.

Get ready: Prepare storytelling figures (see Activity Pak—p. 2).

- Tell the Bible Story, Activity 2a
- Retell the Bible Story, Activity 2b
- Use an Action Verse, Activity 2c
- Enjoy Music, Activity 4a

God Made the Plants

When God made the world, there were no plants anywhere—just dirt and rocks.

God said, "This is not good."

So God made plants to grow out of the dirt. There were little bitty plants that grew around the rocks and great big trees that grew straight and tall.

And God said, "This is very, very good."

 **Prepare**

··

for the Story

a **Welcome Each Child**
Do this as each child enters.

Stoop to the child's eye level and welcome each child by name.

Say to each child: "I am so happy you have come to church today."

Be prepared to involve children in an interesting or comforting activity.

b **Play With Puzzles**
Do this in the Discovery Center.

Gather two or three children. Help the children play with the fruits and vegetables puzzles (Activity Pak—p. 16). Help them notice clues in the pictures to find the matching half of the picture.

When each puzzle is put together, help the children name the picture.

c **Examine Plants**
Do this in the Discovery Center.

Have a variety of plants available for the children to examine. Be sure that you only have plants that children can touch. Check with a gardener to make sure that you do not bring in any plants that are toxic to young children. Remember, some of your children are still at the stage of examining things by putting them in their mouths!

Engage the children in conversation about the plants: What colors do they see? Can they feel that the tops of leaves are smooth and the bottoms of leaves are bumpy?

What fruits and vegetables do the children recognize? Help younger children name the vegetables and fruits. Make sure that you have washed the fruits and vegetables thoroughly, because at least one of your children will want to take a bite.

 **Tell**

··

the Story

a **Tell the Bible Story**
Do this in the Storytelling Center.

Gather two or three children. If needed, repeat last week's Bible story. Look at the "God Made Plants" picture (Activity Pak—p. 22) and notice the detail. What kind of plants do the children find? Are there some they have never seen before?

Tell the Bible story. Open a Bible and **say** the verse: "We give thanks to you, O God." Have the children say the verse with you.

This week before you say the prayer, encourage the children to say the prayer with you. Put up the picture of the sun, earth, water, and sky from last week (figures 1–4) as you say the prayer. Then add the picture of the plants (figure 5) as you continue the prayer. **Pray:**

Thank you, God, for light.
Thank you, God, for sky.
Thank you, God, for dirt.
Thank you, God, for water.
Thank you, God, for plants. Amen.

b **Retell the Bible Story**
Do this in the Storytelling Center.

Gather two or three children. Show the children the bare dirt.

Say: "When God made the world, there were no plants anywhere—just dirt and rocks. So God said, 'This is not good.' And God made plants to grow out of the dirt."

Quickly place plants into the dirt. Let the children help you fill the bare planter with lots of silk or plastic plants.

When the planter or dishpan is full, **say:** "And God said, 'This is very good.'"

c **Use an Action Verse**
Do this in the Storytelling Center.

Gather two or three children. Say the action verse "God Planned For Light" (Songbook).

 Connect
with the Story

a Paint Leaves
Do this in the Conversation Center.

Gather two or three children. Protect clothing by putting a shirt on each child, buttoned down the back.

Give each child a piece of paper. Paint the back of a leaf and give it to the child. Show the child how to press the leaf on the paper to make a leaf print. Let the child make several prints on the paper.

b Play With Blocks
Do this in the Building Center.

As the children play with blocks, encourage the children to use the trees and flowers in their play.

Engage in conversation as you play: "Oh, look! Jamail put a tree beside his block tower! Can Sheena use this flower on top of her blocks?"

c Plant a Seed
Do this in the Discovery Center.

Gather two or three children. Let the children put stickers on their cups.

Wad a couple of paper towels and place them in each cup. Place a bean in the paper towels, making sure that the bean is covered. Let the children pour about two teaspoons of water into their cups.

Tell the children to take their cups home and see what happens.

d Take a Walk
If possible, take the class outside to look at plants around your church. Or walk around the inside of the church and notice plants.

If the sanctuary is not being used, go and inspect the floral arrangement on the altar.

Celebrate
the Story

a Enjoy Music
Do this in the Storytelling Center.

Gather two or three children. Play the Bible verse song, "We Give Thanks" (Songbook, CD).

Sing the song and add verses that are appropriate to this week.

We give thanks to you, O God.
We give thanks to you, O God.
We give thanks to you for plants.
We give thanks to you for plants.

b Enjoy a Snack
Do this in the Conversation Center.

Check with parents for allergies before giving children fresh fruits or vegetables, particularly strawberries.

Have a selection of apple and orange slices or other fruits and vegetables that the children enjoy. As the children eat, **say:** "I am so glad that God planned for food!"

c Say Goodbye
Recall today's Bible story, encouraging the children to say the Bible verse with you.

Say: "We enjoyed God's gift of plants today. (*Child's name*) made a leaf painting." Repeat each child's name and mention an activity in which he or she took part.

Pray: "Thank you, God, for plants."

Be sure to have a teacher or helper at the door to match children with their caregivers.

Tell parents about today's Bible story and make sure that each child has today's Bible Story Picture Card. Show parents the "Nurturing Your Child's Faith" section of the card.

Be sure the children take home their leaf print picture.

Tip
Whenever you take your class on a field trip, make sure you have one adult for every two children. Insist that the children hold the hands of the adult assigned to them.

Look Back
What activities went particularly well today? With what activities did you or the children have trouble?

What activities will you want to repeat next week?

Did all of the children have a chance to experience the Bible story this week? Can the children retell the story?

Look Ahead
Next week we will continue our study of plants. Plan to repeat any activity that the children responded to well. Toddlers thrive on repetition.

195

We praise God for plants.

Bible Verse:
We give thanks to you, O God.
(Psalm 75:1a)

Resources:
Bible
CD
Activity Pak (Summer)
  page 9 (figures 1–5)
  page 16 (fruits and
  vegetables puzzles)
  page 22 ("God Made
  Plants" picture)
Songbook
Bible Story Picture Cards

Supplies:
CD player
building blocks
tempera paint (several
  colors plus green)
3- to 5-oz. paper cups
paper
big chunky paintbrush
short-sleeved adult shirts
  that button down the
  front
fruits and vegetables for
  a snack
toy trees and flowers
planter or dishpan
  filled with dirt or sand
silk or plastic flowers
several different plants
collection of leaves, cut
  flowers, vegetables,
  and fruits
brightly colored scarfs
clay pots or unbreakable
  vases
napkins
newspaper
plastic foam

Thank, You, God, for Plants........

Enter the Bible Story

Read Psalm 75:1: We continually give thanks to God for creating the plants, sun, and moon.

Think About It: Because much in this lesson is the same as last week's lesson, think again about the interconnectedness of plants and people. How do we lead toddlers to praise God for plants? According to Genesis 1:11, God did not directly create plant life, but God's word allowed the earth to become fertile, and vegetation began sprouting on it. We see later that one reason God caused plants to appear was to provide food for the animal life that was to follow.

Plants have a variety of uses. We use them for food both directly and indirectly as seasonings for meats. We use them for shelter: Trees give us wood for our houses, and bricks are much stronger when they are made with straw. We use them for clothing: Most of our modern fabrics have at least a touch of cotton, flax, or another plant. We weave baskets from plants and use plants to make soaps and dyes. We are rediscovering the many medicinal uses of herbs in our daily lives. We use plants in celebrations. Florists have to stock up for holidays such as Valentine's Day or Mother's Day. Most churches use live plants in their worship service to represent God's creative power. Plants brighten up many a hospital room and funeral parlor, sending good wishes and warm thoughts through their mere presence.

Through the Week: Psalm 104 praises God as the creator of the earth. In a marvelous recounting of the seasonal rhythms, the psalmist portrays the human interdependence with all creation and with God. Take quiet time to read this psalm and to reflect upon your own dependence upon creation and God.

Pray: We are truly thankful, O God, for the many varieties of plants you created. From the smallest fungus to the largest tree, your creation is wonderful. Help us enjoy and appreciate it.

The Story and Young Children

Toddlers are fascinated with plants. They know very well how to "stop and smell the roses." They bring us leaves that they have found on the ground and touch the pretty flowers they find growing in the cracks of the sidewalk. At my church we made the mistake of planting a bed full of impatiens while the two-year-old class was on the playground. They watched the gardeners with rapt attention, and as soon as the gardeners left, they began pulling up the plants to look at the roots and putting them back into the ground. Needless to say, the impatiens bed did not last long. Bring out this wonder by exposing the children to many kinds of plants. Recognize that the entire world is a wonder to them.

Learning Centers

Work with two or three children at a time in each learning center.

Conversation Center

You will need: tempera paint (several colors plus green); small cups; paper; big chunky paintbrush; short-sleeved adult shirts that button down the front; fruits and vegetables; newspaper; napkins.

Get ready: Pour paint into small cups. Cover the table with newspaper.

- Paint Handprint Flowers, Activity 3a
- Enjoy a Snack, Activity 4b

Building Center

You will need: building blocks, toy trees and flowers.

Get ready: Set out several toy trees and flowers for play.

- Play With Blocks, Activity 3b

Storytelling Center

You will need: Bible; Activity Pak—p. 9 (figures 1-5) and 22 ("God Made Plants" picture); CD and CD player, Songbook; planter or dishpan filled with dirt or sand; silk or plastic flowers; scarfs.

Get ready: Prepare storytelling figures (see Activity Pak—p. 2).

- Tell the Bible Story, Activity 2a
- Retell the Bible Story, Activity 2b
- Use an Action Verse, Activity 2c
- Do a Flower Dance, Activity 3c
- Enjoy Music, Activity 4a

Family Living Center

You will need: silk flowers; clay pots and/or unbreakable vases; plastic foam cut to fit inside the containers.

Get ready: Make sure that the flowers will easily push into the plastic foam.

- Play Flower Shop, Activity 1d

Discovery Center

You will need: several different plants; collection of leaves, cut flowers, vegetables, and fruits; Activity Pak—p. 16 (fruits and vegetables puzzles).

Get ready: If you did not do it last week, prepare the fruits and vegetables puzzles.

- Play With Puzzles, Activity 1b
- Examine Plants, Activity 1c

Thank You, God, for Plants, Sun, and Moon

Susanna was helping her mother in the garden.

They put water on the baby plants. They pulled weeds away from the bigger plants. They picked beans and tomatoes off of the biggest plants.

Then they gathered flowers for their table.

"I am glad God planned for plants," Mother said. "I am glad we can help take care of the plants too."

Prepare

for the Story

a Welcome Each Child
Do this as each child enters.

Stoop to the child's eye level and welcome each child by name. **Say** to each child: "I am so happy you have come to church today."

Be prepared to involve children in an interesting or comforting activity.

b Play With Puzzles
Do this in the Discovery Center.

Gather two or three children. Help the children play with the fruits and vegetables puzzles (Activity Pak—p. 16). Help them notice clues in the pictures to find the matching half of the picture.

When each puzzle is put together, help the children name the picture.

c Examine Plants
Do this in the Discovery Center.

Have a variety of plants available for the children to examine. See the instructions on p. 194 for special cautions.

d Play Flower Shop
Do this in the Family Living Center.

Set up the Family Living Center as a flower shop. Encourage the children to "purchase" flowers to give to their friends.

Let the children pot and re-pot the plants, using the plastic foam and plastic flowers. Talk about how flowers help us feel loved.

Tell

the Story

a Tell the Bible Story
Do this in the Storytelling Center.

Gather two or three children. If needed, repeat last week's Bible story. Look at the "God Made Plants" picture (Activity Pak—p. 22) and notice the detail. What kind of plants do the children find? Are there some they have never seen before?

Tell the Bible story. Open a Bible and **say** the verse: "We give thanks to you, O God." Have the children say the verse with you.

Before you say the prayer, encourage the children to say the prayer with you. Put up the pictures of the sun, earth, water, and sky from last week (figures 1–4) as you say the prayer. Then add the picture of the plants (figure 5) as you continue the prayer. **Pray:**

Thank you, God, for light.
Thank you, God, for sky.
Thank you, God, for dirt.
Thank you, God, for water.
Thank you, God, for plants. Amen.

b Retell the Bible Story
Do this in the Storytelling Center.

Gather two or three children. Show the children the bare dirt.

Say: "When God made the world, there were no plants anywhere—just dirt and rocks. God said, 'This is not good.' So God made plants to grow out of the dirt."

Quickly place plants into the dirt. Let the children help you fill the bare planter with lots of silk or plastic plants. When the planter or dishpan is full, **say:** "And God said, 'This is very good.'"

Tell the story of Susanna and her mother again, this time acting out what they did. (Use pretend water!)

c Use an Action Verse
Do this in the Storytelling Center.

Gather two or three children. Say the action verse, "God Planned for Light" (Songbook).

3 Connect
with the Story

a Paint Handprint Flowers
Do this in the Conversation Center.

Gather two or three children. Protect clothing by putting a shirt on each child, buttoned down the back.

Give each child a piece of paper. Use a paintbrush to paint the child's hand.

Show the child how to press their hand down on the paper to make a handprint. Let the child make several prints on the paper, using different colors.

Later, use green tempera paint to paint stems and leaves below the handprints to make a bouquet of flowers.

b Play With Blocks
Do this in the Building Center.

As the children play with blocks, encourage the children to use the trees and flowers in their play.

Engage the children in conversation as you play: "Oh, look! Jamail put a tree beside his block tower! Can Sheena use this flower on top of her blocks?"

c Do a Flower Dance
Do this in the Storytelling Center.

Gather two or three children. Give each child a brightly colored scarf. Play "God Has Made Everything Beautiful" (CD, Songbook).

Encourage the children to dance like flowers as the music plays.

d Take a Walk
If possible, take the class outside to look at plants around your church. Or walk around the inside of the church and notice plants. If the sanctuary is not being used, go and inspect the floral arrangement on the altar.

4 Celebrate
the Story

a Enjoy Music
Do this in the Storytelling Center.

Gather two or three children. Play the Bible verse song, "We Give Thanks" (CD, Songbook). Sing the song and add verses that are appropriate to this week.

We give thanks to you, O God.
We give thanks to you, O God.
We give thanks to you for plants.
We give thanks to you for plants.

b Enjoy a Snack
Do this in the Conversation Center.

Check with parents for allergies before giving children fresh fruits or vegetables, particularly strawberries.

Have a selection of apple and orange slices or other fruits and vegetables the children enjoy. As the children eat, **say:** "I am so glad that God planned for food!"

c Say Goodbye
Recall today's Bible story, encouraging the children to say the Bible verse with you.

Say: "We enjoyed God's gift of plants today. (*Child's name*) made a painting." Repeat each child's name and mention an activity in which he or she took part.

Pray: "Thank you, God, for plants."

Be sure to have a teacher or helper at the door to match children with their caregivers.

Tell parents about today's Bible story and make sure that each child has today's Bible Story Picture Card. Show parents the "Nurturing Your Child's Faith" section of the card.

Be sure the children take home their Handprint Flowers.

Tip
Whenever you take your class on a field trip, make sure you have one adult for every two children. Insist that the children hold the hands of the adults assigned to them..

Look Back
What activities went particularly well today? With what activities did you or the children have trouble?

What activities will you want to repeat next week?

Did all of the children have a chance to experience the Bible story this week? Can the children retell the story?

Look Ahead
Next week we move onto animals. Many of the activities the children have enjoyed may be adapted and repeated. Take it easy on yourself. As long as the children are interested in an activity, keep repeating it. Toddlers enjoy repetition and familiarity. To be presented with a whole new lesson each week can be unsettling.

Session

49

Genesis 1:20-25

God made a wide variety of animals.

Bible Verse:
We give thanks to you, O God.
(Psalm 75:1)

Resources:
Bible
CD
Activity Pak (Summer)
  page 9
  (figures 1–7)
  page 20 (dogs, cats,
  birds sorting cards)
  page 23 ("God Made
  Animals" picture)
  Songbook
Bible Story Picture Cards

Supplies:
play dough
CD player
building blocks
animal cookie cutters
pine cone
two gallon-size plastic
  freezer bags
peanut butter
bird seed
yarn
toy animals
toy pets
pet items such as
  feeding dishes, bed,
  and grooming items
sand table

God Created Living Creatures......

Enter the Bible Story

Read Genesis 1:20-25: The Bible story for today focuses on the creation of animals. God made the fish and the birds first and then made land animals.

Think About It: Do you ever wonder why God created certain animals? It is so easy to understand why God made our favorite cuddly pets. What about snakes, spiders, or rats? What about insects such as roaches or silverfish? God had a reason or purpose for making every single creature. As we learn about each one's role in nature, we understand a little more about balance, not just in the animal kingdom, but in all of life.

This story tells us something of the power of God. God cannot be afraid of the scary sea monsters, because they are simply a part of creation. Does it help you to know that God is in charge of all of the animals?

Genesis means beginning. The first word in the Hebrew text is "Genesis" or "in the beginning." This book tells us about the beginning of the universe as we know it, the beginning of humanity, and the beginning of the natural realm of living creatures.

Genesis is also one part of the great book, the Bible, where we attempt to fathom the magnitude of almighty God. Refresh your memory and your spirit. Read Genesis 1 and 2.

Through the Week: Rediscover the good in your accomplishments today. Graciously accept the good you do. As you teach and play with a toddler, find ways to say, "Good job!" along the way. Can you look back on your day and say it was good? How are the words *good* and *acceptable* the same? different?

Pray: All creation sings praises to you, O God, each day. Thank you for loving us so much, for giving us the companionship of your living creatures, great and small. Amen.

The Story and Young Children

We know that love, acceptance, and ritual are at the core of the toddler's spiritual formation. Developmentally, we know that every child struggles between two tasks, dependence and independence. The same is true of the toddler. Yet in the midst of it all, the child needs structure. You can create a refreshing, interesting environment—encouraging autonomy while providing clear boundaries and rules. Your loving, caring, helpful responses can develop a sense of balance and acceptance to each child's God-given spirit.

Learning Centers

Work with two or three children at a time in each learning center.

Conversation Center

You will need: play dough, animal cookie cutters; pine cone, two freezer plastic food storage bags (gallon-size), peanut butter, bird seed, yarn.

Get ready: Put one cup of peanut butter in one resealable plastic bag and one cup of bird seed in another.

- Play With Play Dough, Activity 1d
- Make a Bird Feeder, Activity 3a
- Play With Blocks, Activity 3b

Building Center

You will need: building blocks, toy animals.

Get ready: Provide enough blocks for toddlers to share.

- Play With Blocks, Activity 3b

Storytelling Center

This should be an open area where you may gather children for storytelling, or to listen and respond to music. It would be helpful to have this center on a carpeted area.

You will need: CD and CD player, Songbook; Activity Pak—pp. 9 (figures 1-7) and 23 ("God Made Animals" picture); Bible.

Get ready: Prepare storytelling figures (see Activity Pak—p. 2).

- Tell the Bible Story, Activity 2a
- Use an Action Verse, Activity 2b
- Retell the Bible Story, Activity 2c
- Enjoy Music, Activity 4a

Family Living Center

You will need: toy pets and pet items such as feeding dishes, bed, and grooming items.

- Take Care of Pets, Activity 1b

Discovery Center

You will need: sand table (see p. 234 for instructions); toy animals.

- Play With Sand, Activity 1c

God Created Living Creatures

When God made the world, there were lots of plants, dirt, and water. But there were no animals anywhere. Just plants, dirt, and water.

God said, "This is not good."

So God made lots of animals. God made great big elephants and little bitty bugs. God made slow, slow turtles and very fast cats. God made cute, cuddly puppies and big scary alligators. God likes lots of animals.

And God said, "This is very, very good."

 # Prepare

for the Story

 Welcome Each Child

Do this as each child enters.

Have the CD playing as children arrive. Stoop to the child's eye level and welcome each child by name.

Say to each child: "I am so happy you have come to church today."

Be prepared to involve children in an interesting or comforting activity.

 Take Care of Pets

Do this in the Family Living Center.

As the children play, invite them to care for the pets. Engage the children in conversation as they play: Do the children have pets at home? How do they care for them?

Play with Sand

Do this in the Discovery Center.

Gather two or three children. Let the children play in the sand with the toy animals. As they play, engage the children in conversation about the animals: Do they know what the animal is that they are playing with? What sound does it make? Have they ever seen that animal in real life?

Play With Play Dough

Do this in the Conversation Center.

Gather two or three children. Talk with the children as they play. Encourage the children to make animals, especially snakes, which older two-year-olds often can do quite well.

 # Tell

the Story

Tell the Bible Story

Do this in the Storytelling Center.

Gather two or three children. If needed, repeat last week's Bible story. Look at the "God Made Animals" picture (Activity Pak—p. 23). Talk about the animals in the picture. Are any unfamiliar to them? Can they name the animals? Tell the story for this week.

Open a Bible and **say** the Bible verse: "We give thanks to you, O God." Have the children say the Bible verse with you. Before you say the prayer, encourage the children to say the prayer with you. Put up the pictures from last week (figures 1-5) as you say the prayer. Then add the pictures for this week (figures 6-7) as you continue the prayer. **Pray:**

Thank you, God, for light.
Thank you, God, for sky.
Thank you, God, for dirt.
Thank you, God, for water.
Thank you, God, for animals.

 Use an Action Verse

Do this in the Storytelling Center.

Gather two or three children. Say the action verse, "God Planned for Light" (Songbook).

 Retell the Bible Story

Do this in the Storytelling Center.

Gather two or three children. Tell the story and use the motions. Have the children do the motions with you.

God made lots of animals.

God made great big elephants (*Clasp hands together; straighten your arms and wave them back and forth like an elephant trunk.*) and little bitty bugs. (*Put two fingers very close together as if holding a tiny bug.*)

God made slow, slow turtles (*Move arms as if dog paddling, very slowly.*) and very fast cats. (*Same movement, but very fast.*)

God made cute, cuddly puppies (*Pretend to pet a puppy in your arms.*) and big scary alligators. (*Extend arms and clap hands together like an alligator's mouth.*)

God liked lots of animals.

Ask: "What other animals did God make?" As the children name the animals, make a sound or a motion for that animal.

3 Connect
with the Story

a Make a Bird Feeder
Do this in the Conversation Center.

Ahead of time, put one cup of peanut butter in one storage bag and one cup of bird seed in the other storage bag. Tie one end of the yarn to the top of the pine cone, leaving about a two-foot length to tie to the limb of a tree. Secure.

Gather two or three children. **Say:** "We are going to make a bird feeder. I will start, but I can't do it all by myself. I need helpers. Will you be my helper? Ellie, will you put the pine cone into the peanut butter bag?" Seal the bag. **Say:** "Shameeka, will you rub the bag with me? Look, we are rubbing peanut butter into the pine cone." Let others also rub the pine cone. **Say:** "Now the pine cone is full."

Take the pine cone out of the bag and place it in the seed bag and seal. Now **say:** "Ben, will you help me rub the bag? Look, we are rubbing bird seeds on the pine cone." Let others have a turn at rubbing. **Say:** "Now the pine cone is full of seeds. Now we can go outside and hang our bird feeder."

If desired, let each child make a bird feeder. If so, tell the children to leave the feeder in the bag until they get home.

b Play With Blocks
Do this in the Storytelling Center.

As the children play with blocks, encourage them to use the animals in their play.

4 Celebrate
the Story

a Enjoy Music
Do this in the Storytelling Center.

Gather two or three children. Play the Bible verse song, "We Give Thanks" (CD, Songbook). Sing the song and add verses that are appropriate to this week.

We give thanks to you, O God.
We give thanks to you, O God.
We give thanks to you for cats,
We give thanks to you for dogs.
We give thanks to you for birds,
We give thanks to you for snakes.

Add other animals.

b Go On a Nature Walk
If it is safe to do so, take the children outside. Invite enough parents to go along that you have one adult for every two or three children, unless you have a fenced-in playground.

Bring bread crumbs or bird seed to throw on the ground. If you made a bird feeder, take it outside and hang it in a tree. While you walk, look for all of the things God made.

Stop often to **say** a prayer of thanksgiving for the things you see: "Thank you, God, for the pretty yellow flower."

c Say Goodbye
Recall today's Bible story, encouraging the children to say the Bible verse with you.

Say: "We enjoyed God's gift of animals today. (*Child's name*) made a play dough snake." Repeat each child's name and mention an activity in which he or she took part.

Pray: "Thank you, God, for animals."

Be sure to have a teacher or helper at the door to match children with their caregivers.

Tell parents about today's Bible story and make sure that each child has today's Bible Story Picture Card. Show parents the "Nurturing Your Child's Faith" section of the card.

Be sure the children take home their bird feeder, if you made individual ones.

Tip
Make the stories more personal. Substitute your name and that of the children in the contemporary stories.

Look Back
What activities went particularly well today? With what activities did you or the children have trouble?

What activities will you want to repeat next week?

Did all of the children have a chance to experience the Bible story this week? Can the children retell the story?

Look Ahead
Next week will be much the same as this week. Plan to repeat many of the activities the children enjoyed this week. Look over the lesson to get any necessary supplies.

Session

Psalm 75:1a

We are thankful that all of the animals God created are good.

Bible Verse:
We give thanks to you, O God.
(Psalm 75:1a)

Resources:
Bible
CD
animal patterns (pages 243-244)
Activity Pak (Summer)
  pages 9, 12
  (figures 1–7)
  page 20 (dogs, cats, birds sorting cards)
  page 23 ("God Made Animals" picture)
  Songbook
Bible Story Picture Cards

Supplies:
play dough
animal cookie cutters
CD player
building blocks
tagboard or heavy construction paper
clear self-adhesive paper
paper punch
long shoelaces, one per child
toy animals
stuffed toy puppies
pet items such as feeding dishes, beds, and grooming items
sand table (see p. 234)
bird feeder made last week
three small shoeboxes

Thank You, God, for Living Creatures

Enter the Bible Story

Read Psalm 75:1: The psalms help us praise God for all living creatures.

Think About It: How do you spend your summer evenings? It is so easy to walk into the warmth of a summer night and gaze at the star-filled, moonlit skies. Even in the city, where lights sometimes dim the stars, the warm summer breezes after the sun goes down bring relief from the daytime heat.

Listen. Are any of God's creatures speaking to you? This beauty and harmony was created for you, as part of the human race. Living each day anew takes on a special meaning.

What animals do you encounter in your daily life? Do you see God's plan in the pigeon? the pet dog? the squirrel? God has created this wonderful universe and everything in it for us. God's creation is here to enjoy. We should be grateful for it. With each step we take, we should offer a prayer of thanksgiving to God. The Book of Psalms is full of prayers and songs of praise and adoration. This book contains thoughts and feelings that are common to all of us, from total despair to total ecstasy. It can be a great resource to you in your spiritual journey.

Through the Week: Take some time to rediscover God's handiwork. Read Psalm 19 and then feast your eyes upon creation.

Pray: God, thank you for all creatures, great and small. Thank you for the children who will come to Sunday school this week. Bless their families. Help me share my gratitude to you with them. Amen.

The Story and Young Children

Children need to feel competent. In today's lesson you have an opportunity to show each child, a step at a time, how to lace a card. It is important to allow the children to try on their own at some point. Encourage each child, but let the child try things for himself or herself. When we do a child's work, we are saying, "Your work wasn't good enough."

Your children are just beginning to learn. With each new attempt, they will improve. Let each child attempt the task at hand. Then say, "Good try."

You may discover that some children are afraid of certain animals. A little bit of fear is good - it helps keep children safe. But reassure the children that God loves all animals because all animals are a part of creation.

Learning Centers

Conversation Center

You will need: play dough, animal cookie cutters; animal patterns (pp. 243-244); 8½-by-11 pieces of tagboard or heavy construction paper (tagboard is available at teacher or art supply stores); clear self-adhesive paper; paper punch; long shoelaces, one per child.

Get ready: Make copies of the animal patterns, enough for each child.

- Play With Play Dough, Activity 1b
- Make Lacing Cards, Activity 3a

Building Center

You will need: building blocks, toy animals.

- Play With Blocks, Activity 3c

Family Living Center

You will need: toy pets and pet items such as feeding dishes, beds, grooming items.

- Take Care of Pets, Activity 1c

Storytelling Center

You will need: Bible; Activity Pak—pp. 9, 12 (figures 1-7) and 23 ("God Made Animals" picture); stuffed toy puppies; CD and CD player, Songbook.

Get ready: Prepare storytelling figures (see Activity Pak—p. 2).

- Tell the Bible Story, Activity 2a
- Use an Action Verse, Activity 2b
- Retell the Bible Story, Activity 2c
- Enjoy Music, Activity 4a

Discovery Center

You will need: Activity Pak—p. 20 (dogs, cats, birds sorting cards) sand table (see p. 234), toy animals; bird feeder made last week; three small shoeboxes.

- Play With Sand, Activity 1d
- Find the Bird Feeder, Activity 3b
- Play a Game, Activity 4b

Thank You, God, for Living Creatures

"I have a surprise," Daddy said. "We have a new puppy!"

Adam and Abigail jumped up and down when they saw the cute funny puppy. He was so little that Daddy could hold him in his hands.

"God planned for puppies, but God wants us to take take of her," Daddy said. "We need to give her food and water. We need to walk her outside. We need to give her a soft bed to sleep on. We need to pet her and love her. Can you do these things?"

"Yes, we will help to take care of our new puppy," Adam and Abigail said. They were glad that God planned for puppies.

1 Prepare

for the Story

a Welcome Each Child
Do this as each child enters.

Have the CD playing as children arrive. Stoop to the child's eye level and welcome each child by name. **Say** to each child: "I am so happy you are here today."

b Play With Play Dough
Do this in the Conversation Center.

Gather two or three children. Talk with them as they play. Let the children make animals, especially snakes, which older two-year-olds often do quite well.

c Take Care of Pets
Do this in the Family Living Center.

Invite the children to care for the pets. Talk with them as they play. Do they have pets at home? How do they care for them?

d Play With Sand
Do this in the Discovery Center.

Gather two or three children. Let them play in the sand with the animals. Talk about the animals: Do they know what the animal is? What sound does it make? Have they ever seen that animal in real life?

2 Tell

the Story

a Tell the Bible Story
Do this in the Storytelling Center.

Gather two or three children. Repeat last week's Bible story. Talk about the "God Made Animals" picture (Activity Pak—p. 23). Can they name the animals? Tell this week's story. Use the toy puppies as you tell the story.

Open a Bible and **say** the verse: "We give thanks to you, O God." Have the children say the Bible verse with you.

Encourage the children to say the prayer with you. Put up the pictures from last week (figures 1-6) as you say the prayer. Then add this week's picture (figure 7) as you continue. **Pray:**

Thank you, God, for light.
Thank you, God, for sky.
Thank you, God, for dirt.
Thank you, God, for water.
Thank you, God, for animals. Amen.

b Use an Action Verse
Do this in the Storytelling Center.

Gather two or three children. Say the action verse, "God Planned For Light" (Songbook).

c Retell the Bible Story
Do this in the Storytelling Center.

Gather two or three children. Tell the story and do the motions. This is an adaptation of "Going on a Bear Hunt," but in this version the bird is not scary. Adapt this story to any animal you wish.

We're going on a bird hunt. We're going to find a bird. (*Place your hand above one eye, like a visor.*) Are you ready? Let's go. (*Pat your knees to imitate the sound of walking.*)

Walk quietly, so we don't scare the bird.

Look, there's very tall grass! Let's walk through it. (*Push tall grass aside.*) Do you see a bird? No! (*Shake head.*) I guess we're not there yet.

Look, there's a lake. Let's swim to the other side. (*Pretend to swim.*) Do you see a bird? No! (*Shake your head.*) I guess we're not there yet.

Look, there's a tree! Let's climb up. (*Stand up and pretend to climb with your arms and legs.*) Do you see a bird? Yes! (*Nod and point.*)

Oh, the bird is beautiful.

OK, we're ready to go home.

Climb down the tree. (*Pretend to climb down.*)

Swim across the lake. (*Pretend to swim.*)

Let's walk through the tall grass. (*Pretend to push grass aside.*)

Now we're home! (*Sit still.*)

Thank you, God, for birds. (*Fold hands in prayer.*)

Connect

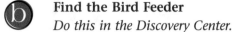

with the Story

a Make Lacing Cards

Do this in the Conversation Center.

Ahead of time, make copies of pp. 243 and/or 244 for each child. Glue the copies to pieces of tagboard or heavyweight construction paper. Cover the tagboard with clear self-adhesive paper. Using a paper punch, put holes at the designated circles. Be sure the shoelace will easily lace through the holes. Put a knot in one end of each shoelace.

Gather two or three children. **Say:** "I am lacing with this shoelace. See, I'm taking the end up through this hole and pulling it until it stops. See, the knot in the shoelace stops it from going through the hole. Now I'm lacing the shoelace down through the next hole. Can you try it? Show me. Yes, I'll work with you. Look what you are doing. You're lacing! Good for you!"

If the child misses a hole or laces different holes than you would, that is OK. Be sure the child feels successful in this activity.

b Find the Bird Feeder

Do this in the Discovery Center.

Check the bird feeder you made last week. Take the children on a bird-watching expedition to the feeder. Take a quilt to sit on. Sing "Can you find our bird feeder?" to the tune of "Do You Know the Muffin Man?"

Can you find our bird feeder,
Our bird feeder, our bird feeder?
Can you find our bird feeder,
So early in the morning?

As you see other animals, airplanes or insects, sing the song and insert the name of the item you are looking for.

c Play With Blocks

Do this in the Building Center.

As the children play with blocks, encourage them to use the animals in their play.

Tip

Make the stories more personal. Substitute your name and that of the children in the contemporary stories.

Look Back

What activities went particularly well today? With what activities did you or the children have trouble?

What activities will you want to repeat next week?

Did all of the children have a chance to experience the Bible story this week? Can the children retell the story?

Look Ahead

Next week we will learn about a special kind of animal: human beings. Plan to repeat any of the activities the children enjoyed this week. Look over the lesson to get any necessary supplies.

Celebrate

the Story

a Enjoy Music

Do this in the Storytelling Center.

Gather two or three children. Play the Bible verse song, "We Give Thanks" (CD, Songbook). Sing the song and add verses that are appropriate to this week.

We give thanks to you, O God.
We give thanks to you, O God.
We give thanks to you for cats,
We give thanks to you for dogs.
We give thanks to you for birds,
We give thanks to you for snakes.

Add other animals.

b Play a Game

Do this in the Discovery Center.

Gather two or three children. Show the children the pictures of dogs, cats, and birds. Show the children how to classify the pictures, placing the dog pictures in the first shoebox, the bird pictures in the

second shoebox, and the cat pictures into the third shoebox. **Say:** "Thank you, God, for plants and animals."

c Say Goodbye

Recall today's Bible story. Encourage children to say the Bible verse with you.

Say: "We enjoyed God's gift of animals today. (*Child's name*) laced a teddy bear." Repeat each child's name and mention an activity in which he or she took part.

Pray: "Thank you, God, for animals."

Be sure to have a teacher or helper at the door to match children with their caregivers.

Tell parents about today's Bible story and make sure that each child has today's Bible Story Picture Card. Show parents the "Nurturing Your Child's Faith" section of the card.

Be sure the children take home their lacing cards.

We are made in the image of God.

Bible Verse:
We give thanks to you, O God.
(Psalm 75:1a)

Resources:
Bible
CD
Activity Pak (Summer)
  pages 9,12
  (figures 1-10)
  page 24 ("God Made People" picture)
  Songbook
Bible Story Picture Cards

Supplies:
play dough
CD player
hand mirror
building blocks
gingerbread people cookie cutters
fingerpaint and paper
short-sleeved adult shirts that button down the front
small toy dolls
clear two-liter, plastic soda bottle
glitter or confetti
water
collection of rocks
magazines
teacher scissors
(optional: glue that is not water-soluble)

God Created People...............................

Enter the Bible Story

Read Genesis 1:26-30: The Bible story for today focuses on the creation of humankind.

Think About It: In the first story of creation, on which this session is based, the human beings were created last, as the crowning touch of all creation. People were special. At the culmination of creation, human beings were created "in the image of God," a reflection of God on earth. What does it mean to you to be created in God's image? How do you reflect God to those you meet daily? God creates human beings and gives them dominion over all creation, but with limits. They are supposed to care for creation and subdue it. The humans are supposed to be vegetarian (verse 29). In fact, it even appears that the animals were intended to be vegetarian (verse 30).

In the second story of creation, told in Genesis 2, the human being is created first, and all creation was created in order to benefit him. Furthermore, while God formed all of the animals, it is only the human that directly receives the breath of God. Again, there are limits put on the humans. They are not to eat of the tree in the midst of the garden, but the rest of creation is theirs.

In both stories the human being is given special status in creation. Whether people were created first or last, the whole of the Bible teaches us that humans are special in the eyes of God. Creation was not made for God's benefit, but to benefit the "image of God." We were not created as a part of creation, but creation was created for us! It was the human being that God wanted a personal relationship with, so much so that God became one of us in the birth of Jesus.

Through the Week: Think about the fact that you are created in God's image. What does that mean to you? How do you reflect God to those you meet daily? How do you reflect God to the toddlers you teach?

Pray: God, it is an awesome responsibility to be made in your image. Help me to be more like you every day. Help me to pass along your word to the children I teach. Help me to represent you in my own world. Amen.

The Story and Young Children

As has been said before, toddlers cannot conceive of a God they cannot see. And to be made in the image of God is a very abstract concept that adults still do not fully understand. Nevertheless, toddlers can hear that God made them and that they are very good. Older infants and young toddlers are fascinated with their own bodies. Help the children examine their hands and their feet. In what ways do they bend? Let them feel your hair and compare it to theirs. Delight in the fact that God made us and made us good!

Learning Centers

Conversation Center

You will need: play dough, gingerbread people cookie cutters; fingerpaint and paper, short-sleeved adult shirts that button down the front.

Get ready: Prepare play dough and fingerpaint (see pp. 232-233)

- Play With Play Dough, Activity 1b
- Fingerpaint, Activity 3a

Building Center

You will need: building blocks, small toy dolls.

Get ready: Provide enough blocks for toddlers to share.

- Play With Blocks, Activity 3b

Family Living Center

You will need: dolls.

- Play With Dolls, Activity 1d

Storytelling Center

You will need: Activity Pak—p. 12 (figures 8–10) and 24 ("God Made People" picture); CD and CD player, Songbook; Bible; small hand mirror.

Get ready: Prepare storytelling figures (see Activity Pak—p. 2).

- Tell the Bible Story, Activity 2a
- Sing a Song, Activity 2b
- Use an Action Verse, Activity 2c
- Enjoy Music, Activity 4a

Discovery Center

You will need: magazines, teacher scissors, clear two-liter plastic soda bottle, glitter or confetti, water; collection of rocks (optional: glue that is not water-soluble).

Get ready: Cut pictures of people from magazines. Gather rocks with many different characteristics—some smooth, some bumpy, some shiny, some dull. Gather as many different colors as you can.

- Look at Pictures, Activity 1c
- Play With a Water Bottle, Activity 3c
- Look at Rocks, Activity 4b

God Created People

When God made the world, there were lots of plants, lots of dirt, lots of water, and lots and lots of animals. But there were no people anywhere.

God said, "This is not good."

So God made people. God made big, tall people and short, little people. God made people with brown hair and black hair and yellow hair and white hair and no hair! And God made children—lots and lots of children.

And God said, "This is very, very good."

1 Prepare

for the Story

a Welcome Each Child
Do this as each child enters.

Have the CD playing as children arrive.

Stoop to the child's eye level and welcome each child by name.

Say to each child: "I am so happy you have come to church today."

Be prepared to involve children in an interesting or comforting activity.

b Play With Play Dough
Do this in the Conversation Center.

Gather two or three children. Engage the children in conversation as they play.

Say: "I wonder what God felt like making people? Look, I made a little boy (or a little girl). Can you make one too?"

c Look at Pictures
Do this in the Discovery Center.

Have the children look through the pictures of people that you cut out of magazines. Notice the similarities and differences. How many of the people have noses? How many of the people have brown hair? How many of the people wear glasses?

Talk to the children about similarities and differences in the people in the classroom.

d Play With Dolls
Do this in the Family Living Center.

As the children play with the dolls, notice the similarities and the differences in the dolls.

2 Tell

the Story

a Tell the Bible Story
Do this in the Storytelling Center.

Gather two or three children. If needed, repeat last week's Bible story.

Show the children the "God Made People" picture (Activity Pak—p. 24). Notice the wide variety of people in the picture. Are there any that look like your children? Then tell the story for this week.

Open a Bible and **say** the Bible verse: "We give thanks to you, O God." Encourage the children to say the Bible verse with you.

This week before you say the prayer, encourage the children to say the prayer with you. Put up the pictures from past weeks (figures 1-7) as you say the prayer. Then add the pictures from this week (figures 8-10) as you continue the prayer. **Pray:**

Thank you, God, for light.
Thank you, God, for sky.
Thank you, God, for dirt.
Thank you, God. for water.
Thank you, God, for animals.
Thank you, God, for people. Amen.

b Sing a Song
Do this in the Storytelling Center.

Gather two or three children. Pass around the hand mirror and let the children look at themselves in it.

Ask the children where their nose is. Where are their eyes? their ears? their mouths?

Sing the following song to the tune of "London Bridge."

Look in the mirror, I see me.
I see me, I see me.
Look in the mirror, God made me.
I am someone special!

c Use an Action Verse
Do this in the Storytelling Center.

Gather two or three children. Say the action verse, "God Planned For Light" (Songbook). Add the verse about people this week.

 Connect
with the Story

a Fingerpaint
Do this in the Conversation Center.

Gather two or three children. Protect clothing by putting a shirt on each child, buttoned down the back. Give each child a piece of fingerpaint paper and a blob of fingerpaint.

As the children paint, talk about fingers and hands and all that they can do.

b Play With Blocks
Do this in the Building Center.

As the children play with blocks, encourage them to build houses for the dolls.

Notice the similarities and differences in the dolls. Are some older or younger? Are some larger? Do some have different hair?

c Play With a Water Bottle
Do this in the Discovery Center.

Ahead of time, pour glitter or confetti into the bottle and fill it with water.

Securely screw the lid on. You may wish to pour some glue that is not water-soluble into the cap before screwing it on.

Let the children play with the water bottle. Notice that if you shake the bottle, the glitter or confetti seems to fill the bottle.

Or you can gently pour the glitter or confetti from the bottom to the top of the bottle by moving it very slowly.

Thank God for eyes that can see the pretty glitter. Remember that glitter is an eye hazard for young children and must stay in the bottle.

Celebrate
the Story

a Enjoy Music
Do this in the Storytelling Center.

Gather two or three children. Play the Bible verse song, "We Give Thanks" (CD, Songbook). Sing the song and add verses that are appropriate to this week.

We give thanks to you, O God.
We give thanks to you, O God.
We give thanks to you for people.
We give thanks to you for people.

b Look at Rocks
Do this in the Discovery Center.

Gather two or three children. Examine the rocks. Encourage the children to talk about the rocks and their characteristics.

Put the rocks inside a large sock or a cloth bag and see if the children can find the smooth one or the bumpy one by touch alone. Thank God for fingers that can touch.

c Say Goodbye
Recall today's Bible story, encouraging the children to say the Bible verse with you.

Say: "We enjoyed God's gift of people today. (*Child's name*) played with the rocks." Repeat each child's name and mention an activity in which he or she took part.

Pray: "Thank you, God, for people."

Be sure to have a teacher or helper at the door to match children with their parents or caregivers.

Tell parents about today's Bible story and make sure that each child has today's Bible Story Picture Card. Show parents the "Nurturing Your Child's Faith" section of the card.

Be sure the children take home their finger painting.

Tip
Toddlers are just beginning to learn about senses. Encourage them to use their eyes, ears, tongues, fingers, and noses as they explore their world.

Look Back
What activities went particularly well today? With what activities did you or the children have trouble?

What activities will you want to repeat next week?

Did all of the children have a chance to experience the Bible story this week? Can the children retell the story?

Look Ahead
Next week will be essentially the same as this week. Be sure to repeat any activities that went well this week, and substitute activities for those that did not go well.

We praise God
for all people.

Bible Verse:
We give thanks to
you, O God.
(Psalm 75:1a)

Resources:
Bible
CD
Activity Pak (Summer)
  pages 9, 12
  (figures 1-10)
  page 24 ("God Made
  People" picture)
  Songbook
  favorite puzzles
Bible Story Picture Cards

Supplies:
play dough
people-shaped cookie
  cutters
CD player
building blocks
paper plates
3- to 5-oz. paper cups
construction paper
glue
toy people
paper streamers or silk
  scarfs
large sock or cloth bag
several small toys with a
  distinct shape
water bottle (see p. 211)
teacher scissors

Thank You, God, For People.......

Enter the Bible Story

Read Psalm 8. We are each unique in all of creation, and we are each different from everyone else.

Think About It: Across the street from my apartment there are identical twins. These women are in their sixties and are always dressed alike. The casual observer cannot tell them apart. But I can. One of them is much more interested in the plants that grow around their front door; the other one is the one I will see washing the windows while her sister tends the plants. One of them usually drives. Their walk is ever-so-slightly different. It is the same with every set of identical twins that I know. Those who know them well can always tell them apart, precisely because they are not identical. They are each unique human beings.

What are the differences in the children in your class? Which ones are more active? Which ones are more talkative? Which ones are shy and cling to their caregiver when they are dropped off? Which ones bound into the room and greet everyone with a "Hello, world, aren't you happy to see me?" attitude? What about physical characteristics? Notice the difference in skin tones, hair color, height, and build. What about differing abilities? Are some more advanced in certain areas than others? Be careful not to place any value on differing abilities among your children. Remember that God pronounced all people—with their varying abilities—"good."

Through the Week: Spend some time "people watching." Notice how different people react to the same situation. Notice how different personality styles affect behavior. Which people always seem to want to be the center of attention? Which try to blend into the woodwork?

Pray: Loving God, thank you that even though I may not be as attractive as some, or as smart as some, or even as thoughtful as some, you love me just the way I am. Help me to look beyond appearance, ability, or age and see the children that you created and called "good." Amen.

The Story and Young Children

Children at this age are just learning the concept of body parts. A favorite game of toddlers is "Where's Your Nose?" They are not far from being able to sing "Head and Shoulders, Knees and Toes." So it is appropriate to point out to them that everyone has a nose. Everyone has eyes, hair, and a mouth. You can talk to them about the differences in other bodies. "Look, my hand is bigger than yours! Your hair is brown, and my hair is white. And Mr. Don has hardly any hair at all!" As you notice differences be sure not to place any value on the difference. For example, do not contribute to early ageism by wishing that your hair were still brown like theirs, or that there is something funny about "Mr. Don" not having hair. It is simply different.

Learning Centers

Work with two or three children at a time in each learning center.

Conversation Center

You will need: play dough (see p. 232), people-shaped cookie cutters. paper plates. construction paper circles and arcs for mouths, glue; small paper cups.

Get ready: Cut out construction paper circles for eyes and noses and arcs for mouths. With older children you may wish to add large ovals for ears and yarn for hair.

- Play With Play Dough, Activity 1b
- Make Paper Plate Faces, Activity 3a

Building Center

You will need: building blocks; toy people.

- Play With Blocks, Activity 3b

Discovery Center

You will need: favorite puzzles from the Activity Pak, such as the fruits and vegetables puzzles or the day and night sorting cards; large sock or cloth bag, several small toys with a distinct shape; water bottle made for Session 51.

Get ready: Prepare the water bottle if you did not use it last week. Make sure that the children do not have access to glitter. Gather toys that are too large for the children to swallow. Place one of them in the "feely bag."

- Play a Game, Activity 1b
- Play With Puzzles, Activity 1d
- Play With a Water Bottle, Activity 3c
- Use a Feely Bag, Activity 4b

Storytelling Center

You will need: CD and CD player, Songbook; Bible; Activity Pak—pp. 9, 12 (figures 1–10) and 24 ("God Made People" picture); paper streamers or silk scarfs.

Get ready: Prepare storytelling figures (see Activity Pak—p. 2).

- Tell the Bible Story, Activity 2a
- Retell the Bible Story, Activity 2b
- Use an Action Verse, Activity 2c
- Enjoy Music, Activity 4a

Family Living Center

You will need: dolls.

Set out dolls for play. Talk to the children about the dolls. In what way are they like the children? How are they different?

A New Baby Sister!

Caleb had a new baby sister! Her name was Elizabeth. She had two ears, just like Caleb's. She had two hands, two feet, and a belly button, just like Caleb's.

But she was different from Caleb. She was very tiny, and Caleb was big. She could not walk, talk, or play with toys like Caleb could. Caleb's eyes were dark brown, and Elizabeth's were light blue. Caleb's hair was brown, and Elizabeth had hardly any hair at all!

Caleb was glad that God planned for baby sisters.

1 Prepare

for the Story

Welcome Each Child
Do this as each child enters.

Have the CD playing as children arrive. Stoop to the child's eye level and welcome each child by name. **Say** to each child: "I am so happy you have come to church today."

Play With Play Dough
Do this in the Conversation Center.

Gather two or three children. Talk with the children as they play.

Say: "I wonder what God felt like making the dirt. Maybe the dirt felt like this dough. What do you think God did with it?"

Play a Game
Do this in the Discovery Center.

Play "Where's Your Nose?" **Ask:** "Where's your nose?" and ask the children to point to theirs. Then ask about eyes, hair, mouth, ears, chin, and other body parts. If you have older children, they may want to ask you to find your own nose. As you play, thank God for making different parts of the body.

Play With Puzzles
Do this in the Discovery Center.

Gather two or three children. Let the children play with puzzles. Talk with the children about the things pictured in the puzzle. **Say:** "God made everything good."

2 Tell

the Story

Tell the Bible Story
Do this in the Storytelling Center.

Gather two or three children. Repeat the past weeks' Bible stories. Look at the "God Made People" picture (Activity Pak—p. 24). Talk about the differences in the different people.

Tell the story for this week. If any of your children have baby brothers or sisters, be sure to use their names in the story.

Open a Bible and say the Bible verse: "We give thanks to you, O God." Have the children say the Bible verse with you.

Before you pray, encourage the children to say the prayer with you. Put up the pictures from past weeks (figures 1–10) as you say the prayer. **Pray:**

Thank you, God, for light.
Thank you, God, for sky.
Thank you, God, for dirt.
Thank you, God. for water.
Thank you, God, for animals.
Thank you, God, for people. Amen.

Retell the Bible Story
Do this in the Storytelling Center.

Gather two or three children. Tell the story and use the motions. Encourage the children to do the motions with you.

God made the trees. (*Stand straight and tall, arms raised and outstretched like branches.*)

God made the stars. (*Hold your hands high and wiggle your fingers like twinkling stars.*)

God made the fish. (*Put palms together; move your hands back and forth like a fish swimming.*)

God made the cows. (*Make "moo" sounds.*)

Let the children come up with ideas. End with "God made me!" (*Jump up and down; clap hands.*)

Use an Action Verse
Do this in the Storytelling Center.

Gather two or three children. Say the action verse, "God Planned For Light" (Songbook).

 Connect

with the Story

 Make Paper Plate Faces
Do this in the Conversation Center.

Gather two or three children. Give each child a paper plate. Show the child how to "touch" the glue with their finger and then "touch" the piece of construction paper they wish to glue.

Say: "We are going to make a face. Here's an eye. Where does the eye go?"

Be sure to accept all answers. However, if the children place eyes, mouths, and noses in particularly awkward places, you may **say:** "What a silly face you are making! The eyes are not together, and the nose is under the mouth!"

Do not, however, tell the child that he or she is wrong.

b **Play With Blocks**
Do this in the Building Center.

As the children play with blocks, encourage them to build houses for the dolls. Notice the similarities and differences in the dolls. Are some older or younger? Are some larger? Do some have different hair?

c **Play With a Water Bottle**
This can begin in the Discovery Center.

Let the children play with the water bottle. Notice that if you shake the bottle, the glitter or confetti seems to fill the bottle. Or you can gently pour the glitter or confetti from the bottom to the top of the bottle by moving it very slowly. Thank God for eyes that can see the pretty glitter.

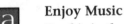 Celebrate

the Story

a **Enjoy Music**
Do this in the Storytelling Center.

Gather two or three children. Play the Bible verse song, "We Give Thanks" (CD, Songbook). Sing the song and add verses that are appropriate to this week.

Give each child a paper streamer or silk scarf. Play "God Has Made Everything Beautiful" (CD, Songbook).

Encourage the children to dance as they listen to the song, waving their streamers in the air.

b **Use a Feely Bag**
Do this in the Discovery Center.

Gather two or three children. Hold up the bag.

Say: "I wonder what is in here?"

Feel the object from the outside of the bag. Encourage the children to guess about what they feel. Then let the children put their hands inside the bag to feel the objects and guess about them.

Finally, let the children remove the objects and examine them. You may repeat this game with different objects. Thank God for fingers that can touch.

c **Say Goodbye**

Recall today's Bible story. Have the children say the Bible verse with you.

Say: "We enjoyed God's good gifts today. (*Child's name*) played in the water." Repeat each child's name and mention an activity in which he or she took part.

Pray: "Thank you, God, for everything."

Be sure to have a teacher or helper at the door to match children with their caregivers.

Tell parents about today's Bible story and make sure that each child has today's Bible Story Picture Card. Show parents the "Nurturing Your Child's Faith" section of the card.

Be sure the children take home their collages.

Tip
Make the stories more personal. Substitute your name and that of the children in the contemporary stories.

Look Back
What activities went particularly well today? With what activities did you or the children have trouble?

What activities will you want to repeat next week?

Did all of the children have a chance to experience the Bible story this week? Can the children retell the story?

Look Ahead
The next four weeks will be summaries of the entire summer. Recall what activities went well this summer and repeat them..

Everything God created is good.

Bible Verse:
We give thanks to you, O God. (Psalm 75:1a)

Resources:
Bible
CD
Activity Pak (Summer)
   pages 9, 12
   (figures 1–10)
   page 4 (God Made
   Everything Good
   picture)
   Songbook
   favorite puzzles
Bible Story Picture Cards

Supplies:
play dough
CD player
building blocks
construction paper
glue
toy boats and/or fish
toy animals
toy people
large piece of blue fabric
paper streamers or
   silk scarfs
silk flowers and pots
toy pets and pet items
items for water table
   activities
plastic grocery bags
magazines
teacher scissors
3- to 5- oz. paper cups

God Made Everything Good......

Enter the Bible Story

Read Genesis 1:31: God looked at the whole of creation and pronounced it "good."

Think About It: We have no problem believing that God created everything. Even the Christians who believe in evolution believe that God created the creatures to evolve. Believing that God is the Creator of all poses no problem to us. Believing that God created everything "good," however, sometimes poses a big problem. I have a hard time thinking that there is anything good in roaches. And surely God did not create ragweed! Nevertheless, the Bible clearly states that God looked over all of creation and pronounced it not only "good" but "very good." Reflect on the following as you prepare to tell the story of creation this week: What things do you have no trouble believing are good in creation? What things in creation do you have a lot of trouble believing are good?

As we read the story of God's creation, we must keep in mind that this story tells us how the world was to be in God's plan. However, we know that within a few chapters, the human beings begin to exercise the free choice given to them by God, and the world is never the same. Even though God created everything good, it does not mean that everything in the world *is* good. Many things— murder, pollution, treachery, political indifference to the powerless—are creations of human will, not God's will. We must be careful to attribute only the things that God created with the goodness of God.

Through the Week: Think of yourself as a good creation of God. Remember that God delights in you and in your talents. It is easy for us to focus on all the things we would like to change (our hip size, our height, our singing ability). Focus instead on all the wonderful things that God has given you. Love yourself as God loves you.

Pray: Creator God, help me to see good in all your creation. Remind me once again of the interconnectedness of the universe, and that all parts of creation have a plan. Amen.

The Story and Young Children

We know that children cannot understand all that is encompassed in the creation, but then, what adult can understand this wonder? The children can know that God created all things and that "it was very good." Sometimes we tell young children to be good, or we ask the parents of an infant if this is a good baby. The Bible tells us clearly that all children are good as they are created. Sometimes they choose to do bad things, but that does not make them bad children. Reinforce this teaching in young children.

Learning Centers

Conversation Center

You will need: play dough, magazines, teacher scissors, construction paper; glue, small cups.

Get ready: Cut pictures of things God made from magazines.

- Play With Play Dough, Activity 1c
- Make a Collage, Activity 3a

Building Center

You will need: building blocks; toy boats and/or fish, toy animals, toy people, large piece of blue fabric.

- Play With Blocks, Activity 3b

Storytelling Center

You will need: CD and CD player, Songbook; Bible; Activity Pak, pp. 9, 12 (figures 1-10) and p. 4 ("God Made Everything Good" picture); paper streamers or silk scarfs.

- Tell the Bible Story, Activity 2a
- Use an Action Verse, Activity 2b
- Retell the Bible Story, Activity 2c

- Sing a Song, Activity 2d
- Enjoy Music, Activity 4a

Family Living Center

You will need: silk flowers and pots, toy pets and pet items.

- Play House, Activity 4b

Discovery Center

You will need: items for water table activities (see p. 234); favorite puzzles from the Activity Pak, such as fruits and vegetables puzzles or the day and night sorting cards; plastic grocery bag for litter.

Get ready: Prepare the water table activities (see p. 234). Recruit parent volunteers for your walk. If you are going to pick up litter, do a quick walk through the area where you will take the children to make sure there is no broken glass or other items that might be dangerous.

- Play With Water, Activity 1b
- Play With Puzzles, Activity 1d
- Take a Walk, Activity 3c

God Made Everything Good

When God made the world, there was nothing to start with.

God said, "This is not good." So God made daytime and nighttime. And God said, "This is good." God made the sky, and dirt, and water. And God said, "This is GOOD!" God made plants and the sun and the moon. And God said, "This is very good." God made animals and lots of people. And God said, "This is VERY, VERY GOOD."

Everything God made was very, very good.

1 Prepare

for the Story

a Welcome Each Child
Do this as each child enters.

Have the CD playing as children arrive. Stoop to the child's eye level and welcome each child by name. **Say** to each child: "I am so happy you have come to church today."

b Play with Water
Do this in the Discovery Center.

Let the children play in the water. Notice how water pours through funnels and squirts from meat basters. See what floats in the water and what sinks. Thank God for water.

c Play With Play Dough
Do this in the Conversation Center.

Gather two or three children. Talk with the children as they play.

Say: "I wonder what God felt like making dirt. Maybe the dirt felt like this dough. What do you think?

d Play With Puzzles
Do this in the Discovery Center.

Gather two or three children. Let the children play with puzzles. Talk about the things pictured in the puzzle. **Say:** "God made everything good."

2 Tell

the Story

a Tell the Bible Story
Do this in the Storytelling Center.

Gather two or three children. Repeat the past weeks' Bible stories. Look at the "God Made Everything Good" picture (Activity Pak—p. 4). Can the children find the sky? Can the children find the water? the animals? the people? Tell the story for this week.

Open a Bible and **say** the Bible verse: "We give thanks to you, O God.'" Have the children say the Bible verse with you.

Before you pray, have the children say the prayer with you. Put up the pictures from past weeks (figures 1–10) as you say the prayer. **Pray:**

Thank you, God, for light.
Thank you, God, for sky.
Thank you, God, for dirt.
Thank you, God, for water.
Thank you, God, for animals.
Thank you, God, for people.
Thank you, God, for everything. Amen.

b Use an Action Verse
Do this in the Storytelling Center.

Gather two or three children. Say the action verse, "God Planned For Light" (Songbook).

c Retell the Bible Story
Do this in the Storytelling Center.

Gather two or three children. Tell the story and use the motions. Encourage the children to do the motions with you.

God made trees. (*Stand straight and tall, arms raised and outstretched like branches.*)

God made stars. (*Hold hands high; wiggle your fingers like twinkling stars.*)

God made fish. (*Put palms together; move hands back and forth like a fish swimming.*)

God made cows. (*Make "mooing" sounds.*)

Let the children come up with ideas. End with "God made me!" (*Jump up and down and clap hands.*)

d Sing a Song
Do this in the Storytelling Center.

Gather two or three children. Sing "God Planned for Fish" (Songbook, CD). Add the verses below and others that you and the children make up.

1. God planned for dogs to bark this way. (*Make barking sounds.*)

2. God planned for flowers to grow this way. (*Crouch down low, then stand up.*)

3. God planned for water to move this way. (*Wave hands up and down.*)

3 Connect
with the Story

a Make a Collage
Do this in the Conversation Center.

Gather two or three children. Show the children how to "touch" the glue in a paper cup and then "touch" the picture they wish to glue. Help the children glue different pictures to their papers. Write across the top of the paper: "God Made Everything Good!"

b Play With Blocks
Do this in the Building Center.

As the children play with blocks, spread out the blue fabric and pretend that it is a large lake.

Play with the toys. Encourage conversation as you play. **Say:** "God created everything good."

c Take a Walk
This can begin in the Discovery Center.

If the weather permits, and you have a safe place to walk outdoors, take the children on a walk. Be sure that you have at least one adult for every two to three children.

As you walk, notice all of the things that God made. Help God take care of the earth by picking up litter and putting it in the plastic bag.

4 Celebrate
the Story

a Enjoy Music
Do this in the Storytelling Center.

Gather two or three children. Play the Bible verse song, "We Give Thanks" (CD, Songbook). Sing the song and add verses that are appropriate to this week.

Give each child a paper streamer or silk scarf. Play "God Has Made Everything Beautiful" (CD, Songbook). Encourage the children to dance as they listen to the song, waving their streamers in the air.

b Play House
Do this in the Family Living Center.

As children play in the Family Living Center, encourage conversation about the things God made. Thank God for the pretty plants and for the animals.

c Say Goodbye
Recall today's Bible story, encouraging children to say the Bible verse with you.

Say: "We enjoyed God's good gifts today. (*Child's name*) played in the water." Repeat each child's name and mention an activity in which he or she took part.

Pray: "Thank you, God, for everything."

Be sure to have a teacher or helper at the door to match children with their caregivers.

Tell parents about today's Bible story and make sure that each child has today's Bible Story Picture Card. Show parents the "Nurturing Your Child's Faith" section of the card.

Be sure the children take home their collages.

Tip
There is no way to do all of the activities listed in a single session. Pick and choose from your favorites.

Look Back
What activities went particularly well today? With what activities did you or the children have trouble?

What activities will you want to repeat next week?

Did all of the children have a chance to experience the Bible story this week? Can the children retell the story?

Look Ahead
We are winding up our unit on Creation. Be sure to plan to repeat any activities the children have particularly enjoyed. Discard activities that no longer interest the children.

Thank You, God, for Everything..........

Enter the Bible Story

Read Psalm 75:1: The Bible verse reminds us to praise God for all that we have.

Think About It: Too often we take God's creation for granted. We expect the trees to bud in the spring, and we expect the eggs to hatch in the nest. We know that the air we breathe will be good for us and that water will come out of the faucet. And we know without a doubt that the sun *will* rise in the morning. But we need to remember to thank God for creation. We believe that all babies will be born healthy, until one is born with a problem. We expect to live until we are in our eighties, until one of our friends has a heart attack at thirty-eight. We should praise God for every healthy child that comes along and for all the healthy characteristics of the one with a problem. We should give thanks for every day we are privileged to live on this earth. And every morning we should shout "Hallelujah!" when we see the sun. Living in an attitude of praise gives us the perspective God wants us to have.

How often we stand amazed at a beautiful sunset, an ocean, or a mountain view. Do we see God's wondrous works in the ordinary, small things? The psalmist tells us to "give thanks." Paul writes in I Thessalonians 5:18 that we are to "give thanks in all circumstances: for this is the will of God in Christ Jesus for you." Read Psalm 104 for another example of how the psalmist thanked God for creation.

Through the Week: Try to live in an attitude of praise every day. This does not mean to have a "Pollyanna" type attitude where everything looks lovely even when it is not, but to avoid a pessimistic attitude and to see the good that God has created.

Pray: God, thank you for life, and for love, and for all that you have created. Help us to see signs of your love in our daily lives. And when things do not go well, give us the strength to right the wrongs we see. Amen.

The Story and Young Children

Young children are very accepting and curious about differences. While they may be frightened when confronted by a grownup that looks different from them, they do not have the same reservation about children who are different. In my church we have a child who has cerebral palsy, and he has been active since birth in the life of the church. The children his age did not notice that he was different until they were four years old. Draw on this acceptance of difference to help instill in children a sense of celebration for diversity.

Bible Verse:
We give thanks to you, O God. (Psalm 75:1a)

Resources:
Bible
CD
Activity Pak (Summer)
pages 9, 12
(figures 1–10)
page 4 (God Made Everything Good picture)
Songbook
favorite puzzles
Bible Story Picture Cards

Supplies:
play dough
CD player
building blocks
large piece of butcher paper or newsprint
crayons
toy boats and/or fish
toy animals
toy people
large piece of blue fabric
paper streamers or silk scarfs
silk flowers and pots
toy pets and pet items
items for water table activities
plastic grocery bag

Learning Centers

Work with two or three children at a time in each learning center.

Conversation Center

You will need: play dough, large piece of butcher paper or newsprint, crayons.

Get ready: Gather the children around a table and sit down with them; engage them in conversation.

- Play With Play Dough, Activity 1c
- Make a Scribble Banner, Activity 3a

Building Center

You will need: building blocks, toy boats and/or fish, toy animals, toy people, large piece of blue fabric.

Get ready: Provide enough blocks for toddlers to share.

- Play With Blocks, Activity 3b

Discovery Center

You will need: items for water table activities (see p. 234); favorite puzzles and games from the Activity Pak or simple wooden puzzles; plastic grocery bag.

- Play With Water, Activity 1b
- Play With Puzzles, Activity 1d
- Take a Walk, Activity 3c

Storytelling Center

You will need: CD and CD player; Songbook; Bible; Activity Pak—pp. 9, 12 (figures 1-10) and p. 4 ("God Made Everything Good" picture); paper streamers or silk scarfs.

Get ready: Prepare storytelling figures (see Activity Pak—p. 2).

- Tell the Bible Story, Activity 2a
- Use an Action Verse, Activity 2b
- Retell the Bible Story, Activity 2c
- Sing a Song, Activity 2d
- Enjoy Music, Activity 4a

Family Living Center

You will need: silk flowers and pots, toy pets and pet items.

- Play House, Activity 4b

A Happy Walk

Jesse and Caitlin and Drew and Elizabeth ran onto the church playground. They were happy to be outside.

"I am glad that God made the trees and the sun and the breeze," said Ms. Jodie. "It is good to be outdoors."

"Oh, oh!" said Jesse. "Trash!" He saw a paper cup underneath the picnic table.

"Thank you, Jesse, for finding the trash," Ms. Jodie said. "You are helping take care of God's world. Let's put the cup in this plastic bag."

Jesse was glad to help clean up the playground.

1 Prepare

for the Story

 Welcome Each Child
Do this as each child enters.

Have the CD playing as children arrive. Stoop to the child's eye level and welcome each child by name. **Say** to each child: "I am so happy you have come to church today."

 Play With Water
Do this in the Discovery Center.

Let the children play in water. Notice how the water pours through funnels and squirts from meat basters. See what floats in the water and what sinks. Thank God for water.

c **Play With Play Dough**
Do this in the Conversation Center.

Gather two or three children. Talk with the children as they play. **Say:** "I wonder what God felt like making dirt. Maybe the dirt felt like this dough. What do you think?"

d **Play With Puzzles**
Do this in the Discovery Center.

Gather two or three children. Let the children play with puzzles. Talk to the children about the things pictured in the puzzle. **Say:** "God made everything good."

2 Tell

the Story

 Tell the Bible Story
Do this in the Storytelling Center.

Gather two or three children. If needed, repeat past week's Bible stories. Look at the "God Made Everything Good" picture (Activity Pak—p. 4) and notice the detail. Can the children find the sky? Can the children find the water? the animals? the people? Then tell the story for this week.

Open a Bible and **say** the Bible verse: "We give thanks to you, O God." Encourage the children to say the Bible verse with you. Put up the pictures from the past weeks (figures 1-10) as you say the prayer. **Pray:**

Thank you, God, for light.
Thank you, God, for sky.
Thank you, God, for dirt.
Thank you, God, for water.
Thank you, God, for animals.
Thank you, God, for people.
Thank you, God, for everything. Amen.

 Use an Action Verse
Do this in the Storytelling Center.

Gather two or three children. Say the action verse, "God Planned For Light" (Songbook).

c **Retell the Bible Story**
Do this in the Storytelling Center.

Gather two or three children. Tell the story and help the children do the motions.

God made trees. (*Stand straight and tall, arms raised and outstretched like branches.*)

God made stars. (*Hold your hands high and wiggle your fingers like twinkling stars.*)

God made fish. (*Put both palms together; move hands back and forth like a fish swimming.*)

God made cows. (*Make "mooing" sounds.*)

Let the children come up with ideas. End with "God made me!" (*Jump up and down and clap hands.*)

 Sing a Song
Do this in the Storytelling Center.

Gather two or three children. Sing "God Planned for Fish" (Songbook, CD). Add the verses below and others that you and the children make up.

1. God planned for dogs to bark this way. (*Make barking sounds.*)

2. God planned for flowers to grow this way. (*Crouch down low, then stand up.*)

3. God planned for water to move this way. (*Wave hands up and down.*)

 Connect

....

with the Story

a Make a Scribble Banner
Do this in the Conversation Center.

Gather two or three children. Let the children draw things that God made on the banner. Write across the top of the banner: "Thank You, God, for Everything!"

b Play With Blocks
Do this in the Building Center.

As the children play with blocks, spread out the blue fabric and pretend that it is a large lake. Play with the toys. Encourage conversation as you play. **Say:** "God made everything good."

c Take a Walk
This can begin in the Discovery Center.

If the weather permits, and you have a safe place to walk outdoors, take the children on a walk. Be sure that you have at least one adult for every two to three children.

As you walk, notice all of the things that God made. Help God take care of the earth by picking up litter and putting it in the plastic bag.

4 Celebrate

....

the Story

a Enjoy Music
Do this in the Storytelling Center.

Gather two or three children. Play the Bible verse song, "We Give Thanks" (CD, Songbook). Sing the song and add verses that are appropriate to this week.

Give each child a paper streamer or silk scarf. Play "God Has Made Everything Beautiful" (CD, Songbook). Encourage the children to dance as they listen to the song, waving their streamers in the air.

b Play House
Do this in the Family Living Center.

As the children play in the Family Living Center, encourage conversation about the things God made.

Thank God for the pretty plants and for the animals.

c Say Goodbye
Recall today's Bible story, encouraging children to say the Bible verse with you.

Say: "We enjoyed God's good gifts today. (*Name of child*) played in the water." Repeat each child's name and mention an activity in which he or she took part.

Pray: "Thank you, God, for everything."

Be sure to have a teacher or helper at the door to match children with their parents or caregivers.

Tell parents about today's Bible story and make sure that each child has today's Bible Story Picture Card. Show parents the "Nurturing Your Child's Faith" section of the card.

Be sure to show parents the scribble banner the children made. If you wish, cut the banner apart and let each child take home a piece.

Tip
Make the stories more personal. Substitute your name and that of the children in the contemporary stories.

Look Back
What activities went particularly well today? With what activities did you or the children have trouble?

What activities will you want to repeat next week?

Did all of the children have a chance to experience the Bible story this week? Can the children retell the story?

Look Ahead
Next week we will talk about resting. Feel free to change the session plan to reflect the needs and desires of your particular group.

God made rest.

Bible Verse:
We give thanks to you, O God.
(Psalm 75:1a)

Resources:
Bible
CD
Activity Pak (Summer)
    pages 9, 12
    (figures 1–10)
    page 4 ("God Made
    Everything Beautiful"
    picture)
    Songbook
    favorite puzzles
Bible Story Picture Cards

Supplies:
play dough
CD player
building blocks
cookie cutters
large absorbent paper
    towels
food coloring in squirt
    bottles
toy boats and/or fish
toy animals and people
large piece of blue fabric
paper streamers or silk
    scarfs
dolls and doll beds
pet beds or blankets
items for sand table
    activities (see p. 234)

God Rested...............

Enter the Bible Story

Read Genesis 2:2-3: And on the seventh day, God rested.

Think About It: We are faced with many good choices every day. We work hard at our daily tasks. There are plays to see, sporting events to watch, television shows that our friends will be talking about, sick people to visit, shopping and laundry to finish, and meals to prepare. Then we are bombarded with pleas for help. "Be a Big Brother!" "Come read a story to preschoolers." "Please be a Girl Scout leader." "Won't you teach Sunday school for another year?" We often get to the end of our day totally exhausted and then get up the next morning to start all over again. Surely this is not God's plan! As a matter of fact, it is not. God set an example for all of us. After a full six days of work, we are to rest. The concept of "sabbath rest" seems to be an old-fashioned, out-of-date oddity. And yet we know that rest is important for our physical and spiritual well-being. Reflect on the following as you prepare to teach the lesson this week: How do you get your rest? What activities do you find restful? How do you schedule rest time in your life? What would be a realistic schedule for you to have sabbath rest?

Through the Week: What activities would you be willing to give up in order to have rest? Remember that anything could fit in here. It is not the end of the world if you do not make your bed every day, or if you eat out or use paper plates for dinner. Each of these substitutes has drawbacks, of course. Many people are not comfortable if they cannot crawl into a "made" bed every evening, and paper plates are not always eco-friendly. But the important thing is that you get the rest you need.

Pray: Dear God, please help me find rest in my daily life. Help me set aside time for prayer, for meditation, and for being still and knowing that you are God. Amen.

The Story and Young Children

Sometimes children at this age do not like to rest. They fight sleep because they are so sure that they will miss something important if they close their eyes. But it is easy to see what a day without rest will do to a toddler. They become cranky, easily provoked, and often forget to use words instead of fists or teeth to convey their dissatisfaction with the world around them.

Teaching children that rest is good is sometimes a hard concept. The Parent Leaflet today has some suggestions for how we can teach children the goodness of rest at home. Read it and reinforce to children the need for daily rest.

We, as adults, know that God is not like us - we are like God. We know that God does not behave or react like human beings. We know that God does not get tired or need rest. But young children do not know this yeat, nor can they conceive of an abstract God. The Bible story that we have been using all summer tends to give God human characteristics. This is appropriate for preschoolers. By the time these children reach adolescence, they should know that being made in the image of God does not in any way imply that God is human.

Learning Centers

Work with two or three children at a time in each learning center.

Conversation Center

You will need: play dough, cookie cutters; large absorbent paper towels, food coloring in squirt bottles.

Get ready: Gather the children around a table and sit down with them; engage them in conversation.

- Play With Play Dough, Activity 1c
- Make a Rest-time Blanket, Activity 4b

Building Center

You will need: building blocks; toy boats and/or fish, toy animals and people, large piece of blue fabric.

Get ready: Provide enough blocks for toddlers to share.

- Play With Blocks, Activity 3b

Storytelling Center

You will need: CD and CD player, Songbook; Bible, Activity Pak, pp. 9, 12 (figures 1-10) and p. 4 ("God Made Everything Good" picture); paper streamers or silk scarfs.

Get ready: Prepare storytelling figures (see Activity Pak—p. 2).

- Tell the Bible Story, Activity 2a
- Retell the Bible Story, Activity 2b
- Use an Action Verse, Activity 2c
- Pantomime Rest and Play, Activity 3a
- Enjoy Music, Activity 4a

Family Living Center

You will need: dolls and doll beds, pet beds or blankets on which pets may rest.

- Play Rest Time, Activity 3c

Discovery Center

You will need: items for sand table activities (see p. 234); favorite puzzles from the Activity Pak, such as the cats, dogs, and birds sorting cards or the happy/sad sorting cards.

- Play With Sand, Activity 1b
- Play With Puzzles, Activity 1d

God Rested

When God made the world, there was nothing to start with. So God said, "This is not good." And God made daytime and nighttime. God made the sky, dirt, and water. God made plants and the sun and the moon. God made animals and lots of people.

And God said, "This is very, very good."

But then God was tired. So God made "rest." And God sat down and stretched out and just rested. And God said, "*This* is very good."

1 Prepare

for the Story

a Welcome Each Child
Do this as each child enters.

Have the CD playing as children arrive. Stoop to the child's eye level and welcome each child by name. **Say** to each child: "I am so happy you have come to church today."

b Play With Sand
Do this in the Discovery Center.

Let the children play in the sand. Talk about the toys they are playing with. Encourage the children to keep the sand in the sandbox.

c Play With Play Dough
Do this in the Conversation Center.

Gather two or three children. Talk with the children as they play. **Say:** "I wonder what God felt like making the world. Look! I made a star!"

d Play With Puzzles
Do this in the Discovery Center.

Gather two or three children. Let the children play with puzzles. Talk to the children about the things pictured in the puzzle. **Say:** "God made everything good."

2 Tell

the Story

a Tell the Bible Story
Do this in the Storytelling Center.

Gather two or three children. Look at the "God Made Everything Good" picture (Activity Pak—p. 4). Can the children find the sky? Can the children find the water? the animals? the people? **Say:** "God created everything good." Tell the Bible story.

Open a Bible and **say** the Bible verse: "We give thanks to you, O God.'" Have the children say the Bible verse with you.

Have the children say the prayer with you. Put up the pictures from past weeks (figures 1-10) as you say the prayer. **Pray:**

Thank you, God, for light.
Thank you, God, for sky.
Thank you, God, for dirt.
Thank you, God, for water.
Thank you, God, for animals.
Thank you, God, for people.
Thank you, God, for everything. Amen.

b Retell the Bible Story
Do this in the Storytelling Center.

Gather two or three children. Tell the story and do the motions. Encourage the children to do the motions with you.

When God made the world, there was nothing to start with. (*Hold hands out, palms up, and shake your head.*)

So God said, "This is not good." (*Put your hands on your hips.*)

And God made daytime (*Hold arms in a big circle for the sun.*) and nighttime. (*Lay your head on your hands as if asleep.*)

God made the sky, (*Sweep one arm up high.*) and dirt, (*Sweep same arm down low.*) and water. (*Put hands waist high, palms down, and move up and down to denote waves of water.*)

God made plants. (*Put your right elbow on your left hand and hold your right hand up. Shake your right hand slightly.*)

God made animals (*Put your hands on your head to make animal ears.*) and lots of people. (*Point to yourself and the other children.*)

And God said, "This is very, very good." (*Put hands on hips.*)

But then God was tired. (*Stretch and yawn.*)

So God made rest. And God sat down and stretched out and just rested. And God said, "This is very good." (*Sit down and stretch out; put your hands behind your head.*)

c Use an Action Verse
Do this in the Storytelling Center.

Gather two or three children. Use the action verse, "God Planned for Rest."

 **Connect**

with the Story

 Pantomime Rest and Play
Do this in the Storytelling Center.

Gather two or three children. Tell the children that you are going to play some music and they should decide if the music is telling them to rest or to play. Play one of the lullabies on the CD ("Little Baby Moses," "Naomi's Lullaby," or "Sleep Baby Jesus). Then follow it with one of the livelier songs ("If You're Happy and You Know It," "Having Fun Today," or "This Little Light of Mine").

When the music is lively, they should get up and dance. When the music is soft and quiet, they should lay down and pretend to go to sleep. Continue this game as long as the children have interest.

 Play With Blocks
Do this in the Building Center.

As the children play with blocks, spread out the blue fabric and pretend that it is a large lake. Play with the toys. Encourage the children to create beds for the people and barns for the animals for their rest time. Encourage conversation as you play: "What kind of bed would an elephant need?"

Play Rest Time
Do this in the Family Living Center.

As the children play in the Family Living Center, encourage them to provide for rest for the dolls and the pet animals. **Say:** "It is good to have rest time."

 Celebrate

the Story

Enjoy Music
Do this in the Storytelling Center.

Gather two or three children. Play the Bible verse song, "We Give Thanks" (CD, Songbook).

Give each child a paper streamer or silk scarf. Play "God Has Made Everything Beautiful" (CD, Songbook). By now they should be able to sing along.

Encourage the children to dance as they listen to the song, waving their streamers in the air. After dancing, **say:** "Whew! I am tired. Let's sit down and rest!"

 Make a Rest-time Blanket
Do this in the Conversation Center.

Gather two or three children. Show the children how to squeeze the food coloring bottles just enough to make a drop come out and fall on the paper towel.

Use several colors to make a design on the paper towel. If necessary, hang the paper towel up to dry.

Say: "We can use these pretty blankets to cover our dolls for rest time. When we see these blankets, we will remember that it is good to rest."

 Say Goodbye

Recall today's Bible story, encouraging children to say the Bible verse with you.

Say: "We enjoyed God's gift of rest today. (*Child's name*) made a rest blanket." Repeat each child's name and mention an activity in which he or she took part.

Pray: "Thank you, God, for rest."

Be sure to have a teacher or helper at the door to match children with their parents or caregivers.

Tell parents about today's Bible story and make sure that each child has today's Bible Story Picture Card. Show parents the "Nurturing Your Child's Faith" section of the card.

Be sure the children take home their rest blankets.

Tip
Provide a corner of your room with a soft blanket and pillows. If a child is particularly cranky, sit with that child in this corner and encourage him or her to rest (with lots of lap time!)

Look Back
What activities went particularly well today? With what activities did you or the children have trouble?

What activities will you want to repeat next week?

Did all of the children have a chance to experience the Bible story this week? Can the children retell the story?

Look Ahead
Next week is the last one for this year. You may want to plan a party and ask parents to come and see all of the things you have been playing with for the summer. If so, send invitations home this week.

Session

Psalm 118:24

We praise God every day.

Bible Verse:
We give thanks to you, O God.
(Psalm 75:1a)

Resources:
Bible
CD
Activity Pak (Summer)
    pages 9, 12
    (figures 1-10)
    Songbook
    favorite puzzles
Bible Story Picture Cards

Supplies:
play dough
CD player
building blocks
cookie cutters
shaving cream
toy boats and/or fish
toy animals and people
large piece of blue fabric
streamers or scarfs
rhythm instruments
items for sand table
    activities
short-sleeved adult shirts
that button down the
front)
bath towel
simple snack such as
    fruits and vegetables
napkins
cups and juice
dolls and doll furniture
(optional: powdered
    paint in a shaker)

Every Day Is God's Day...........

Enter the Bible Story

Read Psalm 118:24: Because God has created this day, we may rejoice.

Think About It: I was taught as a child that six days of the week were mine to spend as I wished, but the seventh day (Sunday) belonged to God. But now I believe that each and every day belongs to God and that I have choices every day in how to spend God's day. Contemplate the following as you prepare to teach the lesson this week. How can you live each day as if it belonged to God? How do we continually rejoice in each day? How do we teach toddlers to praise God? Psalms 113-118 are known as the "Egyptian Hallel" and were used in Jewish liturgical tradition at the great festivals. For example, at Passover, it was the custom to sing Psalm 113 and 114 before the meal and then to sing 115-118 afterwards. Remember that after Jesus and his disciples had eaten the Passover meal shortly before his execution, they sang a hymn before leaving (see Matthew 26:30). Many of the verses in this "Hallel" have been set to music, including our verse for today.

Through the Week: Spend some time meditating on the Doxology. Many churches sing it every Sunday: Praise God from whom all blessings flow! Praise God, all creatures here below! Praise God above, ye heavenly hosts! Praise Father, Son, and Holy Ghost! Praise God!

Pray: Dear God, truly this is your day. Whether it be Sunday, Wednesday, or Thursday, today belongs to you. Help me to live my life rejoicing because you have made this day. Amen.

The Story and Young Children

This teacher book is written as if you have started teaching in the fall. If so, this is the last Sunday before your class will move on into the preschool classes. It is time for a party! Celebrate all that you have learned this year. If your church, as many churches do, has promotion at the end of May, or if you receive new children all year long as they turn two, it is still time for a party! You have been learning all summer long about God's wonderful creation, and it is time to invite parents to come into the room and see all the things you have done for the past three months. So celebrate! Prepare a special snack (or better yet, let one of your parents do it) and decorate the room with all the posters from the Activity Pak. Let the children demonstrate the activity verse, "God Planned For Light" (Songbook), that you have been rehearsing all summer. Encourage parents to play with the play dough or the blocks with their child. Celebrate the end of the quarter. Young children love parties and celebrations. Teach them to praise God in all that they do.

Learning Centers

Conversation Center

You will need: play dough, cookie cutters; shaving cream, short-sleeved adult shirts that button down the front, bath towel, simple snack such as fruits and vegetables, cups and juice (optional: powdered tempera paint in a shaker).

Get ready: Gather the children around a table and sit down with them; engage them in conversation.

- Play With Play Dough, Activity 1c
- Fingerpaint With Shaving Cream, Activity 3a
- Have a Snack, Activity 4b

Building Center

You will need: building blocks, toy boats and/or fish, toy animals and people, large piece of blue fabric.

Get ready: Provide enough blocks for toddlers to share.

- Play With Blocks, Activity 3b

Family Living Center

You will need: dolls and doll furniture.

Encourage the children to praise God as they play. When they play with the dolls, **say:** "Thank you, God, for babies."

Storytelling Center

You will need: CD and CD player, Songbook; Bible; Activity Pak—pp. 9, 12 (figures 1-10); streamers or scarfs, rhythm instruments.

- Tell the Bible Story, Activity 2a
- Use an Action Verse, Activity 2b
- Sing a Song, Activity 3c
- Enjoy Music, Activity 4a

Discovery Center

You will need: items for sand table activities (see p. 234); favorite puzzles from the Activity Pak, such as cats, dogs, and birds sorting cards or the happy/sad sorting cards.

- Play With Sand, Activity 1b
- Play With Puzzles, Activity 1d

Every Day Is God's Day

Jacob woke up and ran to the table for his breakfast. Before they ate, Jacob's mother said, "Thank you, God, for today."

"Why do you say the same prayer every morning?" Jacob asked.

"Because I want to remind myself that today, and every day, belongs to God," Jacob's mother said. "God made the world, and God made you, and God made me. And I want to thank God for everything."

Jacob bowed his head and said, "Thank you, God, for today."

1 Prepare

for the Story

a Welcome Each Child
Do this as each child enters.

Stoop to the child's eye level. Welcome each child by name. **Say** to each child: "I am so happy you have come to church today."

b Play With Sand
Do this in the Discovery Center.

Let the children play in the sand. Talk about the toys they are playing with. Have the children keep the sand in the sandbox.

c Play With Play Dough
Do this in the Conversation Center.

Gather two or three children. Talk to them as they play. **Say:** "I wonder what God felt like making the world. Look! I made a star!"

d Play With Puzzles
Do this in the Discovery Center.

Gather two or three children. Let the children play with puzzles. **Say:** "God made everything good."

2 Tell

the Story

a Tell the Bible Story
Do this in the Storytelling Center.

Gather two or three children. Tell the story for this week. Open a Bible and **say** the Bible verse: "We give thanks to you, O God." Have the children say the verse with you.

Encourage the children to say the prayer with you. Put up the pictures from past weeks (figures 1-10) as you say the prayer. **Pray:**

Thank you, God, for light.
Thank you, God, for sky.
Thank you, God, for dirt.
Thank you, God, for water.
Thank you, God, for animals.
Thank you, God, for people.
Thank you, God, for everything. Amen.

b Use an Action Verse
Do this in the Storytelling Center.

Gather two or three children. If parents are present, encourage them to join in as you say the following action verse:

God planned for light so I can see.
(*Point to eyes.*)
God planned for light to help warm me.
(*Hug arms.*)
God planned for light to make the day.
(*Spread arms.*)
I am so glad God planned that way.
(*Hand to chest as you say, "I."*)

God planned for sky and wind to blow..
(*Wave arms as in the wind.*)

God planned for water down below.
(*Wave hands as if making waves.*)
God planned for dirt so I can play.
(*Run in place.*)
I am so glad God planned that way.
(*Hand to chest as you say, "I."*)

God planned for trees to grow so tall.
(*Stretch up high.*)
God planned for flowers very small.
(*Touch the ground.*)
God planned for food for every day.
(*Rub stomach.*)
I am so glad God planned that way.
(*Hand to chest as you say, "I."*)

God planned for birds up in the sky.
(*Flap arms.*)
God planned for goats to climb so high.
(*Pretend to climb.*)
God planned for fish down in the bay.
(*Place palms together and wiggle hands back and forth.*)
I am so glad God planned that way.
(*Hand to chest as you say, "I."*)

God planned for eyes so I can see.
(*Point to eyes.*)
God planned for hair to cover me.
(*Put hands on head.*)
God planned for hands to help me pray.
(*Fold hands as in prayer.*)
I am so glad God planned that way.
(*Hand to chest as you say, "I."*)

3 Connect
with the Story

a Fingerpaint With Shaving Cream
Do this in the Conversation Center.

Gather two or three children. Protect clothing by putting a shirt on each child, buttoned down the back. Squirt shaving cream on the table. Let the children enjoy the shaving cream. Sprinkle tempera paint on the shaving cream for color. When finished, wipe the table with a bath towel.

b Play With Blocks
Do this in the Building Center.

As the children play, spread out the blue fabric and pretend it is a lake. Play with the toys. Thank God for making everything.

c Sing a Song
Do this in the Storytelling Center.

Sing "God Made the Sun and Moon and Stars" to the tune of "This is the Way." Have children (and parents) do the motions as you sing.

4 Celebrate
the Story

a Enjoy Music
Do this in the Storytelling Center.

Play favorite songs (CD). Let children (and parents, if present) to dance and sing along. Have rhythm instruments and scarfs or streamers available.

b Have a Snack
Do this in the Conversation Center.

Provide snacks. If possible, use natural snacks such as fruits or vegetables. Talk about how God provides food such as carrots or apples. If your class is old enough, let the children serve their parents a snack.

c Say Goodbye

Encourage the children say or sing the Bible verse. If parents are present, teach them the song.

Say: "We enjoyed all of God's gifts today. (*Child's name*) sang and danced." Repeat each child's name and mention an activity in which he or she took part.

Pray: "Thank you, God, for everything."

Have a teacher or helper match children with parents or caregivers.

Make sure that each child has today's Bible Story Picture Card. Show parents the "Nurturing Your Child's Faith" section of the card.

Tip
Make the stories more personal. Substitute your name and that of the children in the contemporary stories.

Look Back
What activities went particularly well today? With what activities did you or the children have trouble?

Did all of the children have a chance to experience the Bible story this week? Can the children retell the story?

Look Ahead
This is the last session in this book. Some of you will be continuing to teach toddlers and two-year-olds next year. If so, look back to Session 1 to begin planning for a new year. If you are not continuing, be sure to leave all relevant materials, such as this teacher book and the CD, in a place where the new teacher can find it. File games and activities away so that they will be available for new groups of children in the coming year. Thank God for the opportunity to teach this year.

Molding Doughs and Messy Mixtures

No-Cook Play Dough

2 cups flour
1 cup salt
1 tablespoon cooking oil (or baby oil)
Water
Food coloring
Oil of wintergreen

- Mix together the flour, salt, oil.
- Add up to 1/2 cup water gradually, kneading to the desired consistency.
- Add food coloring until desired color is achieved.
- If you use baby oil or add a few drops of oil of wintergreen, dough does not need to be refrigerated between uses.
- Store in an airtight container.

Oil-based Play Dough

3 cups flour
1 cup salt
3 Tablespoons oil
1 cup water

- Mix flour and salt in a bowl.
- Stir in oil and water.
- Add more water if necessary to form soft dough.

Cooked Play Dough

1 cup flour
1 cup water
1/2 cup salt
2 teaspoons cream of tartar
2 Tablespoons oil
Pan
- Mix all ingredients in the pan.
- Cook over low heat until thickened.
- Cool.
- Knead.

Peanut Butter Play Dough

1/2 cup peanut butter
1/2 cup non-fat dry milk
2/3 Tablsepoon honey, optional
- Mix equal parts of peanut butter and dry milk.
- Add honey (optional)
- Knead and mix until a good dough-like consistency.

Keeps well in covered container in refrigerator. It is edible, but be cautious of children who have a peanut allergy. Does not harden well.

Fun Fingerpaint

Liquid starch
Tempera paint

- Mix tempera paint with liquid starch.
- Dampen paper with sponge.
- Spoon out a small amount of paint on the paper.

Soap Bubbles

1 cup dish washing liquid
3-4 Tablespoons glycerine (available in most pharmacies)
10 cups cold water
- Mix dishwashing liquid, glycerine, and water together.
- Add food coloring to create different shades of colors

Hints: The higherpriced brands of dishwashing liquid tend to make the best bubbles.)

Waterproof Cover Up

1 heavy plastic trash bag
Scissors
Spring-type clothespin

- Lay a bag flat on a table, with the bottom of the bag away from you.
- Cut the bag open along the center of one of the two large sides.
- Make a neck opening in the bottom of the bag.
- Make two armholes, a few inches down on both sides of the bag.
- Have a child slip on the vest, putting the opening in the back. Fasten the back opening with a clothespin.

Sand and Water Play

Toddlers and Twos love to play in the dirt and in the sand. You can let them do these things in your classroom. Just follow these simple instructions to give your children hours of fun in Sunday school!

Sand Box

Place a large plastic bin, such as an under-bed storage box, on a low table. Fill it with play sand available at hardware stores and garden centers. Place toys such as plastic cups, funnels, spoons, in the bin. Caution: make sure that there are enough toys in the box for each child to have a couple, but know that too many choices confuse young children. You may need to leave it out a few weeks before you get a handle on how many toys are optimum. With young twos, a teacher will need to remain beside the box to help teach children to leave the sand in the box. A large plastic tablecloth spread underneath the table will help you in cleanup. Have fun!

Water Play

Place another large plastic bin, or several dishpans on a low table. Fill with no more than 2 inches of water. Again, until children are used to the water play area, a teacher will need to closely supervise this activity, to teach children not to splash. Place cups, pitchers, funnels and other items that can teach children how to measure and pour. Also place items that will float, like corks and ping pong balls, along with items that will sink. Waterproof coverups (see p. 233) will protect clothing from all but the most rambunctious water play. Let the children play!

Heart Pattern

Sheep Pattern

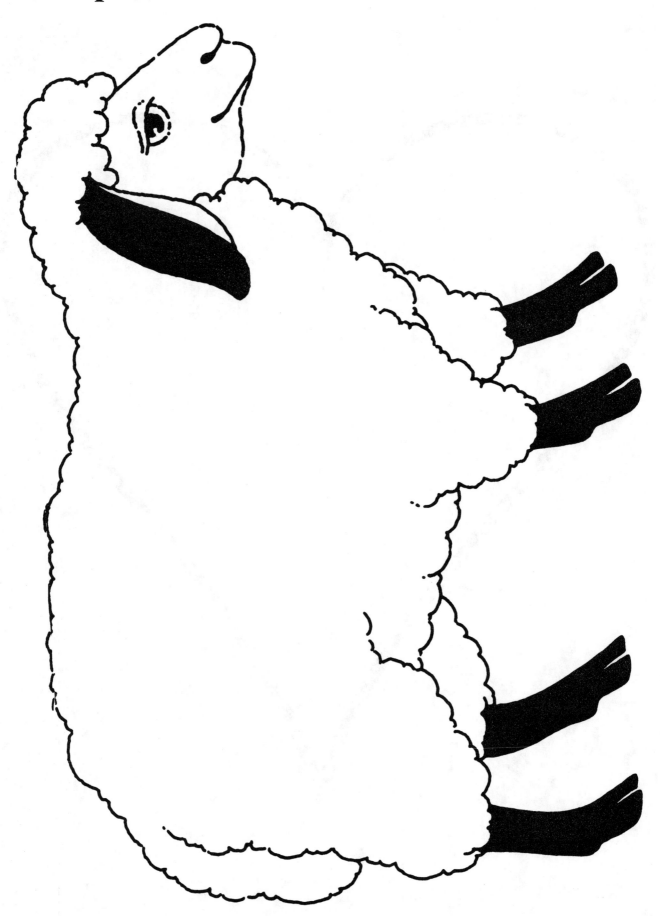

Crown Pattern

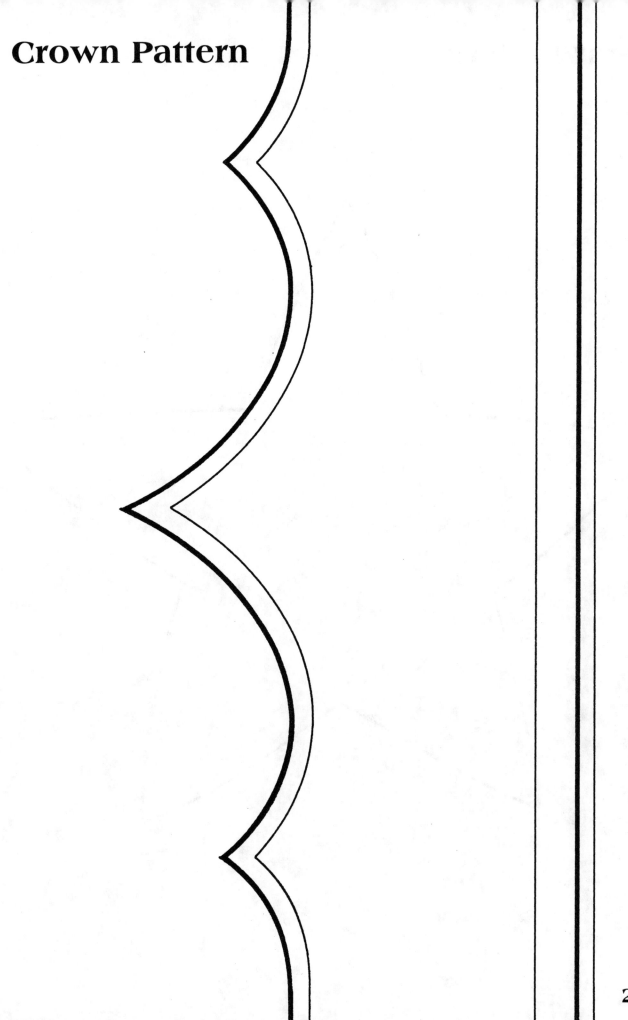

Star Pattern

Bell Pattern

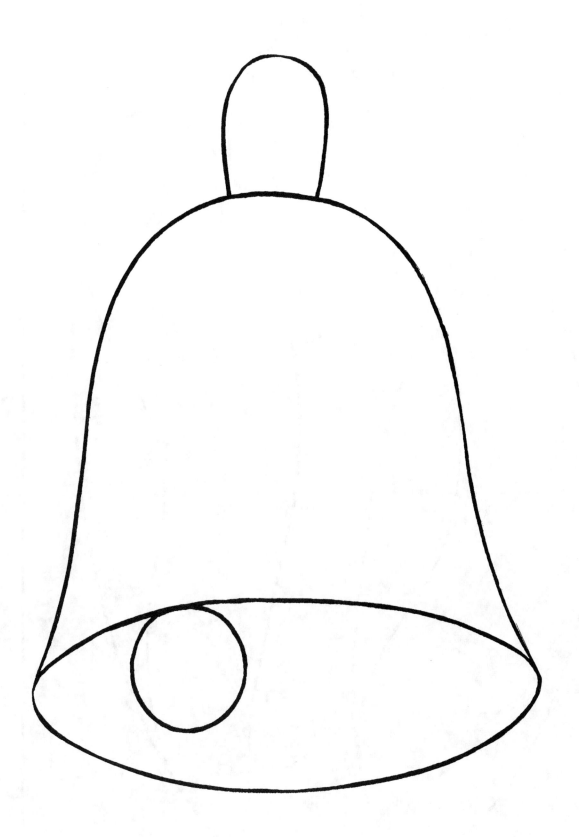

Donkey Ears Pattern

Copy this pattern on brown or grey paper.
Cut out the ears..

Cut the two strips apart and tape the ends together.
This will give you one long strip to use as a headband.
Measure strip to childs head for correct size and mark.

Help child attach ears to strip in places that would be
on either side of childs head.

Tape strip together with the excess to the inside.

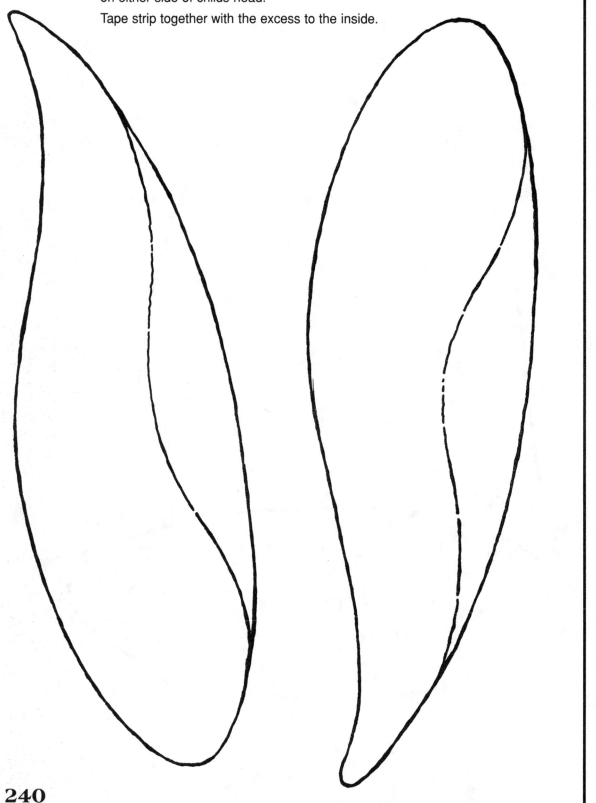

Christmas Ornament Pattern

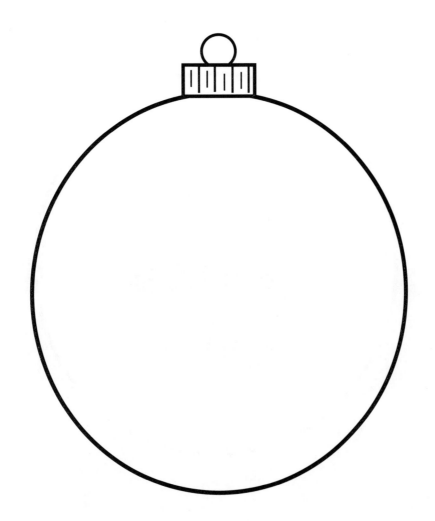

Helper Badge Pattern

Animal Sewing Card Pattern

Animal Sewing Card Pattern

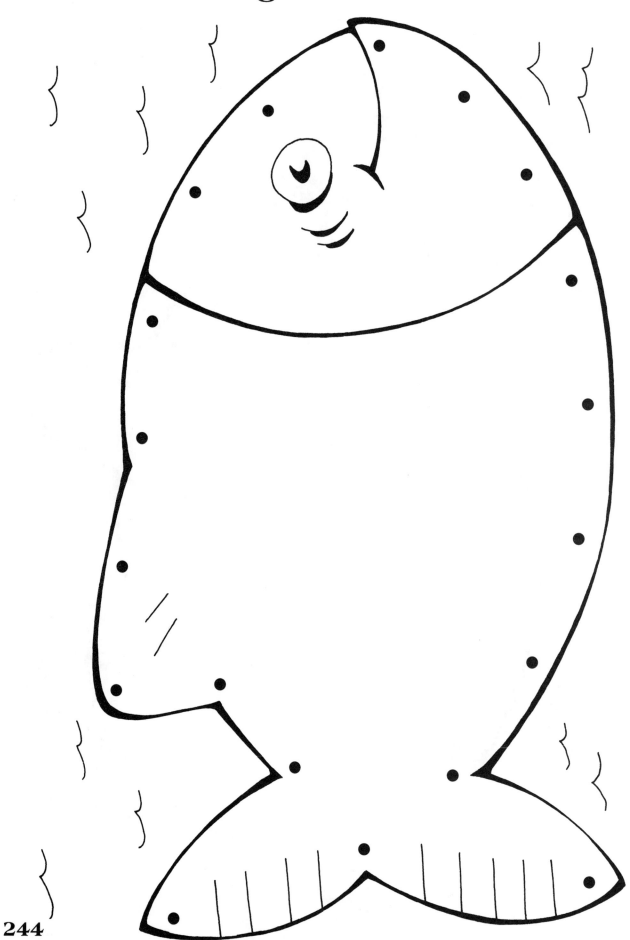

Noah's Ark Pattern

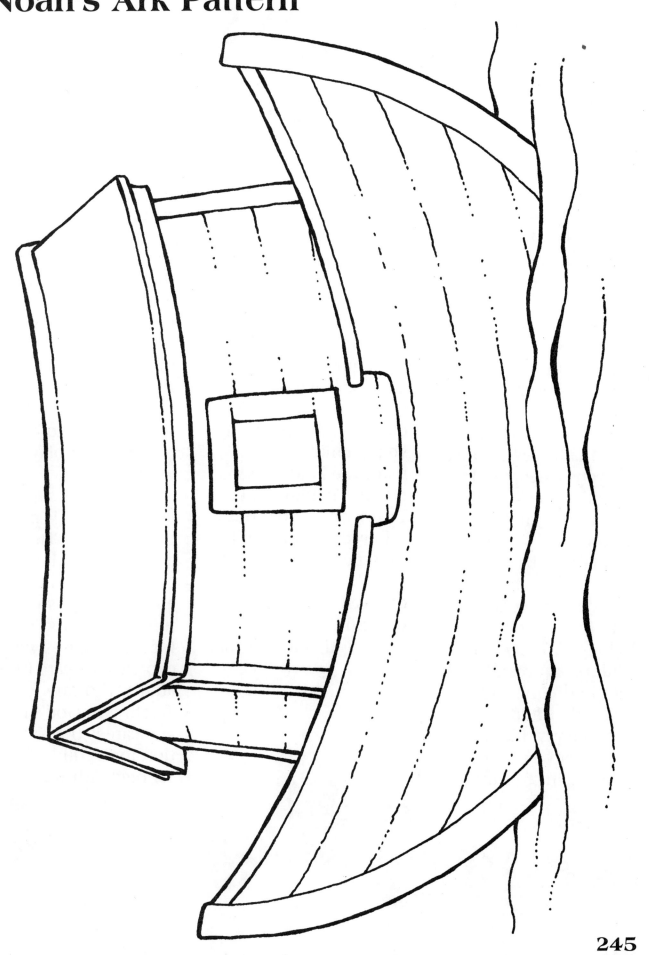

Children's Spiritual Growth

by MaryJane Pierce Norton

Parents bring young children to church to help the children grow in faith.

Parents don't expect church to be just a place where young children are cared for during meetings, Sunday school, and worship. While much faith development happens when children are older, the foundation for faith begins in infancy.

All faith is based on basic trust. As an infant or toddler the child says with a cry: "I'm hungry. Help me!" When an adult picks up and feeds the child, time and time again, the child says "I'm hungry. I know you'll help me." The child begins to trust as she learns that adults can be trusted to satisfy her basic needs. This becomes the basis for trusting God.

As adults we often separate our physical selves from our spiritual selves (*at least in our minds*). We forget how intertwined our *whole* selves are. A young child does not make the kinds of separations an adult makes. To respond to the physical needs of the child is to respond to the *whole* child. Fulfilling a physical need also nurtures the child's mental, psychological, and spiritual needs.

• **Respond to the needs of the child.** The first step in faith growth for this age group comes when adults pay attention to the children's needs. Seek to respond in good time as a teacher to the needs of toddlers to be changed, to be fed, to be rocked, to be talked to, and to be played with.

Such actions say to the child that "This person cares for me." The actions build the foundation for the child to be able to say "I know what it is like for God to care for me because I have experienced care from adults who care for me." Trusting in God's love and care is the foundation for a child's faith. Through attitudes,

feelings, and actions we teach the child about *God's love* and *love for one another*.

• **Talk about God.** Children can recognize words and know what they mean long before they can talk. Children learn how to recognize words as adults use the same words again and again. We help children grow in faith as we help them build the language of faith. Use records or tapes with simple songs about God and Jesus. Say short prayers to God as you hold the child and talk with the child.

• **Talk about the child.** Every child is a child of God. Beginning with the youngest child we say over and over again "You are a child of God. God loves you. You are important." This helps the child begin to make the connection between God and himself or herself. And having caring adults tell a child over

and over "You are a child of God" provides the basis for feelings of healthy self-worth for that child.

• **Play with the child.** It always makes me sad to walk into a Sunday school room and observe adults talking and interacting with *one another* instead of with the *children* in their care. This gives a message to children: "You really don't matter very much to me. I would rather talk to other adults than to *you*. Maybe when you're an adult, you'll be important enough to get my attention."

As children feel your arms around them, feel your body rocking their bodies, see the pictures you point to, and play with toys with you, they learn that they *matter*. We build faith because we are teaching this message—"You matter. You are important. I enjoy you. I like helping you learn. God loves *you* too."

Practice Christian values in the classroom.

We teach values in every word we say and in every action we take. We teach forgiveness as we lovingly clean up a spill instead of saying angrily "Now look at the mess you've made!" We teach hope as we say "Just look at you stretch! My, just look how you're growing! Thank you, God, for growing children." Ask yourself the following question: "Do the children in my class learn in everything that I do and say the values that show love for God and love for neighbors?"

Most toddlers have begun to communicate through words and actions, cries, and laughter. Their religious concepts are related to concrete experiences. So, much of the way we teach is through the experiences we provide in the classroom.

• **Provide a climate of trust.** Toddlers don't like change. They need to see the same teacher week by week. They need the same classroom week by week. They like hearing the same stories, singing the same songs, and enjoying the same activities again and again. This kind of dependability allows growing and changing toddlers to feel safe, although *we* might become bored. It leads them to say "I know who I can count on. I know what's waiting for me." And since you, the teacher, are trustworthy and you speak of God as trustworthy, the toddler says "I can trust God because I trust my teacher and my teacher tells me that God loves me."

• **Model caring.** Toddlers have little regard for other children except as objects to explore. During the toddler years the child grows in the *ability* to *play with* and to *interact with* others. As the teacher *you* model caring and concern for others. And children do mimic adults. They learn to show caring and concern as they see you hug a child, bandage a scraped knee, or guard a child from being hurt by another child.

• **Pray with the children.** Children learn their first prayers early. My son Bradford was saying two- and three-letter word prayers long before I would have believed this was possible. Often the only recognizable word was 'God'. But he had learned the *attitude* of

prayer and the *places* of prayer even before he could clearly speak his prayers. He learned these at church and at home.

As you pray you *teach* prayer. Pray often with the children. Pray short prayers of thanks for what you do and what you see.

• **Sing with the children.** Songs help us express our faith in God. Pair *words* with *actions* so that toddlers can learn the songs more quickly.

Sing and listen to songs about Jesus, about God, about the church, and about the children.

• **Tell and read stories.** Books that talk about God, about Jesus, and about the church help toddlers and twos grow in knowledge and in faith. Young children enjoy "reading" books and hearing stories. Short Bible stories about God's love and care are good choices. Keep a Bible in the room and refer to the Bible as the book that adults read to help them know more about God.

• **Play with the children.** *Religious* growth cannot be separated from *total* growth. The child's *spiritual growth* is nurtured as the *whole child* is nurtured. Play is the work of the child. Young children learn through play about God's Creation and their place in Creation. Toddlers learn through *play* that *they too* can create. As you play with the toddlers you teach faith to them.

Will You Please Sign In?

by MaryJane Pierce Norton

Even though we're a small church—often fewer than fifty in Sunday school on Sunday morning—we don't know *everything* about *every one* of our members. That fact was brought home to us by an incident that happened with one of our toddlers.

Allison tripped and fell while walking across the floor. Nothing was on the floor that would have made her fall. As so often happens with toddlers, however, her shoes got in the way and she fell— with such force that she split her lip. Blood and tears began to pour.

One of the teachers picked her up and started searching for her parents. But neither parent could be immediately located. They were soon found, though not without much anxious movement through the halls and in and out of classrooms. The parents could have

been found more quickly and Allison could have been comforted by them in a more timely manner if we had been using an information sheet.

Using an information sheet gives you as teacher an extra bit of security. This way teachers can tell at a glance where parents will be. Teachers will have ready information about medications, feedings, and naps to help them know how best to minister to the child.

A sample information sheet is included on the following page. Duplicate it and use a new sheet each week.

Photo by Digital Vision

249

Toddler Information

Please give us the following information.
This will allow us to take better care of your child.

Child's Name _____

Name of parent(s) or caregiver(s) _____

Where will parent(s) or caregiver(s) be? _____

_____

Will your child need a snack? _____

Will your child need a nap? _____

Has your child had any medication today? _____

Will your child need medication? _____

If so, what and when? _____

_____

Reading *and* Books

by MaryJane Pierce Norton

"**M**iss Jan, Miss Jan, book, book!" An eighteen-month-old pulls at his teacher's leg, holding a book to be read. "Go find your Jesus book," a mother says to her eleven-month-old. Anna toddles over to the shelf and returns with the correct book. A nine-month-old crows with delight as he pats the picture of a book held by his teacher. Book reading is an important part of any infant and toddler class.

Reading is one of our most important skills. Children who see adults reading and who are read to are more likely to develop a love of reading. This love can begin at an early age. By six months of age children need to be read to. The purpose of this early reading is not so much to understand what the adult is reading but to build experiences of trust and comfort and security around reading.

• **Toddlers like bright, colorful books.** They enjoy books with pictures of babies doing many of the same things they do. Toddlers like bold outlines. Pictures of toddlers with lots of detail may be too "busy" to hold the attention of infants. The text of books for infants needs to be simple.

Even if there is a lot of text you can simply call out one or two words on each page. Toddlers don't often like to linger over a page. They like to move quickly through a book. In fact the book may become a source of fascination as a hinged object that stays together. Toddlers will taste and pull on the book to explore this new kind of object. Paper books often become "food of the day" in the hands of toddlers. Look for cloth, plastic, and laminated books— these will have a longer classroom life.

Twos like colorful picture books. Photographs of familiar objects like animals, toys, and people are often favorites of twos. Rhyming books are important as twos grow in language. Their attention is held by the *patterns* of the rhymes. They will begin to *mimic* this rhyming and will even begin to repeat some of the rhymes.

Twos continue to taste and experiment with books. Books with thick pages are easier for them to use by themselves. And they too enjoy the plastic, cloth, and laminated books.

• **Choose carefully your times for reading.** Children choose their own times for moving, sitting, and listening as they grow and become more mobile. Pressuring or forcing a resistant twenty-three-month-old to sit and read can have a dampening effect on children's desire to read. If children are more interested in *climbing* than *reading* at a particular moment—that is perfectly okay. With interesting books around they will soon become eager listeners.

Read to one or two children at a time. *Reading time* is often *cuddle time*. Reading will then become a time for children to be comfortable and relaxed while enjoying books with you and the other children.

Suggest a book to read as you see that children are beginning to get tired. Looking at a book allows twos in particular to stay active and involved even as they relax and wind down.

- **Find a comfortable spot for reading.** Be true to your particular style. Sit in the chair to read if you are more comfortable sitting in a rocker rather than flopping down on the floor. The children will be comfortable and relaxed if *you* are comfortable and relaxed.

Point to pictures and to words as you read. Invite the children to point out objects in the book. "Show me the horse. Show me the baby. Where is the flower?" you might ask. These directions allow the children to participate in the reading of the book.

Encourage the children to make sound effects for the story. Claps, clicks, animal sounds, and cries help the children *own* the story if you use sounds as part of the storytelling experience.

- **Find a place in your classroom where a few books can be kept.** A low shelf will enable young children to pick up books themselves. Cover the pages with clear self-adhesive vinyl to prolong the lives of the books and make them easy to clean.

Set out only a few books at a time for toddlers. Toddlers can become overwhelmed if you have lots of books. They may simply sweep the books off the book shelf and onto the floor! Twos, on the other hand, need more choices.

Include a variety of books in your classroom. Simple Bible stories, stories based on Christian values, rhyming books, books about what babies do, books with animals, and homemade touch books can all add to the reading pleasure of the children in your classroom.

We rely on reading the Bible to help us know more about God and about Jesus as we grow in the Christian faith. But people who do not enjoy reading as they grow up may avoid it later—including Bible reading. Building an early love for reading lays the foundation for later Bible reading and enjoyment.

Getting the Help You Need

Don't have time to cut out 50 pictures from magazines for next Sunday's lesson? Or need to locate a Noah's ark toy, or people-shaped cookie cutters? How about someone to mix up a fresh batch of play dough? Or cut out construction paper shapes for art? Use the following form to solicit help from your parents.

Dear Parents:

Helping children grow as Christians is definitely a team effort! You will receive a leaflet each week to help you carry through on the lesson at home. Occasionally, we will also need extra hands to help out. Please return this form to me to let me know of your interest.

Yes! I will help! Please call on me to:

_____ Collect magazine pictures for collages

_____ Locate specialty toys (Noah's Ark, dress up clothes)

_____ Mix play dough or paint for class (recipe provided)

_____ Cut out construction paper shapes

_____ Help during Sunday school with walking trips through the church or outdoors

_____ Prepare other materials for children's use

Name (please print) _____

Phone _____

Best time to reach me _____

Your Comments *Please*

Use the following scale to rate Toddlers & Twos resources.
If you did not use a section, write "Did not use" in the comments space.

1 = No Time   2 = Some Times   3 = Most Times   4 = All Times

Teacher Guide and CD

1. Enter the Story provided information that helped me teach this session's Bible story.
Comments:

1 2 3 4

2. The Story and Young Children helped me connect the Bible story with the children I teach.
Comments:

1 2 3 4

3. The Learning Centers provided an opportunity for all the children to find activities that suited them during the session.
Comments:

1 2 3 4

4. The supplies necessary to do the activities were easily located in my home or church.
Comments:

1 2 3 4

5. The Teacher's Guide provided easy-to-follow instructions for the learning activities.
Comments:

1 2 3 4

6. My children were able to understand the Bible story.
Comments:

1 2 3 4

7. The activities matched the abilities and learning level of my children.
Comments:

1 2 3 4

8. The number of activities in the session guide worked for the time I had available.
Comments:

1 2 3 4

9. I used the CD in my classroom.
Comments:

1 2 3 4

10. I sent home the Bible Picture Story Cards to parents.
Comments:

1 2 3 4

Toddler & Twos Activity Pak

11. The pictures and posters and games in the Activity Pak were age-level appropriate.
Comments:

1 2 3 4

12. The Activity Pak provided creative helps for teaching the lessons.
Comments:

1 2 3 4

Additional Comments

Activities my children enjoy the most are.

Activities my children enjoy the least are.

About My Class

Number of children at each age in my class:

_____ 12 to 18 months,   _____ 18 months to 2 years,   _____ 2 years +

Average number of children who attend my class each week. _____

Number of helpers in my class. _____

About My Church

_____ Rural,   _____ Small Town,   _____ Downtown,   _____ Suburban

_____ Under 200 Members,   _____ 200-700 Members,   _____ Over 700 Members

Church Name and Addresss:

My Name and Address:

Extra Comments

Please return this form to: Amy Smith
Research Department
201 8th Ave., So.
P.O. Box 801
Nashville, TN   37202